Improving Medication Use and Outcomes with Clinical Decision Support:

A Step-by-Step Guide

Jerome A. Osheroff, MD, FACP, FACMI, Editor

Sponsors
Agency for Healthcare Research and Quality
Scottsdale Institute
Epic Systems Corporation
Advocate Health Care
Eclipsys Corporation
Memorial Hermann Healthcare System
Computer Programs and Systems, Inc. (CPSI)

HIMSS Mission

To lead healthcare transformation through the effective use of health information technology.

Printed in the U.S.A. 5 4 3 2

Requests for permission to reproduce any part of this work should be sent to:

Permissions Editor
HIMSS
230 E. Ohio St., Suite 500
Chicago, IL 60611-3270
cmclean@himss.org

ISBN: 978-0-9800697-3-0

For more information about HIMSS, please visit www.himss.org.

Contents

Acknowledgments

Editorial and Project Leadership

Editor-in-Chief
Jerome A. Osheroff, MD, FACP, FACMI
Chief Clinical Informatics Officer, Thomson Reuters
Adjunct Assistant Professor of Medicine, University
    of Pennsylvania
Cherry Hill, NJ

Associate Editors
*These individuals played a leadership role in helping
shape both the content and processes that led to this
book:*

Chuck Appleby
Principal
Appleby Ink Strategic Communications
Benicia, CA

Anne M. Bobb, RPh
Clinical Informatics Pharmacist
Northwestern Memorial Hospital
Chicago, IL

John Chuo, MD, MS
Neonatal Quality Officer
Children's Hospital of Philadelphia
Philadelphia, PA

Carol Leighton, MBA, BPharm, MRPharmS
Vice President, Data & Analytics
Cardinal Health
San Diego, CA

Louis E. Penrod, MD
Medical Director, eRecord Clinical Decision
    Support
University of Pittsburgh Medical Center
Pittsburgh, PA

Luis Saldana, MD, MBA, FACEP
Medical Director, Clinical Decision Support
Texas Health Resources
Arlington, TX

**Edward J. Septimus, MD, FIDSA, FACP,
FSHEA**
Ed Septimus, MD Consulting
Houston, TX

Joel S. Shoolin, DO, MBA, FAAFP
Vice President, Clinical Informatics
Advocate Healthcare
Oakbrook, IL

Anwar Mohammad Sirajuddin, MS, MBBS
Clinical Decision Support Lead, Medical Informatics
Memorial Hermann Healthcare System
Houston, TX

Dean F. Sittig, PhD, FACMI
Associate Professor, University of Texas School of
    Health Information Sciences at Houston
UT-Memorial Hermann Center for Healthcare
    Quality and Safety
Houston, TX

Ferdinand T. Velasco, MD
Chief Medical Information Officer
Texas Health Resources
Arlington, TX

Raymond Trenor Williams, MD
Senior Manager
Deloitte Consulting, LLP
Washington, D.C.

Adam Wright, PhD
Medical Informatician
Partners HealthCare System, Inc.
Boston, MA

Contributors

These individuals made substantial contributions across one or more chapters:

Tonya Hongsermeier, MD, MBA
Corporate Manager II, Clinical Knowledge
    Management and Decision Support
Partners HealthCare System, Inc.
Boston, MA

Saverio Maviglia, MD, MSc
Senior Medical Informaticist
Partners HealthCare System, Inc.
Boston, MA

Dona Stablein, RN, MBA
Senior Lead
Deloitte Consulting
McLean, VA

Douglas I. Thompson, MBA, FHIMSS
Principal Strategy Expert
CSC
Mesa, AZ

Eileen Yoshida, RPh, MBA
Medication Informaticist
Partners HealthCare System, Inc.
Boston, MA

These individuals participated in working project calls, made significant contributions to content development in those calls, and/or contributed directly to the unfolding body of text during content development:

May Alomari, BSPharm
Medication Safety Coordinator
St. John Hospital and Medical Center
Detroit, MI

Tony Avery, DM, FRCGP
Professor of Primary Health Care
University of Nottingham
Nottingham, UK

David W. Bates, MD, MSc
Chief, General Internal Medicine Division,
    Brigham and Women's Hospital
Medical Director, Clinical and Quality Analysis,
    Partners HealthCare System, Inc.
Professor of Medicine, Harvard Medical School
Boston, MA

Jane M. Brokel, PhD, RN
Assistant Professor, College of Nursing, University
    of Iowa
Iowa City, IA
Informatics Consultant, Trinity Health
Novi, MI

Daniel R. Brown, RPh
Clinical Informatics Pharmacist, Knowledge and
    Content Team
Memorial Hermann Healthcare System
Houston, TX

David C. Classen, MD, MS
Senior Partner and CMO, CSC
Associate Professor of Medicine, University of Utah
Salt Lake City, UT

Beverly Collins, RN, MS
Manager, Research & Technology, Clinical Decision
    Support
Allina Hospital & Clinics
Minneapolis, MN

Jonathan S. Einbinder, MD, MPH
Corporate Manager, Quality Data Management
Partners HealthCare System, Inc.
Boston, MA

William Galanter, MD, PhD
Medical Director, Clinical Information Systems
University of Illinois Medical Center at Chicago
Chicago, IL

Jay M. Goldstein, MBA, CMPE, CSSGB
Administrative Director, Special Projects
Hackensack University Medical Center
Hackensack, NJ

Mary Lou Guy, MBA, RRT, CHT
Manager, Cardiopulmonary and Neurodiagnostic
    Services
Saint Luke's Northland Hospital
Kansas City, MO

Patricia L. Hale, MD, PhD, FACP
Deputy Director, Office of Health Information
    Technology and Transformation
New York State Department of Health
Albany, NY

Sharon A. Henry, RN
Former Director Clinical Decision Support
Allina Hospitals & Clinics
Minneapolis, MN

Terry K. Kirkpatrick, MS, RPh
Director of Pharmacy Services
Saint Mary's Health Care
Grand Rapids, MI

Paul Kleeberg, MD, FAAFP
Medical Director, Clinical Decision Support
HealthEast Care System
Saint Paul, MN

Gil Kuperman, MD
Director, Quality Informatics
New York Presbyterian Hospital
New York, NY

Catherine Lai, PharmD
Knowledge Development Manager
Thomson Reuters
Greenwood Village, CO

Thomas Landholt, MD
Medical Director for Health Information
    Technology
MassPRO
Boston, MA
Family Practice
Springfield, MO

Joyce Anne LeMaistre, MD
Chief Medical Information Officer
Seton Family of Hospitals
Austin, TX

Stuart Levine, PharmD
Informatics Specialist
Institute for Safe Medication Practices
Horsham, PA

David M. Liebovitz, MD
Chief Medical Information Officer, Northwestern
    Medical Faculty Foundation
Northwestern Memorial Hospital
Chicago, IL

Martha Muffie Martin, MSN, RN
Senior Project Specialist
Clinical Informatics Research and Development
Partners HealthCare System, Inc.
Boston, MA

Jason Maude
CEO & Co-founder
Isabel Healthcare, Inc.
Falls Church, VA

Jane B. Metzger
Principal, Emerging Practices
CSC
Lexington, MA

Steven J. Meurer, PhD, MBA, MHS
Vice President, Clinical Data & Informatics
University HealthSystem Consortium
Oak Brook, IL

Rhodes Moxley, MPA
National Director, Clinical Improvement
Thomson Reuters
Santa Barbara, CA

Robert E. Murphy, MD
Chief Medical Informatics Officer, Memorial
    Hermann Healthcare System
Adjunct Assistant Professor, University of Texas
    School of Health Information Sciences
Houston, TX

Brian D. Patty, MD, FAAEM
Vice President and Chief Medical Informatics
    Officer
HealthEast Care System
St. Paul, MN

Thomas Payne, MD, FACP
Medical Director, IT Services, UW Medicine
University of Washington
Seattle, WA

Danielle Przychodzin, PharmD
Clinical Terminology Specialist
Thomson Reuters
Greenwood Village, CO

Gordon Schiff, MD
Associate Director, Center for Patient Safety
    Research and Practice
Brigham and Women's Hospital
Boston, MA

Robert A. See
Clinical Decision Support
Allina Hospitals & Clinics
Minneapolis, MN

Manisha Shah, MBA, RT
Director Patient Safety & Harm Prevention
Hospital Corporation of America
Nashville, TN

Brian F. Shea, PharmD, BSPharm, FCCP
Senior Manager and Director, National Patient
    Safety Practice
Accenture
Boston, MA

Ann Slee, MSc, BPharm, MRPharmS
Clinical Lead, National ePrescribing Programme
NHS Connecting for Health
England

Mark Van Kooy, MD
Medical Director of Informatics
Virtua Health
Marlton, NJ

Tammy Williams, RN, BSN
Director, Product Management
Thomson Reuters
Greenwood Village, CO

Reviewers

These individuals were enlisted for the review process largely through their response to request for reviewers circulated to listservs maintained by several of the co-publishing organizations. Those individuals whose names are marked with an asterisk (*) provided particularly extensive and helpful input.

Thomas C. Bailey, MD
Professor of Medicine, Washington University
    School of Medicine
Director, Medical Informatics, BJC Healthcare
St. Louis, MO

Michael B. Blackman, MD, MBA
Chief Medical Information Officer, Berkshire
    Health Systems
Assistant Professor of Medicine, University of
    Massachusetts School of Medicine
Pittsfield, MA

Jane M. Brokel, PhD, RN*
Assistant Professor, College of Nursing, University
of Iowa
Iowa City, IA
Informatics Consultant, Trinity Health
Novi, MI

**Steven J. Davidson, MD, MBA, FACEP,
FACPE**
Chairman, Department of Emergency Medicine,
Maimonides Medical Center
Professor of Clinical Emergency Medicine, SUNY-
Downstate Medical Center
Brooklyn, NY

Paul R. Dexter, MD
Associate Professor of Clinical Medicine, Indiana
University School of Medicine
Research Scientist, Regenstrief Institute
Chief Medical Information Officer, Wishard
Health Services
Indianapolis, IN

Ruth M. Flores, RPh, MBA
Practice Manager, Eclipsys Consulting Services
Eclipsys Corp.
Fort Worth, TX

William Galanter, MD, PhD*
Medical Director, Clinical Information Systems
University of Illinois Medical Center at Chicago
Chicago, IL

Jay M. Ginsberg, MD
Southeastern Connecticut Nephrology Associates
Lawrence and Memorial Hospital
New London, CT

Robert A. Greenes, MD, PhD
Ira A. Fulton Chair and Professor, Department of
Biomedical Informatics
Arizona State University
Phoenix, AZ

**Karl F. Gumpper, RPh, BCNSP, BCPS,
FASHP**
Director, Section of Pharmacy Informatics &
Technology
American Society of Health-System Pharmacists
Bethesda, MD

Steve Hasley, MD, FACOG
Associate Medical Director, Interoperability Clinical
Decision Support, and Visiting Clinical Associate
Professor, Department of Obstetrics, Gynecology,
Reproductive Services
University of Pittsburgh Medical Center
Pittsburgh, PA

Kevin B. Johnson, MD, MS*
Associate Professor and Vice Chair, Department of
Biomedical Informatics, and Associate Professor
of Pediatrics
Vanderbilt University Medical Center
Nashville, TN

Rainu Kaushal, MD, MPH
Chief, Division of Quality and Clinical Informatics
Associate Professor of Pediatrics, Medicine and
Public Health, WCMC
Executive Director, HITEC
Director of Pediatric Quality and Patient Safety at
KCCH of NYPH
New York, NY

LuAnn Kimker
Manager, Health Information Technology
Masspro
Waltham, MA

Paul Kleeberg, MD, FAAFP*
Medical Director, Clinical Decision Support
HealthEast Care System
St. Paul, MN

Margaret Ross Kraft, PhD, RN*
Assistant Professor, Niehoff School of Nursing,
    Loyola University Chicago
Research Associate, Veterans' Information Resource
    Center, VA Edward Hines Hospital
Hines, IL

Thomas Landholt, MD
Family Practice
Springfield, MO
Medical Director for Health Information
    Technology
MassPRO
Boston, MA

Barbara L. Lanzara, MD, FACOG*
Attending Physician OB/GYN
Harlem Hospital Center
New York, NY

Harold P. Lehmann, MD, PhD
Director, Research and Training, Division of
    Health Sciences Informatics
Johns Hopkins School of Medicine
Baltimore, MD

Stuart Levine, PharmD*
Informatics Specialist
Institute for Safe Medication Practices
Horsham, PA

David M. Liebovitz, MD
Chief Medical Information Officer, Northwestern
    Medical Faculty Foundation
Northwestern Memorial Hospital
Chicago, IL

David F. Lobach, MD, PhD, MS, FACMI, FACP
Associate Professor and Chief , Division of Clinical
    Informatics, Department of Community and
    Family Medicine
Duke University Medical Center
Durham, NC

Steven Luxenberg, MD, FACP
Chief Medical Information Officer
Piedmont Healthcare
Atlanta, GA

Kathleen A. McCormick, PhD, RN, FACMI*
Chief Scientist, Vice President
SAIC
Rockville, MD

Edward D. Millikan, PharmD*
Assistant Director, eHealth Solutions
Clinical Informaticist, American Society of
    Health-System Pharmacists
Bethesda, MD

Thomas Minich, RPh
Lead Pharmacist
Cincinnati Children's Hospital Medical Center
Cincinnati, OH

James W. Mold, MD, MPH
Professor and Director of Research, Department of
    Family and Preventive Medicine
University of Oklahoma Health Sciences Center
Oklahoma City, OK

Donald Nelson, MD, ABFP
Director of Medical Informatics, Cedar Rapids
    Medical Education Foundation
Cedar Rapids, Iowa
Director of Clinical Informatics & Research,
    Clinical Content Consultants
Concord, NH

Matvey B. Palchuk, MD, MS*
Senior Medical Informatics Specialist
Partners HealthCare System, Inc.
Boston, MA

Luzviminda C. Ross, MA, HIM (Candidate)
The College of Saint Scholastica
Duluth, MN

Eleanor Bimla Schwarz, MD, MS
Assistant Professor of Medicine, Epidemiology,
    Obstetrics, Gynecology and Reproductive
    Sciences, Center for Research on Health Care
University of Pittsburgh
Pittsburgh, PA

Brian J. Stehula, PharmD, BS
Medication Safety Manager, Department of
    Pharmacy
Gundersen Lutheran Medical Center
La Crosse, WI

Steven J. Steindel, PhD, FACMI
Director, Data Standards and Vocabulary
Centers for Disease Control and Prevention
Atlanta, GA

Dona Stablein, RN, MBA*
Senior Lead
Deloitte Consulting
McLean, VA

Harris R. Stutman, MD, FIDSA
Executive Director, Clinical Informatics
Memorial Health Services
Fountain Valley, CA

Sarah R. Tupper, MS, RN-BC
Consultant
Taylor-Tupper & Associates, LLC
Woodbury, MN

Robert A. Vinti, RPh, MS
Product Manager
HealthCare Systems Inc.
Montgomery, AL

Doris Wong, PharmD*
Pharmacy Operations Manager
Washington Hospital Healthcare System
Fremont, CA

Paul Zlotnik, MD, FAAP
Chief Medical Informatics Officer
Children's Specialists
San Diego, CA

Other Acknowledgments

The following organizations and individuals provided substantial support for the processes required to develop this book's content:

Scottsdale Institute

Major support to multiple key logistic and other components from project inception were provided by the Scottsdale Institute.

Shelli Williamson
Executive Director
Scottsdale Institute
Chicago, IL

Ricki A. Levitan
Project Manager
Scottsdale Institute
Frisco, TX

Margaret M. Hahn
Administrative Assistant
Scottsdale Institute
Minneapolis, MN

Nancy Navarette
Webmaster
Scottsdale Institute
Hermosa Beach, CA

Editorial Solutions

Content structuring, editing and guidance throughout the development process was provided by Editorial Solutions.

Mary Kelly
President and Project Manager
Editorial Solutions, LLC
Arlington Heights, IL

Becky Thompson
Editorial Support and Permissions
Editorial Solutions, LLC
Arlington Heights, IL

Healthcare Information and Management Systems Society

Support for various key project and content development components was provided by HIMSS.

Fran Perveiler
Vice President, Communications
Healthcare Information and Management
    Systems Society
Chicago, IL

Patricia B. Wise, RN, MS, MA, FHIMSS, Col. (USA Ret'd)
Vice President, Healthcare Information Systems
Healthcare Information and Management
    Systems Society
Evans, GA

Cari McLean
Coordinator, Communications
Healthcare Information and Management
    Systems Society
Chicago, IL

More than a dozen individuals from Scottsdale Institute member provider organizations and a few other institutions participated in early discussions that helped to shape and ultimately to launch this project. Their support and engagement at that early project stage is acknowledged and appreciated, as is the encouragement and input of others along the way not mentioned by name.

The editors also acknowledge: Douglas Goldstein (eFuturist, iConecto - Gaming4Health.com, Alexandria, VA) for his input at several key stages in the collaborative process; Janet Guptil, FACHE (President, KM At Work Inc., Chicago, IL) for pointing us early on to models for collaborative book development (especially wearesmarterthanme.org, which helped inspire this project's transition to a "mass collaboration" effort); and Patricia Osheroff for facilitating the manuscript peer review process.

Sponsors

The following organizations provided generous unrestricted grants to help engage editorial support for gathering and synthesizing input from the many individuals with their diverse perspectives that contributed to this project:

- Agency for Healthcare Research and Quality (www.ahrq.gov)
- Scottsdale Institute (www.scottsdaleinstitute.org)
- Epic Systems Corporation (www.epicsystems.com)
- Advocate Health Care (www.advocatehealth.com)
- Eclipsys Corporation (www.eclipsys.com)
- Memorial Hermann Healthcare System (www.memorialhermann.org)
- Computer Programs and Systems, Inc. (CPSI) (www.cpsinet.com)

Co-publishers' Statements

The other co-publishers of this book listed next supported HIMSS in this publishing effort by endorsing the work product, facilitating broad access to their membership for participation in content development and/or directly supplying subject matter expertise, and assisting with dissemination of the material to their constituencies.

The following are brief statements by co-publisher executives about the relevance of this publication to their organization and membership.

Scottsdale Institute

Shelli Williamson, Executive Director, and
Stan Nelson, Chairman

The challenge of implementing and managing CDS systems, technologies, and governance and their ongoing management will continue to be of critical importance to Scottsdale Institute members, many of whom are leaders in the development and use of these systems. In addition, the public outcry for drug safety creates an urgent platform for this specific application of CDS. The creation of this book means bringing the knowledge and experience of many CDS leaders to the industry and thus supports our 501c3 mission: sharing best practices and lessons learned is at the heart of our purpose. The resulting book content and the process of developing it is also a perfect example of the use of virtual collaboration tools such as wiki and SIWebII. Ultimately, we believe this virtual way of working together across organizations and industries will be expected and demanded for all those engaged in operations and quality improvement: both knowledge and its workers are becoming increasingly decentralized. Initially working virtually, the collaborators in this project have shown that these tools can play an essential supporting role in information exchange and professional relationship building. We are proud to co-sponsor and co-publish this important work and

are confident that its use and impact will be ongoing and widespread.

Healthcare Information and Management Systems Society (HIMSS)

Patricia Wise, RN, MS, MA, FHIMSS,
Vice President, Healthcare Information Systems

As the healthcare industry's membership organization focused on providing global leadership for the optimal use of healthcare information technology and management systems for the betterment of healthcare, HIMSS is keenly interested in promoting CDS as a highly effective method to improve outcomes related to medication management. HIMSS was proud to publish the original *Clinical Decision Support Implementer's Workbook* in 2003 as a Web-based tool, and in 2004 a follow-up book designed to assist healthcare organizations in using CDS to measurably improve quality outcomes. HIMSS' Physician Community continues to support and guide clinicians in the selection, customization, and implementation of CDS.

This book is the result of a groundbreaking collaboration of individuals and organizations, as evidenced by the large number of its reputable co-editors and contributors and esteemed co-publishers. Together, all have contributed to this practical guide that will surely assist CDS implementers in improving medication use and associated outcomes in their organizations.

American Medical Informatics Association (AMIA)

David W. Bates, MD, MSc, Chairman, and
Don E. Detmer, MD, MA, President and Chief
Executive Officer

AMIA, as the professional home for informaticians engaged in transforming patient care, research, and public health, is currently directing substantial attention to CDS and believes this current development represents an important contribution in an area that is central to realizing benefit from clinical systems. In 2006, an AMIA steering group worked with a wide range of collaborators to create a robust Roadmap for National Action on Clinical Decision Support that identified key steps for progress with respect to knowledge management (KM) and CDS in the United States. This publication contributes to a realization of that Roadmap. AMIA is involved in many CDS-related efforts—a new AMIA CDS work group now complements groups on clinical information systems (CISs) and clinical research, and we are a partner in the Morningside Initiative that seeks to create a public-private partnership for a KM repository of shared, broadly available, executable knowledge.

AMIA is committed to continued leadership and collaboration on pivotal health informatics challenges, such as CDS, that will shape the future of healthcare. Although these challenges are complex and significant, the potential for improvement and progress to date justifies our commitment.

The Institute for Safe Medication Practices (ISMP)
Michael Cohen, RPh, MS, ScD, President
This book represents the current wisdom and thinking on successful use of CDS from a variety of practitioners representing many different healthcare disciplines. It is testimony to the power of multi-disciplinary thinking in our approach to preventing medication errors. ISMP's primary focus has always been on the dissemination of practical, implementable, high-leverage medication error prevention strategies, which include CDS as an essential element. ISMP has long promoted computerized prescriber order entry (CPOE), "smart" pumps, and other technology tools to improve safety, recognizing that their true value can only be achieved when CDS is embedded in their application. This book provides readers from hospitals and other healthcare organizations with the basic fundamentals to create, maintain, and monitor superior CDS systems that optimize medication use and reduce risk. It is our hope at ISMP that hospitals and other healthcare

organizations will use the information presented to not only help build their systems but also better utilize data from their error reporting programs and technology reports to guide the committees responsible for CDS in concentrating on those areas of the greatest concern and value. This will provide a strong starting point for improving the use of current technology to deliver clinical knowledge and decision making at the most critical points to prevent medication errors and adverse events, which ultimately will help us better protect patients.

American Society of Health-System Pharmacists (ASHP)
Henri R. Manasse, Jr, PhD, ScD, Executive Vice President and Chief Executive Officer
ASHP is a 35,000-member national professional association that represents pharmacists who practice in hospitals, health maintenance organizations, long-term care facilities, home care, and other components of healthcare systems. ASHP and health-system pharmacists have a long history of improving medication use and enhancing patient safety. Recognizing the transformational power of the technology information revolution, ASHP established a Section of Informatics and Technology for the purpose of improving health outcomes through the use and integration of data, information, knowledge, technology, and automation in the medication-use process. We believe that pharmacy expertise is a key element of the multidisciplinary collaboration required to create, implement and maintain effective CDS systems. We are therefore pleased to co-publish this book and commend HIMSS for its collaborative approach to bringing this resource to fruition.

Association of Medical Directors of Information Systems
William F. Bria, MD, President
The Association of Medical Directors of Information Systems is a 2,000-member organization of clinicians with formal responsibility for healthcare information technology leadership. In particular, AMDIS is dedicated to the education and networking of Chief

Medical Information Officers (CMIOs). In the last decade, the CMIO role has evolved to become the central architect of the implementation of computerized CDS in American healthcare. Over the same period of time, medication errors have been identified as the single most important target for application of CDS in the United States. This guidebook has been developed because of the urgency and importance of minimizing medication errors and the potential for patient suffering that may occur as a result of those errors. We believe that only through the routine application of evidence-based policies and practices, as described here, can an effective and lasting solution to medication errors in American healthcare be achieved.

Foreword

From today's perspective, the 1991 Institute of Medicine (IOM)* report that called for patient records to serve as more than vehicles to store patient data but to also support the clinical decision process and help improve the quality of care, might appear to have been stating the obvious. Yet, at the time it was forward thinking. Since then, myriad organizations and individuals have contributed to evolving the vision for patient records to include CDS, quality healthcare, and how information and communications technology can and should support healthcare delivery. Other efforts, such as the collaboration that led to this volume, have focused on translating that vision into practice. Dr. Osheroff and his collaborators are to be commended for this important contribution to the field of CDS.

This volume provides assistance for organizations grappling with the pressing issue of improving medication safety. It also highlights two broader issues for the future of CDS. The first issue of extending the benefits of CDS to more patients requires that we continue to invest sufficient intellectual energy and financial resources to build the infrastructure that will foster efficient development and application of clinical knowledge across the country. That infrastructure will encompass mechanisms for converting existing clinical knowledge into computer-executable formats, as well as speed the creation of new knowledge by feeding experiences from local organizations into regional, national, and global databases. It will also include a variety of delivery mechanisms for decision support, with particular emphasis on electronic health records (EHRs), and continuing education for clinicians on effective use of decision support. A series of recent activities (for example, development of the Roadmap for National Action on Clinical

Decision Support, formation of the Federal CDS Collaboratory, and discussions about creation of a public-private knowledge management repository) are helping to lay the foundation for the infrastructure. We must maintain momentum toward this important objective for the health sector.

The second broad issue facing CDS will require that we continue to push the boundaries in our thinking about CDS so that the vision remains vital and responsive to the needs of clinicians and patients. Just as our notion of EHRs has evolved from a focus on clinicians to include patients through personal health records (PHRs), we are challenged to consider the issue of bringing patients and informal caregivers into the CDS process. We will be further challenged to do so as clinical knowledge becomes more complex. We can expect that over time, rather than providing global evidence-based knowledge for a general proxy of an individual, cutting-edge CDS will offer customized knowledge that considers genetic and environmental evidence for a particular individual. The prospects are both exciting and daunting.

Today, 17 years after the IOM recommended that all healthcare providers adopt EHRs within 10 years, the use of EHRs is increasingly common in the United States but are, by no means, exclusively used. Similarly, the path to widely used, robust CDS capabilities is going to take longer to travel than we would wish. Over the past two decades, we have made progress on multiple fronts, including information and communication technology capabilities, increased technical skills in the workforce, development of standards that enable data to be shared across settings, clearer understanding of the impediments to adoption of clinical information systems, and recog-

---

* *Computer-Based Records: An Essential Technology for Health Care.*

nition that the performance of healthcare practitioners is far better when data and relevant knowledge support are available in decision making. Although much remains to be accomplished for both electronic EMRs and CDS, this progress shows we are headed in the right direction. Further, efforts such as those that resulted in this book suggest that there is reason to hope that the pace of progress will accelerate.

Don E. Detmer, MD, MA
President and CEO,
American Medical Informatics Association

Preface

This Is Not a Book!

Rather than thinking of the guide you now hold as static, as you would a typical book, we hope you will consider it, and the time you spend perusing and applying its guidance, as a portal to engagement in an important experiment in healthcare. The experiment postulates that many individuals and organizations, with diverse perspectives and competencies, can come together and collectively accelerate the process whereby urgently needed improvements in healthcare are realized—at both local and wider levels.

Other efforts, such as the 100K and 5 Million Lives Campaigns launched by the Institute for Healthcare Improvement (IHI), are already demonstrating the compelling power of collective action toward performance improvement (PI). The pages in this guide represent a snapshot of the evolving work product derived from an initiative focused on driving improvements in medication use (and associated outcomes) with CDS. Scores of individuals, healthcare organizations, professional societies, and others have come together in this initiative to produce this work product.

The sincerest hope of all those involved is that you will find the material helpful in your related efforts. We acknowledge that the subject matter at hand—measurably improving medication management with CDS—is complex and fraught with challenges. Further, despite the efforts of many thoughtful experts and other stakeholders, at times the guidance in this edition offers best guesses about successful implementation strategies, which may raise as many questions as they answer. Nonetheless, we expect that this broad base of organized insight on useful approaches will significantly enhance implementers' efficiency and success. Likewise, we hope that the details and challenges outlined in this guide will serve as a useful framework for accelerated collaborations toward better CDS tools among implementers, CIS and CDS content vendors, and other key stakeholders. Your experience with this material will help test this hypothesis and will serve as a springboard for what we envision as your contribution to a maturing body of best practices and solutions. Before we get to how that might happen, a few words on the path that lead to the current collaboration and its output.

How We Got Here

The general approach for improving outcomes with CDS used in this book is based on a previous collaborative effort that culminated in the 2005 guide published by HIMSS, *Improving Outcomes with Clinical Decision Support: An Implementer's Guide.* This previous book has been widely used in healthcare provider organizations by CMIOs, other health information technology (IT) and PI leaders, and their teams. Rather than focusing on specific improvement targets, it provides broad guidance on successful CDS implementation. The material was synthesized from the five authors' experiences, combined with insights from many others who had also provided input on a previous Internet-based version and on draft manuscripts of the subsequent print-based edition.

Shortly after that book was published, several forces set the stage for the current initiative. First, a large group of diverse stakeholders outlined a national CDS strategy in their Roadmap for National Action on Clinical Decision Support. This roadmap identified six strategic objectives that should be realized to optimize CDS value, along with suggested actions. Recommendations include "…identifying and disseminating best practices for CDS deployment."[1] Around the same time, users of the 2005 CDS guide began asking for more detailed guidance on CDS strategies for improving specific, high-priority objectives. These included imperatives, such as better use of medications and enhanced performance on core measures of quality care. Also during this period, informal discussion occurred among CMIOs and others (including many leaders of this project) around identifying better strategies for successful CDS deployment. This dialog took place in various forums, including professional society meetings and electronic discussion groups provided by several co-publishers of this guidebook.

The Scottsdale Institute, for example, had launched "Web 2.0" infrastructure to support collaboration among its members on pressing topics of broad interest, and a community focused on CDS formed and began sharing successful deployment strategies. The CDS group quickly recognized that the "pearls" that were being exchanged would likely be of widespread value. The group agreed early on that the previous CDS implementers' guide would provide a useful framework for compiling the pearls and that medication management would be a valuable domain on which the group should focus its efforts.

This community initially had a dozen or so participants from a variety of Scottsdale Institute (SI) member organizations. It held active discussions on the SI Web II forum, jointly developed and enhanced an outline to convey best CDS implementation practices for medication management, and organized regular working teleconferences to discuss best practices and project management. SI conferences were similarly leveraged for in-person content development and planning. Through networking by project participants, others (besides SI members) with interest and expertise in the topic learned of the project and expressed interest in joining the effort. Inspired by the example of http://wearesmarterthanme.com/ (a business book developed through an open online collaboration), project leaders established a wiki (as an offshoot to the popular Informatics Review wiki [http://www.informatics-review.com/]) to facilitate collaboration and shared content creation beyond SI members.

Discussions among the project team about how best to share the successful practices that were being synthesized naturally led to contact with HIMSS about a follow-up to the previous CDS guide. As other individuals and healthcare organizations joined the project based on word-of-mouth and shared interest (there were approximately 70 registered users of the project wiki at its peak, though not all were active), so too did other professional societies. AMIA's participation broadened access to deep informatics and CDS expertise; as ISMP did for medication safety, ASHP did for health system pharmacists, and AMDIS did for clinicians who lead information systems deployments. In turn, this project represented an opportunity to further the mission of each respective society (see co-publishers statements, page xiii, for further details).

The project rapidly expanded in other ways as well. When additional financial resources were sought to support the editorial management of input from the large number of participating contributors, several organizations from a variety of sectors—care delivery organizations, CIS vendors, and the federal government—responded generously. When invitations soliciting reviewers for a draft of this manuscript were circulated to listservs of several co-publishers, nearly 200 individuals responded with requests to participate (see Reviewers, page viii).

This story is an example of broader societal trends, well-described in the popular book *Wikinomics: How Mass Collaboration Changes Everything.*[2] Widespread availability of tools that support peer-to-peer knowledge sharing (already leveraged to a significant degree in this project) point toward what could happen in subsequent chapters of the story.

What's Next

Hopefully this project's history will motivate you to consider your role in it as beyond that of a passive reader and even beyond that of actively implementing and evaluating this guide's recommendations. Ideally, you will become an engaged member of the stakeholder community, seeking to jointly find and deploy improved ways to leverage CDS in medication management. The stakes are high, and the time for action is now. Together we can more effectively focus CDS on medication use to help stop unnecessary harm, missed opportunities to help people when we know well how to do so, and wasted scarce resources—all to the unacceptable levels today that are well-documented.

So, how do you do all that? The first step, as previously mentioned, is to think of your efforts related to the subject matter of this book from a collaborative, community perspective, rather than from a more parochial one. There are many tools to help with this, including the online and in-person forums established for these exchanges by organizations such as those acknowledged earlier, and many others. Explorations are already underway into whether and how some of the guidance contained in this edition—or at least stakeholder discussions about that content—can be made freely and globally available for use and enhancement (for example, through a wiki).

The goal would be to provide, in a manner somewhat like Wikipedia.org or wikinomics.com, a dynamic community and resource for continually expanding and refining the best practices for leveraging CDS to improve the poor outcomes too often associated with medication use. This would enable those who have asked for deeper coverage than we have provided, in areas such as pediatrics, geriatrics, ambulatory care, and the like, to work with those who developed the current material and others with the necessary expertise to build out that needed information.

We believe that the CDS enhancement approaches outlined in this project should be scalable to more participants and topics, especially if we build upon the hard-won lessons from producing this guide. For example, we have begun using enhanced guidance frameworks and collaboration mechanisms to synthesize and disseminate best practices for applying CDS in even more focused areas. A follow-on collaboration among HIMSS, SI, and some of their provider organization members has been created to share and augment strategies for applying CDS to highly specific national healthcare PI targets (starting with preventing venous thromboembolism [VTE], a major cause of preventable inpatient death).[3]

It seems appropriate to recall the closing words of the last CDS guide preface in the conclusion to this one, reinforcing that this ending, too, is a beginning: "For us, this book is not a finished work; rather, it is a springboard into a number of other activities designed to help CDS fulfill its original promise: to be a vitally important, routinely used tool that helps bring the best care to the largest number of patients. We hope you will continue to be our partners in the journey."[4]

Jerome A. Osheroff, MD, FACP, FACMI
Chief Clinical Informatics Officer, Thomson Reuters
Adjunct Assistant Professor of Medicine,
University of Pennsylvania
Cherry Hill, NJ

REFERENCES

1   Osheroff JA, Teich JM, Middleton B, et al. American Medical Informatics Association. *A Roadmap for National Action on Clinical Decision Support.* 13 Jun 2006. www.amia.org/inside/initiatives/cds/, accessed 10/8/08.

2   Wikinomics. www.wikinomics.com, accessed 10/8/08.

3   Keep an eye on the HIMSS CDS web page for further information about the various HIMSS initiatives mentioned in this preface: www.himss.org/cdsguide, accessed 10/8/08.

4   Osheroff JA, Pifer EA, Teich JM, et al. *Improving Outcomes with Clinical Decision Support: An Implementer's Guide.* Chicago: HIMSS; 2005.

Introduction

The framework this book uses to synthesize and convey clinical decision support (CDS) best practices for supporting appropriate, safe, and cost-effective drug use is based on the HIMSS guide, *Improving Outcomes with Clinical Decision Support.*[1] This approach closely parallels performance improvement (PI) methodologies increasingly applied in healthcare delivery organizations.[2] Guidance presented in this book addresses the following key tasks:

- Understanding basic definitions, concepts, and CDS approaches
- Building the foundation by defining processes, opportunities, priorities, and baselines
- Considering workflow, available clinical information systems (CISs), and specific targets in setting up CDS interventions (in three chapters)
- Deploying CDS interventions to optimize acceptance and value
- Measuring results and refining the program

In addition, a chapter that outlines a systematic approach to CDS knowledge management in the medication management program has been included, as well as appendices that address considerations specifically pertinent to office practice and medico-legal issues.

Worksheets with sample data are provided at the end of Chapters 2 through 8 to help inform your approach to systematically gathering, applying, and sharing with stakeholders the critical information necessary to address the various PI steps. You should consider consolidating key worksheets that reflect the status and results for all interventions in your program throughout their life cycle. Such a physical binder and/or online portal can be an important element of knowledge management activities as outlined in Chapter 8.

Those of you who have used the previous book in this series, *Improving Outcomes with Clinical Decision Support: An Implementer's Guide,* will rec-ognize key figures and a few selected passages and worksheets that have been brought forward. In every case, the material has been carefully reviewed and updated as needed to specifically address the issues and insights from this current effort.

Figure 1 illustrates, with a slightly more detailed breakdown, how key tasks outlined in this guide interrelate and flow across chapters.

This book is different from most IT implementation guidebooks in that each component reflects the experiences and expertise of many and varied stakeholders. You will hear these voices in the structure and content of this material, with extensive editing to make those voices fairly clear and harmonious. Keep in mind that, despite broad input into these recommendations for improving medication management with CDS, in many cases what those voices have to say reflects informed opinion and anecdotal experience. This field is relatively early in its development, and such syntheses are a work in progress. No one has mapped out all the territory (which is in flux anyway), and definitive answers about everything that should (or should not) be done do not yet exist. As discussed in the preface, project leaders are planning to create an online community that will further accelerate the synthesis and dissemination of effective CDS approaches, a community in which we hope you will participate.

SCOPE OF BOOK

This book covers applying CDS to improve care processes and various outcomes associated with the medication-use cycle, including safety, clinical effectiveness, and cost-effectiveness. A major focus is on medication safety—for example, reducing errors of commission. Considerable attention is also paid to errors of omission—for example, failure to use specific medications in appropriate patients as indicated by various core measures and other PI priorities. Strategies for improving cost-effectiveness are included as well.

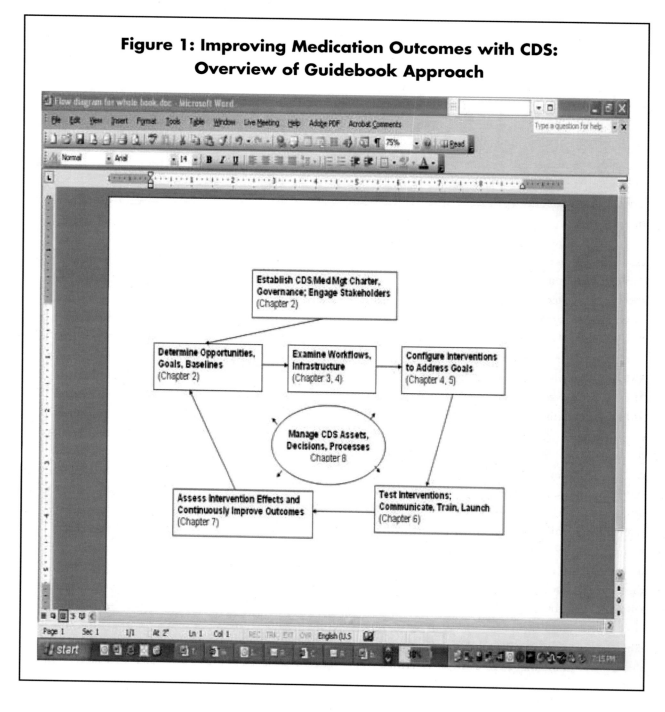

Figure 1: Improving Medication Outcomes with CDS: Overview of Guidebook Approach

Our goal is to cover issues pertinent to CDS in diverse care venues, including both inpatient and outpatient settings, with many of the approaches applying across the care continuum. However, much of the detailed guidance will be most pertinent to the inpatient and health system environments, although the appendix includes some additional considerations for smaller ambulatory practices.

Similarly, since most of the information is derived from individuals who work in larger organizations, it will resonate most strongly with others from similar settings. Nonetheless, we hope that many of the concepts and approaches will prove useful by extrapolation to those in other clinical environments, such as smaller hospitals, ambulatory surgery centers, and the like. Further build out of recommendations specific to such sites will hopefully become a focus of the online community we are working to develop to expand this base of CDS implementation best practices for medication management.

This book is not intended to be a comprehensive guide to improving medication safety or related outcomes. Although CDS can be a powerful and important component of an organization's medication-management program, many other elements are key to these initiatives that are beyond the scope of this book. Broader components that are not covered include establishing a culture of safety (though aspects pertinent to CDS will be mentioned) and deploying technologies for medication safety not specifically related to CDS, such as many aspects of smart pumps, bar-code medication administration, dispensing cabinets, and the like.

AUDIENCE

This book is primarily intended for those responsible for, or participating in, a care delivery organization's efforts to use CDS to improve medication use and outcomes. These include roles such as chief medical information officer (CMIO), pharmacy and therapeutic (P&T) committee member, pharmacy director, nursing informatics officer, quality and/or safety officer, chief nursing officer (CNO)/chief medical officer (CMO), and IT staff responsible for deploying pertinent systems, among many others. Physicians or practice managers in smaller practices with active electronic medical record (EMR) or electronic prescribing initiatives underway will also likely find valuable guidance. Secondary audiences include CIS and CDS vendors and suppliers. The strategies and challenges outlined here will hopefully facilitate richer dialog between these suppliers and CDS implementers, and thereby accelerate the availability of even more powerful and workflow-friendly CDS solutions. We also hope that health informatics trainees and researchers, along with others interested in medication management and health IT, will find this book informative and useful.

HOW TO USE THIS BOOK

Working through this book linearly will provide the reader with a comprehensive overview and a systematic approach to applying CDS in medication management. However, many organizations will already be deeply engaged in some phase of deploying CDS to support medication management. Individuals in these organizations may, therefore, want to delve into specific components of the book pertinent to their stage in the process. Skimming the tasks and key lessons in the beginning of each chapter will help readers focus on material that will be of greatest relevance to their most pressing needs.

CMIOs and others with substantial CDS experience may find that material in this book reinforces many insights already gleaned. Those who read our previous guide pointed out that in those instances, they still found the material useful in bringing their organizations and teams along. We hope this guide will be similarly helpful in not only introducing promising approaches into your strategy, but also in conveying useful concepts and tactics to other key stakeholders in your organization.

Those who primarily work in small office settings might consider first reading Appendix A: Using CDS to Enhance Safe and Effective Medication Use in the Small Practice Environment, and using it as a guide for navigating the rest of the book. Similarly, questions about legal matters related to CDS deployment frequently arise at various points throughout the process. Readers may wish to review the brief overview and references in Appendix B: Some Medico-legal Considerations to be prepared for when such issues arise.

Keep in mind that this guide is a snapshot of collective insight on how to approach this complex arena; although we all might wish otherwise, it is not a recipe for guaranteed success. Hopefully, the ideas presented will accelerate your learning, and help you and your organization efficiently achieve desired outcomes related to CDS and medication use.

REFERENCES

1 Osheroff JA, Pifer EA, Teich JM, et al. *Improving Outcomes with Clinical Decision Support: An Implementer's Guide.* Chicago: HIMSS; 2005.

2 For example, see iSix Sigma. *Six Sigma DMAIC Roadmap* for an overview and tools related to Six Sigma, one of several formal approaches to performance improvement being used increasingly in healthcare organizations. http://www.isixsigma.com/library/content/c020617a.asp, accessed 10/8/08.

Chapter 1
Approaching Clinical Decision Support in Medication Management

TASKS

- Begin by developing a clear picture of central processes and concepts, such as the medication management cycle, CDS intervention types, and challenges and opportunities related to medication management.
- Consider how the "CDS Five Rights" apply to improving processes related to medication use and outcomes throughout the medication management cycle.

> ### KEY LESSONS
>
> - Take a broad perspective on opportunities to support end users with CDS; the toolkit contains many important CDS tools in addition to interruptive alerts and reminders.
> - Go into your efforts bearing in mind what optimal, CDS-facilitated medication management might look like.

DISCUSSION

How well are tasks related to the medication use cycle typically accomplished in healthcare delivery today? Because you are reading this book, you probably sense that there is vast opportunity for improvement. Each step in the medication management process is fraught with opportunities for suboptimal outcomes, even with the best trained/educated/intended participants. CDS interventions offer promise for shoring up many of these weak spots. In typical practice today, however, CDS is used in relatively few components of the medication management process and is generally not optimally executed. A recent report from the Institute of Medicine (IOM) (see page 14) hints at the extensive opportunity for improvement.

To set the stage for the CDS implementation guidance offered in the remainder of this book, this chapter will walk you through the following related elements:

- The Five Rights of CDS—a framework for supporting clinical decisions to improve outcomes
- How CDS can be applied within the medication management cycle
- The types of CDS interventions that can be used to support medication management
- How key terms are used in this book

This chapter also briefly summarizes the current state of medication management to help you place your environment and challenges within a broader context. We provide a glimpse of a future characterized by more optimal CDS-enhanced medication management to inspire and guide your improvement efforts. We conclude this chapter with a literature sampling on medication errors and CDS in medication management as a springboard for those interested in deeper research on these topics.

Overview of CDS Five Rights

CDS interventions can be applied throughout the medication management cycle to optimize medication safety and other pertinent outcomes. A useful framework for achieving success in this effort is the "CDS Five Rights" approach. This should not be confused with the Five Rights of medication use, which speak to ensuring that the right patient gets the right drug, at the right dose, via the right route, at the right time.[1]

The CDS Five Rights model states that we can achieve CDS-supported improvements in desired healthcare outcomes if we communicate:

1. The *right information:* evidence-based, suitable to guide action, pertinent to the circumstance
2. To the *right person:* considering all members of the care team, including clinicians, patients, and their caretakers
3. In the *right CDS intervention format:* such as an alert, order set, or reference information to answer a clinical question
4. Through the *right channel:* for example, a clinical information system (CIS) such as an electronic medical record (EMR), personal health record (PHR), or a more general channel such as the Internet or a mobile device
5. At the *right time in workflow:* for example, at time of decision/action/need

For each step in the medication management process, one can consider how to apply these CDS Five Rights to ensure that the step is negotiated with optimal effectiveness, safety, and resource use. Chapters 3 through 5 will explore in detail how to address these parameters to achieve specific objectives associated with medication management, such as decreasing drug-drug interactions (DDIs) and supporting proper drug selection and dosing.

Applying CDS to Medication Management

The following outlines tasks in the medication management cycle and related CDS opportunities; typical parties responsible for each step in the cycle are listed in parentheses. This outline underpins further discussion on applying CDS to improving medication use and outcomes in this and subsequent chapters.

- **Medication Selection/Reconciliation** (prescriber, nurse, pharmacist)

– Select, for a clinical condition, a medication that is safe and effective, appropriate for a specific patient and circumstance, and available within an organizational formulary. The selection should be based on clinical evidence, best practice, patient characteristics, and cost-effectiveness.[2] The selection process requires access to pertinent patient information (such as clinical history, weight, height and age), as well as pertinent disease management knowledge (for example, evidence-based best practice treatment approaches) and drug information (addressing dosing, side effects, costs, interactions, contraindications and the like).

– Support medication reconciliation with an accurate list of the patient's medications, along with medication identification and therapeutic use information.

• **Ordering** (prescriber)

– Create a medication order/prescription (ideally linked to the indication) for the patient to take a drug or for the drug to be administered.

– Provide dosing recommendations, ideally specific to patient and clinical condition.

– Conduct automatic checks (or at least communicate reference information when appropriate) for contraindications, duplications, DDIs, drug-lab interactions, clinically significant allergies, right dose/route/frequency.

• **Verification/Dispensing** (pharmacist, pharmacy staff)

– Double check for interactions, appropriateness/contraindications, right dose/route/frequency/timing.

– Match prescription/order to correct dose and dose form.

– Check for proper concentration and volume to minimize pump programming errors, incompatibilities, and dispensing waste—important especially in pediatrics (for example, using 500-mL instead of 1000-mL bags when appropriate, and the like).

• **Administration** (patient or caretaker, nurse, and/or other clinician)

– Make positive medication and patient identification.

– Assess patient and document pertinent parameters (such as blood pressure, heart rate, blood glucose, pain level) prior to administration.

– Check for incompatibilities/interactions, such as between parenteral medications, between medications and foods, etc.

– Recheck right dose/route/frequency, administration technique and timing, monitoring guidelines.

– Provide reminder/guidance when medications are not administered at the appropriate time or are delayed or missed.

• **Education** (patient or caretaker, pharmacist, nurse, prescriber, other clinicians)

– Engage patient in effective medication use; help patient understand how and why to properly take medications (including indication, administration, and desired effects), how to appropriately store and handle medications, and potential adverse effects to be vigilant for and how to address them; ensure patient understanding of information (whether communicated via discussion, handouts, patient portals/kiosks, PHRs, and/or audio/video material and other media). Engage caregiver/parent when needed to support patient.

• **Monitoring** (patient or caregiver, nurse, other clinicians, pharmacist, prescriber, health system)

– Verify proper patient adherence to the medication regimen.

– Anticipate and monitor individual desired and adverse effects, for example, through history/symptoms, examination, and checking appropriate labs with notification of critical labs/adverse effects.

– Track adverse events across populations, for example, (ideally) via robust structured data-reporting system that incorporates medication error taxonomy standards, and updating the patient record with any new allergy/side effect/interaction.

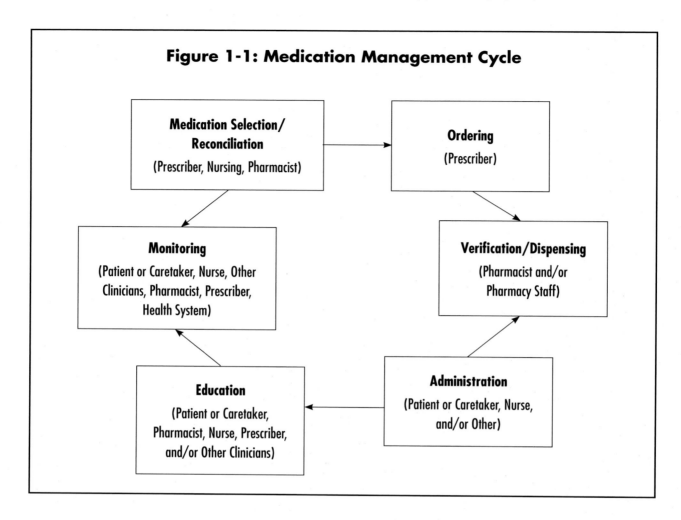

Figure 1-1: Medication Management Cycle

Medication Selection/ Reconciliation
(Prescriber, Nursing, Pharmacist)

Ordering
(Prescriber)

Monitoring
(Patient or Caretaker, Nurse, Other Clinicians, Pharmacist, Prescriber, Health System)

Verification/Dispensing
(Pharmacist and/or Pharmacy Staff)

Education
(Patient or Caretaker, Pharmacist, Nurse, Prescriber, and/or Other Clinicians)

Administration
(Patient or Caretaker, Nurse, and/or Other)

— Provide feedback and input about patient medication use—across care settings—into the medication reconciliation/selection step, and thus help close the medication management loop.

Figure 1-1 illustrates how all the individuals and components of the medication management cycle are connected. It is important to remember these connections going forward to avoid the tendency to isolate key tasks in silos; this approach plagues the traditional medication management process and supports errors and inefficiency. You do not want to create or continue an environment in which people take a narrow view of this interdependent process and respond with, "That's not my job," or, "The pharmacist or nurse will take care of that"—thereby creating a breeding ground for poor outcomes. As we will show in this chapter and in Chapters 3

through 5, well-executed CDS can support knowledge and data flows that help optimize care quality and efficiency throughout this cycle.

Types of CDS Interventions

The medication management cycle just described defines the "when," or workflow step, and the "who" for applying CDS; the palate of available CDS intervention types addresses the "how," or format for delivering information to support decisions.

Table 1-1 outlines several major CDS intervention types and subtypes along with their benefits. These categories are not meant to be rigid or mutually exclusive. Rather, the intent is to paint a rich picture of opportunities for guiding decisions through targeted information delivery. In practice, CDS interventions often combine several elements from these basic types. For example, an order set

Table 1-1: Clinical Decision Support Intervention Types

1. Documentation forms/templates

Benefits: Provide complete documentation for care quality/continuity, reimbursement, legal requirements; reduce omission errors by displaying items for selection; reduce commission errors by ensuring critical data—such as allergies—are captured; provide coded data for other data-driven CDS. Provide prompts to acquire specific information in the format desired (for example, displaying "kg" for weight to ensure capture in the metric system as needed for subsequent dose calculation).

Subtypes:	Examples:
Patient self-assessment forms	• Previsit questionnaire, for example, that captures health problems and current medications • Health risk appraisal
Clinician patient assessment forms	• Inpatient admission assessment • Assessment of medication-related parameters, such as pain, bleeding, blood glucose, blood pressure, breathing difficulty and the like, pre- and postmedication administration (possibly prepopulated with pertinent data)
Clinician encounter documentation forms	• Structured history and physical examination template • Problem-specific assessment template • Intelligent referral form
Departmental/multidisciplinary clinical documentation forms	• Emergency department (ED) documentation • Ambulatory care documentation • Combinations of the above
Data flowsheets (usually a mixture of data entry form and relevant data presentation; see next entry)	• Immunization flowsheet • Health maintenance/disease management form • Pay-for-performance form (such as for tracking pertinent quality measure parameters for individual patients)

2. Relevant data presentation

Benefits: Optimize decision making by ensuring all pertinent data are considered; organize complex data collections to promote understanding of overall clinical picture and to highlight needed actions.

Subtypes:	Examples:
Relevant data for ordering, administration, or documentation	• Patient allergies, relevant lab test results, formulary status, and/or drug costs when ordering a medication • Key parameters such as heart rate, pain level prior to medication administration • Patient rounding or action lists organized to highlight items needing attention, such as abnormal or new values • Longitudinal display of key patient information to highlight trends and issues requiring attention

Table 1-1: *continued*

Retrospective/aggregate reporting or filtering	• Data on patient adherence to prescribed medication regimen • Physician practice audit and feedback/physician report cards; for example, outlining rates at which highly indicated drugs are used in specific situations, such as treating heart attack • List of all patients overdue for a key preventive care intervention • List of all patients in disease management program with abnormal test results indicating poor disease control • Adverse drug event (ADE) tracking • List of all patients currently prescribed a medication newly withdrawn from the market
Environmental parameter reporting	• Recent hospital antibiotic sensitivities
Choice lists	• On-formulary display for a drug class, sequenced with preferred items listed first • Suggested dose choice lists, possibly modified as needed for patient's kidney or liver function and age
Practice status display	• Operating room (OR) scheduling and status display • ED tracking display

3. Order/prescription creation facilitators

Benefits: Promote adherence to standards of care by making the right thing the easiest to do.

Subtypes:	*Examples:*
Single-order completers including consequent orders	• Prompts for appropriate orders and documentation (for example, for additional meds when only one drug from a medication cocktail is selected or for reasons when ordering certain highly toxic drugs) • Suggested drug and/or dose choice lists integrated into ordering function — possibly modified by patient's kidney or liver function and age • Consequent order suggestions (for example, for drug levels when ordering certain antibiotics or for premedication when ordering certain drugs or procedures)

Table 1-1: *continued*

Order sets	• General order sets (for example, for hospital admission or problem-oriented ambulatory visit) • Condition-specific order sets (for example, for heart attack) • Pre- or postoperation order sets • Order sets containing orders that are fully specified (order sentences), contain parameter choices, have "fill-in-the-blank" fields for user-specified components of a recommended order, or a combination of the three • Active guidelines
Tools for complex ordering	• Guided dose algorithms based on weight, body surface area (BSA), kidney function, etc. • Total parenteral nutrition (TPN) ordering forms with built-in calculators

4. Protocol/pathway support

Benefits: Provides support for multistep care plans, pathways, and protocols that extend over time.

Subtypes:	*Examples:*
Stepwise processing of multistep protocol or guideline	• Tools for monitoring and supporting inpatient clinical pathways (for example, for pneumonia admissions) and multiday/multicycle chemotherapy protocols in the inpatient or outpatient setting
Support for managing clinical problems over long periods and many encounters[4]	• Computer-assisted management algorithm for treating hyperlipidemia over many outpatient visits

5. Reference information and guidance

Benefits: Addresses recognized information needs of patients and clinicians.

Subtypes:	*Examples:*
Context-insensitive	• General link from EMR or clinical portal to a reference program (at table of contents or general-search level)

Table 1-1: *continued*

Context-sensitive	• Direct links to specific, pertinent reference information (which can be mediated using the HL7 infobutton standard[5]); for example, link from medication order screen to display of side effects and/or dosing for that medication; link from problem-list entry to recent evidence-based treatment overviews for that problem • Link from immunization flowsheet to table of standard immunization intervals • Link within patient-messaging application to relevant patient drug information leaflets • Calculators/nomograms, such as for drug dosing • Diagnostic decision support driven by patient-specific data

6. Alerts and reminders (typically unsolicited by patient or clinician recipient)

Benefits: Provide immediate notification of errors and hazards related to new data or orders entered by CIS user or the CIS itself (such as when abnormal lab result is posted), or passage of a time interval during which a critical event should occur; help enforce standards of care. Effectiveness requires careful attention to workflow, high value of information to end user, and other factors as discussed in subsequent chapters.

Subtypes:	*Examples:*
Alerts to prevent potential omission/commission errors or hazards	• Drug allergy alert • Drug interaction alert; for example, with drugs, pregnancy, laboratory, food • Under/overdose alert (single dose, total dose, frequency, etc.; general, or specific for age, weight, laboratory results) • Wrong drug route alert • Patient-specific contraindication for a medication or other clinical intervention, such as due to pregnancy or genetic test result • Inappropriate therapeutic duplication • Incorrect test or study for an indication or inappropriate testing interval, such as for drug-level monitoring • Potential omission error detection, such as checking for a result from a follow-up test that is indicated after a medication is given • Critical lab test result notification • High-risk medication, such as chemotherapy agent or intravenous cardiovascular drug triggers reminder to nurse to obtain second witness before administration • User-requested notification when lab result is available or other key event has occurred

Table 1-1: *continued*

Alerts to foster best care	• Disease management; for example, alert for needed therapeutic intervention based on guidelines/evidence and patient-specific factors • Wellness management; for example, alert for patient needing flu shot • Risk management; for example, alert to document patient risk factor and/or obtain consults/interventions to address documented risk for suicide, physical abuse, falls, nutrition or smoking-related problems, etc. • Medication order triggers display of more cost-effective drug, regimen, or formulary-compliant option • Suggestion to add patient to a medication study or protocol

might highlight—through a non-interruptive alert—an essential intervention that should routinely be ordered and provide an infobutton link to more detailed reference information that supports the clinical recommendation.

Table 1-2 illustrates how the material discussed in the previous sections on the CDS Five Rights, the medication management loop, and CDS intervention types can provide a framework for developing a CDS intervention strategy to improve medication outcomes. Information in the table is not intended to be comprehensive and include every CDS option and objective but rather serves as a strawman to consider as you develop your approach to aligning CDS interventions with targeted goals (as discussed in Chapters 2 through 5).

How Key Terms Are Used in This Book

Many specialized clinical and information technology (IT) terms come into play in addressing the subject matter of this book, some of which may be jargon to those unfamiliar with a particular topic being discussed. Readers can consult online or print-based dictionaries[6] for clarification of such terms. There has been a national effort to standardize

definitions of several key health IT terms.[7] We have generally followed these definitions, though they have not yet been widely adopted.

In CDS and medication management, words shape thinking, which translates to action that changes the environment in which we operate. We therefore define several key terms that are fundamental to the subject at hand. Although these terms can be used differently in other contexts, the definitions presented here serve as the foundation for the guidance provided in this book.

Clinical decision support. We use this term, broadly defined, to encompass a wide variety of approaches—increasingly but not exclusively computer-based—for delivering clinical knowledge and intelligently filtered patient information to clinicians and/or patients for the purpose of improving healthcare processes and outcomes. CDS includes knowledge-delivery interventions, such as targeted documentation forms and templates, relevant data presentation, order and prescription creation facilitators, protocol and pathway support, reference information and guidance, and alerts and reminders (see Table 1-1).

Table 1-2: Using CDS to Improve Medication Use and Outcomes

		Medication Management Cycle Steps					
CDS Five Rights	**WHY (Goal)**	Optimize EBM/quality/ regulatory, cost, safe transition	Safer use: DDI, dosing, allergies, etc.	Safety/ appropriateness check	Safe administration	Optimize patient self-care	Track intention/ unintentional effects
	WHEN (Workflow)	Reconcile/Select	Prescribe/Order	Verify/Dispense	Administer	Educate	Monitor
	WHO (Person)	Prescriber, nurse, pharmacist, (patient)	Prescriber	Pharmacist	Nurse, other clinician, (patient)	Clinicians, patient	Clinicians, patient, health system
	WHAT (Information)	Reference on drugs (selection, dosing, ID, pricing, etc.), diseases (treatment), condition-specific recommendations	Condition-specific order sets and order sentences; order checks and references	Reference/ alerts on dosing/interactions	Reference information (e.g., administration, IV compatibility)	Patient-oriented reference (drug, disease, lab)	Reference drugs (effects/ monitoring), diseases (course), labs (interpretation); effect monitoring
	HOW (Format)	Order sets, reference (lookup/ infobutton)	Reference (lookup/ infobutton), order sets/ sentences, unsolicited alerting	Reference (lookup/ infobutton), unsolicited alerting	Reference (lookup/ infobutton)	Reference (lookup/ infobutton)	Reference (lookup/ infobutton); rule checking/ unsolicited alerting/ relevant data
	WHERE (Channel)	Internet, EMR/CPOE, mobile, med rec applications, formulary tools	CPOE, EMR, Internet, mobile, paper/ electronic order forms	Pharmacy system, Internet, EMR	eMAR, EMR, bar coding, dispensing cabinets, IV pumps, Internet, mobile, PHR	Internet, EMR, PHR	EMR/surveillance systems, PHR, Internet, mobile

Clinical information systems. This term broadly refers to computer-based systems that manage patient-related data, for example, EMR, PHR, CPOE (computerized practitioner order entry), and the like. As previously noted, early attempts have been made to standardize the definitions of selected key systems, although widely accepted definitions do not generally exist.

Medication errors. The National Coordinating Council for Medication Error Reporting and Prevention (NCC MERP)[8] has defined a medication error as "...any preventable event that may cause or lead to inappropriate medication use or patient harm, while the medication is in the control of the healthcare professional, patient, or consumer. Such events may be related to professional practice, healthcare products, procedures, and systems, including prescribing; order communication; product labeling, packaging and nomenclature; compounding; dispensing; distribution; administration; education; monitoring; and use."[9,10] NCC MERP has developed a taxonomy for categorizing medication errors and the associated harm to patients, summarized next.[11] This taxonomy informs medication error reporting programs, such as that provided by U.S. Pharmacopeia (USP) and the Institute for Safe Medication Practices (ISMP):[12]

- No Error
  - Category A - Circumstances or events that have the capacity to cause error.
- Error, no harm
  - Category B - Error did not reach patient (an "error of omission" *does* reach the patient).
  - Category C - Error reached patient but did not cause harm.
    - Medication reaches patient and is administered.
    - Medication reaches patient and is not administered.
  - Category D - Error reached patient and requires intervention to preclude harm (i.e., monitoring, lab tests).
- Error, harm
  - Category E - Error may have contributed to or resulted in harm that required intervention.
  - Category F - Error may have contributed to or resulted in harm that required initial or prolonged hospitalization.

  - Category G - Error contributed to or resulted in permanent patient harm.
  - Category H - Error contributed to or resulted in intervention necessary to sustain life.
  - Category I - Error contributed to or resulted in death.

Medication management. This term includes the full medication-use cycle in inpatient, ambulatory care and/or home settings, with emphasis on opportunities for CDS (see discussion and Figure 1-1 on page 2). Note that, in addition to helping optimize these process steps individually, a medication-management CDS program should continually measure and improve how CDS-mediated information delivery optimizes overall medication-related outcomes, such as pertinent morbidity, mortality, cost-effectiveness, and efficiency (see Chapter 7).

Medication use (appropriate). Ideally medications are used in a manner that minimizes, to the greatest extent possible, preventable harm caused by both errors of omission (such as failing to obtain appropriate follow-up data about a patient's response to a medication) and commission (such as providing a medication to a patient for which they have a known life-threatening allergy). It likewise includes using medications effectively and efficiently to optimize health (such as ensuring that patients receive medications that are strongly indicated to minimize disease complications). This appropriate use is accomplished, in part, by applying the best evidence, clinical information, and care practices to decisions and actions throughout the medication use cycle—all of which can be supported through well-executed CDS.

Outcomes related to medication use. For the purposes of this book, medication use outcomes include the extent to which the therapeutic (or diagnostic) intent for the medication is achieved; the safety with which medications are used—for example, avoiding preventable adverse events; and the financial implications of medication use—for example, cost-effectiveness compared with alternatives.

Typical State of Medication Management Today

As noted previously in this chapter, each step in the medication management process is fraught with opportunities for suboptimal outcomes, even with the best trained/educated/intended participants. The current state of affairs is roughly described as follows:

- The most common form of CDS applied to medication management is typically DDI and drug-allergy checking modules. Alert fatigue and general dissatisfaction with these interventions is common.

- Relatively limited diffusion of advanced CISs, such as CPOEs and EMRs, further limits the opportunities for fully optimizing the CDS Five Rights. Even when organizations have these systems in place, interoperability barriers across systems—for both patient data and CDS interventions/knowledge—frustrates successful implementation.

- Standard terminologies for clinical information, such as LOINC®,[13] SNOMED-CT®,[14] and RxNorm[15] are still underutilized across CIS and further limit data and knowledge interoperability across pertinent systems.

- Medication-error reporting channels exist but capture only a small fraction of errors.
  - USP-ISMP,[12] MEDMARX®, and Federal (MedWatch) are prominent examples among others. There has been progress in standardization and terminology (defining contributing factors, nodes, NCC MERP error categories) and electronic submission into large databases at national, regional, and hospital levels. However, federal mandatory error reporting only contributes a relatively few reportable sentinel events. Hence, there is still dependency on voluntary reporting mechanisms that are highly variable, with reporting volume depending on the care quality and culture across different delivery organizations.

- Sharing information about successful strategies for applying CDS to improving medication-related outcomes is relatively limited.

- Many institutions customize their CDS assets, such as DDI databases, to address current problems with excessive alerting; however, these customized—and potentially more practical—solutions are not readily available to other institutions due to lack of interoperability standards and other barriers.

- The lack of widespread plug-and-play interoperability of CDS interventions with CIS typically makes CDS deployment more difficult than it should be and slows the pace of innovation. These factors exacerbate the potential workflow difficulties that arise when CIS and CDS and systems are not developed and deployed with end-user needs and constraints in mind.

- Historically, misaligned financial incentives, an unclear business case, low capital availability, and/or fragmentation between quality/medication efforts and CDS activities have prevented a coordinated and systematic approach to CDS and medication management.

- In some cases, clinicians resist use of medication decision support tools for fear they will reduce autonomy or increase liability, or because of the perception (often justified) that the interventions (typically unsolicited alerts) are more annoying than useful.

- Conflicts between guidelines from multiple sources regarding appropriate medication use are not infrequent, which creates challenges for implementers attempting to facilitate guideline-based care with CDS.

A Vision for Optimal, CDS-Enabled Medication Management

The future state outlined next is adapted from the Roadmap for National Action on CDS:[16]

- The most current and applicable evidence and best practices for proper medication use underpin guidance throughout the medication management cycle. This guidance is easily accessed and accurate and is used appropriately as needed.

- Clear, evidence-based information about treatments that work best for specific patients and circumstances is readily available.[17]
- Widely used, standardized, and practical formats are available for expressing specific health-related knowledge and medication-specific interventions in both human and machine-readable form. These formats are used to create a plug-and-play environment wherein CDS guidance is readily deployed in CISs and sharable across systems and organizations.[18]
- Knowledge is readily customizable for location and facility-specific needs.
- Data needed for medication-related CDS (for example, drug terminologies and patient drug sensitivities, allergies, clinical problems, and the like) are managed using richly expressive and widely adopted standards.[19]
- Repositories make CDS knowledge more readily accessible for incorporation into CDS interventions and information systems (IS).

- Certified CISs and related tools that support medication management are widely implemented throughout the medication management cycle with high adoption rates by clinicians and patients.[20] This use provides a rich substrate for deploying CDS interventions that drive desired outcomes, such as eliminating preventable medication-related harm.
  - Principles of user-centered design are fully applied by developers in producing CIS and CDS systems, fostering more rapid and successful workflow integration and high end-user acceptance.
  - Electronic prescribing functionality is widely adopted. A 2005 white paper[21] has outlined a current state and future state related to electronic prescribing and environmental changes—standards, certification requirements, etc.—that need to be implemented to realize the future state for e-prescribing systems. These include:
    - Accurate, complete, patient medication list available at all times in all settings.
    - Accurate, complete, allergy list with associated reactions readily available.
    - Implementation of standard medical vocabularies across all systems and data assets.
    - Drug of choice suggestion or lookup function tied to diagnostic impression
    - Benefits and formulary confirmation.
    - Use of TALLman lettering and predefined order strings to prevent transcription and interpretation errors.
    - Drug of choice refinement based on other diagnoses, problems, age, weight, physiologic status (renal, cardiac, pulmonary, cognitive function), and medications.
    - Drug-interaction checking (for example, drug-drug, drug-lab, drug-food, etc.).
    - Monitoring activities (such as recommended surveillance of laboratory parameters) suggested by system and initiated at time of prescription.
    - Electronic prescription transmission to pharmacy.
    - Patient education communicated at encounter with clinician review, at prescription dispensing with pharmacist review, and via online link to further information and educational resources.

- CDS functionality—especially within ISs that underpin workflow—provides a favorable return on investment (ROI) for system purchasers and is welcomed and widely used by all pertinent recipients.
  - The Five CDS Rights are optimized to ensure this information delivery is workflow/user-friendly and supports improved outcomes.
  - Such effective deployments produce data that demonstrate the ability of CDS to reduce medication errors, increase user efficiency and satisfaction, and improve other key outcomes of great interest to stakeholders. This further drives the business case for, as well as uptake and adoption of, effective approaches.
  - Local implementations are characterized by a variety of key elements for success, including:

- Organizational structures to provide governance and gain clinician buy-in.
- Robust knowledge assets, such as evidence-based content, rules, and order sets, etc. that are explicitly focused on addressing priority targets.
- Rich knowledge management (KM) processes and tools to manage these assets and ensure their appropriateness (currency, evidence base, consistency, etc.) and value.
- Substantial attention to end-user needs and constraints to optimize acceptance and usability.
- Rigorous attention to measuring deployed CDS performance, including rich feedback loops with affected stakeholders, and to seeking opportunities for program enhancement.

- A continuous-improvement cycle of knowledge related to medication management and corresponding CDS deployment—within and across many institutions nationally/globally—drives rapid and widespread CDS-supported advances in desired outcomes.
  - Anonymous reports of medical errors and near-misses are used to identify points at which medication-focused interventions should be applied.
  - Medication errors are reported and stored in databanks to monitor for error spikes that can trigger appropriate responses, including new or modified CDS interventions that could be applied locally where spikes occur, or more widely as indicated.
  - Experiences from deploying CDS (including incorporating these interventions into CISs) to improve medication-related outcomes are systematically tracked and synthesized, further adding to the dynamic body of best implementation practices. These best practices are widely disseminated and continually enhanced, for example, through mechanisms such as this book and extensions of this work as outlined in the preface.

A Peek at the Literature on Medication Use and CDS

There is fairly rich evidence that details challenges associated with medication use and application of CDS in specific improvement opportunities. Journals such as those in general internal medicine,[22] medical informatics,[23] and other disciplines are increasingly devoting theme issues and other coverage to such topics. A comprehensive literature review is beyond this guide's scope, but a sampling helps set the stage for the guidance that follows.

Medication errors, which indicate breakdown in the medication use cycle and may cause bad outcomes, are increasingly the focus of public attention and local and national improvement efforts. A recent report from the IOM highlights the challenges and opportunities.

Summary of the 2006 IOM Report on Medication Errors

In 2006, the IOM released a landmark report on medication safety entitled *Preventing Medication Errors,* as part of their Quality Chasm series.[24] The report looked at both prescribing and administration errors. Prescribing error rates ranged from 12.3 to 1,400 errors per 1,000 admissions. The wide distribution reflects varying methods for finding errors—estimates at the lower end were generally based on error reports filed by clinicians. The study that estimated the error rate at 1,400 errors per 1,000 admissions was based on chart review and estimated approximately 0.3 errors per patient per day.[25] Although most of these errors were unlikely to result in patient harm, 7.5% of them either resulted in a preventable ADE or could have resulted in one.

Administration errors also occur with significant frequency. The IOM report reviewed five studies that estimated administration error rates as between 2.4 and 11.1 errors per 100 medication administrations. The IOM committee estimated that between all sources of errors, a hospital patient is subject, on average, to one medication error per day.

The IOM report also synthesized research on medication errors in the outpatient setting, citing studies which found that 21% of all prescriptions contain at least one error,[26] 3% of doses in an outpatient chemotherapy unit contained an error,[27] and between 1.7% and 24% of community pharmacy prescriptions were dispensed incorrectly.[28,29]

Beyond error incidence, the IOM report also reviewed research on the incidence of ADEs. They found three studies that met their inclusion criteria. These studies estimated the preventable ADE rate at 1.2 preventable ADEs per 100 admissions,[30] 1.8 preventable ADEs per 100 non-obstetric admissions,[31] and 5.57 ADEs per 1,000 patient days.[32] Preventable ADEs in hospitalized patients increased length of stay (LOS) by 4.6 days and total costs by $5,857 (1993 cost data).[33] In ambulatory Medicare patients at least 65 years old, the cost (in 2000 dollars) per preventable ADE is estimated at $1,983.[34]

Based on this literature synthesis, the IOM report concludes that, in the United States, 1.5 million people suffer preventable injury every year as a result of medication errors. Roughly 530,000 preventable drug-related injuries occur each year among Medicare recipients in outpatient clinics alone. The extra annual medical costs for treating patient injuries that occur in hospitals alone is $3.5 billion.

"The Future Is Already Here, It's Just Unevenly Distributed"[35]

As outlined previously in this chapter, CDS holds great promise for addressing the pressing challenges related to medication use that have been identified by the IOM and others. A growing collection of studies demonstrates that this promise is currently being realized in leading organizations to varying degrees. In developing this guidebook, an effort has been made to base implementation recommendations on evidence from such literature on successful practices; therefore, references are included throughout. Given the practical focus and largely volunteer nature of this effort, the literature analysis has been more opportunistic than exhaustive.

Perhaps a more important barrier to providing strongly evidence-based implementation guidance than extensive literature review is that, although

there have been a number of studies on medication-related CDS, this literature only covers, and in a somewhat limited manner, the full medication management cycle. Even in relatively well-studied areas, such as CPOE to reduce ADEs, major gaps still exist.[36,37] Further, much of the published literature is derived from leading academic organizations with locally developed systems; 70% of the studies in this review examining ADE rates used homegrown CPOE with CDS.[37]

There is much to be learned from these pioneers, but the CDS functionality and results from custom-crafted systems in academic settings may not be directly transferred elsewhere. In this guide, we have tried to extrapolate lessons from groundbreaking efforts to healthcare delivery settings in which vendor supplied systems are the norm and organizational dynamics may be different. Where evidence is not specifically cited, the guidance provided is drawn from the experience of the editors, contributors, and reviewers, based on success strategies (or at least thoughtful approaches) gleaned in the course of their efforts.

In subsequent chapters, we occasionally reference CDS studies to reinforce specific recommendations. For example, Chapter 5 contains references to studies exploring the issues in applying CDS to various specific targets, such as reducing drug-allergy, DDI, and drug dosing problems. In addition, the following is a sampling from the literature on applying CDS to medication management. Studies of this sort have been loosely summarized in various sources such as the Roadmap for National Action on CDS,[16] the IOM report, *Preventing Medication Errors,*[24] and systematic reviews of CPOE with CDS as previously mentioned.[36,37]

Sampling of Literature on CDS in Medication Management

• Utilizing CDS has been shown to improve adherence to guidelines. Traditionally, clinical guidelines are left "on the shelf" and, as a result, errors and suboptimal care persist. Using CDS to communicate the guidance within clinician workflow, and hence increase adherence, has resulted in an absolute increase in influenza and pneumococcal vaccination of 12% and 20%, respectively.[38] Another study demonstrated a 3.3% absolute decrease in the primary endpoint of deep vein thrombosis (DVT) or pulmonary emboli (PE) within 90 days after hospitalization.[39]

- CPOE with CDS has improved physician prescribing practices, formulary adherence, and cost savings[40] and produced an 86% absolute reduction in non-intercepted serious medication errors.[41]

- CDS for empiric preoperative antibiotic selection decreased postoperative wound infections.[42]

- CDS-supported medication dosing produced a 21% increase in appropriate medication prescribing in renal insufficiency and a 4.5% reduction in length of stay (LOS).[43]

- EMR use does not appear to be associated with improved performance on ambulatory care quality indicators without focused CDS features.[44] Basic computer prescribing (which improves legibility and completeness) was not associated with a reduced rate of errors in an outpatient setting unless combined with advanced systems with CDS (drug-drug, drug allergy, and drug-interaction checking).[45] Similarly, even hospitals with highly computerized medication management processes experience high rates of ADEs without CDS focused specifically on drug selection, dosing, and monitoring.[46] To realize benefits of CDS within CPOE, authors have suggested a two-stage approach: (1) basic CDS (drug-allergy testing, basic dosing guidance, duplication checking, and DDI checking), followed by (2) advanced CDS (dose-lab, renal dosing, drug-disease checking).[47]

- A systematic review found that CPOE reduces medication errors and ADEs.[48] Extensive tables featured in this review outline the CDS functionality examined in various studies, whether the systems were homegrown or commercial, and the risk ratio for ADEs with the system.

We will take a closer look at literature-suggested CDS targets in Chapter 2.

CONCLUDING COMMENTS

Deploying CDS in a manner that effectively addresses priority objectives doesn't generally occur in a piecemeal manner (for example, through entirely separate initiatives for each target, such as medication use, regulatory compliance, and the like). Typically, a variety of targets are addressed in a somewhat integrated fashion within a broader organizational CDS program. Nonetheless, since improving medication management with CDS is such a widespread (perhaps universal) and important healthcare goal, we are focusing this book on this specific topic. Keep in mind, however, that insights conveyed here may be applicable to your broader CDS efforts and, likewise, pearls you may have gleaned from CDS initiatives focused on other targets may well help accelerate your medication management CDS efforts.

In any case, a systematic performance improvement (PI) approach based on careful attention to the CDS Five Rights, the full spectrum of CDS intervention types, and the interdependent nature of the medication management cycle should help provide solid footing for your efforts. Inspiration from a vision of what optimal CDS-enabled medication management could be should further help you enhance your program so that it delivers optimal benefit today and in the future.

REFERENCES

1   Institute for Healthcare Improvement. *The Five Rights of Medication Administration.* http://www.ihi.org/IHI/Topics/ PatientSafety/MedicationSystems/ImprovementStories/ FiveRightsofMedicationAdministration.htm, accessed 9/30/08.

2   Institute for Safe Medical Practices (ISMP) stresses that if all of the other aspects mentioned are achieved, then the drug will be cost effective.

3   Tang PC, Young CY. ActiveGuidelines: Integrating Web-based guidelines with computer-based patient records. *AMIA Proceedings.* 2000; 843-847.

4   Maviglia SM, Zielstorff RD, Paterno M, et al. Automating complex guidelines for chronic disease: lessons learned. *J Am Med Inform Assoc.* 2003; 10(2):154-165.

5   Background on infobuttons and the version of the HL7 standard approved in May 2008 can be found here: Health Level 7. *HL7 V3 Infobutton, R1.* http://www.hl7.org/ v3ballot2008may/html/domains/uvds/ uvds_Context-awareInformationRetrieval(Infobutton). htm#REDS_DO010001UV-Infobutton-ic, accessed 9/30/08.

6   For example, Wikipedia (http://en.wikipedia.org/wiki/ Main_Page, accessed 10/1/08), and the HIMSS dictionary of HIT terms. (http://marketplace.himss.org/acct618b/ Default.aspx?tabid=44&action=INVProductDetails&args= 585&BookTitle=HIMSS%20Store%20-%20HIMSS%20 Dictionary%20of%20Healthcare%20IT%20Terms,%20 Acronyms, accessed 10/1/08).

7   NAHIT Releases HIT Definitions; http://www.nahit .org/pandc/press/pr5_20_2008_1_33_49.asp, accessed 12/12/08.

8   National Coordinating Council for Medication Error Reporting and Prevention. http://www.nccmerp.org/, accessed 9/30/08.

9   The Institute for Safe Medication Practices. *Frequently Asked Questions (FAQ).* www.ismp.org/faq.asp, accessed 9/30/08.

10 National Coordinating Council for Medication Error Reporting and Prevention. *About Medication Errors.* www.nccmerp.org/aboutMedErrors.html, accessed 9/30/08.

11 National Coordinating Council for Medication Error Reporting and Prevention. *About Medication Errors. Taxonomy of Medication Errors Now Available.* http:// www.nccmerp.org/medErrorTaxonomy.html (see items 30-34), accessed 9/30/08. See also links to diagrams under NCC MERP Index for Categorizing Medication Errors. http://www.nccmerp.org/medErrorCatIndex.html, accessed 12/12/08.

12 *USP-ISMP Medication Errors Reporting Program.* https:// www.ismp.org/orderforms/reporterrortoISMP.asp, accessed 12/12/08.

13 Standard terminology for laboratory information. See Logical Observation Identifiers Names and Codes (LOINC). http://loinc.org/, accessed 9/30/08.

14 A very rich, standardized, multi-lingual clinical healthcare terminology. See Systematized Nomenclature of Medicine-Clinical Terms. *SNOMED CT.* http://www.ihtsdo.org/ snomed-ct/, accessed 9/30/08.

15 A standard terminology for clinical drugs. See U.S. National Library of Medicine. *Unified Medical Language System: RxNorm.* http://www.nlm.nih.gov/research/umls/rxnorm/, accessed 9/30/08.

16 Osheroff JA, Teich JM, Middleton B, et al. A roadmap for national action on clinical decision support. *J Am Med Inform Assoc.* 2007; 14(2):141-145. See also American Medical Informatics Association. CDS Roadmap. http:// www.amia.org/inside/initiatives/cds/, accessed 9/30/08.

17 The Institute of Medicine has recently developed a detailed roadmap for this. See Institute of Medicine. *Knowing What Works in Health Care: A Roadmap for the Nation.* http:// www.iom.edu/CMS/3809/34261/50718.aspx, accessed 9/30/08.

18 The standards development organization HL7 (http:// www.hl7.com.au/FAQ.htm, accessed 10/2/08) has a Clinical Decision Support Technical Committee that produces standards for CDS capabilities such as rules and alerts, infobuttons, and order sets; further work is needed to produce a robust suite of widely used standards for the full suite of CDS interventions.

19 The Health Information Technology Standards Panel (HITSP: http://www.hitsp.org/about_hitsp.aspx, accessed 10/1/08) has begun work on this. See, for example, The Medication Management Interoperability Specification: http://www.hitsp.org/InteroperabilitySet_Details.aspx?Ma sterIS=true&InteroperabilityId=54&PrefixAlpha=1&APre fix=IS&PrefixNumeric=07, accessed 10/1/08. This work is supporting the medication management use case (see Health Information Technology. *Medication Management Use Case:* http://www.hhs.gov/healthit/usecases/ medicationmgmt.html, accessed 10/1/08), developed by Office of the National Coordinator for Health IT.

20 The Certification Commission for Health Information Technology (CCHIT) has begun this work. See, for example, the clinical decision support requirements related to medication management in the latest inpatient and

ambulatory certification requirements and test scripts, available at http://www.cchit.org/, accessed 10/1/08.

21 Teich JM, Osheroff JA, Pifer EA, et al. Clinical decision support in electronic prescribing: recommendations and an action plan: report of the joint clinical decision support workgroup. *J Am Med Inform Assoc.* 2005; 12(4):365-376.

22 See, for example, Clancy CM, White PJ. Introduction to the JGIM special issue on health information technology. *J Gen Intern Med.* 2008; 23(4):353-4. http://www.springerlink.com/content/g10768345264, accessed 10/1/08.

23 See, for example, Focus on Safe e-Prescribing. *Journal of the American Medical Informatics Association.* 2008; 15(4). http://www.jamia.org/content/vol15/issue4, accessed 10/1/08.

24 Institute of Medicine. *Preventing Medication Errors: Quality Chasm Series.* Washington, DC: National Academies Press; 2006. http://www.iom.edu/?id=35961, accessed 10/1/08.

25 Bates DW, Boyle DL, Vander Vliet MB, et al. Relationship between medication errors and adverse drug events. *J Gen Intern Med.* 1995; (10)4:199-205.

26 Shaughnessy AF, Nickel RO. Prescription-writing patterns and errors in a family medicine residency program. *J Fam Pract.* 1989; 29(3):290-295.

27 Gandhi TK, Bartel SB, Shulman LN, et al. Medication safety in the ambulatory chemotherapy setting. *Cancer.* 2005; 104(11):2477-2483.

28 Allan EL, Barker KN, Malloy MJ, et al. Dispensing errors and counseling in community practice. *Am Pharm.* 1995; NS35(12):25-33.

29 Flynn EA, Barker KN, Carnahan BJ. National observational study of prescription dispensing accuracy and safety in 50 pharmacies. *J Am Pharm Assoc* (Wash). 2003; 43(2):191-200.

30 Classen DC, Pestotnik SL, Evans RS, et al. Adverse drug events in hospitalized patients. Excess length of stay, extra costs, and attributable mortality. *JAMA.* 1997; 277(4):301-306.

31 Bates DW, Cullen DJ, Laird N, et al. Incidence of adverse drug events and potential adverse drug events. Implications for prevention. ADE Prevention Study Group. *JAMA.* 1995; 274(1):29-34.

32 Jha AK, Kuperman GJ, Rittenberg E, et al. Identifying hospital admissions due to adverse drug events using a computer-based monitor. *Pharmacoepidemiol Drug Saf.* 2001; 10(2):113-119.

33 Bates DW, Spell N, Cullen DJ, et al. The costs of adverse drug events in hospitalized patients. Adverse Drug Events Prevention Study Group. *JAMA.* 1997; 277(4):307-311.

http://jama.ama-assn.org/cgi/content/abstract/277/4/307, accessed 10/2/08.

34 Field TS, Gilman BH, Subramanian S, et al. The costs associated with adverse drug events among older adults in the ambulatory setting. *Med Care.* 2005; (12):1171-1176. http://www.ncbi.nlm.nih.gov/pubmed/16299427, accessed 10/2/08.

35 Quotation attributed to William Gibson: http://en.wikiquote.org/wiki/William_Gibson#Attributed; 1999; Nov 30, accessed 10/1/08.

36 Eslami S, Abu-Hanna A, de Keizer NF. Evaluation of outpatient computerized physician medication order entry systems: a systematic review. *J Am Med Inform Assoc.* 2007; 14(4):400-6. http://www.jamia.org/cgi/content/abstract/14/4/400, accessed 10/2/08.

37 Wolfstadt JI, Gurwitz JH, Field TS, et al. The effect of computerized physician order entry with clinical decision support on the rates of adverse drug events: a systematic review. *J Gen Intern Med.* 2008; 23(4).

38 Dexter PR, Perkins SM, Maharry KS, et al. Inpatient computer-based standing orders vs. physician reminders to increase influenza and pneumococcal vaccination rates: a randomized trial. *JAMA.* 2004; 292(19):2366-2371.

39 Kucher N, Koo S, Quiroz R, et al. Electronic alerts to prevent venous thromboembolism among hospitalized patients. *N Engl J Med.* 2005; 352(10):969-977.

40 Teich JM, Merchia PR, Schmiz JL, et al. Effects of computerized physician order entry on prescribing practices. *Arch Intern Med.* 2000; 160(18):2741-2747.

41 Bates DW, Teich JM, Lee J, et al. The impact of computerized physician order entry on medication error prevention. *J Am Med Inform Assoc.* 1999; 6(4):313-321.

42 Evans RS, Classen DC, Pestotnik SL, et al. Improving empiric antibiotic selection using computer decision support. *Arch Intern Med.* 1994; 154(8):878-884.

43 Chertow GM, Lee J, Kuperman GJ, et al. Guided medication dosing for inpatients with renal insufficiency. *JAMA.* 2001; 286(22):2839-2844.

44 Linder JA, Ma J, Bates DW, et al. Electronic health record use and the quality of ambulatory care in the United States. *Arch Intern Med.* 2007; 167(13):1400-1405.

45 Gandhi TK, Weingart SN, Seger AC, et al. Outpatient prescribing errors and the impact of computerized prescribing. *J Gen Intern Med.* 2005; 20(9):837-841.

46 Nebeker JR, Hoffman JM, Weir CR, et al. High rates of adverse drug events in a highly computerized hospital. *Arch Intern Med.* 2005; 165(10):1111-1116. http://archinte.ama-assn.org/cgi/content/abstract/165/10/1111, accessed 10/2/08.

47 Kuperman GJ, Bobb A, Payne TH, et al. Medication-related clinical decision support in computerized provider order entry systems: a review. *J Am Med Inform Assoc.* 2007; 14(1):29-40.

48 Ammenwerth E, Schnell-Inderst P, Machan C, et al. The effect of electronic prescribing on medication errors and adverse drug events: a systematic review. *J Am Med Inform Assoc.* 2008; 15(5):585-600.

Chapter 2

Build the Foundation by Defining Processes, Opportunities, Priorities, and Baselines

TASKS

- Identify the stakeholders responsible for medication safety and utilization and CDS, and ensure that a shared vision and appropriate governance around applying CDS to medication management is in place. Develop/use a charter to formalize these CDS activities.
- Examine local and national sources of information to identify opportunities to improve medication safety, utilization, and outcomes.
- Establish/use a formal process within governance structures (noted in the first bullet above) to identify and prioritize CDS targets.
- Establish baseline performance on medication use issues targeted for improvement, against which the effects of CDS interventions will be evaluated.

KEY LESSONS

- Applying CDS to medication safety and management is not solely a pharmacy or IT initiative; it requires a broad multidisciplinary team and approach, which includes end users and their champions.
- Prioritizing specific goals on which to focus CDS efforts and resources is critical; these medication and CDS priorities should be closely aligned with organizational imperatives and business goals established by senior leadership.
- CDS efforts need to be transparent and provide a built-in feedback mechanism that supports continuous improvement.

DISCUSSION

Processes such as medication management, CDS, goal setting, and the like are driven by individuals and committees, so a key initial activity is to understand the people and environment that serve as the context for CDS efforts.

Identify the Stakeholders, Roles, and Activities in CDS and Medication Management

Improving medication safety, utilization, and outcomes with CDS is not just a pharmacy or IT activity—although these functions certainly play a critical role. In fact, many additional and diverse stakeholders are essential for success, and their efforts and priorities must be well-integrated. A first step in this coordination is understanding who the players are and what challenges and goals they are addressing.

Inventory CDS and Medication Management Activities

Medication management is an important and problematic component of healthcare delivery for which CDS can be a powerful improvement tool. As such, it deserves focused attention as part of an organization's overall CDS program.

Typically there will already be, devoted at some level to CDS initiatives, infrastructure, people, resources, and management priorities; likewise for medication safety, utilization, and related areas. A first step in fully leveraging CDS to optimize medication management is to conduct an inventory of pertinent organizational activities within each of these two spheres (that is, CDS initiatives and efforts to improve medication utilization). This might include determining answers to the following:

- What pertinent CDS and medication management governance structures and processes are in place? How do they interrelate?
- Who are the key pertinent individuals and their roles and challenges?

- What are the current priorities being addressed around CDS and medication management, separately and jointly?
- What resources (such as people and IS infrastructure) are being applied to tackling these priorities?

The current state of these issues will be the foundation for performance enhancements that hopefully can be realized by executing the recommendations in this book. Worksheet 2-1 in this chapter may be helpful in your approach to gathering and documenting this type of information.

Your inventory can help determine whether any modifications to governance, management, infrastructure, resources, and roles may be needed to optimize the next round of your CDS activities focused on medication management. In the next few sections, we consider individuals and groups that play key roles in these activities.

Leadership Engagement in CDS, Quality, and Medication Management

Ultimately, the context of medication-management initiatives should trace back to boards of directors and their responsibility for quality oversight.[1] While some leading organizations have already created this top-down context, in others it is the chief medical/nursing officer (CMO/CNO), chief medical information officer (CMIO), quality/safety officers, and others who can serve as change agents for helping senior leadership fully address this oversight responsibility. This may play out, for example, through efforts related to developing and gaining approval for a CDS charter, which will be discussed shortly. The following key questions assess the degree of board engagement—and thus top-down impetus for CDS-focused improvements in medication management.

- Is there a quality committee?
- How much time does the issue of quality in general, and medication management in particular, have on their agenda?
- How engaged are the board's influential leaders, and the group overall, in quality matters?
- What level of detail about medication-related issues is presented and discussed?

- To what extent is CDS discussed and regarded as a strategic organizational tool?

Although hospital governing boards are typically engaged in quality oversight to some degree, there appears to be substantial room for improvement. For example, fewer than half of CEOs responding to a survey considered their organization's board very effective in its quality oversight function, and only 61% indicated their boards had a quality committee. Such quality committees appear to be important, since they were associated with lower mortality rates for six common medical conditions and improved use of various quality oversight practices.[2]

However your organization's board of trustees handles quality, ideally, CDS-supported medication-management strategy and objectives should flow from the quality and safety imperatives it has established. These imperatives should be developed and executed in conjunction with other pertinent leadership structures, such as the pharmacy and therapeutics (P&T) committee, quality council, medical executive committee, and other stakeholders as outlined in Table 2-1. As responsibilities and activities pertinent to CDS efforts—such as those handled by nursing, IT, pharmacy, physician staff, quality/safety and others—may often occur in silos, executive leadership may have to play a key role in helping bridge these silos to ensure the effective coordination needed for successful improvement efforts.

CDS and Medication Management Stakeholders

Typically positions such as CMO, CMIO, chief safety/quality safety officer, CNO/director of nursing informatics, and/or pharmacy director should play leadership roles in the medication-related components of the CDS program. Table 2-1 outlines several pertinent stakeholder roles and committees.

Legal counsel is included as an entity on the stakeholders list because legal issues tend to arise at several points in the CDS program lifecycle. Appendix B: Some Medico-legal Considerations, provides a brief introduction to these issues and lists suggestions for additional resources.

As noted earlier, optimal success in improving outcomes requires bridges between the traditional vertical silos that exist between stakeholders and their respective activities. Ideally, the CDS program focus (both related to medication management and more broadly) should be patient-centered (as opposed to departmentally oriented), yet should simultaneously address the business needs of the organization and its component functions.

Involving CDS end users, whose behavior will be targeted for change by improvement efforts (for example, rank and file clinicians and patients, and the champions among them), very early in the process is vital. These constituencies should likewise be kept closely engaged in an ongoing manner as CDS development and deployment unfolds.

Patients and their caregivers also are central players in medication use, outcomes, and improvement opportunities, so they should have a voice in strategy, as well as in execution. Table 2-2 outlines the various groups involved and their respective roles.

Figure 2-1 illustrates how the different stakeholder groups and functions interrelate in a CDS program.

Builders and Managers of CDS Interventions Focused on Medication Management

A typical core team executing CDS interventions for medication management might consist of a physician, pharmacist, nurse, IT specialist, and a team leader (who may also fill one of the other roles). It is very helpful to have one or more team members with formal clinical informatics skills and experiences; that is, expertise in how clinical and technology capabilities can be applied together in addressing care delivery needs.

Informatics professionals play an important role in serving as a liaison between CDS users and developers, among other responsibilities. CDS recipients (such as clinicians or patients) do not always know all the possibilities for optimizing CDS interventions to meet their needs. In addition, they might not be able to convey their insights, needs,

Table 2-1: Stakeholders for Individual CDS Interventions and Overall CDS Program

Committees

- Board of directors
- Pharmacy and therapeutics (P&T)
- Quality improvement (organization-wide)
- Quality (departmental)
- Patient safety
- Utilization review (organization-wide or departmental, such as blood product use)
- Medical staff/executive
- Residency/training
- Clinical information systems (for example, implementation, oversight, benefits realization)
- Guideline/practice standards, clinical strategy, disease/care management
- Medical records
- Infection control
- Service line-focused

Positions

- Medical director of CDS
- CMO/medical director
- CMIO/medical director of information systems
- Chief Information Officer (CIO)
- Pharmacy director/ chair of P&T committee
- CNO/director of nursing informatics
- Quality officer
- Patient/Medication safety officer
- Risk management officer
- Department chairs
- Residency/training directors
- Independent Practice Association (IPA)/physician group chairs
- Legal counsel

Other CDS Stakeholders

- Clinicians vocal on clinical computing/CDS issues (positively or negatively)
- Clinical thought leaders
- Patients/patient representatives
- Other clinician, trainee, and non-clinician end users of CDS interventions
- Non-end users who will be affected by a CDS intervention (such as radiology staff that will have to accommodate interventions that will increase the frequency of particular imaging studies)

Table 2-2: Generic Outline of CDS Program Stakeholder Groups and Responsibilities

Board and Executive Leadership: Set Strategy and Priorities, Clinical Standards, Allocate Resources
- Overall board and members with quality/safety interests: help set overall organizational agenda (including quality/safety focus), improvement priorities, resource allocation
- Executive leadership: sets a more specific improvement agenda, priorities, resource allocations

Management/Oversight: Manage Processes Related to CDS Program
- Healthcare organization departments/functions: responsible for processes/outcomes that will be affected by CDS program (see Table 2-1)
  - Clinical departments (for example, laboratory, pharmacy, nursing, medicine, surgery, infection control) and service lines
  - Organized medical staff
  - Cross-cutting functions (for example, quality, safety, disease management, case managers, risk management)
  - Clinical director of information systems/medical informatics
  - Other organizational committees and departments
- CDS oversight/benefits realization committee: supports execution and evaluation of CDS initiatives; educates senior executives and board of directors on importance and impact of CDS efforts
- CIO/IT steering committee and IT department: responsible for IT infrastructure that underpins CDS interventions

Implementation/Project Management: Develop, Deploy, Monitor CDS Interventions
- CDS-specific: overall responsibility to deploy/maintain CDS knowledge assets, collect and analyze evaluation data
- General IT: overall responsibility to support/maintain CISs

End Users and Related Positions: Perform Patient Care Activities Affected by CDS
- End users: recipients of CDS interventions (for example, patients, nurses, pharmacists, physicians, others on the care team, case managers)
- Related staff: generate data for, or are affected by, interventions
- Subject matter experts: clinical authorities for content in CDS interventions
- Clinical thought leaders and champions (such as clinicians respected and listened to by colleagues): help ensure interventions meet needs and are successfully adopted

and constraints in a way that translates easily to the technical staff. Likewise, communication challenges may exist in the opposite direction, for example in conveying technical limitations on CDS capabilities to intervention recipients. Informatics professionals who have appreciation for both perspectives can be exceedingly helpful in bridging this gap. Organizations such as the American Medical Informatics Association (AMIA) are developing robust training programs to ensure that individuals with appropriate qualifications are available to fill these positions.[3]

The clinical and/or informatics team members should ideally be familiar with local IT development and deployment issues, have working knowledge of the pertinent clinical applications used within their healthcare system, and be familiar with organizational culture issues that could potentially impede successful CDS approaches to medication management. The team should understand pertinent work-

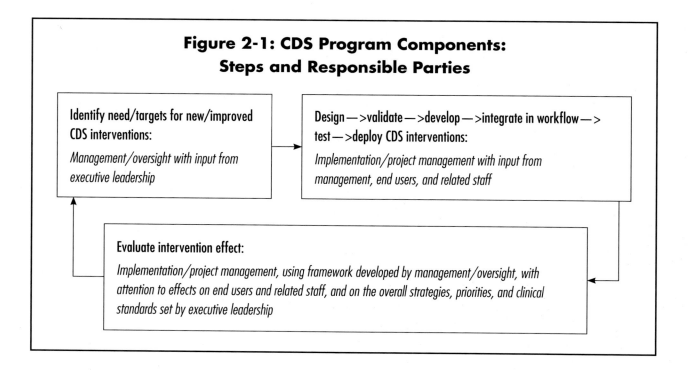

Figure 2-1: CDS Program Components: Steps and Responsible Parties

Identify need/targets for new/improved CDS interventions:

Management/oversight with input from executive leadership

Design —>validate —>develop —>integrate in workflow —> test —>deploy CDS interventions:

Implementation/project management with input from management, end users, and related staff

Evaluate intervention effect:

Implementation/project management, using framework developed by management/oversight, with attention to effects on end users and related staff, and on the overall strategies, priorities, and clinical standards set by executive leadership

flows (see Chapter 3) and continually seek to provide CDS interventions that improve, rather than hinder, work processes (see Chapter 7). To ensure that this core team has an accurate and broad appreciation of these critical issues, close and frequent communication about the project should be maintained with those who will be affected by its output.

Consumers of CDS (Patients, Nurses, Pharmacists, Physicians, Case Managers, Others)

As we emphasize throughout this guide, CDS interventions are done *with* end users to achieve *shared* goals, rather than done *to* them in a Draconian fashion. It is therefore essential to make sure that the full spectrum of CDS consumers is represented on the appropriate teams—or at least that a communication channel with each is established. For each intervention, consider which end-users groups are pertinent. In addition to top-of-mind recipients, such as patients, nurses, pharmacists and doctors, also consider house staff, pharmacy technicians, respiratory therapists, patients' families and other caregivers, and all other potential recipients as appropriate.

Similarly, end-user champions play important roles in intervention development and adoption, as is described in subsequent chapters. End users respect these peers and consider them to be spokespersons for their needs and constraints. These champions can therefore serve as liaisons between the development team and end users, helping to ensure that both groups' needs and constraints are addressed. To bridge the gap between users and developers, champions ideally should have some appreciation for the capabilities and limitations of CDS to support medication management. To successfully represent and support their colleagues, it is essential that champions are influential and highly regarded among their end-user peers. An optimistic but realistic perspective regarding CDS value, and excellent communication skills (both listening and conveying), can also be very helpful. Though it may be challenging to find individuals with all these qualifications, keeping this list in mind can help in identifying and enlisting the most suitable candidates.

CDS Oversight Committee and Its Relation to Other Teams

CDS efforts related to medication management typically unfold as part of an organization's broader CDS program. Different organizations approach CDS governance and management in various ways. Many organizations either already have or are developing a CDS oversight committee of some type, with responsibility for managing the organization's efforts to apply CDS in improving targeted outcomes. Having such an entity oversee activities related to CDS and take responsibility for their value is important. Without some type of accountability, it is far less likely that this value will be optimized.

Well-rounded CDS oversight committees should be comprised of representatives from a variety of key departments. These can include physicians from various specialty groups, pharmacists, nursing, risk management, infection control, quality, case management, administration, IS, and other stakeholders as appropriate. (See Tables 2-1 and 2-2 for more potential participants.) There should be adequate authority and mandate so that this group has access to the necessary people, infrastructure, and other resources to ensure that CDS interventions are developed and deployed in a manner that delivers the expected, measurable value in targeted areas.

This committee should meet regularly to develop strategy, guide execution, monitor progress and results, and address challenges that arise in the CDS program. These responsibilities extend continuously throughout planning, implementation, evaluation, and continuous improvement phases. As opposed to only including clinicians who primarily function in administrative roles, it is important to include representation from actively practicing physicians, nurses, pharmacists, and other clinicians (and ideally champions from these groups) on the CDS oversight committee. Involving actual users of the interventions that will be deployed will help ensure that the needs and constraints of that critical constituency are addressed.

The CDS oversight committee should be the gatekeeper for all CDS functionality implementation. It should work in close coordination with other entities (for example, the quality, P&T, and IT committees) that are responsible for CDS-related processes and outcomes. This coordination may include explicitly appointing members of the CDS oversight committee and/or CDS project team to follow or serve on pertinent committees as a liaison between the related activities. For example, a CDS committee member sitting on a quality improvement committee can follow the specific quality-related policies, procedures, and priorities and help identify points at which CDS approaches could support the quality goals and compliance using the new policies and procedures. Similarly, a formal liaison between the CDS oversight committee and the P&T committee can be highly beneficial for optimizing CDS efforts focused on medication management.

Organizations may develop a formal CDS subcommittee or function to specifically focus on medication management. Alternatively, they can just handle the many medication-specific targets and interventions in a fully integrated way within the rest of their CDS portfolio. In a similar fashion, the CDS management structures dealing with medication issues can interface with medication-related components of pertinent quality, safety, pharmacy and other committees.

Figure 2-2 is an example of a CDS governance model successfully employed at an academic medical center over the past several years. This example illustrates the close interplay between clinical, medication, IS, and CDS activities and governance. This coordination has served the organization well in enhancing the efficiency and effectiveness of its CDS and medication management initiatives.

Develop a Charter to Formalize the Program

Conducting the inventory of pertinent initiatives and management structures (such as is outlined in Worksheet 2-1) helps determine the most fruitful focal point or "home" for coordinating and executing the activities outlined in this book. For example, existence of a high-priority organizational initiative

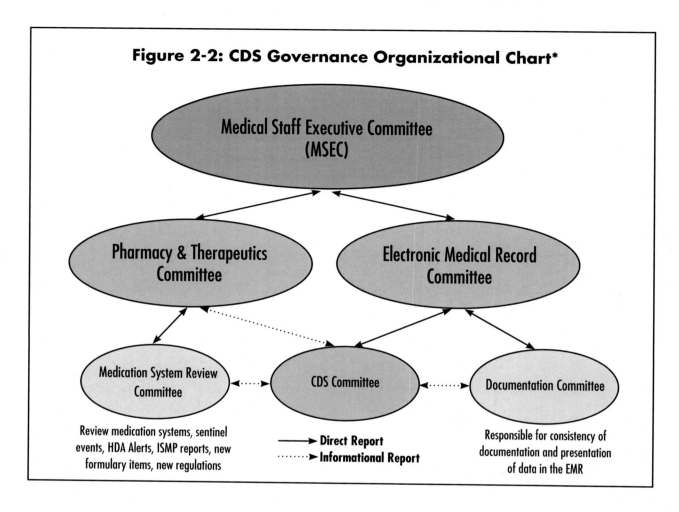

Figure 2-2: CDS Governance Organizational Chart*

to deploy CPOE to improve key outcomes means there may already be in place the staffing, infrastructure, and momentum to serve as a logical home for next-round efforts to leverage the tool's CDS capabilities to improve medication management. It is important, however, to balance being opportunistic with the need to install the right people and processes to ensure a comprehensive, long-term approach to leveraging CDS to enhance medication management. An effective CDS charter, developed and managed by a CDS oversight committee that has appropriate representation, authority and resources, can play a central role in this long-term plan for your organization.

The Overall CDS Charter

The shared vision and coordinated effort required to successfully apply CDS in addressing priority needs

does not happen by accident. As opposed to a document with no real buy-in or execution, a living CDS charter or mission statement can help, especially when this charter is managed within a governance model that fully leverages and optimizes pertinent organizational resources in carrying out the charter.

Successful CDS efforts often use such a CDS mission statement, or charter, to formalize the program's goals and overall approach. When appropriately developed with stakeholder input, and supported and incorporated into an organization's culture, such a statement can add focus, credibility, and urgency to CDS initiatives. When available, such a charter will provide a natural framework for CDS activities specifically focused on medication management. On the next three pages are sample generic CDS charters that might be of use in developing or enhancing one in your organization.

---

* Source: University of Illinois Medical Center at Chicago. Used by permission.

Sample Generic CDS Charter*

Overview
Well-executed Clinical Decision Support (CDS) is essential for Health System to realize
full value from its substantial investments in health information technology (HIT) and to
address Health System's overall Mission and Vision.

Mission Statement
The mission of Health System's CDS program is to continuously improve the safety, quality, and efficiency of patient care at Health System by ensuring that the care delivery
team has the information needed to drive good decisions and actions that lead to optimal
outcomes.

Principles
- Aim to measurably improve key organizational performance metrics.
- Leverage the full spectrum of CDS interventions and the full capabilities of the deployed
  health information technology to maximize CDS usefulness and benefits.
- Develop and deploy CDS in a user-focused manner to optimize user acceptance and
  clinical workflow; use best evidence and documented best practices when available.
- Proactively manage CDS knowledge assets to ensure their currency, relevance, and
  consistency, and continuously monitor and enhance their effectiveness.

Methods
Governance
- Core CDS efforts are focused on addressing goals established and prioritized by the
  Health System clinical and executive leadership.
- The Decision Support Strategic Planning Committee (DSSPC), a subcommittee of the
  system-wide HIT Physician Advisory Council (PAC), is responsible for the oversight and
  direction of the Health System CDS Program.
- The Decision Support Working Group (DSWG) is responsible for managing the CDS
  program execution and operates under the direction of the DSSPC.
- Specific DSWG responsibilities include prioritizing and addressing requests for CDS
  support received from various departments, developing and maintaining CDS interventions, monitoring CDS system implementation and results, and ensuring currency,
  consistency, and appropriateness of Health System CDS assets.

CDS Intervention Strategy
- *Begin with the end in mind:* the starting point for considering CDS interventions is a
  clear, shared understanding by pertinent stakeholders of the target that the planned
  CDS approach is intended to address.
- *Key parties at the table:* the intended users and other affected parties play a key role
  in each step of the development, launch, evaluation, and improvement loop. There is

* Adapted from: The University of Pittsburgh Medical Center CDS Mission Statement. Used with permission.

meticulous attention to affected workflows and processes during each of these steps in the CDS intervention lifecycle. Good use is made of champions.

- *Right tool for the job:* a range of possible CDS intervention types (for example, alerts, order sets, referential information, focused data gathering, review tools, etc.) are considered in developing an optimal strategy for ensuring that targeted goals are achieved most efficiently and effectively.
- *Deliver high-value information:* patient- and context-specific information available in deployed HIT systems is fully leveraged to optimize the applicability and usefulness of CDS information and guidance delivered to the recipient.
- *Measure and improve:* intervention monitoring is considered at each step of the intervention lifecycle. Effects of deployed interventions (both desirable and otherwise) are monitored; progress toward each intended objective is tracked, and the portfolio of interventions focused on the objective is refined, as needed.

Knowledge Asset Portfolio Management and Value
- The DSWG maintains an inventory of deployed CDS interventions and regularly monitors their currency, appropriateness, and consistency. For example, there is at least a yearly review of each CDS rule.
- To complement the review of interventions focused on specific objectives, the DSWG monitors overall performance of the Health System CDS program on an ongoing basis to ensure continued function as intended.
- DSWG will collaborate with pertinent experts within the Health System, affiliated academic programs, and outside agencies, as appropriate, in evaluating the CDS program.

A Charter for CDS in Medication Management

Once you identify the right stakeholders and organization structures to support CDS efforts to enhance medication management, you might consider developing a CDS charter focused on this domain to clarify why and how these efforts will proceed. Although it probably would be impractical and overkill to develop a charter for every goal within the CDS program, medication management is so closely tied to the core mission of care delivery, and such a high stakes activity, that a separate charter might be useful. It can help obtain buy-in and resources (especially time) from all pertinent stakeholders. It can also help ensure that everyone clearly understands

the goals, roles, and steps involved in implementing CDS to improve medication management.

The medication management charter should be a subset of the organization's broader CDS charter, if one exists. If there is not yet a broad CDS charter and your organization is prepared to adopt one specifically for medication management efforts, consider adapting the generic one in the sidebar shown earlier for this purpose. It could then serve as the kernel from which a broader CDS charter can be developed at the appropriate time.

The charter for applying CDS to medication management may outline broad goals and approaches as found in the generic sample previously discussed. It may also cover more specific

A More Concise CDS Charter Sample*

- Focus on clinical interventions for which strong evidence and/or best practices have been demonstrated.
- Develop solutions that are useful and usable, focusing on those things that truly make a difference. Align priorities with overall organizational goals for safe, timely, effective, efficient, and equitable patient-centered care.
- Recognize the applications and limitations of decision support, while respecting the clinical expertise of nurses, physicians, and other staff.
- Pursue systemness when it enhances value, allowing latitude for legitimate local variation.
- Create an organizational model that is sustainable over the long-term and offers rapid support and problem-resolution for Texas Health Resources' (THR) clinicians.

CDS targets, such as those pertinent to addressing specific clinical objectives (as discussed in Chapter 5) or related to deploying specific CISs (as discussed in Chapter 4). The charter may include a combination of optimizing the value from currently deployed interventions (for example, DDI alerting in CPOE) and launching new, high-value interventions to address priority medication targets.

Specific goals contained in, or referenced by, the medication-focused CDS charter should ideally have target dates with measurable outcomes. For example, an overarching objective might be reducing all

* Source: Texas Health Resources, Arlington, TX. Used with permission.

preventable medication adverse events by half within three years. Narrower targets with shorter timelines might include reducing avoidable allergic reactions or anticoagulation drug overdoses by 20% within one year. Worksheet 2-2 contains a checklist of items to consider in developing charter components that address specific targets.

Identify Opportunities for Improvement

A primary objective for CDS initiatives addressing medication management should be to *drive measurable improvement in specific areas identified as top priorities for the organization.* As the stakes are high in terms of both the outcomes involved and organizational resources required, it is imperative to carefully select the specific areas the program will address. In addition, the expected outcomes and benefits should be articulated in advance, based on thoughtful analysis. This will help ensure (though not guarantee) adequate support and resources required for successful execution and monitoring.

How does an organization determine top-priority medication targets on which to focus CDS efforts? Two general sources of information can help: publicly available information about particular points at which problems have been found to occur in medication management broadly, and analysis of local medication use patterns and problems specific to your organization.

National Sources for Opportunities to Improve Medication Management

External information sources that are useful in identifying and prioritizing medication-related targets for CDS intervention can be considered in three categories. In order of decreasing potential influence for decision making, these categories include mandatory initiatives, market-driven opportunities, and literature-suggested targets.

Provider organizations can approach such external sources for setting priorities in a manner suited to the maturity and capability level of the CDS program. An organization with an already established and well-functioning CDS program might consider targets suggested by external sources in all three categories. A less mature CDS program would do well to initially focus on meeting regulatory and other mandatory requirements. On the other hand, an organization that has identified an area of opportunity internally could benefit from researching the literature to determine if others have already implemented and studied CDS interventions designed to address that particular problem area. Literature pertinent to specific targets discussed in Chapter 5 should help with clarifying such opportunities as well. We now explore in further detail each of these three external types of sources for improvement opportunities.

Mandatory Initiatives

External agencies impose explicit requirements that healthcare provider organizations must meet to maintain accreditation status or receive reimbursement for services provided. These include, but are not limited to the following:

- Regulatory/Reporting—for example, the Centers for Medicare & Medicaid Services (CMS) has rules regarding core-measures reporting requirements. These metrics include various medication-related issues, such as whether indicated drugs have been given to patients with specific conditions.

- Required for accreditation—for example, The Joint Commission's National Patient Safety Goals. The 2008 goals, as a case in point, added reducing patient harm from use of anticoagulant drugs.[4] In addition, several prior and ongoing goals relate directly to medication use and have CDS implications; for example, preventing errors related to look alike/sound alike (LASA) drugs, reconciling medications across the continuum of care, and standardizing dose designations *not* to be used throughout the organization, among others.

- Payment—for example, non-payment by CMS and other payers for treating complications related to certain preventable complications acquired during hospitalization,[5,6] such as inpatient falls (which can be exacerbated by improper medication use) and venous thromboembolism (VTE) (which can be prevented with appropriate drugs).

These mandatory initiatives provide compelling motivation for provider organizations to leverage CDS in meeting the imposed requirements. Scientific evidence and/or broad support for the goal is well-established, and there may be rich CDS opportunities to address pertinent targets, as we will discuss in Chapter 5.

Market-driven Opportunities

Formal, voluntary programs that healthcare provider organizations can opt to participate in (typically for market differentiation purposes and/or supplemental reimbursement) include:

- Pay-for-performance demonstration programs, such as that sponsored by CMS,[7] or employer programs that focus on physician practices.[8]

- National patient safety initiatives, such as those offered by the Institute for Healthcare Improvement (IHI), Leapfrog, and others (as described in next sections).

Along similar lines, the National Committee for Quality Assurance (NCQA) evaluates health plan performance and publishes this information in the Quality Compass database.[9] This evaluation includes several measures on how medications are managed, which may be useful in selecting improvement targets.

Many medication-safety campaigns are underway across the country. You may want your CDS efforts to address some of the issues highlighted by those campaigns. For example, the 5 Million Lives Campaign includes a variety of goals related to medication management that can be supported by CDS, including appropriate perioperative medication use, preventing harm from high-alert medications, and delivering evidence-based care for heart attack and heart failure.[10]

The Leapfrog CPOE test (see also Chapter 7) assesses several key areas that should be addressed by CDS, including the following:[11]

- Therapeutic duplication

- Single and cumulative dose limits
- Allergies and cross allergies
- Contraindicated route of administration
- Drug-drug and drug-food interactions
- Contraindications/dose limits based on patient diagnosis
- Contraindications/dose limits based on patient age or weight
- Contraindications/dose limits based on laboratory studies
- Contraindications/dose limits based on radiology studies
- Corollary orders
- Cost of care
- Lack of nuisance alerts

Leapfrog also maintains a compendium of incentive and reward programs[12] that provide information about various pay for performance programs currently underway. The National Quality Foundation (NQF) has identified "serious reportable events," or "never events" that include medication issues, such as death or serious disability resulting from healthcare facility-acquired hypoglycemia or medication error (wrong dose, for example).[13]

Market-driven opportunities, such as those previously outlined in this chapter, can highlight fruitful areas for provider organizations to focus CDS efforts. Scientific evidence and/or broad support for the target is generally well-established, and useful and relevant CDS approaches are often available or are rapidly emerging.

Literature-Suggested Targets

There are numerous areas for which clinical research and/or aggregated clinical experience suggest that improved approaches to medication use are needed. Provider organizations may wish to consider this literature in efforts to select promising targets and CDS interventions. These external sources can be further classified into the following two groups:

- Problem-oriented [P]. These sources call attention to challenges in the medication management cycle (such as with safe drug administration) or with specific medications or drug classes (such as

drugs that are toxic to the kidneys). This literature can suggest opportunities for CDS intervention and may or may not describe specific intervention approaches.
- Intervention-focused [I]. These sources explicitly describe how CDS interventions can be used to improve medication safety, such as for geriatric patients in a long-term-care facility.[14]

Common sources (and their subclassification) include:

- Studies published in peer-reviewed journals [P,I]
- Clinical guidelines published by medical societies [P]
- Reports published by panels of subject-matter experts—IOM reports, for example [P,I]
- Advisories from patient-safety organizations, such as ISMP [P,I]
- CDS content from third-party providers [I]
- Peer organizations exchanging clinical challenges, opportunities, targets and CDS strategies via forums, such as online communities offered by co-publishers of this book and many others [P,I]

These sources can supplement the more essential regulatory/payment drivers in generating candidate medication targets to address with CDS. For example, when considered in light of improvement opportunities and priorities in your organization, they may help identify additional fruitful areas on which to focus. Keep in mind that the scientific evidence and/or broad support for addressing these targets range from that which is immature to well-established. Similarly, desirable CDS interventions range from available to in development to non-existent. As will be discussed shortly, any target candidates you identify from the three categories outlined earlier should be formally prioritized for execution, based on explicit criteria. The Sidebar on the next page presents further details on CDS targets suggested by available literature.

Identify Pertinent Local Data Sources and Examine Them for Problems/Opportunities

In addition to considering external drivers for improving specific aspects of medication use, it is

More on Literature-Suggested Targets

IOM

The IOM report, Identifying and Preventing Medication Errors,[15] outlined causes for drug errors that are widely prevalent in healthcare delivery, including the following:

- Wrong dose/rate/frequency/patient
- Contraindications due to co-morbidities
- Effects of drug on pregnancy or vice versa not considered
- Allergies
- Drug interactions
- Failure to monitor response pre-, during, and post-therapy
- Therapeutic duplication
- LASA drugs

   In addition, IOM, NQF, and others are defining priority conditions and activities[16,17] on which to focus national efforts for performance improvement (PI). CDS can support appropriate medication use in managing these conditions and issues, as outlined in the sampling that follows.

- Asthma—using appropriate treatment for persons with specific types of asthma, such as mild/moderate persistent asthma
- Cancer management—for example, implementing evidence-based therapy for colorectal cancer
- Diabetes—for example, appropriately managing early disease and preventing complications
- Frailty associated with old age—preventing falls (for example, by careful use and monitoring of sedatives) and maximizing function (by minimizing polypharmacy)
- Hypertension—focusing on appropriate management of early disease
- Immunization—providing as indicated for both children and adults
- Ischemic heart disease—preventing, reducing recurring events, and optimizing functional capacity through appropriate medication use
- Major depression—effectively treating according to type and duration
- Medication management—preventing medication errors and overuse of antibiotics
- Pain control—utilizing medication effectively, such as in advanced cancer
- Pregnancy and childbirth—appropriately implementing pharmaceuticals in preconception, prenatal, and intrapartum care
- Severe and persistent mental illness—focusing on treatment in the public sector
- Stroke—focusing on early intervention and rehabilitation, including role for medications
- Tobacco dependence—implementing treatment in adults, including role for medications

Institute for Safe Medication Practices (ISMP)

This medication-safety focused organization provides various data and tools useful for selecting targets. For example, their Medication Safety Tools and Resources Web page[18] includes links to a list of drugs with heightened risk of patient harm ("high alert" medications for which errors may be less common than others, such as those identified by IOM but which may produce greater harm), an error-prone abbreviation list, a confused drug name list, error report investigation tools, and a Failure Mode and Effects Analyses (FMEA) overview and sample. Carried out by a multidisciplinary team, FMEA is an ongoing quality improvement approach that involves carefully examining processes to determine potential points of failure and their effects *before* they actually occur. This allows proactive refinement of processes to help eliminate sources of error and harm, which can include applying CDS interventions.

Literature on CPOE and ADEs

Because high ADE rates can persist unless appropriate targets are addressed—even in highly computerized hospitals with CPOE and other technologies[19]—implementers must select and approach targets thoughtfully. Research on the role of CPOE in addressing specific priority improvement objectives can therefore be helpful in identifying promising opportunities. For example, non-intercepted serious medication errors, such as wrong dose/choice/route/frequency, as well as problems with allergy/interactions/monitoring, have been decreased by 55%.[20] Other studies similarly point to the role of CPOE with CDS in decreasing errors related to dosing, route, selection, and the like.[21,22]

Other useful data for selecting targets to be addressed with CPOE are provided by results from the review of 4,200 paper patient charts reported by the Massachusetts Technology Collaborative and New England Healthcare Institute.[23] This analysis revealed a 10.4% average baseline level of preventable ADEs and quantified the expected clinical and financial return from addressing such harms. The distribution of ADEs is shown in the Table 2-3. Only 19% of the ADEs were deemed "not preventable" with a robust CPOE plus CDS system. ADEs that occur with the most frequency and have been shown to be preventable with CDS might be good candidates for initial targets. Chapter 4 provides further information on setting up CDS in CPOE, and Chapter 5 discusses CDS interventions targeted on the issues outlined in the table.

Table 2-3: Distribution of ADEs Judged to Be Amenable with a Robust CPOE/CDS System*

Drug-lab check	27%
Renal check	19%
Drug dose suggestion	9%
Drug-age	9%
Drug-specific guidelines	7%
Drug-allergy	4%
Drug frequency	3%
Drug-drug	2%
Duplicate med check	1%

* Source: Massachusetts Technology Collaborative and New England Healthcare Institute. Saving Lives, Saving Money. The Imperative for Computerized Physician Order Entry in Massachusetts Hospitals. Westborough, MA: Massachusetts Technology Collaborative, 2008. Used with permission.

Patient characteristic	1%
Subtotal	**81%**
ADEs NOT judged preventable by CPOE/CDS	19%

Analysis by the United Kingdom National Health Service (NHS)

The NHS Connecting for Health initiative set up a working group to identify a small number of important medication-related harms that could be mitigated by e-prescribing/CDS systems.[24] The objectives of the group were to:

- Identify those drugs commonly associated with preventable patient harm;
- Identify the most common reasons they cause harm; and
- Identify CDS support that would have the greatest likelihood of reducing this risk.

The notable drugs included antiplatelets, diuretics, non-steroidal anti-inflammatory drugs (NSAIDs), anticoagulants, opiates, beta-blockers, ACE inhibitors, insulin, and a small number of others. These comprised 86.4% of all drug-related admissions associated with ADEs.

The most common events that occur appear to be associated with dosing, contraindications and cautions, allergies, drug interactions and monitoring problems. Table 2-4 highlights that the top four classes of drugs account for more than half of preventable ADEs that caused hospital admissions. Table 2-5 identifies the drug classes associated with preventable ADEs in secondary care.

Table 2-4: Drug Groups Most Commonly Associated with Preventable Admissions to Hospital Caused by Preventable ADRs and Over-Treatment*

Drug Group	Drug-Related Admissions Associated with Preventable ADRs and Over Treatment Number (%) (n = 1263)
Antiplatelets (including aspirin when used as an antiplatelet)	219 (17.3)
Diuretics	202 (16.0)
Non-steroidal anti-inflammatory drugs	151 (12.0)
Anticoagulants	113 (8.9)
Opioid analgesics	68 (5.4)
Betablockers	56 (4.4)
Drugs affecting the rennin-angiotensin systems (e.g., angiotensin converting enzyme inhibitors)	58 (4.6)
Drugs used in diabetes	40 (3.2)
Positive inotropes	41 (3.2)

* Adapted from: Howard RL, Avery AJ, Slavenburg S, et al. Which drugs cause preventable admissions to hospital? A systematic review. *Br J Clin Pharmacol.* 2007; 63(2):136-147.

Corticosteroids	41 (3.2)
Antidepressants	41 (3.2)
Calcium channel blockers	34 (2.7)
Antiepileptics	11 (0.9)
Nitrates	15 (1.2)
Potassium channel activators	1 (0.1)
Total	*1,091 (86.4)*

Table 2-5: Drug Classes Most Commonly Associated with Preventable Adverse Drug Events in Secondary Care*

Drug Class	Median Percentage of All Preventable Adverse Drug Events (Data from 6 Studies)
Cardiovascular events	17.9
Psychoactive and CNS drugs	15.3
Analgesics	12.8
Anticoagulants	9.8
Antiinfectives	9.6
Antidiabetic agents, insulin	6.7
Antiasthmatic agents	3.1
Electrolytes	3.0
Antineoplastics	2.8
Antiseizure agents	2.1

Some of the specific CDS approaches for addressing common and important medication safety challenges that were recommended by this NHS report are incorporated into the discussion in Chapter 5.

Other Pertinent Literature

Extending the potential targets suggested by the summary sources noted earlier are research reports from investigators, and press releases from safety-related organization, that appear regularly and focus on specific drugs or improvement opportunities. Examples include information about the drugs identified as most frequently responsible for voluntary reports of serious medication errors;[25] high-risk medications given frequently, yet inappropriately to pregnant women;[26,27] and common causes of medication errors in children.[28] Similarly, it has been noted that the use of potentially toxic drugs, such as warfarin, digoxin, and insulin, causes many times more ED visits for ADEs by patients at least 65 years old than drugs that are prescribed despite being inappropriate for this age group.[29] Again, additional pertinent literature that may be helpful for identifying targets is outlined in other chapters.

---

* Adapted from: Kajanarat P, Winterstein AG, Johns TE, et al. Nature of preventable adverse drug events in hospitals: A literature review. *Am J Health Sys Pharm* 2003; 60(17):1750-1759.

Table 2-6: Some Internal Sources for Identifying CDS Targets

- Institutional analyses of quality, safety, patient satisfaction, cost, and regulatory problems (for example, from committees, such as P&T, quality assurance, patient safety, utilization review, or others)
- High-level committees that prepare the overall response to environmental drivers, such as accreditation requirements (for example, related to care safety and quality), pay-for-performance, and related quality measurement/improvement initiatives
- Analyses of available data on care and outcomes at the organization (see details in discussion that follows)
- Interviews with clinicians, medical directors, and other stakeholders; review/discuss with pharmacists the data on interventions they are providing to avoid medication errors
- Surveys assessing stakeholders' (such as clinicians) CDS-related activities, needs, and priorities related to medication management
- Direct observation of information needs and related obstacles creating medication use challenges in clinical settings
- Community-based priorities and programs related to medication use, such as local smoking cessation initiatives that include a drug-therapy component

---

important to conduct an internal review to uncover priority improvement opportunities. Table 2-6 outlines several general sources from within an organization that can be useful in determining fruitful areas on which to focus medication-related CDS efforts.

Analyzing local data about care and outcomes can be a rich—though sometimes challenging—source to guide CDS target selection. Data may be incomplete and/or difficult to synthesize because of disparate data definitions and sources, and the like. Nonetheless, think broadly about sources for pertinent care process and outcomes data, including clinical, financial, and administrative systems. Items of interest include, among many others:

- Medication-related outcomes from pertinent patient safety indicators and core measures
- Self-reported medication errors and near misses and data on interventions by pharmacists
- Root-cause analyses and FMEAs conducted by the risk/quality management department
- Medication-related legal action taken against the organization
- Drug cost data (including most expensive and most frequently used drugs, which may suggest opportunities for improvement) and comparisons with benchmarks

Be sure to leverage broader patient safety infrastructure, activities, and reports available in your organization. Consider also pertinent data analytic tools that might be available in-house or from vendor partners, as well as pertinent staff that can help use these tools to uncover improvement opportunities.

"Trigger tools" can also be helpful for identifying points at which safer medication use may be needed. For example, the IHI Trigger Tool[30] (and derivatives for populations, such as pediatric patients[31]) involves retrospective patient chart review looking for signals that an ADE may have occurred. Triggers include clues such as administration of a drug used to treat overdose or toxicity from another drug. Twenty charts per month are examined—either in paper format or electronically when available—for evidence of these triggers. The frequency with which they occur is used to estimate the number of ADEs per 1,000 doses and the percent of admissions with an ADE.

Careful chart review to assess triggers and otherwise delve into improvement opportunities can be very revealing but difficult, costly, and time-consuming. This approach does, however, provide more reliable quantitative data than self reports, since a relatively small portion of errors and ADEs are voluntarily reported. Nonetheless, when available, incident-reporting or tracking systems (which typically include information about medication errors and ADEs) are a useful source of information about the types of recognized errors that are occurring in your organization. Note that data in these systems tend to skew toward administration and possibly dispensing errors, as they typically represent voluntary reports from nurses and, perhaps, pharmacists.

The sidebars that follow on the next two pages illustrate two approaches that specific health systems have adopted in their efforts to systematically identify opportunities for improving medication use with CDS. Worksheet 2-3 can be used to document potential improvement priorities for your organization and the rationale for each as determined by the opportunity analysis outlined earlier.

Prioritize Medication Management Goals and Objectives to Be Addressed with CDS

The inventory of internal initiatives pertinent to CDS for medication use, recommended earlier in this chapter, will likely identify a variety of current and planned activities. For example, initiatives to implement CISs, such as CPOE, will likely have significant components related to medication CDS. Examining local and national sources for improvement opportunities listed earlier will likely suggest many additional important and promising focus areas. On top of all this, department representatives and others often present urgent requests for CDS to support medication use issues in their areas.

Prioritizing these opportunities is essential because there probably will not be sufficient resources to address them all, and there will likely be different benefit-cost ratios for each. The CDS governance processes discussed earlier in this chapter provide the framework and mechanisms for setting priorities. We have seen that CDS targets will arise from a variety of sources and evolve over time, but the CDS prioritization process should be relatively stable, explicit, and well-connected to organizational

governance structures and processes. It should also be well-integrated with related organizational PI initiatives and priorities.

Select Broad Medication-related Goals and More Specific Objectives within Each

Because there are so many specific opportunities to improve medication management with CDS, it is helpful to first identify broad-based medication-related goals that align with priority organizational targets. For example, if increasing performance on core measures is a top organization-wide focus, then helping to improve outcomes related to appropriate medication use is a logical focal point for CDS efforts. Similarly, if decreasing preventable harm is a top priority, then focusing CDS efforts on common and dangerous avoidable ADEs (with specifics defined through the internal and external sources as outlined earlier) will be a fruitful approach. These key organizational initiatives will hopefully have become clear during the analysis of stakeholders and activities recommended in the beginning of this chapter.

Many organizations are approaching as a strategic priority the deployment of clinical systems, such as CPOE, to enhance clinical performance. In such situations, pursuing CDS-related opportunities to ensure that expected benefits are realized may be a logical starting point for medication-related CDS. Again, specific objectives within this broader goal can be defined by considering opportunities revealed by examining internal and external sources of information about performance gaps. For example, improper drug dosing is a common and important prescribing error that CPOE may logically be expected to reduce. However, even with wide CPOE use, the occurrence of specific types of errors, including those related to dosing, will remain high unless CDS interventions that specifically focus on these are deployed.[19] Chapters 4 and 5 provide guidance on deploying CDS in CPOE and on reducing dosing errors, should this emerge as a priority in your program.

Managing drug costs is generally an important issue that is intertwined with specific clinical targets.

AVIATOR Model Used at Memorial Hermann*

AVIATOR is a simple step-by-step approach to help identify key areas in the medication process that could be the focus of PI using CDS interventions. Developed and used at the Memorial Hermann Healthcare System (MHHS), Houston, TX, the AVIATOR process could easily be used in other healthcare organizations. AVIATOR is an acronym, with the following components: (A) Analysis of (V) Variance reporting (I) ISMP data (A) Adverse drug event reporting (T) Top 100 drugs (O) One source pharmacy interventions (R) Root-cause analyses.

Variance reporting: This is done on a voluntary basis across all facilities at MHHS. Although all types of variances are reported, we focused our attention on variances related to medication administration: (a) missed dosage, (b) delay, (c) different dosage, (d) adverse medication reaction, (e) wrong medication.

ISMP data: We used ISMP's high-risk medication list that is available online. We quickly saw a trend in our data, which closely resembled the items in this list.

Adverse drug event reporting: This is voluntary reporting that is done by the pharmacists at our biggest facility in the medical center. Some data from the variance reporting can be duplicated in this database. However, since these are both voluntary reporting systems, we did find some unique cases.

Top 100 drugs: We identified by volume the top 100 drugs that are dispensed in our system. This was done using a simple query against our formulary and orders entered into the order management system. The top 100 drugs constituted more than half of all medication orders entered into the system.

One source pharmacy interventions: This is a third-party database that was used by our system pharmacists to document any intervention they did to correct ADEs that may have occurred or had the potential to occur.

Root cause analyses: These are conducted at our facilities to identify the root cause of any serious adverse event.

We compiled all of the data obtained from these analyses and came up with our own "AVIATOR" list of drugs. All drugs in this list were targeted for all current and future CDS functionality.

Summary of key AVIATOR model elements:
• Identify the high-volume drugs that are ordered pertaining to the hospital system.
• Reconcile with ISMP high-risk drug list.
• Look at the voluntary variance reporting database within your system; if you don't have one, developing one is an option.
• Explore pharmacists' intervention database, which is a rich source of identifying opportunities for improvement.
• Root-cause analyses and FMEAs also reveal gaps that may be corrected with the help of simple-to-complex CDS interventions.

---

* Source: Memorial Hermann Healthcare System, Houston, TX. Used with permission.

Identifying Medication Safety Issues at Advocate Healthcare*

Eight hospitals participate in a system P&T committee. Members include site pharmacy directors, physician chairs of the site P&T committees, clinical pharmacists, and drug information specialists. Review of new—or class review of current—formulary medications always includes discussion of safety risks and how the EMR and order entry system can be used to prevent potential ADEs.

Recognizing problems with medication ordering, a specific workgroup on medication optimization was developed. It included physicians, respiratory therapists, nurses, and pharmacists. This group identified high medication risks and improvement opportunities from incident reporting on medication safety issues by quality departments and other sources.

Problems with anticoagulant drug use emerged as a top issue across the enterprise. The group developed CDS tools, such as an anticoagulation tab in the EMR that provides a single quick view of the patient's current anticoagulant doses, along with current anticoagulation monitoring results (such as INR [International Normalized Ratio] or PTT [Partial Thromboplastin Time]). Assembling this information in a single, convenient location improves decision making on safe and effective dosing.

* Source: Advocate Healthcare, Oakbrook, IL. Used with permission.

Make sure you discuss with pertinent stakeholders how this figures into target selection and prioritization, that is, the extent to which controlling specific drug costs is a primary target for CDS, as well as a secondary consideration with other targets. Costs are important, but care quality and safety goals should not be compromised as primary goals.

Prioritize PI Activities

Many CMIOs feel that once they have the core CISs implemented and stabilized, prioritizing the myriad requests for CDS interventions from various stakeholders is the major challenge. It is, therefore, best to have the institutional leadership endorse priority goals and an organizational framework for setting and achieving the CDS targets, as outlined earlier. This management intervention can help coordinate priorities and focus actions taken by the diverse medication management stakeholders on the most important organizational targets. Such a governance approach enables formal methods for receiving, vetting, and prioritizing improvement opportunities to ensure that the organizations' resources are used most effectively in addressing top-priority needs.

Your prioritization scheme should be transparent, formally adopted by the organization, and ideally accepted (or at least understood) by all pertinent stakeholders. When this has been accomplished, all those who have requested CDS attention for specific targets will understand where their project fits in the queue and why it occupies that position. To the extent possible, the prioritization process should provide reliable estimates about when the various initiatives will be addressed; this can be very helpful for managing both expectations and timely delivery of desired outcomes.

Because addressing priority goals can require a significant investment, it is useful to consider the ROI—both financial and non-financial—for addressing each goal with CDS. ROI data for CDS are relatively scant, but some are available. This organizational return is an explicit factor in Table 2-7, which highlights some considerations in prioritizing CDS objectives. Brigham and Women's Hospital,

Table 2-7: Factors Affecting the Desirability of a CDS Objective

Clinical Objective Value Score* = (P+O+C+N+G)-(D+C)

P= Patient impact (individual/population) (positive, for example, quality, safe, cost-effective care; improved morbidity and mortality; of interest to patients)

O= Organizational impact (positive, for example, regulatory or audit compliance, appropriate resource use, liability, financial return)

C= Clinician impact (favorable, for example, enhanced workflow/compensation, consistent with consensus, local standards, feasible to address, of interest to clinicians)

N= Number of patients positively affected

G= Gap between ideal and actual behavior pertinent to the intervention

D= Difficulty associated with addressing the objective

C= Cost of addressing the objective

_____

* The strength of systematic evidence about the magnitude of the variable should be considered when practical.

Boston, MA, has reported some details on CDS ROI (total benefit per year listed in parentheses after each item):[32]

- Renal dosing ($2.24 million)
- ADE prevention ($1.05 million)
- Guidance related to special or expensive drugs, such as Human Growth Hormone and vancomycin ($880,000)
- ADE monitoring ($760,000)
- Converting medication route from intravenous to oral ($740,000)
- Automated medication summary at hospital discharge ($100,000)
- Guidance for dosing in the elderly ($50,000)
- Guidance on need-to-order drug levels ($20,000)

An extension of these findings is provided in the report cited earlier entitled "Saving Lives, Saving Money" from the Massachusetts Technology Collaborative.[23]

Table 2-7 summarizes several key factors that affect the relative value of addressing a particular objective with CDS. Although not necessarily meant to suggest a numerical calculation, the equation can help you assess the various components that contribute positively and negatively to the benefit-cost ratio. For example, when prioritizing targets, it reinforces the importance of keeping in mind very rare but very serious problems, which might still warrant CDS attention. In these cases, the exceedingly high patient impact (P) might outweigh the very low number of patients positively affected (N) to yield an overall value that warrants some CDS effort (depending also on the other variables, such as the level of difficulty and the expense the interventions would entail).

The CDS driver categories mentioned in the previous section—mandatory, market-driven, and literature-driven—can be incorporated into this prioritization approach. For example, mandatory initiatives have an organizational impact so great that they will typically surpass the threshold for action within the CDS program.

If you have a prioritization process that specifically covers medication-related goals, and a medication CDS charter, you might want to include the prioritization approach (and perhaps resulting improvement priorities) in that charter, an example of which appears in the following sidebar.

CDS Prioritization Approach at Memorial Hermann Healthcare System*

The approach to prioritizing CDS interventions at MHHS has the following key components:
- The Quality committee identifies six to eight high-level attributes against which CDS intervention will be evaluated.
- The CDS oversight committee members vote on the extent to which each candidate CDS intervention addresses the key attributes.
- The CDS team ensures that data and functionality needed for the intervention are available in the pertinent CIS/application before prioritization.
- The CDS oversight committee prioritizes for action a few CDS interventions at a time to ensure there is a continuous flow of CDS interventions focused on important objectives ready to deploy.

Further details and examples are as follows:
- Identifying intervention attributes and establishing relative weights
  - The first column in Table 2-8 lists the attributes that the Quality Committee selected. Each member of this committee divided a total score of 1.0 between the attributes in increments of 0.1. Committee members were not required to assign a score to every attribute; for example, they could assign patient safety 0.5 and quality measures 0.5 and the remaining attributes 0. The relative weights that the committee assigned are given in the second column of Table 2-8. Assigning weights in this way is a one-time process, though organizations may wish to periodically review the assignments to ensure that circumstances haven't changed in a way that would suggest that the weights should be modified.
- Ranking individual interventions
  - The CDS implementation team leads filter proposed CDS interventions (for example, to ensure technical feasibility). A survey is then sent to members of the CDS oversight committee for each proposed CDS intervention that passes the initial filter. Respondents assign a score indicating how well the proposed intervention addresses each of the attributes (No-1, Partially-5, and Yes-10). Each of these scores is then multiplied by the attribute weight defined by the Quality Committee. Figure 2-3 shows a scoring sheet for a particular intervention.
- Collating individual intervention scores and prioritizing interventions for deployment
  - Table 2-9 shows the top scores for candidate interventions (in this case, focusing on rules) at a specific point in time. This ranking determines the order in which resources will be applied to developing and deploying the rules.

* Source: Memorial Hermann Healthcare System, Houston, TX. Used with permission.

Table 2-8: Attributes of a CDS Implementation and their Relative Weight as Determined by the Quality Committee*

Selection Attribute	Rating of Importance
Patient safety (no adverse events)	3.48
Quality measures (The Joint Commission, CMS, AHRQ)	2.13
Waste reduction	0.87
Increase in user satisfaction	0.805
Minimal process change	0.77
Higher percentage of population impacted	1.305
Minimal physician behavior change	1.64

Figure 2-3: Candidate Intervention Scoring Sheet used by CDS Oversight Committee*

Blood glucose monitoring alert for ICU and Post Surgical patients

Rank this rule request based on how it will help to achieve the listed criteria
- No (1)
- Partially (5)
- Yes (10)

✱ 8. As part of the Surviving Sepsis Campaign strict glycemic control in the post surgical patients and ICU patients is a quality measure that we are looking to focus on. To help identify patients with hyperglycemia in the ICU and post-surgical patients if 2 consecutive readings of Blood Glucose >200 are posted for a patient who is not on an insulin infusion, a message is sent to the printer/inbox on the ICU floor/post surgical unit as well as the Pharmacy ADE inbox for the clinical staff to monitor and action accordingly.

Rule Type: Asynchronous, message to inbox or printer

	No	Partially	Yes
Impacts high percentage of population	○	○	○
Improves Quality (JCAHO, CMS, AHRQ)	○	○	○
Requires minimal process change for implementation	○	○	○
Improves Patient Safety (No Adverse Events)	○	○	○
Increases User Satisfaction	○	○	○
Reduces wastage /Improves Revenue	○	○	○
Requires minimal physician behavior change for implementation	○	○	○

Comments (Please enter any comments or thoughts you may have on this request)

* Source: Memorial Hermann Healthcare System, Houston, TX. Used with permission.

Table 2-9: Prioritization Results: Ranking Rules by Their Scores*

Order	Rule Title	Score
1	Glycemic control in ICU & post-surgical	87.24
2	Rocephin in hyperbilirubinemic neonates	83.95
3	Vincristine wrong route rule	81.79
4	Diuretic-induced hypokalemia	80.28
5	Drug-induced hepatotoxicity	79.40
6	Elevated troponin I/T rule	78.88
7	Antibiotic-induced hypernatremia	77.83
8	Antiviral-induced lactic acidosis	76.05
9	Dofetilide-induced Torsade de Pointes	75.65
10	Drug-induced hyperuricemia	65.60

To the extent possible, realistic and quantifiable improvement targets should be established for each objective you will address with CDS. Worksheet 2-3 can be used to help with thinking through this task and documenting the results. Appropriate targets and prioritization will depend to some degree on baseline performance and its relationship to desired performance. We turn next to measuring these baselines.

Establish Baseline Values for Targeted Objectives

As will be discussed in Chapter 7, it is critical to carefully evaluate the effects that the CDS interventions you deploy have on the medication management targets you aim to address. This requires having a clear "before picture" of pertinent process and outcome measures. These measures include rates such as how often drugs are used inappropriately (or not used when indicated) and the frequency with which resulting adverse clinical consequences occur. These pre-intervention measurements serve as a baseline against which you can assess CDS results.

Sources for this information include clinical and administrative databases, each of which may pres-

ent challenges to optimally and easily obtaining the needed information. For example, available clinical systems might not have all the needed data readily accessible. To be useful, the data in administrative sources need to be properly captured and coded. In any case, a first step is to consider which specific rates you plan to track in assessing CDS effects, the detailed equations that will be used to determine those rates, and the sources from which you will gather the data for the equations (see Chapters 4 and 7).

Look carefully for sources in which key data, such as patient problem lists and medication administration information, are available electronically as a direct byproduct of care delivery. These sources might include EMRs and electronic Medication Administration Records (eMARs). Because data in these systems are generated during care, they may be more reliable than claims data in administrative systems (depending on the details of how each is recorded). For environments in which electronic clinical data are not readily available and administrative data are used, it may be helpful to conduct focused, manual medical chart reviews as an adjunct to supplement or validate baseline trends derived from administrative sources.

---

* Source: Memorial Hermann Healthcare System, Houston, TX. Used with permission.

Table 2-10: Sample Adverse Drug Event Categories*

Complications Relating to Sntibiotics	
ICD-9-CM Code	Explanation
9600	Poisoning by penicillins
9601	Poisoning by antifungal antibiotics
9602	Poisoning by chloramphenicol group
9603	Poisoning by erythromycin and other macrolides
9604	Poisoning by tetracycline group
9605	Poisoning by cephalosporin group
9606	Poisoning by antimycobacterial antibiotics
9607	Poisoning by antineoplastic antibiotics
9608	Poisoning by other specified antibiotics
9609	Poisoning by unspecified antibiotic

Check to see if your pharmacy department tracks information useful for baseline determination, for example, related to ADEs, drug costs, and utilization. Databases with this information may already be used for reporting to hospital quality improvement entities and could be used for CDS-related efforts as well. Consider the extent to which these data are voluntarily submitted, and develop plans and workflows to review/validate the information as appropriate before using it to establish and monitor baseline rates. The trigger tools mentioned earlier also provide quantitative data about ADEs that can be used in establishing baselines. Literature reports of ADE PI initiatives can be another source of strategies for determining initial and follow-up event rates.[33]

For those organizations without rich access to electronic clinical information, we detail next how administrative data can be used in assessing key baseline rates. Again, the appropriate mix of clinical and administrative sources for baseline rates will depend on local needs and infrastructure.

Administrative data, such as billing information from the hospital Universal Billing forms (UB) 92 or 04, can help assess ADE rates and use of particular medications for indicated conditions. These data sets contain patient level information, including demographics, medical record number, and the ICD-9-CM code associated with the principle diagnosis and secondary diagnoses. The ICD-9-CM diagnosis codes, when applied correctly and consistently, can be used to categorize specific types of ADEs. Available guides[34] and/or healthcare analytics vendors and consultants can assist with this coding and analysis. Properly documenting and coding these events as needed for measurement and reporting is absolutely essential. This effort involves cultural and workflow challenges, which can be addressed through the governance and management mechanisms discussed earlier in this chapter. Some technical components related to these measurement tasks are mentioned in Chapters 4 and 7.

Table 2-10 illustrates ICD-9-CM codes related to adverse events (termed "poisoning" in the code description) by different antibiotics. If such ADE-related codes have been appropriately applied to patient charts, they can be used in queries to help

---

* Source: National Center for Health Statistics. *Classifications of Diseases and Functioning & Disability.* http://www.cdc.gov/nchs/icd9.htm#RTF.

Table 2-11: Sample Adverse Drug Event Incidence Report

Complication	Observed ADE cases	Observed ADE rate
Complications relating to CNS stimulants and drugs affecting the autonomic nervous system	33	0.10
Complications relating to anesthetic agents and CNS depressants	20	0.07
Complications relating to anti-asthmatic drugs	19	0.07
Complications relating to anti-convulsants and anti-Parkinsonism drugs	16	0.04
Complications relating to anti-neoplastic and immunosuppressive drugs	11	0.03
Complications relating to antibiotics	11	0.03

establish pertinent ADE rates. Selecting patients with these codes as a secondary diagnosis increases the probability that these events occurred during the hospitalization (and may therefore represent a preventable complication), as opposed to being present on admission. Present on Admission (POA) codes now required by Medicare and others may further help with isolating the complications of interest.[35]

Once the codes of interest have been identified, the next step is to evaluate how often these ADEs are occurring. Table 2-11 illustrates this analysis. Patients with an ICD-9-CM code suggesting an ADE should be excluded if a POA flag is set, since this indicates that the complication did not occur during the admission and thus is not pertinent to the baseline for improvement. For each ADE category, further analysis is required by Diagnosis Related Group (DRG) or the Medicare Severity Adjusted Diagnosis Related Group (MS DRG), physician, surgeon, location in the hospital, and other variables that may isolate or identify patterns of these events.

If a pattern is identified in a patient group, then the next step is to retrieve the medical records for these patients and review the care process that may have contributed to the ADE. If analysis does not result in isolating any specific pattern, then review of all the patients by category type is required. The overall goal of this approach (and related modeling and analytic approaches) is not only to determine

the baseline ADE rates but also to uncover insights that can be used to identify the point at which things are breaking down and why. This can help inform development of supportive CDS interventions, as outlined in the next several chapters.

Categorizing ICD-9-CM codes from administrative data—or corresponding clinical data from clinical systems—can be used in similar ways to assess complication rates for other medication management outcomes as well. For example:

- Hemorrhage, hematoma or seromas (suggesting possible excessive anticoagulation)
- Postoperative septicemia, abscess, and wound infection (suggesting possible inappropriate antibiotic use)
- DVT and PE (suggesting possible underuse of venous thromboembolism prophylaxis drugs)

Besides assessing the baseline rates for complications, related approaches and systems can be used to assess baselines for appropriate and effective medication use. As discussed earlier in this chapter, be sure to cultivate synergies between these CDS assessment efforts and related organizational activities, such as Drug Utilization Evaluation, resource management, and quality improvement initiatives.

Baseline data on high cost, high frequency medications are typically obtained with support from the medication formulary. This list provides the cost per dosage or volume, which can then be combined with data on the units of service actually delivered and other sources that indicate appropriateness of use. If both costs and units of service are available from a single source, such as the patient billing system, a top-down analysis can be designed. Analyzing costs and units of service for each drug code will identify patterns by clinical service, MS DRG, physician, surgeon and when possible, the ordering physician. Again, nuances of how data are coded and billed versus what is actually done need to be considered to ensure that the results are reliable. For example, interesting patterns that help focus CDS efforts can be seen when analyzing medication use by MS DRG and physician or ordering physician. For some conditions, there may be a wide variety of use, suggesting no clinical consensus about appropriateness. Sharing these data can be helpful in establishing both the clinical policies and CDS interventions to optimize appropriate use.

Table 2-12 illustrates such a sample baseline data report. It can help identify and further characterize potential medication overuse and serve as a basis for exploring deeper patient level data to validate and refine hypotheses about use. This information can then be considered with pertinent stakeholders to design clinical policies, pathways, and supportive CDS tools to optimize medication use.

The approach to gathering baseline data outlined in this table is a limited and simplified introduction, which omits consideration of important issues such as severity and risk adjustment, internal and external benchmarking, standardizing definitions, and the like. See page 217 in Chapter 7, "Who Will Measure," for ideas on accessing the expertise needed to address all the various baseline measurement issues outlined in this section.

Table 2-12: Sample Attending Physician Antibiotic Utilization for Simple Pneumonia

Att Phys	PT* Count	Ave. Age	Average Pharmacy Charges	% Amino-glycosides	% Cephalosporins	% Macrolides	% Quinotones	% Vancomycin	% Staph Aureus Pneumonia (sec DX)
A	167	4	1,472.60	6.00%	87.40%	41.30%	2.40%	6.00%	1.20%
B	36	61.9	3,037.20	5.60%	50.00%	13.90%	72.20%	5.60%	2.80%
C	32	62.1	2,702.80	3.10%	37.50%	28.10%	68.80%	3.10%	3.10%
D	27	82.9	3,261.50		63.00%	3.70%	59.30%	22.20%	
E	25	61.6	3,435.70		56.00%	16.00%	52.00%	16.00%	4.00%
F	25	62.6	6,399.90		32.00%	20.00%	64.00%	20.00%	20.00%
G	24	60.7	11,886.70		62.50%		83.30%	12.50%	8.30%
H	23	60.6	3,219.10		47.80%	30.40%	73.90%	8.70%	8.70%
I	17	65.8	2,960.30		35.30%	29.40%	82.40%	29.40%	
J	17	63.6	3,346.90		35.30%	11.80%	82.40%	11.80%	
K	17	70.9	3,630.50	5.90%	52.90%	29.40%	70.60%	17.70%	
L	16	70.2	3,863.20		81.30%	18.80%	75.00%	18.80%	12.50%
M	14	67.4	4,449.20	7.10%	71.40%	50.00%	35.70%	14.30%	
N	13	66.2	3,236.20		23.10%	30.80%	76.90%		
O	13	71.1	5,767.60	7.70%	38.50%	7.70%	76.90%	23.10%	15.40%
P	12	71.9	3,299.50	8.30%	41.70%	25.00%	83.30%		
Q	12	77.8	4,414.50		50.00%	16.70%	75.00%	25.00%	8.30%
R	11	81.9	3,494.20		63.60%	18.20%	72.70%	9.10%	
S	11	75.1	1,928.50		54.60%	9.10%	90.90%		
T	11	70.8	5,632.80	9.10%	72.70%	27.30%	72.70%	36.40%	
U	11	61.1	2,916.80		63.60%	36.40%	90.90%	9.10%	
V	10	79.9	3,092.80	10.00%	70.00%	30.00%	80.00%		
W	10	58.1	5,971.10		70.00%	50.00%	40.00%		
X	10	71.7	4,016.20		40.00%		100.00%	10.00%	10.00%

* PT = patient.

WORKSHEETS

Worksheet 2-1

Stakeholders, Goals, Objectives

*This worksheet is used to document your discussions with stakeholders in the medication management process, and their high-level medication management goals and specific objectives, as outlined in this chapter. Careful attention to **all** key stakeholders cannot be overemphasized. With Tables 2-1 and 2-2 as guides, list the stakeholder names and titles in the first column.*

In the second and third columns, indicate the role that this person or group currently plays and will play in the medication management process (for example, from Table 1-1) and in the CDS program (for example, from Table 2-2). As the project unfolds, each stakeholder often takes on a new role in either the medication management process and/or the CDS program. It is useful to consider such crossover roles at the beginning of this exercise. You should also note whether each is a potential champion or resistor/detractor for addressing a particular goal or objective (the answer to which you will list in the next columns) with CDS interventions and whether they might play a role in obtaining resources or funding.

In the fourth column, list the high-level medication management goals that emerged from your discussions as important to this person or committee. These goals define broad care processes or outcomes that you will address with CDS interventions. In particular, listen for spontaneously-offered stakeholder priorities. In this column, try to answer the question, What do you want to achieve regarding medication management processes and outcomes?

In the fifth column, break down the goals you have elicited into their component clinical objectives. The question to answer is, To achieve your goal, what objectives will have to be completed? The more specific and quantifiable you make these objectives, the more likely you will be to devise interventions that produce measurable results. For example, an objective such as "improve prescribing practices for heparin" will likely be less useful than a more specific one, such as "decrease incidence of heparin overdose." These objectives will be tied to specific CDS interventions in Chapter 5. Also begin identifying the objectives that have potentially similar CDS solutions. In our example, the stakeholder interviews resulted in identifying a common high-level goal of reducing preventable ADEs. At a more specific level, a common medication management objective is preventing patients from getting medications to which they have a known allergy. Note, however, the CFO's goal is to reduce medication error cost to the hospital. In the course of the interview, we are able to extract an objective from him that complements the predominate objective of reducing preventable allergic drug events, that is, since the additional hospital costs associated with these events may not be reimbursable. In practice, you may want to have several columns of goals and objectives, as it is unrealistic to assume that stakeholders will converge as tightly on improvement issues as has been done in this example.

Worksheet 2-1 *continued*

Stakeholder	Current Role in Medication Management Process	Current Role in CDS Program	High-Level Medication Management Goals	Medication Management Objectives
Terry E. (CQO)	Clinical thought leader in medication safety	CDS oversight committee	Organization-wide initiative to reduce ADE	Ensure accurate and updated patient allergy information in the EMR
Nathan W. (CMO)	None: Clinical thought leader	Clinical thought leader	Organization-wide initiative to reduce ADE	Prevent prescription of medications to allergic patients
Rubin R. (CIO)	None: IT thought leader	CDS oversight committee, VP of IS	Deploy technology to improve patient care	Increase staff satisfaction with CDS aspect of CPOE
Kari R. (CNO)	None: Clinical thought leader	Clinical thought leader	Organization-wide initiative to reduce ADE	Increase compliance with medication safety 5 rights: "Right patient, right route, right med, right time, right dose," double-check procedure before medication administration
Michael G. (CFO)	Budget owner	Budget owner	Reduce medication error cost	Avoid costs associated with preventable allergic reactions
John S. (Chief of medical staff)	Clinical thought leader on medication selection, reconciliation, and ordering—potential detractor for cumbersome systems	Communication to medical staff, CDS oversight committee	Make physician's prescribing process easier	Make hospital computer systems easier to use
Charley P. (Unit Head Nurse)	Monitoring medication effects; member, Medication Usage Policy committee, PI committee	Clinical thought leader, policy resource	Reduce medication administration errors	More accurate patient allergy documentation by nursing
Tom K. (Director of Intensive Care Unit [ICU])	Neonatal Intensive Care Unit (NICU) budget owner, pharmacy safety committee	None: Clinical thought leader	Reduce preventable ADEs	Prevent staff from prescribing medications to allergic patients

Worksheet 2-1 *continued*

Stakeholder	Current Role in Medication Management Process	Current Role in CDS Program	High-Level Medication Management Goals	Medication Management Objectives
Patty J. (Director of Pharmacy)	Manage pharmacy operations, chair of pharmacy safety committee	None: potential subject matter expert	Minimize dispensing waste and preventable ADEs	Avoid dispensing medication to allergic patients
Adam B. (Pharmacist)	Verification and dispensing	None: potential subject matter expert	Reduce preventable ADEs	Reduce prescription of medications to allergic patients

Worksheet 2-2

Checklist for Medication Management Goal Charter*

Once you have identified medication management goals and objectives on which to focus CDS atten-tion, you might consider making a formal charter for the targets, individually or collectively. Such char-ters should be linked to your broader CDS charter, if you have one. There are different ways to approach templates for project charters, and the following checklist is one example. For this worksheet sample, we have provided notes about the type of information that could be used for some of the elements in a charter focusing on the objective of reducing preventable allergic reactions.

Check		Section	Details
	1.	Overview	
❏	1.1	Purpose Statement	What are the reasons for addressing this goal? For example, antibiotics given to patients who are allergic to them result in significant morbidity and mortality.
❏	1.2	Goals and Objectives/Expected Outcome	What are expected returns from addressing this goal/ objective? They need to be important and worthwhile! For example, prevent patients from getting antibiotics to which they are allergic and reap corresponding returns.
❏	1.3	Scope	What are the boundaries for this project? For example: 1. Actions from this initiative will affect major nodes in the medication management process—Prescription, Dispensing, Administration. 2. Focus will be on antibiotic medications only. 3. Non-antibiotic medications will not be considered, although we may favor actions that are scalable to other medication groups.
❏	1.4	Critical Success Factors	What are factors needed for success? For example: 1. Education to all, especially to frontline stakeholders 2. Easy CDS system use with minimal disruption of current workflow 3. Quantifiable reduction in preventable adverse events

*Adapted from: State of Texas Department of Information Resources. *Project Charter.* http://www.dir.state.tx.us/pubs/framework/gate1/projectcharter/index.htm. Updated 01 June 2008.

Worksheet 2-2 *continued*

Check		Section	Details
❏	1.5	Assumptions	What are assumptions related to the technology, resource, scope, expectation, or timeline assumptions for addressing this goal/objective? For example: 1. Adverse events from antibiotics are detectable and preventable. 2. We have statistical methods that can determine whether our actions are effective, even if the event rate is very low.
❏	1.6	Constraints	What are the constraints related to budget, resources, timeline, and technology? For example: 1. This project needs to be completed within 12 months. 2. Action plan must be efficient for frontline stakeholders. 3. Leadership support is critical.
	2.	Authority and Milestones	
❏	2.1	Funding Authority	Who or what is funding efforts toward this goal? For example, this project is funded by hospital capital budget.
❏	2.2	Oversight Authority	What committee is responsible for this goal/objective? For example, the quality improvement, patient safety, and/or P&T committee could be the oversight authority for an objective that focuses on decreasing preventable allergic reactions.
❏	2.3	Major Milestones	What are the major points of success and deliverables that will define progress toward this objective? For example: 1. Get buy-in from oversight authority and executive committee. 2. Define feasible data management strategy. 3. Formulate action strategy and timeline. 4. Execute action strategy. 5. Analyze and interpret results.
	3.	Organization	
❏	3.1	Committee Structure	Graphically represent committees pertinent to this goal/objective and their interaction.

Worksheet 2-2 *continued*

Check		Section	Details
❏	3.2	Roles and Responsibilities	Three-column table stating the member, their role, and responsibilities
❏	3.3	Facilities and Resources	What are the facilities and resources needed? For example, office space, computers, personnel.
❏	4.	Points of Contact	Who is the primary and back-up contact for the project?
❏	5.	Glossary	Define all terms and acronyms used in the project charter.
❏	6.	Revision History	Track all changes to the charter document.
❏	7.	Appendices	Include any additional relevant information (for example, charts, tables, lists).

Worksheet 2-3

Selecting/Prioritizing Targets for Action

This worksheet helps integrate, prioritize, and refine the survey of clinical goals and objectives into a foundation for action. You can extract from the stakeholder-centric Worksheet 2-1 the strong themes regarding CDS-facilitated improvement opportunities that emerge from your interviews and analysis. To this candidate list, add other potential targets identified from the internal and external survey of improvement opportunities as discussed in the chapter. List the most promising targets in the first column of this worksheet. In the second column, list the rationale for why you've included each target. This might include the stakeholder(s) that emphasized the target, the mandatory external (such as regulatory) or internal (such as Board-level) driver behind it, the pertinent organizational momentum (for example, from a major CIS deployment such as CPOE motivated by addressing the target).

In the third column, record information about the organizational priority for addressing the target through the CDS program. The prioritization approaches outlined in the chapter should be helpful here. In the fourth column, indicate the baseline performance level for the target. Be as quantitative as possible, considering data gathering approaches as outlined in the chapter. In the fifth column, record a desired performance level to be achieved through CDS implementation. Determining this target will require consulting with key stakeholders and governance entities, and the specific goal may be further refined during the subsequent implementation steps outlined in the next chapters. When possible and appropriate, try to specify a timeframe during which the goal will be achieved.

In the Notes column, include items that might be useful in justifying or executing the CDS effort directed toward the target, such as synergies with other organizational initiatives, available information about the benefit/cost ratio of addressing the target, and the like.

Target	Rationale	Priority	Baseline performance	Desired outcome	Notes
Increase appropriate use of venous thromboembolism (VTE) prophylaxis	Part of P4P contract; VTE is a hospital-acquired condition for which CMS is not providing additional reimbursement	1	76% appropriate prophylaxis use	>90% appropriate use within 12 months	Coordinate CDS efforts with major organizational PI effort on this topic
Prevent patients from getting medications to which they are allergic	Recent high-profile sentinel event; significant documented costs associated with this preventable ADE	2	3% of prescriptions are to allergic patients	0% of prescriptions are to allergic patients within 12 months	Coordinate CDS approach with recent launch of CPOE and eMAR system

CONCLUDING COMMENTS

The tasks outlined in this chapter really do provide the critical foundation upon which all subsequent CDS efforts rest. If solid governance structures and processes are in place, they can help buffer and facilitate recovery from any of the inevitable missteps that occur in executing the tasks outlined in the following chapters. Similarly, having a shared and detailed sense of improvement priorities and goals—solidly grounded in major internal and external drivers—is a major part of the road to success in achieving CDS-enabled progress toward desired performance levels. On the other hand, to the extent that these critical foundations are not laid properly, the CDS development and deployment activities that follow will be much less likely to flow smoothly and deliver critically needed value.

REFERENCES

1   U.S. Department of Health and Human Services. *Corporate Responsibility and Health Care Quality: A Resource for Health Care Boards of Directors.* http://www.oig.hhs.gov/fraud/docs/complianceguidance/CorporateResponsibilityFinal%209-4-07.pdf, accessed 10/2/08.

2   Jiang HJ, Lockee C, Bass K, et al. Board engagement in quality: findings of a survey of hospital and system leaders. *J Healthc Manag.* 2008; 53(2):121-134.

3   American Medical Informatics Association. *Training Health Care Professionals to Serve as Local Informatics Leaders and Champions.* http://www.amia.org/10x10/, accessed 10/2/08.

4   The Joint Commission. *2008 National Patient Safety Goals Hospital Program.* http://www.jointcommission.org/PatientSafety/NationalPatientSafetyGoals/08_hap_npsgs.htm, accessed 10/2/08.

5   Centers for Medicare & Medicaid Services. *Fact Sheets: Quality Measures for Reporting.* http://www.cms.hhs.gov/apps/media/press/factsheet.asp?Counter=3044, accessed 10/2/08.

6   Centers for Medicare & Medicaid Services. *Overview: Hospital-Acquired Conditions.* http://www.cms.hhs.gov/hospitalacqcond/, accessed 10/2/08.

7   For an overview of CMS pay for performance initiatives, see Centers for Medicare & Medicaid Services. *Medicare "Pay for Performance (P4P)" Initiatives.* http://www.cms.hhs.gov/apps/media/press/release.asp?counter=1343, accessed 10/2/08. For an update on the successful CMS/Premier Hospital Quality Improvement Demonstration, see Centers for Medicare & Medicaid Services. *CMS/Premier Hospital Quality Incentive Demonstration (HQID).* http://www.premierinc.com/quality-safety/tools-services/p4p/hqi/index.jsp, accessed 10/2/08.

8   For example, see Bridges to Excellence. *High Quality Care Can Also be Cost Effective Care.* http://www.bridgestoexcellence.org/, accessed 10/2/08.

9   Patient Safety and Quality Healthcare. *New medication management data highlight additions to industry-standard health plan performance database.* http://www.psqh.com/enews/0807d.shtml. 22 Aug 2007.

10 Institute for Healthcare Improvement. *Protecting 5 Million Lives from Harm.* http://www.ihi.org/IHI/Programs/Campaign/Campaign.htm?TabId=1, accessed 10/2/08.

11 Kilbridge PM, Welebob EM, Classen DC. Development of the Leapfrog Methodology for evaluating hospital implemented inpatient computerized physician order entry systems. *Qual Saf Health Care.* 2006 Apr; 15(2):81-8. See also the Leapfrog CPOE Evaluation Tool at https://leapfrog.medstat.com/cpoe/, accessed 10/2/08.

12 The Leapfrog Group. *Incentives and Rewards Compendium.* http://www.leapfroggroup.org/leapfrog_compendium, accessed 10/2/08.

13 The National Quality Forum. *National Quality Forum Updates Endorsement of Serious Reportable Events in Healthcare.* http://www.qualityforum.org/pdf/news/prSeriousReportableEvents10-15-06.pdf. 16 Oct 2006.

14 Rochon PA, Field TS, Bates DW, et al. Computerized physician order entry with clinical decision support in the long-term care setting: insights from the Baycrest Centre for Geriatric Care. *Journal of the American Geriatrics Society.* 2005; Oct; 53(10):1780–1789.

15 Institute of Medicine. *Identifying and Preventing Medication Errors.* http://www.iom.edu/?id=35942, accessed 10/2/08.

16 See home page for NQF National Priorities Partners at http://www.qualityforum.org/about/NPP/, accessed 10/2/08.

17 The IOM priority areas for transforming healthcare can be found here: http://www.ahrq.gov/qual/iompriorities.pdf, accessed 10/2/08.

18 The Institute for Safe Medication Practices. *Medication Safety Tools and Resources.* 2008. http://www.ismp.org/Tools/default.asp, accessed 10/2/08.

19 Nebeker JR, Hoffman JM, Weir CR, et al. High rates of adverse drug events in a highly computerized hospital. *Arch Intern Med.* 2005; 165:1111-6. http://archinte.ama-assn .org/cgi/content/abstract/165/10/1111, accessed 10/2/08.

20 Bates DW, Leape LL, Cullen DJ, et al. Effect of computerized physician order entry and a team intervention on prevention of serious medication errors. *JAMA.* 1998; 280(15):1311-1316. http://jama.ama-assn.org/cgi/content/full/280/15/1311, accessed 10/2/08.

21 Bobb A, Gleason K, Husch M, et al. The epidemiology of prescribing errors: the potential impact of computerized prescriber order entry. *Arch Intern Med.* 2004; 164(7):785-792.

22 Oppenheim MI, Vidal C, Velasco F, et al. Impact of a Computerized Alert During Physician Order Entry on Medication Dosing in Patients with Renal Impairment. *Proc AMIA Symp.* 2002; 577-581. http://www.amia.org/pubs/proceedings/symposia/2002/117.pdf, accessed 10/2/08.

23 Massachusetts Technology Collaborative and New England Healthcare Institute. *Saving Lives, Saving Money: The Imperative for Computerized Physician Order Entry in Massachusetts Hospitals.* Executive Director: Mitchell Adams. 14 Feb 2008. http://web3.streamhoster.com/mtc/cpoe20808.pdf, accessed 10/2/08.

24 Avery AJ, Howard R, Barber N, Bates DW, Coleman J, Fernando B, Ferner R, Jacklin A. Report for NHS Connecting for Health on the production of a draft design specification for NHS IT systems aimed at reducing risk of harm to patients from medications (2006). Report available at: http://www.connectingforhealth.nhs.uk/systemsandservices/eprescribing/news/averyreport.pdf, accessed 12/12/08.

25 Moore TJ, Cohen MR, Furberg CD. Serious adverse drug events reported to The Food and Drug Administration, 1998-2005. *Arch Intern Med.* 2007; 167(16):1752-1759. (See especially Table 4, "Most frequent suspect drugs," and Table 5, "Drugs with > 500 ADEs/year.") http://archinte .ama-assn.org/cgi/content/abstract/167/16/1752, accessed 10/2/08.

26 Agency for Healthcare Research and Quality. *Women's Health.* http://www.ahrq.gov/RESEARCH/may07/0507RA19.htm, accessed 10/2/08.

27 Lee E, Maneno MK, Smith L, et al. National patterns of medication use during pregnancy. *Pharmacoepidemiol Drug Saf.* 2006; 15(8):537-545. http://www3.interscience.wiley .com/cgi-bin/abstract/112613557/ABSTRACT, accessed 10/2/08.

28 The Joint Commission. *Sentinel Event Alert—Preventing pediatric medication errors.* http://www.jointcommission .org/SentinelEvents/SentinelEventAlert/sea_39.htm. 11 Apr 2008.

29 Budnitz DS, Shehab N, Kegler SR, et al. Medication use leading to emergency department visits for adverse drug events in older adults. *Ann Intern Med.* 2007; 147(11):755-765.

30 Institute for Healthcare Improvement. *Trigger Tool for Measuring Adverse Drug Events (IHI Tool).* http://www.ihi .org/ihi/topics/patientsafety/medicationsystems/tools/trigger+tool+for+measuring+adverse+drug+events+(ihi+tool).htm, accessed 10/2/08. See also Griffin FA, Resar RK. *IHI Global Trigger Tool for Measuring Adverse Events.* IHI Innovation Series white paper. Cambridge, MA: Institute for Healthcare Improvement; 2007. (Available on www.IHI.org.)

31 Takata GS, Mason W, Taketomo C, et al. Development, testing, and findings of a pediatric-focused trigger tool to identify medication-related harm in US children's hospitals. *Pediatrics.* 2008; 121(4):e927-935.

32 Kaushal R, Jha AK, Franz C, et al. Return on investment for a computerized physician order entry system. *J Am Med Inform Assoc.* 2006; 13(3):261-266. http://web3.streamhoster.com/mtc/cpoe20808.pdf, accessed 10/2/08.

33 See, for example, Jennings HR, Miller EC, Williams TS, et al. Reducing anticoagulant medication adverse events and avoidable patient harm. *Jt Comm J Qual Patient Saf.* 2008; 34(4):196-200.

34 Iezzoni LI, editor. *Risk Adjustment for Measuring Healthcare Outcomes, 3rd edition.* Academy Health & Health Administration Press; 2003 Aug.

35 Centers for Medicare & Medicaid Services. See CMS fact sheet on POA coding at: http://www.cms.hhs.gov/HospitalAcqCond/Downloads/poa_fact_sheet.pdf, accessed 10/2/08.

Chapter 3
Consider Workflows and Other General CDS Intervention Setup Issues

TASKS

- Revisit the CDS Five Rights (see Chapter 1) with special attention to "right stake-holder" and "right point in workflow" for optimizing targeted medication management processes and outcomes identified in Chapter 2.
- Carefully map workflows associated with care processes you plan to enhance with CDS; develop and use case scenarios for mapping practical and helpful "future states" after CDS deployment.
- Document the roles that different stakeholders will play in developing and executing the planned CDS interventions.
- Incorporate strategies for assessing intervention effects throughout the planning and development process.
- Consider sources for CDS content and interventions; build versus buy versus share.

KEY LESSONS

- It is important to think broadly about who the stakeholders are in key workflow processes and be meticulous about mapping workflow—not just what people say they do or should be doing, but what is actually done.
- Many CDS content and intervention components will be purchased; this approach may require significant effort to validate, localize, coordinate, and maintain.

DISCUSSION

This is the first of three chapters—Chapters 3 through 5—that together cover the tasks needed to prepare CDS interventions that will successfully deliver improvements in targeted components of the medication-use cycle. Here we delve more deeply into the "right point in workflow," the fifth of the CDS Five Rights, and discuss approaches to mapping and improving this workflow with CDS interventions. We also begin to consider how alerts affect workflow and the importance of measuring intervention effects—topics we build upon in subsequent chapters. We conclude with thoughts about how to obtain CDS interventions—that is build, buy, or share.

Revisit Medication Management Cycle and CDS Five Rights

In applying CDS to achieve specific medication management objectives—as outlined in Chapter 2—it is important to consider what the CDS Five Rights should be to make this happen. As a reminder, these rights involve getting:

1. The right information
2. To the right person
3. In the right CDS intervention format
4. Through the right channel
5. At the right point in workflow

In an environment as complex as healthcare, identifying the people and the processes associated with each potential improvement target is critical. It is to these individuals and workflows that CDS interventions will provide needed information. Workflow mapping is an invaluable tool to make these care processes explicit, so they can be examined and improved.

Workflow/Process Mapping

In Chapter 2, we considered stakeholders in developing and managing the *CDS program*. For workflow mapping, it is important to carefully consider those involved in the *clinical processes* that you plan to augment with CDS. There are a variety of sources you can use for identifying these individuals, including

consultation with the clinical managers identified as CDS program stakeholders in Chapter 2, page 23, staff lists from ISs used to support staffing, and direct observation of care delivery, among others.

Once you identify the stakeholders in the pertinent care delivery process—including patients, nurses, pharmacists, physicians, and other members of the care delivery team—workflow mapping helps identify the roles they play in addressing the targets. Mapping helps you identify not only the detailed workflows for each stakeholder but also their needs and perspectives pertinent to supporting their medication use activities with CDS.

Workflow/process mapping is a method by which activities pertinent to a specific objective are identified and represented in a visual manner. In the medication-management cycle, the maps depict how information and tasks flow from one stakeholder to another. They help to identify how data originate and are reused and highlight potential areas of vulnerability and improvement related to outcomes, such as care quality, safety, and efficiency. When there are multiple actions taken by multiple users within each process, it is most useful to create a cross-functional process map, as will be illustrated shortly.

When considering and mapping workflows, keep in mind that there may be important differences between how processes are designed to work, how participants describe what they do, and what they actually do. Ideally these should be the same, and workflow mapping can help ensure this is the case. Gathering objective data (for example, based on directly observing care activities) is an important foundation for understanding steps participants *actually take* in a medication management activity. These observations can serve as a foundation for reconciling with participants any differences with their mental models about their workflow and/or with formal organizational procedures for accomplishing the medication-related activity.

A variety of software tools that generate flowcharts can be used for workflow mapping.[1] Worksheet 3-1 in this chapter contains a sample blank flowsheet and symbol key that might be useful for your mapping efforts.

Techniques for gathering the data that underpin creation of workflow maps include *structured interviews* and *observations.*

Structured interviews: This approach involves conducting team sessions or one-on-one interviews to identify individual tasks performed by each stakeholder. Asking about other participants in tasks related to key medication use processes that are CDS targets can help ensure that all pertinent stakeholders are considered.

As an example, pharmacists play a central role in processing medication orders and are a logical starting point for analyzing this task. The following is an example of the different steps that a pharmacist performs in a particular hospital when processing orders using a pharmacy IS. In this case, some prescribers enter orders via CPOE and others handwrite orders or deliver them verbally (that is, as spoken orders). Task lists of this sort, as shown next, might be gathered by interviewing one or more pharmacists:

- Pull up CPOE orders or scanned copy of written orders.
- Pull up correct patient medication profile in pharmacy system.
- Identify drug from the scanned order.
- Pull up the right drug order.
- Enter and verify in the pharmacy system the correct route, dosage, and frequency.

Based on this interview, other non-pharmacy stakeholders and their tasks will be identified. Continuing the example above:

- The physician (or other ordering clinician) gives a written, verbal, or electronic order for medication. (Note that verbal orders can introduce opportunities for error and decrease use of prescriber-focused CDS, so care should be taken to avoid the spoken ordering mode when possible. Interviews and observation can help characterize such improvement opportunities and determine approaches that minimize risks.)
- Nursing accepts the written order, or in the case of the verbal medication order, reads it back

to the ordering clinician, and writes it down. The nurse may scan the written order into the pharmacy application or ask the unit clerk to do this. (Handwritten orders should be avoided when possible, since they can be more prone to misinterpretation.)

- If not already done by the nurse, the unit clerk takes the written medication order and scans the order into the pharmacy application.

Observations: This method involves directly observing all the participants involved in a particular clinical task and documenting workflow and information flow related to the improvement target at hand. The method can also include discussion with those being observed to address observer questions that arise about workflow activities and issues. If you have conducted interviews prior to direct observation, remain alert for any differences between results gleaned from the two methods. Keep in mind the potential for a Hawthorne Effect, where a process temporarily improves or changes due to outside observation.

Interviews and observations should complement each other in creating an accurate "before picture" into which CDS-enabled improvements will be introduced. Smoothing out any identified inconsistencies or rough spots prior to CDS launch can help increase intervention success.

An example: When multiple stakeholders perform one or several steps within a process, it is helpful to illustrate this interrelationship in a cross-functional workflow map in which each functional band represents a different stakeholder. Figure 3-1 illustrates what a cross-functional process map would look like for the previously discussed process.

Once you have identified the workflow steps within a process, you can conduct an in-depth step-by-step analysis to determine which phase of the medication-management cycle should be represented by each workflow step. As outlined in Chapter 1, medication management involves six major phases:

1. Medication selection/reconciliation (based on assessment of clinical problems)
2. Ordering

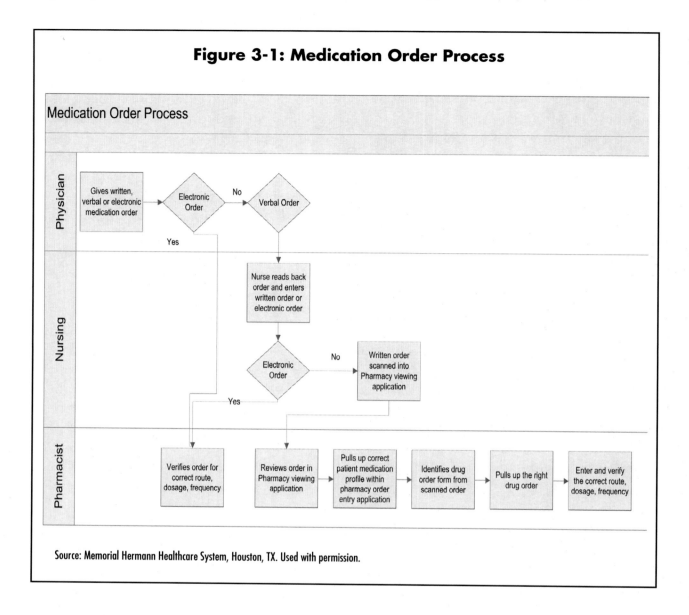

Figure 3-1: Medication Order Process

Source: Memorial Hermann Healthcare System, Houston, TX. Used with permission.

3. Dispensing/verifying
4. Administration
5. Education
6. Monitoring

To illustrate features of a more in-depth workflow analysis and its role in CDS design, we outline the work that one health system has done. This example addresses adjustments to dosing for the drug enoxaparin in a patient with kidney dysfunction. Figure 3-2 illustrates their workflow map for renal enoxaparin dosing in a non-CPOE environment.

As we see in Figure 3-2, functional bands representing several stakeholder roles (physician, nursing, and pharmacist) are again represented. Once the initial map is drafted, the next step is to engage those stakeholders in identifying potential problem areas in the process. For example, some key process issues that were not apparent when the diagram was initially drafted but were identified on subsequent discussion with stakeholders include:

• Physicians do not always check for kidney function (which is needed for proper dosing) when ordering. They assume that the pharmacist will take care of it.

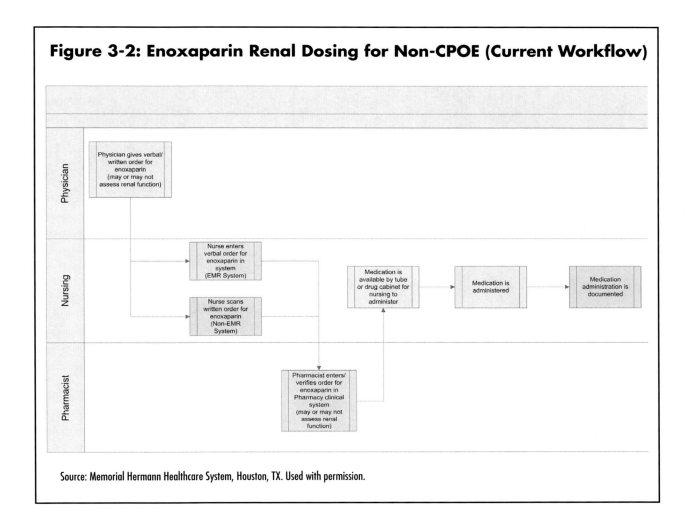

Figure 3-2: Enoxaparin Renal Dosing for Non-CPOE (Current Workflow)

Source: Memorial Hermann Healthcare System, Houston, TX. Used with permission.

- Pharmacists may or may not check for kidney function for dosing as well. They may assume that the physician has taken care of it.
- Nursing does not check for kidney function when enoxaparin is administered. They assume that the physician and/or pharmacist have done so, if needed.

In this case, workflow mapping revealed that typical care routines were not ensuring that critical data needed for safe medication use was reliably available and used. Such details about potential process weaknesses that emerge from workflow mapping provide a backdrop for applying the CDS Five Rights to address those weaknesses. For example, Table 3-1 and the explanatory text that follows highlight some of the potential CDS interventions that could be used. Which specific interventions might be most appropriate at each step in a given

organization depends on a variety of factors. These may include the CDS functionality supported by the available CIS infrastructure, the electronic data that are available to drive specific CDS interventions, and other considerations. (See Chapter 1, page 5, for a detailed list of intervention types and Chapter 5, page 133, for a more detailed discussion of applying CDS to improve medication dosing.) Further explanation of interventions in Table 3-1 follow:

Order Sentences: In CPOE systems, order sentences provide complete information about drug administration. For example, they may indicate a specific dose, route, frequency, etc. for the drug. They can be preconfigured and labeled to cover different levels of renal impairment, thus alerting the prescriber to the need for dosage adjustment, as well as providing guidance on the appropriate dosage in

Table 3-1: Potential CDS Interventions for Supporting Renal Dosing

Stakeholder	Med Management Step	Candidate CDS Interventions
Physician (or other Prescriber or verbal order taker)	Ordering	• Order sentences/sets (ideally presented as appropriate for patient's kidney function and indicated as such) • Patient-specific dosing recommendations • Dosing calculators • Drug dosing reference (for example, via infobutton) • Related results (kidney function) • Kidney function alert • Dose range checking after order is placed
Pharmacist	Dispensing/Verifying	• Related results (kidney function) • Dosing calculators • Drug dosing reference (for example, via infobutton) • Kidney function alert (triggered for inappropriate dose) • Automated dose-range checking
Nursing	Administration	• Pre- and post-administration assessment/documentation tools for signs of drug toxicity • Related results (kidney function) • Kidney function alert (triggered for inappropriate dose)

different circumstances. (See Chapter 4, page 96, for further details.)

Patient-specific Dosing Recommendations: Some CPOE systems can use data about a patient's kidney function available within the CIS to automatically calculate appropriate dosing recommendations and present them to the prescriber.

Related Results: Displaying kidney function information, such as serum creatinine or creatinine clearance, while ordering enoxaparin or other medications can help to alert the prescriber that impaired kidney function may require altered dosing. The intervention can also provide links to information about how to make the necessary adjustment. However, since use of displays and links is a passive form of CDS, it requires the user to be aware of the implications of this kidney function information and to, independently, take appropriate action to adjust the dose.

Dosing Calculators and Drug Dosing Reference: When the prescriber suspects or is aware that a dose adjustment may be needed, reference material can help supply the specifics. Calculators may allow the user to enter in key parameters (for example, those related to kidney function) and then provide a dose recommendation based on these variables. Similarly, drug monographs can provide dosing recommendations in text form that the prescriber then applies. This information may be provided via online references and/or within the CIS environment. Infobutton links (see Chapter 1, page 8) can enable direct one-click access to needed information, thereby providing quick support within workflow when desired by the system user.

Kidney Function Alert: Such an alert could check a patient's creatinine clearance value when enoxaparin is ordered. If the creatinine clearance value is below the set threshold, an alert fires that the dose might be excessive and gives the user the option to change it—ideally with a specific recommended dose and the rationale for the adjustment. Such an alert might be sent to the physician at the time of ordering or to the pharmacist at the time of verification and dispensing, depending on local needs and policies. An important pearl for implementing CDS is to use interruptive alerts sparingly. That is, such alerts should generally serve as a "safety net" for critical issues when other CDS interventions "upstream" in the workflow (such as order sentences accounting for kidney function or dosing reference information) have failed to produce the needed action.

CDS interventions selected as candidates to improve dosing then need to be discussed with each stakeholder to ensure feasibility and acceptance. The following bullets summarize the results from discussions with stakeholders in the workflow mapping example just presented:

- Physicians: Taking extra time to determine whether the medication needs to be adjusted for kidney function in a particular patient does not always fit easily into workflow. May expect that pharmacists will make needed dosage adjustments.
- Pharmacists: Can make dosage adjustments based on laboratory data about kidney function.
- Nursing: As long as physicians and pharmacists determine what needs to be done to check for level of kidney function in regard to dosing, do not foresee any problems from their side.

Based on the feedback from stakeholders, the following was decided:

- Order sentences with renal dosing for enoxaparin would be added for all physicians entering orders using CPOE. If they choose to do renal dosing, they have the option to do so at the point of ordering. Non-CPOE physicians would continue to dose as in the past.
- A rule would be implemented to determine whether the patient's creatinine clearance value was below the threshold and, if so, an alert would be triggered for the pharmacist to adjust dosage

accordingly. If the dosage already met the renal dosing criteria, the alert would not fire.

- For the pharmacist to make this dosing change, a protocol would have to be approved by the pertinent clinical governing bodies. In this case, the protocol would allow the pharmacist to make dosage adjustments to enoxaparin as deemed necessary based on kidney function.

Figure 3-3 is a portion of the revised workflow map after the protocol was approved and the kidney function alert was implemented. For simplicity, it focuses on the pharmacist workflow in a non-CPOE environment.

As suggested by this discussion, many ways exist to address the various CDS Five Rights to ensure appropriate dosing of enoxaparin in patients with decreased kidney function. The workflow map just discussed illustrates one configuration that focuses on pharmacist order verification and dispensing in a particular care delivery organization. In summary, the CDS Five Rights approach in this example addresses the following:

1. The right information: evidence that patient has decreased kidney function suggested by creatinine clearance value (or fact that patient does not have these data available)
2. To the right person: the pharmacist
3. In the right CDS intervention: alert
4. Through the right channel: pharmacy IS
5. At the right point in workflow: during enoxaparin order verification

A full program to ensure appropriate renal enoxaparin dosing could contain several such CDS Five Rights sets, developed and implemented to ensure that the desired outcome is achieved in the most efficient and effective way, given organizational needs and constraints. More detailed guidance on how to accomplish such goals is provided in Chapters 4 and 5. Worksheet 3-2 might be helpful for organizing some initial thoughts about selecting interventions to address specific goals and documenting this thinking.

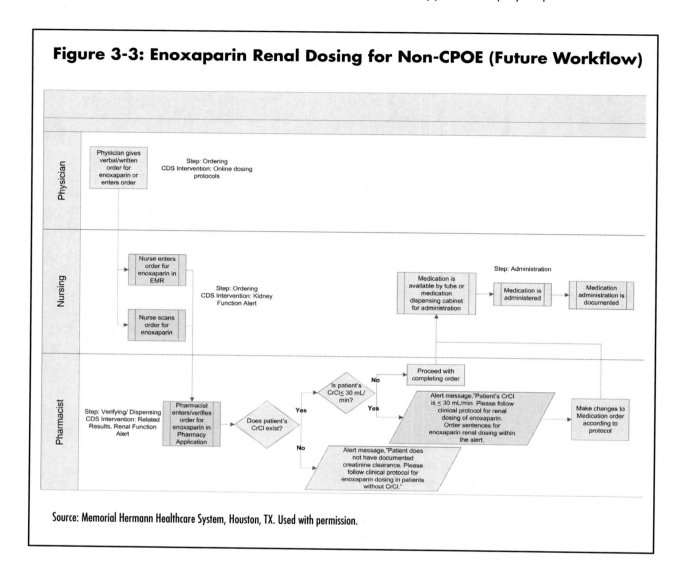

Figure 3-3: Enoxaparin Renal Dosing for Non-CPOE (Future Workflow)

Source: Memorial Hermann Healthcare System, Houston, TX. Used with permission.

Summary Points on Mapping

Key take-away points on workflow/process mapping include:

- Thoughtfully developed workflow/process maps can greatly facilitate identifying the right person, right workflow step, right information, right CDS format, and right channel to achieve a specific objective.

- You may not always get it right the first time; it's important to discuss the workflow map with the stakeholders you have identified to ensure that the process representation is accurate and complete enough to provide a solid foundation for CDS intervention planning.

- Establishing accountability for who is doing what is critical when documenting and enhancing workflows. For example, if key clinical data drive care decisions (such as creatinine clearance in enoxaparin dosing), be explicit about primary and secondary responsibility for checking this information, and focus CDS interventions accordingly to support those roles.

- Once the potential CDS interventions are identified, it is important to perform feasibility studies to determine which of the interventions can be implemented within the organization and available CISs. It is not always possible to implement all of the interventions, usually because the ISs do not have the functionality or the user does not want it.

Additional Points about Workflow Mapping to Keep in Mind

- If you have multiple facilities, don't assume the workflow is identical across all of them. Although it may be an arduous task, it is important to document the pertinent workflow process individually at each facility. Workflow depends on local conditions; that's why workflow analysis is so crucial to ensure that CDS interventions add value given these nuances.

- When you get deep into the details, organizations can vary dramatically in the way they manage medications, even within the same health system or facility. For example, even within the same hospital, the surgery, oncology, and pediatrics departments may differ in their workflows for a particular medication-related task.

- Realize there will be problematic workflows that might be difficult to document or repair; it may be hard to identify these when you start mapping, but good communication with the involved stakeholders is the best tool for overcoming these obstacles.

- Clinical processes are often interrupted, non-linear, or ubiquitous, which may pose challenges to fully documenting all the elements that can be supported by CDS and related CISs.

- Automating bad workflow will not fix a problem and often magnifies it to the point that clinicians think it is an outcome created by the computer.

- Workflow analysis often clarifies how information can literally change hands dozens of times, introducing opportunities for both errors and CDS-mediated improvements. A goal should be to simplify workflow first by reducing unnecessary handoffs and activities; then automate and support those that remain.

- It is also important to simplify workflow during re-engineering because CISs often make workflows less flexible, and large, complex, automated flows will be more difficult to implement and follow.

- You'll also get better adoption if you simplify. Cumbersome workflows may trigger revolts by users.

- Keep in mind, though, that one reason you have complex workflows (prior to re-engineering) is that they account for variations in circumstances. The goal then is to have straightforward, efficient workflows that accommodate different and important needs pertinent to the process at hand.

- Once you automate certain processes, you may eliminate necessary workarounds that provide user options in particular situations; that's why thoughtful but simplified replacement workflows are important. It may still be difficult to overcome or eliminate workarounds altogether. It is important to monitor and address new workarounds that are developed after rounds of enhanced automation and CDS support.

- A detailed workflow analysis is critical to successfully deploying alerts. When alerts are used, careful attention should be given to exactly how, when, and where they will appear and that the messages delivered are consistent; this will help decrease alert overload and promote end-user value and acceptance (also see the sidebar on alerts later in this chapter).

- The CDS Five Rights approach isn't meant to suggest that there's any single combination of right information/stakeholder/format/channel/workflow point that will fully achieve the desired CDS goal. It may take multiple intervention types focused on different stakeholders delivered through a variety of channels.

Outline the Roles That Various Stakeholders Will Play

Although the most highly visible stakeholders in the medication management cycle (besides the patient) are physicians, nurses, and pharmacists, it is imperative to address other stakeholders, such as respiratory therapists, who play important roles in specific medication-use issues. Once you have determined who all these players are, appoint a clinical liaison or champion from each stakeholder group. These individuals ensure those constituents' needs and constraints regarding CDS will be fully addressed as CDS interventions suggested by workflow analyses are developed. It is important to engage the CDS team(s) responsible for change management (see Chapter 2, Stakeholder Roles, Activities, page 22, and Chapter 6, Change Management, page 176) early in the process to help understand and manage the changes that may occur in medication management processes that are handled by each stakeholder type (including patients).

In partnership with project team members, the stakeholder liaisons/champions will help identify current workflows and how a proposed CDS intervention might impact those patient care activities. This feedback helps the CDS team decide whether changes to the CDS intervention specifications might be needed. Remember that, given the functional limitations of CISs, it is not always possible to maintain the same workflow process—some changes may be unavoidable. However, the new CDS-supported workflows should provide important benefits to each stakeholder. You can use Worksheet 3-3 to stimulate your thinking about optimizing the role that various stakeholders will play for individual CDS interventions.

Intervention details and workflow changes should be solidified based on rich collaboration with pertinent stakeholders. As the intervention is finalized, the CDS team can begin communicating about implementation planning with the broader stakeholder community that will be affected by the intervention. This helps reduce the time lag between development and deployment of the CDS intervention and promotes successful adoption (see Chapter 6, page 185 and Worksheet 3-3).

Use-Case Scenarios

Workflow processes mapping, and related analyses, will generate rich hypotheses about CDS interventions that may improve care processes and outcomes. As you translate these hypotheses into intervention designs, use-case scenarios can support the design process by helping make explicit exactly how these improvements will occur. *Use-case scenarios* are step-by-step written descriptions of how users interact with a system, and the results of those interactions. For example, consider the case in which an alert is chosen to reduce a specific commission error, such as ordering a medication to which the patient is allergic. Use-case scenarios can help make explicit how the alert is expected to occur in workflow, what the range of responses is likely to be, and whether these notifications and responses will help achieve the desired objective.

Use-case scenarios for an intervention should cover several different examples of likely user-system interactions and can be divided into a low, medium, and high complexity progression. This hierarchy can help isolate areas in which the intervention might perform well or poorly based on a specific design approach, which can then be modified if needed.

Use cases should be reviewed with all pertinent stakeholder groups to ensure a shared understanding about the intervention purpose and mechanics. This review can help uncover incorrect assumptions about how the interventions will work or what they will accomplish. Obtaining this input early in the development process can make it far easier to address any problematic issues that arise. Keep in mind that as intervention development unfolds, you might need to add additional stakeholders to ensure that all parties affected by the intervention are included in reviewing the use cases.

Use cases developed for design will underpin testing and validation for the corresponding interventions, as will be discussed in Chapter 6, page 182. Often changes to the use cases will occur as review and input broadens during intervention development and vetting. This evolution should be handled through formal governance processes for managing the changes (as discussed in Chapter 2, page 28, and Chapter 8, page 246).

Build in Outcomes Measurement from the Beginning

The measurement component in a CDS program for medication management is discussed in detail in Chapter 7, page 199, and you might consider peeking ahead if more specifics would be useful at this stage in your work. For those working linearly through this book, however, we reinforce some initial concepts here. They will be important to keep in mind throughout the process from identifying specific targets/outcomes (Chapter 2, page 31) through developing and deploying CDS interventions that will successfully address those targets (Chapters 4 through 6).

A Word about Developing Alerts

We provide deeper discussion of using and monitoring alerts in subsequent chapters but offer here some considerations to keep in mind during early intervention planning.

A fundamental premise of the approach embodied in the CDS Five Rights and this guide is that multiple opportunities exist for delivering data and knowledge to drive improved outcomes. Although alerts that interrupt workflow can be a powerful intervention, they also tend to be overused, which exacerbates problems such as alert fatigue and inappropriate alert overrides.

For example, a readily accessible order set, such as for appropriate thromboembolism prophylaxis in patients for whom this is indicated, can make the right thing the easy thing to do. Such an intervention should lead to better clinical outcomes and better staff satisfaction than an unsolicited alert that simply notifies a clinician that the prophylaxis was not given without having provided such up front support. The contrast becomes even more glaring when an alert is inappropriate because it does not account for all pertinent patient factors. This may occur, for example, if the patient has already received the indicated prophylaxis or is not a candidate for some reason.

The key to effective alerting is to deploy alerts sparingly and in situations for which such unsolicited interruptions are deemed (by all stakeholders, especially the recipients) to be the most appropriate approach to achieving desired outcomes. Carefully think through other intervention types that may achieve the same objective with less interruption to workflow and thought flow.

For example, consider non-interruptive alerting, that is, information that is highlighted somewhere on a screen but doesn't require user action, such as closing a dialog box, to continue. This type of alerting may include using colors or bolding in the user interface to call out information requiring special attention. For example, in important but non-critical situations, clinicians might be notified through text highlighted in some appropriate context within the CPOE or EMR user interface that a patient has not received some indicated drug or that the potential for a DDI exists. More intrusive notification is appropriate as the clinical stakes become higher and certainty increases that the information is appropriate to a specific patient. It is important with both interruptive and non-interruptive alerting to ensure that information presented to the user will have the greatest value possible.

Some organizations with custom-developed clinical applications have used non-interruptive notifications for "anticipatory alerting" as well. For example, the system highlights on the screen information (such as a selected drug dose exceeding the recommended maximum or a problematic medication selection on a reconciliation form) that will trigger an interruptive alert in a subsequent workflow step, if not corrected.

Consider various alert recipients as well, to avoid overburdening any specific stakeholder type. For example, Advocate Health Care uses the following approach within their efforts to achieve a desired outcome (VTE prophylaxis) with minimal unnecessary intrusion. At a patient's admission, an alert is triggered for nursing to complete the VTE assessment if this is not already done. Based on the resulting assessment score, nursing calls the physician for VTE prophylaxis orders if they are not already entered.

Alert fatigue tends to be associated with interruptive alerts that fire frequently and are often falsely positive. To avoid this scenario, you should spend extra time in the initial testing phase (when you have concluded that alerts are absolutely necessary) to determine how often and under what circumstances the alert fires. You may need to modify the triggering rule accordingly to make sure the alert fires appropriately when it would be helpful and does not fire otherwise.

Also, when alert overrides are allowed within a CDS intervention, such overrides might be tiered (if the CIS has this functionality) so that the ability to override specific alert types is based on an individual user's role, title, or identity. This might include, for example, not permitting a trainee to override the alert but allowing a more senior clinician to do so. Ideally, reasons for overrides should be captured and tracked in a standardized fashion. Override reasons, along with alert recommendation compliance, should be monitored in an ongoing fashion to identify trends in practice that may require modifications to make the alert more specific and useful (see Chapter 7, page 207, for a more detailed discussion of monitoring alert overrides).

Alerts should be actionable wherever possible. The alert should not only warn the clinician to use caution but specifically indicate what needs to be done to address the situation that triggered the alert and make it easy to take that action. For example:

• Drug interaction warning: "Need to decrease digoxin dose by 25% due to decreased clearance; click [here] to modify the order accordingly."

• Drug-lab warning: "Monitor INR twice a week for the first three weeks of therapy to ensure proper therapeutic effect; click [here] to create this order."

As these examples illustrate, alerts should ideally provide some justification for the recommendation (perhaps with links to more detailed supporting information), as well as the ability to directly act on the recommendation.

Consider whether role-based alerts versus workflow-based alerts should be used for specific interventions. Role-based alerts fire based on the person's role within the medication-management cycle (for example, physician, nursing, and pharmacist). Workflow-based alerts are those that fire based on the workflow step being performed and do not discriminate according to who might be performing the workflow step. Considering the CDS Five Rights and the clinical objective may help determine an approach that is most appropriate.

Many CISs will allow alerts to be tiered, so that different users see alerts in different tiers. For DDIs, tiers may include interaction severity, supporting literature documentation, and other factors. As an example, drug-drug or drug-allergy interactions may be tiered such that pharmacists see all notifications that the rules generate, whereas physicians see only notifications in the most severe categories. Similarly, your organization may decide to only show nurses at medication administration the drug-allergy alerts.

For certain types of alerts (such as those indicating extremely dangerous circumstances), it may be important as a safety net to present every rule firing to all users with different roles at each pertinent point in the workflow. In the situation in which multiple users will see the same alert, it is important to note that each user should be able to see each other's documentation for proceeding with the medication order in spite of seeing the alert. For example, a physician may see an alert and document that it is a "treatment plan requirement, risks outweigh benefits" and proceed with the medication order. When the pharmacist is processing the medication order and sees the same alert, it is useful for him or her to also see the physician override documentation. This access to previous documentation will eliminate in many cases the need for the pharmacist to contact the physician and clarify the potentially problematic medication order.

The CDS Five Rights approach directs you to detail exactly where in the user's workflow the alert will fire. The workflow/process mapping described earlier can be very helpful in determining these specifics. For example, if a physician orders prednisone when it is contraindicated, and an alert is the optimal mechanism for preventing this action, then the alert should be triggered as soon as the drug is pulled up, rather than the point at which the physician is about to sign the order. The latter reflects a greater disruption of workflow and thought flow. Alerts delivered either significantly before or after the critical decision/action they are designed to influence will simply not be as effective and will likely irritate recipients. Carefully considering recipient roles and workflows, together with meticulous attention to ensuring alert pertinence when presented, can help make these interruptions more targeted and effective.

Why is it so important to address measurement beginning with the very earliest CDS activities, such as identifying targets, determining baselines, and planning interventions? If the targeted CDS-related goals are firmly rooted in institutional priorities (as outlined in Chapter 2), then progress toward these objectives really matters, and, therefore, should be accurately tracked. For example, performance on care quality and safety metrics that address appropriate medication use is increasingly a factor in compensation plans for organization leadership and other staff—making careful and accurate metric tracking essential. Inadequate leadership support for assessment activities within your CDS program may be an indicator that its goals are not linked tightly enough to leadership priorities.

By considering early on how you will know whether you have achieved desired results from your CDS interventions (and if the interventions have created any new problems), you can ensure that data needed for these assessments are readily available once the CDS interventions have been implemented. The earlier you embed strategies for measuring key variables in your development and testing plan, the easier it is to avoid delays in implementation (caused, for example, by retrofitting measurement capabilities) and make timely, measurable progress toward goals. Executive support for the targets, and for the resources necessary to measure progress toward them, can be key factors in successfully driving measurable improvement in critical areas.

Early measurement capability also provides valuable feedback during the initial implementation phase. End users might perceive, for example, that every alert is a nuisance. Having data about how alerts are handled early in testing and launch allows you to validate or debunk this perception. It is helpful when assessing alerts during development to run them in "silent" mode in the production system. This means that the user is not automatically presented with any information, but the data pertaining to alert firing circumstances and messages are stored in the database for analysis. The results can help to determine whether the CDS intervention fires appropriately or requires tweaking for optimal performance (for example, by further restricting the circumstances that trigger firing).

What Are the Measurement Factors You Need to Consider Up Front?

Representatives from the CDS oversight committee and the different stakeholder groups can help determine the measures that should be evaluated and reported. These measures should reflect two factors:

use of the CDS intervention and progress made toward the targeted medication-related outcome (as defined in Chapter 2). These same people can also determine how often these data should be reported and to whom.

Once you have identified the specific measurements that will be tracked for the interventions, you should determine whether baseline data are available for them. Typically, a CDS intervention is implemented to improve performance, so it is important to have baseline performance data to show the actual impact of the CDS intervention (as discussed in Chapter 2) in addition to other process-related information.

Are the data for ongoing measures available? You should identify whether the needed information can be readily extracted from systems and processes that are in place. If not, some contingency plan should be developed (for example, applying additional resources to obtain the needed information or considering alternative measures that will still provide needed feedback on process and performance). It is important to ensure that all critical data are accurate and reliably available. Measured data should be recorded and presented in a meaningful and easy-to-understand manner.

The CDS project team might appoint one of their team members, together with core IT team members, to create a CDS-reporting task force. This group can determine whether required data points can be extracted, as needed, to understand the process and outcomes related to each CDS intervention. Creating such a relationship between the CDS project team and the core IT team helps the latter better understand the project team's data need related to CDS and helps the CDS team better understand the availability and limitations of specific data elements. In a similar fashion, adding pertinent clinical representatives to the CDS-reporting group can further ensure that considerations relevant to patient care are addressed in the CDS reporting approach.

When needed data do appear to be available, examining how they are stored and retrieved within the testing environment before implementation into the live environment can help ensure that they will be easily accessible and accurate. By intervention launch, there should be in place team members with clear responsibility for gathering and reporting data on the CDS-related metrics over time. If there is ownership for these results within the organizational leadership, then there will be strong incentives for timely reporting and appropriate responses by the CDS team.

Four Types of Metrics

Keep in mind four types of metrics as you begin the process of developing CDS interventions: system response time measurement, structure metrics, process indicators, and outcomes measures.

System response times refers to the amount of time it takes for a CIS or CDS application to process data from a user, and/or various ISs, and deliver a resulting CDS intervention to the recipient. For example, this may include measuring the time that elapses from the point at which a prescriber enters a medication order into a CPOE system to the time the system provides an alert that the new medication could be dangerous for some reason. Such system-generated wait times should be kept to a minimum because users typically consider delays beyond a very few seconds, at most, as unacceptable.

Structure metrics refers to CDS intervention capabilities, such as the number and nature of interruptive alerts that have been deployed and whether and how end users can override these alerts and document override reasons; the number of order sets deployed and the topics they cover; where and how infobuttons are deployed, and the like.

Process indicators illustrate the extent to which CDS interventions affect care activities and flow. They address questions, such as:

- How often was the CDS intervention used? This metric provides an overview of acceptance and value. For example, how many order sets or order sentences were utilized?
- How often does an alert fire? This metric provides an idea of how often the alert triggers occur, which can be useful in subsequent efforts

to decrease false-positive alerting by fine-tuning the triggers. (Keep in mind that rules and alerts designed to prevent very rare events that should never occur may fire rarely or never, yet still be useful. The prioritization process discussed in Chapter 2 can help determine when such rules might be valuable.)

- Who is receiving the alerts? Specific names and positions can be useful for PI, education, and feedback (though this information should be handled carefully and the evaluation process should involve clinical oversight entities).
- How often are the alerts overridden? This metric provides feedback to the CDS team on the usefulness of the alert to the clinician. That information can be used to drive future revision to the alert or education to users, depending on whether the analysis indicates that the overrides are generally appropriate or not.
- What override reasons are given? This metric can help determine (perhaps in conjunction with further investigation) whether the coded override reasons are only chosen based on their placement on the list or whether they are thoughtful responses. Such assessments also help determine whether the override reasons are specific enough and appropriate for users.

Outcome measures address the extent to which CDS interventions accomplish targeted goals and objectives. At the highest level, these metrics include increasing safe medication use, patient care quality, and patient health. Outcome measures answer questions such as:

- Has there been a measurable positive effect from an order set on patient care outcomes?
  - Is there a reduction in average length of stay (ALOS) for conditions in which order sets are being used?
  - Have medication costs decreased because prescribers are selecting less expensive, equally efficacious drugs?
  - Is there a reduction in drug-resistant organism prevalence through improved antibiotic selection and therapy duration?

It is important to remember that as an intervention is used in clinical settings over time and measurements are made, more questions will likely arise. As this is a fluid process, the CDS team should be ready to modify or enhance data gathering and reporting to support PI, as needed.

Maintain Emphasis on Measurement Throughout

Make sure that all stakeholders are engaged as appropriate in ensuring that measurement is an integral and ongoing part of the CDS effort. This includes planning what will be measured and how; gathering, synthesizing, and reporting the data; and addressing their implications. This process begins with opportunity assessment and baseline determination as outlined in the last chapter, flows through intervention development (for example, in answering the design question "How will we know if these approaches are achieving our objectives?"), and then through results assessment and continuous improvement. This is not an "add on" activity that can be approached as an afterthought to intervention development and launch.

It is difficult to overstate the significance of a well-developed and adequately supported approach to measurement; lacking one makes it far more difficult to realize anticipated benefits and to demonstrate return on investment (ROI) from deployed CDS interventions. We emphasize this point so strongly in this guide because it is such a frequent and powerful opportunity for enhancing an organization's CDS program.

Consider Buy versus Build versus Share Approaches for Acquiring CDS Interventions

Organizations generally wind up using a combination of buy, build, and share strategies to assemble their CDS intervention portfolio. We will next examine issues related to each approach.

However the content for CDS interventions is obtained, it's important to consider consistency in terms of clinical recommendations, underlying vocabularies and coding schemes, ease of integration into CISs, and the like. For example, guidance about medication use provided via CDS applications to patients, physicians, nurses, and pharmacists should not contain conflicting information. Such issues related to managing the CDS asset portfolio are discussed in Chapter 8, page 240.

Buy

Commercial CDS offerings to support medication management can provide significant value with relatively modest investment, compared to costs associated with the CISs in which many are deployed.

Although not readily available today, the most desirable CDS interventions are easily integrated into CIS and supported by regularly updated databases with critical information specifically focused on preventing the most common and dangerous avoidable ADEs. For example, such a high-value database might contain a relatively small set of drug pairs that should never be used together—the somewhat larger set of those pairs that can be used together with careful attention (such as dose adjustments), and the still larger set that require monitoring for signs and symptoms of toxicity. Commercial databases may contain much of this information, but it is typically difficult to identify and use this highly actionable subset of these large databases within CISs.

Advantages of the Buy Strategy include the following:

- Content is ready-made and does not require extensive resources from the deploying institution for initial creation. However, at least some local review and content validation is important for much, if not most, of the CDS content purchased from vendors. For example, several vendors offer evidence-based order sets, but these need to be adapted to local practice, formularies, etc.
- The content is backed by evidence based on research and synthesis done by the vendor. It is important, though, to understand the process whereby the vendor incorporates evidence into the knowledge base. For example, if the vendor

relies heavily on secondary sources that summarize primary clinical research literature, there may be a lag before important, cutting-edge information is incorporated.

- It may take less time to implement CDS interventions with many components, such as DDI detection.

- Content is typically updated on a regular schedule (ideally with timeframes suited to the rate at which information changes, with ad hoc updates for urgent developments as needed); the vendor bears responsibility for addressing recently released drug information, new drugs, national quality and safety measures and standards (for example, core measures from The Joint Commission and CMS, ISMP safety alerts, and the like).

- The strategy may include some canned reports for measurement.

- There may be better consistency among various CDS content sets (such as drug alerts, order sets) coming from a single source, as opposed to a potential potpourri from homegrown and/or shared knowledge being combined.

  Disadvantages of the Buy Strategy include the following:

- Commercial drug databases used to populate the medication master file in the pharmacy ISs and CPOE systems also serve as the basis for medication alerts (drug-allergy, drug-drug, drug-laboratory interactions, for example). Interaction alerts generated from these commercial databases are pharmacologically accurate, though many might be of relatively limited usefulness when delivered as interruptive alerts, since the databases tend to emphasize comprehensiveness over clinical relevance. Knowledgebase vendors may offer mechanisms for filtering alerts by severity and documentation, which can help, but these approaches are generally not yet standardized across many CISs. As a result, many CDS implementers find that commercial drug interaction databases require significant adjustments to medication-alert settings; some suppress these altogether and deploy homegrown alerts tuned to local needs.

- These interaction databases may have limited customizability and thereby lock an organization into the vendor's offering. If customizable, it can be very time consuming to review, recommend changes, and vet with local stakeholders; further, mechanisms for synchronizing user customizations with updates provided by the vendor will be needed. Other CDS interventions, such as order sets provided by vendors, are typically customized and updated more easily, though significant organizational resources may still be needed to manage these functions.

- Because there are currently no widely used standards for integrating drug knowledge bases (and other CDS intervention types) into CISs, the integration process varies by CIS and CDS systems and may require significant effort.

- Liability concerns may arise, for example, through questions such as: Do organizations that choose to adjust interaction settings provided by a third-party vendor place themselves at risk when there is an ADE related to the suppression of a medication alert? (See Appendix B, Some Medico-legal Considerations.)

- Availability or access to customer feedback channels may also be a concern. In contrast to software vendors and locally developed CDS content, the process/mechanism for providing input and feedback to drug content providers may be less apparent to clinical users, especially physicians.

Build Your Own/Homegrown

In many cases, academic organizations that helped pioneer successful CDS use have developed their own content and interventions, sometimes with help from research grants that supported their CDS efforts. Although economies of scale have led to increased commercial CDS application availability and use, there will likely remain a role for developing at least some CDS interventions locally. Also, as noted under Buy Strategy previously discussed, even material purchased from vendors will often require some degree of localization.

Advantages of Build Your Own Strategy include the following:

- Custom-tailor to local needs, practice patterns, formulary, policies/procedures, etc.
- Potentially easier adoption by end users, for reasons in previous bullet
- Deep local knowledge about how the content was developed and why specific information and recommendations are included, potentially making it easier to maintain and modify

Disadvantages of Build Your Own Strategy include the following:

- Effort, expertise, resources, and time may not be readily available. Tasks include the following:
  - Research and synthesize pertinent evidence base and recommendations.
  - Decide on local standards and build consensus.
  - Develop editorial policies and procedures for developing content.
  - Understand and address issues surrounding interoperability; for example, deploying similar content across diverse CISs.
  - Engage local clinicians to develop and vet contents; they typically require incentives for this work, such as career advancement in academic settings but more often as direct financial compensation.
- Content can quickly become outdated, and organizations may lack robust tools to support its management.
- Custom reports are necessary for results measurement.
- This strategy may require richer governance structures and processes earlier on than what is required when purchasing CDS content, since gaining consensus on content development from scratch may be more complex than approving content acquired from a trusted source.
- Development and maintenance costs may significantly exceed those of commercial systems because there is no economy of scale. Many organizations compensate clinicians for their time in developing and vetting content, contributing to these costs. Note that such participants should

generally be actively practicing so that pertinent needs and perspectives are adequately addressed. As noted earlier, incorporating primary literature into CDS knowledge bases can improve intervention value, but may require substantial additional expertise and resources compared with using summary sources for content development.

Share

Currently, many organizations are investing significant resources to create very similar—or even identical—CDS interventions, such as specific rules and alerts to address priority goals. Sharing at least some of these interventions across organizations seems logical and desirable. CIS vendors often allow their customers to share CDS interventions via the libraries they establish. Although some CDS sharing occurs today, lack of widely used interoperability standards, in addition to other obstacles noted next, limits its extent.

Advantages of the Share Strategy include the following:

- Ability to leverage work by others to avoid "reinventing the wheel"
- Low acquisition costs compared with vendor-supplied or local development
- Can theoretically share both content and implementation best practices for that content
- Some confidence in usability based on experience of organization supplying content

Disadvantages of the Share Strategy include the following:

- Unclear content quality, currency
- Still have to adapt for local environment, address ongoing maintenance, and incorporate into CDS governance and management processes (for example, by prioritizing each new intervention among other alternatives in the local CDS program and developing pertinent evaluation metrics and data gathering approach for each intervention)
- Reluctance by some organizations to share, for a variety of reasons including competitive differentiation, liability concerns, and the like

There is increasing national attention on executing recommendations in the Roadmap for National Action on Clinical Decision Support;[2] these recommendations include strategies for making CDS more interoperable across CISs. Execution efforts include activities of AHIC ad hoc CDS Working Group[3] and related entities, the Agency for Healthcare Research and Quality (AHRQ),[4] and others.

Developing national CDS content sources is under consideration, and some initial steps in this direction have occurred. For example, the DailyMed service provides downloadable drug information from FDA-approved drug package inserts,[5] and the Morningside Initiative[6] is a public-private effort to create a CDS KM repository for shared, broadly available, executable knowledge. Once mature, these efforts could be a boon to CDS content sharing, local development, and commercial offerings.

In summary, most organizations use a combination of Build and Buy Strategies to acquire CDS assets needed to support medication management. For interventions such as order sets and alerts, this generally includes vetting and making local modifications to customize the content. Although CIS vendors offer libraries and related mechanisms for sharing CDS content among their customers, such sharing has not yet been extensive compared with the intervention breadth pertinent to medication management.

WORKSHEETS

Worksheet 3-1

Workflow Process Mapping

The following is a flowcharting template example you can use for mapping workflows pertinent to the priority medication management targets you will be addressing with CDS. The chapter text outlines considerations for creating such maps and includes information about identifying software tools available for making these flowcharts.

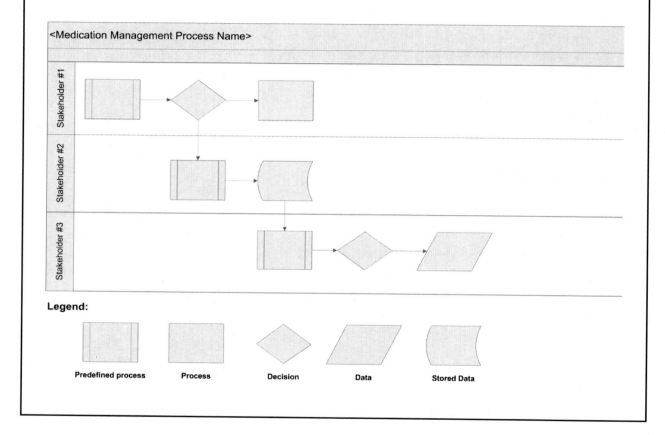

Worksheet 3-2

Selecting Interventions

If you are sequentially working through the chapters in this book, you could begin fleshing out this worksheet now, and return to fill in additional details based on the discussions in Chapter 4 on optimizing interventions in specific CISs and in Chapter 5 on addressing specific targets.

Copy into the first column of this worksheet each target from Worksheet(s) 2-3, page 56, for which you will be developing CDS interventions. If you are addressing more than one high-level clinical goal, you can use one or more versions of this worksheet. In the second column, list decision support actions that can help ensure that the objective is achieved.

Consider the capabilities of your IT and CIS infrastructure (as is documented in Worksheet 4-1, page 107) as a backdrop for intervention opportunities. Filter these intervention candidates with the selection considerations outlined in this chapter and the next two chapters. Document the refined list of targeted workflow steps in the third column and the CDS interventions (including pertinent applications) in the fourth column. The final list should reflect a balance between using multiple interventions to increase the likelihood of achieving an objective and not overloading the care delivery system or participants with excessive interventions.

In the fifth column, assign a name to each intervention that can be used as shorthand notation to identify it, for example, in subsequent worksheets. The sixth column can be used to note important implementation considerations.

Clinical goal: Reduce preventable ADEs					
Medication Management Objective	**Target Action**	**Medication Management Process Step**	**Specific CDS Intervention**	**Intervention Name (ID)**	**Comments**
Prevent prescription of medication to allergic patients	Warn prescriber of patient's allergy at point of medication ordering	Prescribing	Trigger alert window in CPOE when the order is being submitted, requiring prescriber's electronic signature override for order to proceed.	Prescription allergy alert window	Will require careful development to ensure only most critical issues trigger this alert, and "noise" is minimized; need well-vetted override reason list

Worksheet 3-2 *continued*

Clinical goal: Reduce preventable ADEs

Medication Management Objective	Target Action	Medication Management Process Step	Specific CDS Intervention	Intervention Name (ID)	Comments
Prevent prescription of medication to allergic patients	Warn pharmacist of patient's allergy at point of medication dispensing	Dispensing	Pharmacy computer system looks in the EMR for documented patient allergies, triggers an alert to pharmacist who will verify with prescriber before dispensing.	Pharmacy med check system	Will have a lower threshold for alerting than for prescriber, but still need to minimize "noise." Need to develop supporting interventions/strategy to help ensure appropriate allergy documentation at patient intake and updating during stay.

Worsheet 3-3

Roles and Responsibilities of Clinical and Non-clinical Stakeholders

As we have emphasized in the text, front-line clinical participants in the medication management cycle who will be affected by the CDS intervention, such as patients, nurses, pharmacists, and physicians, deserve careful attention. Their successful participation throughout intervention development and deployment can dramatically increase the likelihood that the intervention will produce its intended results. Mapping out the roles that these stakeholders should play in preparing the interventions and in the change management process—in addition to completing corresponding tasks by the CDS team—can help ensure that these stakeholders are effectively engaged and their efforts coordinated. You can use this worksheet to help get that process started; additional change management considerations and tasks associated with intervention launch are addressed in Chapter 6.

Copy into the first column of this worksheet each CDS intervention from Worksheet(s) 3-2 for which you will now detail the principal stakeholders and their roles in the change management process. If you are addressing more than one objective, you can use one or more versions of this worksheet. The clinical goal and medication management objective can be listed at the top of each Worksheet 3-3 to provide further context.

In the second column, outline the tasks that the CDS team needs to address for intervention success. Use the remaining columns to assign corresponding roles in developing the intervention to other stakeholders. Continue adding columns as needed for additional stakeholders, such as quality officers or committees.

Worksheet 3-3 *continued*

Clinical goal: Reduce preventable ADEs

Medication management objective: Prevent patients from getting drugs to which they are allergic

CDS Intervention	CDS Team	Patient	Nurse	Physician	Pharmacist	Clinical IT Advisory Committee
Prescription allergy alert window	• Document and validate changes to workflow • Determine/validate data flows need to manage allergy information • Provide and validate database to be used for checking • Develop/implement evaluation plan • Prepare preliminary training/communications for broader stakeholder community	• Know and communicate their allergies [develop tools and strategies to support this—such as gathering information from previous admissions for prompting]	• Help with testing and validating workflow that involves accurately recording medication list and allergies on admission to floor • Define nursing constraints • Convey the process to other front-line nurses • Help create implementation plans	• Help finalize and accept alerting strategy/logic, • Define prescriber workflow constraints (time, efficiency) • Convey alerting process to colleagues • Help create implementation plans • Advise on alert management such as override handling	• Validate workflow components and identify gaps • Help with intervention testing and validation • Educate colleagues • Verify drug information and alerting strategy • Help create implementation plans	• Coordinate alert management and updates • Oversee development, rollout, and monitoring; help with problem solving
Pharmacy med check system	[Will be similar to above]					

CONCLUDING COMMENTS

To sum up, the following "Ten Commandments for Effective Clinical Decision Support"[7] provide a helpful framework for approaching the CDS intervention design phase.

1. Speed is everything.
2. Anticipate needs and deliver in real time.
3. Fit into the user's workflow.
4. Little things can make a big difference.
5. Recognize that physicians will strongly resist stopping an intended action.
6. Changing direction is easier than stopping.
7. Simple interventions work best.
8. Ask for additional information only when you really need it.
9. Monitor impact, get feedback, and respond.
10. Manage and maintain your knowledge-based systems.

We have explored some of these CDS success factors here, and will address others in the following chapters.

REFERENCES

1. For example, see Wikipedia. *Flowcharts.* http://en.wikipedia.org/wiki/Flowchart, accessed 10/2/08.

2. American Medical Informatics Association. *CDS Roadmap.* www.amia.org/inside/initiatives/cds, accessed 10/2/08.

3. Government HealthIT. *Clinical decision support emerges as a hot topic among feds.* http://www.govhealthit.com/online/news/350287-1.html. 28 Mar 2008.

4. Healthcare IT News. *Brigham and Women's, Yale to launch research on clinical decision support.* http://www.healthcareitnews.com/story.cms?id=8894. 14 Mar 2008.

5. U.S. National Library of Medicine, National Institutes of Health, Health & Human Services. *Daily Med.* http://dailymed.nlm.nih.gov/dailymed, accessed 10/2/08.

6. American Medical Informatics Association. *Engineering a learning Healthcare System: A Look at the Future.* http://www.iom.edu/Object.File/Master/54/014/S4_2-Detmer%20-%20Presentation.pdf, accessed 10/2/08. See slides 16, 21, 22.

7. Bates DW, Kuperman GJ, Wang S, et al. Ten commandments for effective clinical decision support: making the practice of evidence-based medicine a reality. *J Am Med Inform Assoc.* 2003; 10(6):523-530.

Chapter 4
Leverage Available Clinical Information Systems When Developing CDS Interventions

TASKS

- Inventory locally available CISs and CDS interventions/content, and consider the role each will play in using CDS to improve medication utilization.
- Consider opportunities to optimize how CDS is applied to ensure that the key clinical tasks at each step in the medication management process are conducted safely, effectively, and efficiently.
- Keep specific targeted outcomes in mind (from Chapter 2) during efforts to optimize CDS in individual ISs and in steps in the medication management process.

KEY LESSONS

- Focus here on optimizing the "right channel" component of the CDS Five Rights; think broadly about how available CIS might be used to deliver needed information to pertinent stakeholders at appropriate points in workflow.
- Fully leverage the organizational momentum behind deploying CISs to address key business needs; this includes bringing value from CDS to those CIS efforts, as well as harnessing CIS-related resources and energy to enhance CDS capacity and value.

DISCUSSION

In Chapter 3, we reviewed important background considerations, such as careful workflow analysis and use-case development, for implementing CDS interventions to enhance medication management. In this chapter, we examine in more detail how to set up CDS interventions within various CISs. Looking ahead, in Chapter 5 we will build on these themes to provide guidance on applying CDS to address specific clinical improvement targets, considering a cross-cutting perspective across multiple CISs.

Applying CDS to improve medication use can be approached from the perspective of the major CISs that underpin medication management; therefore, in this chapter, we will examine the role CDS can play within several of these major systems at specific points in the medication-use cycle. We provide recommendations about things that "should" be done in these systems, but recognize that systems do not all have the same capabilities and that your ability to implement the guidance may depend on the systems you have in place. Fortunately, certification requirements and processes are emerging that will ensure that systems have a common suite of essential functionality, including elements related to CDS.[1] There are mechanisms for public stakeholders to influence how these requirements evolve, and we encourage implementers to use them.

Inventory Local Information Systems, Pertinent CDS Capabilities, and Related Infrastructure

An initial step in optimizing CDS capabilities in pertinent systems is determining what systems, data and CDS content are available in your organization (see Table 4-1). Core clinical systems are a good starting point; these may include applications that handle documentation, order entry, medication management, and results review. Additional clinical systems of interest include ancillary systems supporting specific departments and clinical areas, such as pharmacy, laboratory, radiology, therapy services, food and nutrition, cardiology (including diagnostic and interventional), blood bank, and operating room (anesthesia, intraoperative documentation, for example). Hospitals and health systems typically use a complex and multifaceted web of systems—often not integrated—to support medication use.[2]

Other IT areas to cover include administrative systems, such as patient-management systems that manage demographic and other administrative data. Clinical content databases and resources (such as drug-reference information, drug interaction databases, order-set content, and online literature sources commonly used by clinicians in the organization) should also be noted since they represent a starting point for your efforts to enhance CDS value and use. Finally, you should inventory clinical and administrative business-intelligence software and associated data warehouses, reporting tools, and dashboards. These will play an important role in assessing CDS intervention results (as we will cover in more detail in Chapter 7).

The task here is to gain an understanding of the information ecosystem available to support CDS functionality. This encompasses identifying the infrastructure that can be leveraged to obtain data needed to drive CDS interventions, providing the user interface to deliver this information, and supplying the content that will be delivered to end users. (See Table 1-1, page 5, outlining CDS intervention types and Worksheet 4-1.) In building the catalog, you should classify the information types entered, managed, and displayed in the CIS (such as lab information, patient demographics, etc.), as well as the underlying terminology/coding system if the information is stored as discrete data. You should list the CIS users and the utilization (adoption) rate. This list will include physicians, nurses, pharmacists, patients and their families, and others. It is also important to identify additional technology infrastructure considerations, such as system performance. For example, as you add additional CDS interventions, you need to ensure that they will not degrade CIS response times for end users. We will offer guidance on assessing CDS impact on CIS performance through pre- and post-implementation measurement in Chapter 7, page 200.

Table 4-1: CIS Applications Pertinent to CDS Interventions

Application Type	Examples
Departmental data management	• Pharmacy ISs • Laboratory ISs/results reporting system • Radiology information/results reporting system
Clinical records and patient management	• EMRs: ambulatory, inpatient, for patients (for example, PHR) • Department-oriented (for example, anesthesia, cardiology) • Care tracking systems: ED, operating room • Medication administration and documentation (for example, bar code medication administration, eMAR, medication reconciliation applications)
Ordering	• CPOE; other order entry systems
Data aggregation	• Data warehouse • Clinical data repository • External and internal registries (for example, disease-specific registries and government immunization registry)
Clinical content	• Reference/knowledge sources for clinicians and patients • CDS interventions incorporated into CIS (for example, order sets, drug-related alerts) • Alerts/advisories about medications withdrawn from the market or new black box warnings; drug shortages • Health information for patients • Health risk assessment tools
Financial/administrative	• Charge capture system • Billing system • Scheduling/registration system • Clinical and related business intelligence systems • Directories: physician on-call and coverage schedules and pager numbers, clinician and patient e-mail addresses

To maximize CDS effectiveness, it is key to ensure that system users have adequate access to devices required to interact with the CISs and their CDS functionality. For example, physicians unable to access a device for CPOE may be forced to give a verbal order or write the order on paper, potentially bypassing prescriber-focused CDS capabilities. Monitoring clinical workflow and speaking to stakeholders will typically indicate whether access to ISs and devices is adequate. Along similar lines,

good wireless connectivity is critical in settings in which wireless systems are used for CDS-related applications. Unreliable wireless access can discourage CIS use at the point of care, and the resulting physical separation between information delivery and targeted care activities can render CDS features less effective.

It is helpful in the IT inventory process to consider how introducing CDS in the various ISs you identify will affect workflow. To optimize care efficiency and user acceptance, the sequence and details for enabling CDS features in each system should be based on a careful workflow assessment for that system and the care processes it mediates (as discussed in Chapter 3). For example, an interruptive alert displayed at an inopportune step in EMR workflow can distract the clinician from the current task, increase the likelihood that the notification will be dismissed without action, and potentially result in an error by disrupting thought flow. The salient point for this discussion is that CIS tools and workflows provide a foundation for CDS-mediated enhancements, so understanding the CIS details is an important starting point for setting up CDS interventions within specific ISs.

User workarounds to avoid CIS imperfections amplifies this point. For example, burdensome workflows for electronically documenting key patient data may adversely affect documentation timeliness. Since usefulness for many CDS interventions (especially alerts) depends on up-to-date patient information, delays in documenting clinical observations or interventions in the CIS could result in inappropriate recommendations for clinicians. In general, when a CDS-related workflow change is required for CIS use (especially adding additional or unfamiliar steps), end users and their champions should be engaged in developing these new workflows. The CDS team should ensure that they thoroughly understand pertinent underlying CIS tools and workflows, as well as desired CDS-mediated enhancements related to the changes.

Additional details to consider in the CIS inventory include how the primary ISs for medication management (for example, from the first three rows in Table 4-1 previously shown) handle the following key CDS intervention types (see Table 1-1, page 5):
- Order sets
- Documentation templates
- Relevant data display
- Alerts
- Multistep protocols
- Reference information, including infobutton capability

Key information types to consider—along with some corresponding terminology and coding schemes—include, among others:
- Diagnosis information (ICD-9-CM);[3] consider also ICD-10-CM/PCS[4]
- Procedure order information (CPT®)[5]
- Medication lists (RxNorm)[6]
- Laboratory results (LOINC®)[7]
- Pathology reports (SNOMED CT®)[8]
- Nursing interventions and education (NIC)[9]

General Considerations about Using CDS in These Systems to Improve Medication Management

As with any IT-supported process improvement, implementing CDS-enabled clinical systems involves social and cultural change. These changes include shifts in care team member roles and relationships. For example, physicians may be required to provide more detailed and complete information during order entry. They may raise concerns about these increased "clerical" responsibilities, pointing out that they are performing tasks more appropriate for nurses, therapists, technicians, and pharmacists. On the other hand, pharmacists, because they are not spending as much time entering orders and requesting clarification from prescribers, might be able to spend more time utilizing CDS tools and performing clinical interventions that enhance safe and effective medication use. The various strategies for gaining shared commitment to CDS goals and strategies that are outlined throughout this guide can help address such concerns.

Similarly, CIS/CDS-induced changes in communication—what, how, when, and between whom—need to be carefully considered, since these changes can introduce unintended, negative consequences.[10] As noted elsewhere in this book, various sources offer guidance on successfully leading organizational change.[11]

Technical considerations are also key. The CIS infrastructure capabilities will influence the CDS interventions that are available to address opportunities for improving medication management. For example, medication order entry in the CIS should include structured data elements, such as discrete dose, unit, route, duration, indication, and frequency. These are necessary to support certain CDS interventions, such as alerts about excessive dosing or wrong route.

Because your CISs and their CDS functionality play such an important role in your CDS efforts, consider enlisting support from applications suppliers. They, as well as those using these same systems in other organizations, are potential allies in your efforts to optimize the value that these tools bring toward accomplishing targeted objectives.

Keep in mind that optimizing CDS within CIS deployments is not a one-time event but rather a continuous refinement process (see Chapter 7, page 198). Prepare end users for, and be ready to respond quickly to, circumstances in which things don't go as expected in the user-CIS-CDS interface (for example, when a wrong order is mistakenly submitted or a key data element is documented incorrectly). Users need to know how to fix such errors properly so that other clinicians do not act on wrong information and so that improvised user fixes don't create additional errors. Educating users before and during launch, and having mechanisms to rapidly respond to their questions (see Chapter 6, page 185), can play an important role in addressing issues that inevitably arise.

Information Consistency and Flow

Seamlessly integrated information flow within the CIS is important for effective CDS but can be elusive. Having separate systems for order entry, pharmacy verification, and medication administration can require vigilance to ensure that CDS remains appropriate and helpful. For example, differences in the patient data handled by these systems may trigger different CDS recommendations. These disparities could confuse providers, slow down care processes when reconciliation is required, and introduce patient safety issues. All pertinent CDS—and related ISs—should be able to exchange data with consistent

meaning to provide the safest environment. When this consistency is managed by tools that automatically map data elements between systems, special care must be applied to ensure that the data mapping process is well-managed and maintained so as not to introduce errors. Similarly, non-integrated systems can result in transcription errors because they require users to re-enter data from one system to another—and every transcription step in the medication-management cycle introduces the potential for error.

Total parenteral nutrition (TPN) processing in a non-integrated system illustrates some of these information flow challenges and opportunities for support. In this setting, a physician may enter a TPN order in the CIS, but the order details are subsequently re-entered by a pharmacist into a TPN compounder. To reduce transcription error risk, the TPN order detail display in the CIS (or in a printed report) should correspond to the sequence of ingredients that must be programmed into the compounder. Also, the ingredient units must match—mEq with mEq, mg with mg, and so on. This thoughtful "relevant information display" can help support this otherwise suboptimal information flow.

Interface engines for automating this handoff can help but also have potential problems. Although they eliminate the need for manual data re-entry, breakdowns can compromise safety and efficiency. For example, a technical failure in the interface can prevent order transmission from the order-entry system to the pharmacy system, and programming errors in the interface (which can result from a variety of causes) can lead to incorrect order mapping from one system to the other. Careful workflow and system configuration—with attention to augmenting error-prone processing steps with supportive information along the lines outlined earlier—can help reinforce safe information flow in environments that are not optimally integrated. Likewise, close follow-up of key processes and outcomes (as discussed in Chapter 7) can help identify and correct information flow problems.

Information Display within CIS as a CDS Intervention

Standardizing information presentation must sometimes trump the desire for flexibility. Standard displays can help reduce medication errors by providing the user with a consistent, and therefore predictable, user interface for receiving and recording critical data items. For example, medication-order details should be presented in logical order and in a consistent manner. That means measure units must be standardized (such as, mEq, mMol, mg, and mcg). Likewise, standard concentrations for high-risk medications should be used, for example, IV drips for high-risk drugs such as epinephrine, dopamine, dobutamine. Flexibility, while preferred by clinicians, also introduces potential safety risks. Having the ability to change units, for example, can result in selecting an incorrect option for a given dose. Consider a prescriber who mistakenly changes the units for a medication order in a selection list from "micrograms" to "micrograms per kilogram." If the medication ordering function fails to constrain the available units options by the specific drug and patient age/weight—a dangerous overdose could be prescribed.

To increase the likelihood that a thoughtful, intended user response is evoked, you should consider option sequencing or defaulting when presenting the user with CDS interventions. For example, preselecting "must do" interventions in an order set, or putting the most frequently used option at the top of a choice list can help make the right thing to do the easiest for users. On the other hand, note that a common reason for dismissing an alert without taking appropriate action is that the default, or first option, makes it easy for this to happen.

Commercial Knowledge Bases for Order Checking

Commercial knowledge bases for checking medication orders are commonly used to support drug allergy, DDI, drug duplication, and dose limit screening in CPOE and pharmacy ISs. Decisions as to where these fit in your CIS-enabled patient-safety plan should ideally be made prior to rolling out provider order entry. Implementers find that most of these order checking systems can produce non-specific alerts and quickly lead to alert fatigue, risking the possibility that users will begin ignoring alerts altogether.[12] However, many systems allow clients to customize the database deployment in such a way that allows more manageable alerting. Implementers will do well to consider this issue early and work closely with their CIS and CDS vendors (or vendor candidates) to determine strategies for optimizing drug order checking to meet safety and user needs.

Although order checking will likely remain a priority strategy in the medication CDS plan, every possible alert need not be active when users are first getting accustomed to the new clinical system. A basic CDS-enabled medication safety net for pharmacy and CPOE systems should incorporate order sentences, order sets, DDI, and drug-allergy alerts. As outlined in Chapter 3, page 69, and throughout Chapter 5, careful attention to what alerting information is being presented to which users, and when and how it is presented, can reduce nuisance alerting and optimize patient safety.

Workflow, Workflow, Workflow

Obviously, addressing workflow is critical to any CIS, CDS-related or otherwise, as has already been emphasized in the discussion about CIS inventory. To begin deploying the CDS tools available within your CIS platform, you should revisit the ideal scenario for medication management described in Chapter 1, page 2, and the workflow mapping discussion, illustrations, and worksheets in Chapter 3, page 60. In a robust IS deployment, the clinician would order medications via a CPOE system fully integrated with the EMR (to support checking and execution). The order would then be presented to the pharmacist for verification and dispensing via the pharmacy system, after it assigns the correct drug product based on the order and formulary. The medication would then become available to the nurse in the patient's room (perhaps via a dispensing cabinet), with the medication bar code identifying

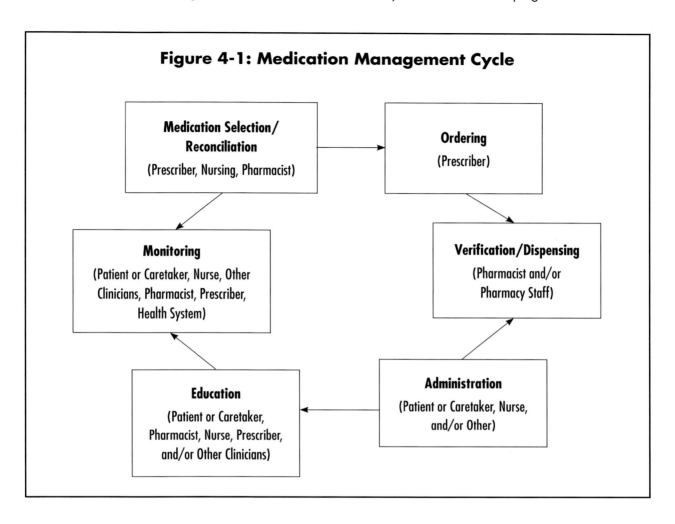

Figure 4-1: Medication Management Cycle

the right patient, drug, dose, route, and time, while the system electronically documents the administration via an eMAR. Most organizations have at least some component technology required for this ideal medication-use process.

Next we consider how CDS can be used to support workflow, quality, and safety within these and other systems that underpin medication use.

CDS in Information Systems at Each Step in the Medication Management Loop

Figure 4-1 is the graphic from Chapter 1 that depicts the medication-management cycle. We use it here as a table of contents for considering the opportunities to incorporate CDS into clinical systems that help mediate this cycle. As you consider the different systems you have in place for supporting medication

management, and how you might configure CDS in these systems to help address priority objectives, you can use Worksheet 4-2 to document notes about these opportunities.

Selection/Reconciliation—Key Systems: EMR, PHR, Medication Reconciliation Applications

Cycles in the medication management loop begin with selecting a drug (or modifying a previous selection) to manage a patient's condition. This selection is driven, of course, by careful clinical analysis of the patient's condition and pertinent management options—which in themselves are important candidates for CDS. To ensure that the drug choice is appropriate for achieving the desired outcomes, prescribers must consider a variety of patient-specific factors including medication history, allergies, and other conditions. Other issues must be considered as well, such as pertinent evidence and best practices about drug therapy for the condition and about the drugs themselves (for example, costs and side effects). Some considerations and opportunities for providing this CDS are outlined later in this chapter and in Chapter 5.

Medication lists for individual patients may span the continuum of care, including both outpatient and inpatient settings. These lists should be obtained from previous hospital admissions when pertinent. Medication lists should indicate whether the drug is actively being used or has been discontinued, including the reason for discontinuation. If possible, additional pertinent items should be included, such as the last prescription fill-date (and/or other information indicating the patient's adherence to the prescribed regimen), the reason (that is, the indication) for which each medication was prescribed, the prescriber, and the fulfilling pharmacy. Medication lists should be comprehensive and should include over-the-counter drugs, herbals, and vitamins. Since the medications that a patient is taking (which may be different from what has been prescribed) form the basis for many safety and quality checks, it is crucial that the combined, working medication list is current and accurate.

Problem lists for clinical conditions should indicate the status of the problem, such as whether it is active or resolved, acute or chronic, hospital-associated or POA. The implication for CDS is that electronically documenting medical problems as discrete data provides the ability to implement disease-specific CDS interventions, such as drug-diagnosis checking. The CIS can also suggest pertinent evidence-based order sets (which will include therapies indicated for best practice care and adherence to quality measures) based on documented problems.

For allergies, the CIS should provide the ability to encode for a true allergy (that is, immunologic hypersensitivity reaction) as distinguished from a drug intolerance or side effect, such as nausea or diarrhea. Reaction type and severity also are impor-

tant dimensions. CDS should likewise be able to differentiate warnings for these types of patient reactions, since the importance and the appropriate response may be quite different for each. Increasingly, CIS certification requirements are speaking to such detailed functionality issues.[13]

Medication reconciliation, a Joint Commission requirement,[14] is a major challenge for many organizations. There are several approaches that incorporate various combinations of electronic and paper-based tools. Systems for medication reconciliation are available from EMR vendors, other workflow solutions vendors, or may be homegrown. Ideally, a patient's shared "home medication list" should be converted to inpatient orders (and vice versa) with a minimum number of steps, maximum efficiency, and greatest support for safety. Accomplishing these goals can be facilitated through tools for comparing previous and new drug lists side-by-side and updating the lists during transitions across care settings, identifying home medications for which the patient doesn't know the name, screening for interactions as the medication lists are changed across settings, and the like. Increasingly, medication lists from patients' PHRs or other external data sources, such as retail pharmacies and pharmacy benefit managers, will become an important information source about what they are actually taking. Fortunately, some information sources about patients' ambulatory medications are beginning to consolidate.[15]

An important issue in supporting medication reconciliation with CDS is how to deal with therapeutic substitution or alternative therapy during an admission, such as when the patient's outpatient medication is not included on the inpatient formulary. For medications that are non-formulary, the CIS should present the recommended substitution and allow the prescriber to select the alternative medication order in one step. Mere notification that a medication is non-formulary is less effective than presenting an alternative. However, the relationship between the non-formulary home medication and the inpatient substitution must remain intact, because this factor is important for medication reconciliation at discharge—to avoid unintended duplications.

CDS can be a powerful tool for guiding medication selection toward preferred, on-formulary medications. One organization increased prescriptions for the preferred medication in a therapeutic class from 15.6% to 81.3% using an alert that both explained the rationale and provided an option to order the preferred agent. The benefit was sustained at the two-year follow-up.[16]

Prescribers consider a patient's current and past clinical problems, medications, allergies, and other factors (for example, medication costs and formularies)—as well as pertinent clinical evidence and best practices—in selecting medications to optimize patient outcomes. CDS interventions that provide such relevant patient data and reference information are important tools for supporting this critical and often complex decision. Consider opportunities to leverage CIS infrastructure to bring information needed for optimal medication selection more efficiently into prescriber workflow. Relevant data presentation via an EMR can be a powerful tool for making pertinent patient data (such as allergies, medications, critical labs, etc.) available to clinicians during the prescribing process. Structuring EMR displays and workflows related to medication selection in a manner that ensures this information is highly visible and readily accessible can support optimal prescribing decisions.

In addition, infobutton links can quickly provide guidance about disease and condition management, medication costs, formularies, and other key prescribing information. A prescriber reviewing a patient's active problem list in an EMR may want additional information about the latest evidence-based medication treatment protocols for the condition. When the EMR has been appropriately configured to link to reference sources that supply this information (for example, using the HL7 infobutton standard),[17] then by clicking a link or icon associated with the condition name, the provider can quickly access the needed information.

Ordering—Key System: CPOE/ePrescribing

Medication ordering—via a written or electronic order/prescription—formally initiates the cascade of events that will determine whether the drug achieves its desired effects and/or causes harm. As such, it is a critical opportunity for using CDS to help ensure that the chosen medication is appropriate and that avoidable errors, such as those that can be anticipated based on medication or patient specific factors, are prevented. CPOE and ePrescribing systems automate many parts of the ordering process and provide very rich opportunities for incorporating CDS.[18] As noted earlier, EMRs contain much of the patient data critical to appropriate ordering, so their tight integration with CPOE/ePrescribing systems is important. Although this section focuses on CPOE and ePrescribing, many of the safety approaches also can be applied in pre-CPOE inpatient environments—for example, one in which administrative staff transcribes written orders from prescribers into a computerized ordering system.

A Framework for Considering CDS Opportunities in CPOE and ePrescribing

Based on their experience and that of other CPOE pioneers, implementers from Vanderbilt University have described a series of stages during which CDS can be incorporated into CPOE.[19] The framework can also be useful for thinking about ePrescribing in the outpatient setting. The stages, along with sample CDS interventions at each, are outlined next.

- CPOE session initiation—users may be informed about new CPOE system features on a one-time-only basis (for example, on logging in).
- Selecting patient from hospital ward census—indicate which beds have new unacknowledged "stat" orders and which have unacknowledged "routine" orders.
- Individual patient session initiation—present summary of past alerts and warnings related to the patient's orders.
- Individual (single) order selection—can trigger protocol-based interventions—such as recommending drug substitutions.

- Individual (single) order construction—highlight recommended drug doses and drug frequencies (for, example, as preconfigured order sentences).
- Individual order completion—suggest corollary orders, that is, "follow-up" tasks clinically indicated after certain orders (for example, measuring drug level after a medication is given).
- Ordering session completion—issue warnings when appropriate monitoring tests have not been issued.
- Clinical events such as a new lab result or vital sign measurement posted in the EMR—asynchronous alerts to the prescriber, which require an event engine to detect clinical triggers (for example, a new positive microbiology culture triggers an alert when the patient is not receiving adequate antimicrobial coverage for the organism identified by the culture).

Miller et al.[19] is a rich resource that provides many useful tips on this topic. Other reviews similarly provide many helpful tips.[20,18]

Data Display within the CPOE/ePrescribing Application

A smooth flow of key patient data items between EMR and CPOE/ePrescribing systems is important for CDS interventions that depend on this information. The elements include:

- Allergies and intolerances
- Complete medication list (as discussed earlier)
- Laboratory results, vital signs, and patient weight (which may not be as simple as the patient's actual current weight; in some instances, related values such as "dry weight" [that is, a patient's weight excluding excess fluid] or ideal body weight may be more pertinent parameters related to medication use)
- Pregnancy status

Other considerations that may be pertinent to medication selection in inpatient and/or outpatient settings include medication formulary information and patient's insurance coverage.

Once available in the CPOE or ePrescribing application, this information can be presented in a prominent but unintrusive manner, as "relevant data" that the prescriber can peruse during the ordering session and address as appropriate. Examples of order-specific data presentation include displaying recent electrolytes when prescribing electrolyte-replacement therapy and displaying heart rate and pertinent electrolytes when prescribing cardiac medications such as digoxin. Non-order-specific information can include continually displaying patient weight, allergy information, and creatinine clearance value (a kidney function measure that can affect medication dosing) in the order entry screen.

If the orders contain critical safety issues related to these data, they can be used to trigger proactive alerts delivered after the order is selected. As will be discussed shortly, other CDS interventions (such as order sets with pertinent annotations) augment data display in helping ensure that the orders entered are safe in the first place.

Some CPOE and ePrescribing systems prompt clinicians to review and complete pertinent clinical details, such as allergies, medication list, problem list, and pregnancy status (if not already done) during order entry. From a workflow perspective, this is less than ideal. It can distract focus from the order entry process, and the prescriber may not have the information needed at that time. It may be preferable to develop policies and workflows in which another care team member documents this information prior to order entry. (See Chapter 3, page 60, for a discussion on workflow mapping—which is helpful for sorting out these details, and see the discussion in Chapter 5, page 122, about whether documentation of patient allergies should be required before allowing medication orders to be entered.)

Selecting the correct patient for whom orders are being entered is obviously a key safety concern to address. To reduce the chances that medication orders will be entered for the wrong patient, a recommended strategy is to automatically populate a physician's patient list in the CIS with those patients with whom there is an established treatment relationship. Another strategy is to clearly display the patient's identifying information—name, age, gender, location, medical record number—in the same view as order entry. You might also limit the number of concurrent patient records that can be simultaneously open in order entry; such multiple open records can increase confusion and errors.

There are several order-selection strategies you can implement to reduce the risk of selecting the wrong medication. Accommodating drug searches using both trade and generic names, and displaying both names together in a standard format during order selection is one approach. When rules such as this one are applied you should still remain vigilant for specific circumstances in which the drug listing might create confusion, and take steps to minimize such problems. In the paragraphs that follow, we explore several additional CDS data display approaches to minimizing drug order selection errors.

Both ISMP and IHI have called attention to the potential medication safety concerns associated with specific medications and drug categories, referred to as "high-alert medications." IHI categorizes these into four basic groups: anticoagulants, narcotics, insulin, and sedatives. For a more comprehensive listing, see the ISMP high-alert medications list.[21]

Many CDS interventions discussed in this book help reduce errors associated with high-alert medications. Some tactics can be specifically applied to address harm resulting from these drugs. For example, ISMP advocates clearly distinguishing high-alert medications from other drugs at the point of order entry. This can be accomplished through naming or other visual indicators, such as graphics or special text formatting. Also, restrictions or special procedures to be followed, such as restricting a drug on formulary to specific indications or patients, should be clearly indicated. Some CPOE systems are able to restrict who can prescribe a particular medication, such as allowing only oncologists to order chemotherapy. Other examples of drugs that can come under such restrictions are certain antibiotics, drotrecogin alfa, and fibrinolytics. (See also discussion in Chapter 5 on Minimizing Adverse Events Associated with Specific Drugs/Classes, page 152.)

TALLman lettering is one such visual indicator approach that can help beyond high-alert medications to more generally distinguish medications with similar names.[22] For example, the use of selected capital/TALLman letters helps decrease the risk for confusing otherwise similarly appearing names, such as:

- DOPamine
- DOBUTamine

You should check on the use of TALLman lettering in the drug databases you develop or acquire from third parties.

Always avoid using drug abbreviations that are ambiguous and likely to be misinterpreted, and be careful in general about the confusion risks associated with such abbreviations. Some (for example, "ASA" often used for acetylsalicylic acid, or aspirin) may be used as a synonym to facilitate drug lookup, but the full medication name should be displayed once it is selected. Helpful guidance can be found in ISMP's *List of Confused Drug Names*[23] and in material from The Joint Commission about the National Patient Safety Goal related to this topic.[24]

In the inpatient setting, prescribers generally do not need to specify a particular dispensable product when selecting medications during order entry. For example, the provider should not need to indicate that to order warfarin 3 mg (the "dose-based" prescription), the pharmacy has to dispense warfarin 2 mg (1 tablet) + warfarin 1 mg (1 tablet) (the "product-based" prescription). On the other hand, in outpatient settings a product-based prescription may be more appropriate. In any case, you should consider using CDS that helps users select proper ordered and dispensed forms as appropriate. RxNorm is a standard for clinical drugs and dose forms that can help make this support possible.[6]

Information displayed in CPOE and ePrescribing systems can help prevent errors by indicating orders that are intended for specific patient populations. One strategy is to provide specialized order sets for specific patient populations, such as pediatrics or geriatrics, and label them accordingly. Or organizations may choose to present appropriately preconfigured order sentences based on a defined context, such as age or gender, or utilize medication-naming conventions to clearly identify medications specially configured for specific patient populations (for example, "calcium gluconate neonatal intravenous"). Finally, you can group specialized orders, such as those for infants or oncology patients, in a separate folder or library in the order catalog.

Order Sentences

A complete medication order contains all the information necessary to deliver the drug to the patient, typically including the following elements:

- Medication name, including generic and brand name, when applicable
- Dose
- Units
- Route
- Frequency
- Indications
- Administration instructions
- Treatment duration—for a specified number of doses, length of time, or open-ended
- Additional free text comments—for example, parameters for holding the medication in situations where it might unsafe to administer, such as when the patient's blood pressure is low when the drug is due to be administered, and it could further lower this pressure
- Other pertinent directions, such as diluent for IV medications

Clear and consistent order sentences are essential. When properly set up, CPOE and ePrescribing systems can help ensure that order sentences support prescribing by minimizing inadvertent errors in assembling the components needed for a safe and appropriate prescription. Certain components of order sentences are necessary for a complete medication order. For example, an order sentence with a blank dose, frequency, or route usually lacks critical information needed to correctly process the order.

Some fields may or may not be required depending on the situation. For example, documenting a drug's indication should be necessary for medica-tions prescribed "as needed" (often designated by "PRN," an acronym from the Latin term) but could remain optional for standing medications. Although treatment duration is ordinarily not required in the inpatient setting, it is required when prescribing outpatient medications. Similarly, prescriptions for some creams might not require an explicit dose per administration. The built-in CPOE or ePrescribing system CDS logic should set required fields based on the order-entry context or responses to other fields.

Some CPOE and ePrescribing systems make an additional distinction between recommended fields (indicated by soft stops) and required fields (indicated by hard stops). Soft stops prompt the prescriber to enter or consider data, but the order can still be signed with missing, non-critical information. In the case of a hard stop, the user cannot proceed with or conclude the ordering session (or other action) until the required information is provided (or the dangerous situation addressed).

We next consider several CDS approaches that can be used within order sentences to enhance pre-scribing safety.

Using defaults. Some order sentence details may be defaulted, that is, completed in the order configuration prior to release into the CPOE system and prescriber ordering. Prescribers can use the preselected parameter, or change the default when appropriate, thereby minimizing clicks or fields required for entry. You can typically determine these defaults using the 80/20 principle. For example, if a drug is ordered with a certain dose at least 80% of the time, the dose may be defaulted in the order sentence.

Defaults are intended to make order entry more convenient for the prescriber, but they can also act as a safety feature since they may decrease the possibility that the prescriber will enter incorrect information. However, defaults can also introduce the potential for medication errors; the prescriber may passively accept an inappropriate default and fail to change it. To mitigate this risk, the lowest dose is typically configured as the default. Typically (but not always), errors of omission that result in underdosing do not impose as significant a patient safety hazard as overdosing. Another default-related unintended consequence that has been noted is when users type an instruction into a free text field component of an order sentence that conflicts with a defaulted element, for example, entering a free text dose instruction that is different from the defaulted dose in the body of the order sentence. You can keep this possibility in mind during development, and be alert for evidence that this problem is occurring after launch.

Restricting options. You should limit the options available for a particular field to those appropriate for the medication being prescribed, typically a much smaller subset than the full catalog of options available for that field. This strategy can include such examples as:

- Oral medications for which you should not allow an intravenous route to be selected
- Intravenous medications, such as vincristine, for which you should not allow an intrathecal route to be selected
- Providing only medication doses that can be practically dispensed and administered, such as not offering a dose of 16 mg if an oral tablet is only available in increments of 5 mg, and not offering an odd liquid medication dose that a patient couldn't practically take in the outpatient setting
- Not permitting a number of characters to be entered in a dosing field that doesn't correspond to an allowable dosage for the medication. For example, if a dose is never more than two digits, the user should not be allowed to enter a three-digit dose. Likewise, if a dose is never less than two digits, do not permit only one digit to be entered.

Managing abbreviations. Certain error-prone abbreviations, in addition to those mentioned earlier for medication names, must be avoided in the order sentence. For example, use "daily" instead of "QD" (an acronym for the Latin "every day"), which can be misinterpreted as "OD" (acronym for the Latin "right eye"). A good reference is the ISMP list of error-prone abbreviations.[25] The Joint Commission, as part of its National Patient Safety Goals,[26] has also published a list of dangerous abbreviations that are to be absolutely avoided, complementing the guidance noted earlier about potentially problematic medication names.

Delivering "inline" dosing guidance. Most CPOE and ePrescribing systems can provide dosing support as users compose an order sentence. For example, when the prescriber selects a "mg/kg" unit dose, the system will automatically calculate the weight-based dose if the weight is available. Guidance can also be provided on whether and how to round such calculated drug dosages to determine a drug quantity feasible to dispense and administer. This can be particularly important—and problematic—in pediatric patients.[27]

In addition, order sentences provide the ability to match correct drug dose form (such as "immediate release" versus "sustained release") to medication strength, particularly important with the many extended-release products available on the market today. For example, if immediate-release diltiazem 180 mg is administered because the CD or XR suffix (which indicates the extended-release formulation) has been omitted in the prescription, an overdose may result.

Order Sets

Order sets are a collection of orders that can be used to guide best practice, evidence-based care, and as such are increasingly a core focus of CDS programs. Typically related to a problem, diagnosis, or condition, order sets are a powerful CDS intervention that can help "make the right thing to do the easy thing to do." Order sets are typically used for situations such as community-acquired pneumonia, postoperative care, cardiac surgery, postpartum care, and other common conditions and settings. They can be particularly helpful for conditions in which there is a strong evidence base to guide prescribing (for example, as in the case with many diseases covered by "core measures").[28]

Order sets may also be generic in nature, such as those for admission to a general adult medicine or pediatric inpatient service. These generic order sets may include PRN medications for pain, constipation, insomnia, and other common symptoms associated with hospitalization. Such medications can be a source of safety issues through interaction with patient conditions or other medications. This should be kept in mind as opportunities for CDS at the ordering stage to address such interactions. Historically, order sets were sometimes customized to individual prescribers, though with the increasing emphasis on evidence-based medicine and standardizing care around best clinical practices, such prescriber-level customizing is discouraged or disallowed in many organizations.

When medical problems are documented for a particular patient, and there are corresponding predefined order sets, these relevant order sets should be presented to the ordering clinician for selection during order entry. This approach minimizes the need for the clinician to search for appropriate order sets. Enabling CPOE and ePrescribing systems to highlight pertinent order sets requires that diagnoses be recorded as structured data elements (rather than free text) and that order sets be linked with the proper diagnoses codes. The configuration work to associate order sets with medical problems can be facilitated through "groupers," which are high-level clusters of related diagnosis codes (for example, "heart failure" for all of the variants of this condition: systolic heart failure, diastolic heart failure, congestive heart failure, etc.). Utilizing groupers reduces the need to specify the large number of available diagnosis codes that need to be associated with several related order sets.

Order sets can facilitate order entry speed, appropriateness, accuracy and safety and therefore are considered a vital CPOE implementation component. Experts recommend against implementing CPOE without a critical mass of order sets. The actual "critical mass" number will vary, depending on the complexity of the order sets (that is, whether a single order set covers multiple care venues), the patient population heterogeneity, and other factors. The appropriate number of order sets needed

at CPOE launch may range from several dozen to many more. A useful starting point for considering initial coverage and content is your organization's existing printed order set library. These can be translated into an electronic format—assuming they are appropriately current and evidence based. The most frequently used paper order sets (together with direct input from key stakeholders, such as end users and quality department staff) can indicate which topics might be most useful (and expected by users) at CPOE launch.

Actual usage can vary considerably between order sets,[29] so it is most efficient to avoid spending resources preparing order sets that won't be used. Once CPOE or ePrescribing is live, carefully monitor order set use and prescriber compliance with recommendations[30] (see Chapter 7, page 203), and be prepared to make adjustments to the initial order set library and create new order sets that were not developed prior to the implementation. Conversely, some order sets that were originally developed may rarely be used. Consider retiring these after a reasonable period of time to minimize the need for ongoing maintenance.[31] Such order set monitoring and modification can also be valuable in the pre-CPOE/ePrescribing implementation phases.

Order sets provide an opportunity to deliver reference information pertinent to orders contained in the order set. This support may include links to material such as clinical evidence, guidelines, core measures details, and relevant organizational policies and procedures. Such information delivery can be accomplished within order entry workflow without resorting to disruptive pop-up alerts. Similarly, links in order sets can be provided to online calculators and other standalone CDS tools. Results from calculators can be useful, for example, to assess patient risks that should be taken into consideration during ordering. These may include risks for preventable hospital-acquired complications, such as VTE, which can be minimized with appropriate medications.

Order sets can help standardize care around specific best practices and performance measures.

For example, compliance with limiting preventative antibiotics use to 24 hours after surgery can be improved by defaulting this duration (which can be modified by the user, when needed) into the pertinent medication orders in all post-op order sets. This approach to guiding and facilitating appropriate prescribing, so that the desired practice is the easier path to take, tends to be received better by prescribers than unnecessarily constraining choices.

Order sets can help implement standardized, evidence-based care practices by including links to other order sets or by embedding specific protocols within the order set. For example, glucose management and sedation-protocol order sets (developed to decrease hospital-acquired infections) can be linked into all ICU-admission order sets, as well as appropriate post-op order sets. In another example, including a VTE-prevention protocol that incorporates both mechanical and pharmacologic prophylaxis reminds prescribers to consider ordering these interventions.

You can also provide visual reminders to place corollary orders to decrease errors of omission. For example, an order set can group a PTT order (to assess the level of anticoagulation) together with a heparin (an anticoagulant) infusion order within an order set, or group appropriate drug level monitoring tests with orders for drugs that require such testing. Alternatively, these necessary corollary orders can be defaulted, as discussed earlier.

Consider during order sets preparation potential problems, such as drug duplication or drug interactions, that may result from the prescriber selecting particular order combinations within the set. To the extent possible, these situations should be anticipated and addressed before finalizing the order set content. Alerts provided as a safety net within the CPOE and/or pharmacy system can be used to catch unavoidable conflicts within the order set. Such conflicts include circumstances where potentially interacting agents need to be included in the set because each might be appropriate for a different clinical situation. In a similar manner, alerts can help identify conflicts between medications ordered within and outside the order set.

As discussed in Chapter 2, page 27, and Chapter 8, page 242, a governance structure and mechanisms to manage the currency, consistency, evidence base, and other critical elements of deployed CDS content are essential. This is especially true for order sets, since their content is so broad, rich, and dynamic. Their maintenance requires input from multiple stakeholders over time as new scientific evidence is published, the status of marketed drugs changes, and the like. These governance mechanisms will also need to establish policies for how much order set customization will be accommodated. Prescribers often seek rich customization to their individual practice style, but too much customization can limit order set value in standardizing care around best practices and can result in a significant maintenance challenge.

Verbal Orders and CDS in a CPOE Environment

Spoken orders (typically referred to as "verbal orders") are a mechanism whereby a prescriber orally communicates an order (such as for the patient to receive a medication) to a nurse or pharmacist, sometimes over the telephone. Verbal orders introduce the potential for communication errors and create an additional layer between the prescriber and knowledge support for safe and effective prescribing. As a result, verbal orders should be discouraged or at least minimized, both through polices and by making order entry via CPOE convenient and efficient. CDS can be applied to verbal orders in a variety of ways.

Ideally, verbal orders should be entered into the CIS in real time, rather than written down and subsequently entered in the system. This affords the nurse or pharmacist entering the order the opportunity to see any alerts presented by the CDS system and inform the prescriber giving the verbal order. Some organizations forbid by hospital policy verbal orders for high-risk but non-urgent medications (such as warfarin). They use CDS rules to warn nurses or pharmacists attempting to enter such verbal orders and to prevent the action.

Providing the capability for remote access to order entry minimizes the need for verbal or telephone orders. Likewise, remote access to the CIS for order review allows the prescriber to more expeditiously review, authenticate (co-sign), and correct erroneous orders. Ideally, this remote access should be accompanied by the full suite of pertinent CDS interventions.

Order Verification/Dispensing—Key Systems: Pharmacy Information System, IV Compounders

In the hospital environment, the pharmacy department and its ISs are an important focus for CDS efforts to support medication management. Many considerations outlined in this section are also pertinent to retail pharmacies in non-hospital settings, though organizational CDS teams to whom this book is primarily directed may have limited opportunity to influence these functions.

The pharmacist's role in verifying a medication order is to double check it for possible interactions; appropriateness; and the right dose, right route, right frequency, and right timing. Similar CDS considerations to those for ordering apply here too. For example, it is essential to thoughtfully present relevant data for these checks on the pharmacy IS order-verification screen. That data include patient clinical information, such as weight, BSA, creatinine clearance value, and many other data types important in specific situations. These may include serum albumin, for example, which helps correctly interpret serum levels for the potentially dangerous anticonvulsant drug phenytoin. You should make it easy for the pharmacist to review and apply this information. Even "one click away" for essential data may be too far, since this may increase the risk that the information will be missed.

As with order entry, positive pregnancy status should be clearly displayed during pharmacy verification. As an added safety check, CDS interventions should alert the pharmacist as well when a specific drug-pregnancy contraindication exists.

Pharmacists should be able to view allergy, DDI, dose, and other alerts prescribers view at order entry. During order verification, pharmacists should also be able to view any reasons the prescriber has given for overriding an alert, which reduces the need to request further clarification. Additional medication alerts—medium or lower severity, for example—that were filtered from the physician during order entry can be displayed to the pharmacist during the verification process as an additional medication safety layer. Careful consideration among the pharmacy staff and other pertinent stakeholders is needed to determine an approach to providing pharmacy with alerts that have a signal-noise ratio that will optimize both pharmacy workflow and patient safety.

In collaboration with pharmacy staff, you should consider configuring system settings and workflow so that certain orders do not require pharmacist review for verification. These orders may include low-risk medications from predefined order sets for which no alerts are fired. Some organizations might consider excluding from pharmacist-verification requirement certain circumstances in which rapid medication turnaround is critical, such as in the ED; this should only be done after carefully reviewing patient safety agency requirements and consulting with pharmacy staff.

As discussed with CPOE earlier, the pharmacy IS should automatically match the medication order with the correct drug and dose form. This can decrease pharmacist burden from having to select the details from a list.

Dispensing is a separate, important pharmacy workflow component. One related technology to consider is automated compounders for IV medications, such as TPN, that use bar codes to ensure that the correct additives in the correct dose are being applied. CDS in these systems can help reduce calculation or incompatibility errors. For example, a soft stop can be added for the user to reconsider a programming or action step that may represent an error, whereas a hard stop may be used to prevent a clearly inappropriate/dangerous action. These systems should be linked to the EMR, so the TPN order entered in CPOE is interfaced with the compounder and does not need to be transcribed. As noted earlier, CDS can come into play when transcription or mapping between systems is required. As additional sophisticated dispensing technologies become available, there will likely be further opportunities to enhance them with CDS.

Administration—Key Systems: PHR, Home Aids, eMARs and Automated Dispensing Cabinets, Bar Coding, Smart Pumps

Technology and CDS to support medication administration are different in the inpatient versus ambulatory settings. In the former, there are generally rich process and technology to support safe administration, whereas in the ambulatory setting, it's often just the patient and the medicine bottle, with few checks on administration. This situation, however, is undergoing important change, thanks to increasingly available home health aides, such as "smart pillboxes" that provide patients with text and voice alerts when medications are to be taken and reminders when doses are missed. PHRs and related tools also can perform similar functions. Readers are encouraged to keep a close eye on these important and evolving ambulatory developments and their CDS implications. For the remainder of this section, we focus on CDS pertinent to drug administration in the inpatient setting.

Electronic Medication Administration Record and Automated Dispensing Cabinets

The eMAR is an important tool for supporting the Five Rights of medication safety: right drug, right dose, right route, right patient, and right administration time. The relevant data display CDS interventions type can be richly used to support safety at the administration step. For example, the date and time that the last dose was administered should be easily visible on the same screen used for subsequent administration. This feature is particularly important for one-time orders or orders that have been modi-

fied. Similarly, highlights or reminders for needed doses can help ensure that nurses administer medications on time and thus reduce an important omission error.

Another relevant data intervention is ensuring that the drug name on the eMAR matches the label on the drug to be administered. This is particularly important for extended-release products with suffixes such as SR, XR, CD, and ER. In addition, advanced CDS systems are able to determine from the doses administered in the eMAR the total dose of a medication that a patient has received over the course of therapy. This cumulative dose information may be important in the case of certain medications, such as doxorubicin, that are associated with toxicity based on cumulative dose.

The eMAR should ideally display drug interaction and other alerts (and override reasons) previously addressed by physicians and pharmacists; this could potentially improve communication and reduce follow-up calls from the nurse. Allergies, pregnancy status, and other key data documented in the EMR should be clearly displayed on the eMAR, as was discussed for CPOE and pharmacy systems. Drug-allergy interactions (particularly when not addressed earlier in the medication management process) need to be presented as alerts, rather than relying on the nurse to view this information based on a less intrusive presentation.

You should set up the eMAR in such a way that pertinent lab values or vital signs are presented to users onscreen to aid in appropriate medication dosing and administration. For example, displaying blood glucose values for insulin administration can help ensure that the drug isn't given when low glucose levels would create a danger. CDS support in the eMAR can also help remind the nurse to perform a related task, such as obtaining a serum drug level following medication administration. Similarly, CDS interventions can prompt and assist the nurse in documenting required pre- and postadministration medication-related patient parameters, such as pain scale around administering PRN analgesics. These prompts could also include tools to help document reasons why the medication could not be delivered, such as vital signs, pain level, bleeding, level of consciousness, patient not available, wrong drug, missed dose, and many others. Such exception information can be highly valuable in understanding this important medication administration step and its implications for improving the overall process.

Warnings for LASA medications or high-alert medications can be helpful on both the eMAR and automated dispensing cabinets. For example, a two-nurse check for insulin is required at retrieval/syringe preparation. The eMAR should support easy-to-use nurse witness co-signature for high-alert medications requiring dual authentication, and an audit trail for both the administering nurse's and the witness' names should be available from the documentation. Likewise, you might consider non-intrusive alerts to highlight key administration information, such as instructions not to crush certain medications in situations for which doing so is not appropriate.

Automated dispensing cabinets and eMARs should provide context-sensitive links to reference information such as indications, administration instructions, typical dose, and side effects. Brigham and Women's hospital used such links in their home-grown eMAR and experienced very rapid uptake by nurse users after little or no training on the intervention. The hospital has unpublished data showing very high use rates for this infobutton-delivered drug information that have been sustained over long periods; it is used an average of once daily for nearly half of the hospitalized patients. There are anecdotes from nurses and managers about various error types avoided, improved nursing satisfaction (and possibly retention), and other benefits as a result of this highly used and useful, integrated CDS intervention. This is a great example of getting the CDS Five Rights right in a manner that improves outcomes for patients, clinicians, and hospitals.

Bar-Coded Medication Administration

Bar-code technology helps ensure that the patient is positively identified and that correct medication and dose are administered at the proper time. Ideally, the devices supporting bar-code point of care medication administration will also provide CDS interventions, such as those available in the eMAR as described earlier. It is important that the bar-code technology and hardware support nurses' workflow. Expecting a nurse to move a computer on wheels into a patient's room to administer medications, for example, may lead to workarounds that bypass CDS-enabled safety checks. You should therefore carefully consider with pertinent stakeholders the effects that new workflows with bar-code systems will require. This can help identify such potential problems with CDS, as well as additional opportunities for CDS to support the bar code-related processes and desired outcomes.

Following are some additional bar code-related activities for which CDS considerations might be useful:

- Assess all policy, procedures, and processes around drug distribution and administration; for example, standardizing and coordinating medication administration times to optimize care delivery efficiency, patient convenience, and medication effectiveness.
- Establish an environment supportive of bar-code technology, such as caregiver bar-coded badges, patient wristbands, and drug packages.
- Review formulary and database for compliance with recommended safety guidelines—limited number of strengths for the same drug, TALLman lettering, unapproved abbreviations, etc.
- Look at alerts and warnings at the administration level being sent from pharmacy system to the point of care system.
- Establish/ensure interface for labs and vitals to point of care system.
- Establish standards for requiring and entering allergies (all types) and "no known allergy" documentation; include allergen, reaction type, and information source.
- Establish standards for requiring and entering basic patient demographics, such as age, birth date, weight, height, and sex.

Smart Pumps

Smart infusion pumps, which use software to support devices that manage intravenous drug delivery, have been shown to decrease errors at the point of administration in the medication management process. You can program smart pumps with soft and hard "guardrails" for medication drips such as epinephrine and dopamine according to ceiling rates, or for pediatric patients, based on the patient's weight. For example, lipid infusion rates in neonates are almost never greater than the parenteral nutrition rate. A recommendation from The Joint Commission Sentinel Event Advisory Group is to establish standard concentrations to be used for programming infusion pumps. There are also opportunities to incorporate CDS associated with smart pump programming and for IV compatibility checking for solutions prior to their use in IV pumps.

ISMP offers a free course on using smart pumps to improve medication safety.[32] IHI provides useful guidance on smart pumps as well.[33] We will next briefly outline items to consider regarding CDS and smart pumps. To the extent that these involve CDS knowledge assets, those assets should be managed in a systematic and coordinated fashion along with all others, as outlined in Chapter 8, page 240.

Guardrails. You should start by establishing dosing limits for what your hospital considers its most critically important IV drugs. Published literature can help identify the most problematic drugs. You can also ask your smart pump vendor to provide this information; they often store aggregate data on problem drugs culled from their customer base. Such drugs typically include propofol, heparin and oxytocin.[34] One issue you may encounter is conflicting protocols: clinicians may have access to more than one IV administration protocol. In those situations, it is important to ensure that clinical practice and the guardrails are consistent.

Installing smart pump guardrails for IV-drug administration and monitoring any overrides electronically allows you to develop alerts to prevent inappropriate overrides. Aggregate data suggest that on average there are 100 reprogramming alerts (the clinician reprograms the pump) for every 1,000 override alerts (the clinician ignores or overrides the alert). As a result, guardrails should be used judiciously to avoid alert fatigue. Once you have a modest amount of data—collected over a one-month period, for example—you can review and refine the guardrails.

Analyzing the information from smart pumps can provide answers to five critical sets of questions:

1. Which clinically significant drugs are getting the most alerts?
2. At what points are these alerts occurring? Which area of the hospital?
3. Which guardrail's limits are being hit for this drug? At what limits did you set the guardrails? Are they reasonable or too narrow?
4. How did clinicians respond to the alerts? Did they review or override the alert?
5. How far are the actual doses from the guardrail's limits? Would they cause a clinically significant event?

Once you have set the guardrails, collect data using the process described earlier, and utilize a continuous-improvement cycle to refine them. The data will allow you, at the end of each month, for example, to provide feedback and education to clinicians involved in the IV drug administration process and to modify the guardrails as appropriate.

The next step is to monitor trends. Is IV medication safety improving? If not, what are the problem areas? Examine these issues over time to determine improvement opportunities (see Chapter 7).

Smart pump programming. This step, which includes establishing a database of best practice dosing recommendations that can be programmed into the pump, requires collaboration among pharmacy, nursing, and the medical staff. You should set up the database so there is minimal calculation required outside of using the pump itself. That may mean changing standard dosing units for particular medications in CPOE if they contain inappropriate measure units. Or, it may mean verifying that the pump database is set up using the same measure units as the particular drugs involved.

For example, a smart pump can be configured to support an infusion rate for dopamine as mcg/kg/min or for heparin as units/hr. While these are two entirely different rate set ups, they are both appropriate because each matches the standard physician order format for the individual drug. If a facility uses a different measure unit for its heparin protocol, it should set up the pump database accordingly.

Clinicians shouldn't have to calculate IV-pump infusion rates. The ordering clinician is responsible for ordering the appropriate dosage, or titration range, for the drug to be administered. The CIS' CDS system should then translate this information into the appropriate rate based on the medication concentration. To minimize the potential for infusion-rate errors, the nurse should also not have to perform this calculation. The nurse merely keys in the desired rate for the drug in the library that matches the physician order dose. If this is not technically feasible, the pharmacist should be responsible for performing these calculations, with nursing conducting a double check.

IV compatibility. CDS should be used to assist nurses and pharmacists in ensuring that drugs administered together intravenously are compatible (for example, that they will not form harmful solid precipitates). The following compatibility checks should be provided through automatic alerting incorporated into a CIS and/or through access to referential information provided via these systems (such as via an infobutton or online resource):
- Single drug with diluent
- Single drug with infusion solution—include potassium in the infusion solutions list
- Multiple drugs
- Multiple drugs and infusion solutions
- Multiple drugs with delivery method—Y-site, admixture, syringe, TPN/TNA (total nutrient admixture)

This information should be presented in an easily readable format. Compatibility parameters such as time-dependency, for example, "do not give within two hours of each other" should be clearly noted.

Education—Key Systems: EMR, CPOE, PHR

Success in the medication management steps outlined earlier to ensure that the patient receives drugs in an optimally safe and effective manner can be undermined if the patient doesn't take the medication or does not take it appropriately. To play their role effectively, patients (and their caregivers, as appropriate) must understand and address the following key issues, among others:
- The clinical condition the medication is designed to treat
- The drug's role in that treatment
- Interactions, contraindications, and warnings (including black box warnings[35]) and what to do about them
- How to handle the drug and take it appropriately
- What intended and unintended effects to watch for and how to respond to each

This information can be communicated in various ways, and because it can be complex (even for healthcare professionals), several channels often are required. For example, messages by the physician, nurse, and/or pharmacist about the bulleted issues just presented can be reinforced through printed patient handouts and online patient resources. Providing patient handouts can be incorporated into clinical workflow through orders in order sets, infobutton links to this content for printing from within CISs, such as EMRs, and the like. Electronic resources can be provided to patients within their PHRs or patient portal, for example, through infobutton links from their problem and/or medication lists.

Getting this information delivery right is increasingly important and critical for patient safety, yet problematic. Increasing public appreciation for the patient's central role in being well-informed about safe medication use, both at home and in the inpatient setting, is evidenced by a recent feature article on this topic in a widely read national newspaper.[36]

A further incentive for doing a good job educating hospital patients about their mediations is the Consumer Assessment of Healthcare Providers and Systems Hospital Survey (H-CAHPS®). Co-developed by CMS and AHRQ, this survey, which is completed by patients about their inpatient experience, incorporates several questions related to effective clinician-patient communication. Hospitals must submit data from this survey, which includes questions about educating patients about medications, or face a penalty in their reimbursement from CMS for Medicare patients. In the survey conducted for patients discharged between October 2006 and June 2007, 42% reported that hospital staff did not always explain drugs before providing them, indicating significant room for improvement on this measure.[37]

Suboptimal communication about medications has documented adverse consequences. For example, a study in pediatric outpatients found that more than two-thirds of the many preventable ADEs were caused by parental administration. The authors concluded, "Improved communication between healthcare providers and parents, and improved communication between pharmacists and parents, whether in the office or in the pharmacy, were judged to be the prevention strategies with greatest potential."[38]

Monitoring—Key Systems: EMR, PHR, Surveillance Systems

Monitoring medication effects is critical so that therapeutic benefits and adverse reactions can be assessed and the treatment plan modified as needed. Various parameters should be monitored, depending on the circumstances.

Monitoring is useful for identifying unintended processes and outcomes. These include medication errors (wrong drug, missed dose), drug interactions (such as drug-allergy, DDI), and drug toxicity (for example, known side effect/patient intolerance, excessive dose/impaired clearance), and idiosyncratic reactions. Monitoring should also identify inadequate therapeutic effects that can result from an insufficient dose and/or augmented drug clearance.

Some medications are safe and effective only when present within narrow ranges in the bloodstream. Therapeutic drug monitoring is used in these cases so that dosages can be adjusted to achieve and maintain the appropriate therapeutic level. As suggested by the interplay between serum albumin and phenytoin serum levels noted earlier, there are rich opportunities to support this monitoring with CDS.

Clinical parameters are also monitored to assess response to medications; these might include signs of infection, symptom palliation, and normalized vital signs, as well as new symptom development that might suggest a toxic or adverse reaction. These assist in titrating medication dose/frequency to achieve desired therapeutic effect while minimizing undesirable effects.

The EMR (and PHR for patients) can play a key role in gathering, presenting, and helping interpret these data. CDS comes into play when data entry forms, flowsheets, and alerts are configured and appropriately delivered to users to ensure that signs of positive and negative medication responses are recognized. Similarly, CDS in the form of referential material can help both clinicians and patients identify and appropriately respond to data about drug effects.

For example, patients with CHF, diabetes, or asthma may track disease activity markers or severity in their PHR. Forms that support collecting this information, presenting it in association with other key parameters such as medication dosage, and providing information to explain the data, can help some patients be more engaged in their care and effective collaborators with their care team.

Along similar lines, in inpatient settings, data presentation for clinicians might include displaying drug levels juxtaposed with medication administration information and clinical parameters, such as temperature and vital signs. A related example is concurrently displaying other relevant laboratory and point-of-care test results together with pertinent medication administration information, such as blood glucose levels paired with insulin injection times/doses. In many cases, graphical data displays can help users (both clinicians and patients) process this information and should be considered as a presentation format if the capability is available.

In outpatient settings, it is particularly important to assess patient adherence to the prescribed medication regimen. Studies that examine how often patients actually fill their prescriptions and take the drugs properly frequently show surprisingly low rates. Non-adherence may indicate a breakdown in the education step or perhaps that a medication has been selected that the patient isn't able to afford (which could potentially have been addressed with CDS upstream during selection/ordering). Technology- and CDS-facilitated approaches for monitoring patient adherence to the prescribed regimen should become increasingly practical as pertinent interoperability standards and health information system (HIS) certification requirements move forward.

Aggregate Assessment and Reporting
ADE detection can be retrospective and/or performed in real time. Medication administration errors and near misses can be gleaned from reviewing and analyzing data from the EMR, medication administration record, medication administration devices, and/or administrative data sources. As we discussed in Chapter 2, adverse event detection using triggers can involve a CIS-facilitated manual chart review or a fully automated process. More information about these tools can be found on the IHI Web site.[39,40]

For more real-time assessment, aggregate reporting on a patient dashboard within the pharmacy IS can help pharmacists monitor medication therapy across several patients. Examples include a list of patients receiving antibiotics and requiring therapeutic drug monitoring and the ICU patient census sorted according to a patient risk assessment score. Similar real-time surveillance tools are available within and across other CISs as well.

A voluntary adverse event/medication error reporting system is a useful adjunct to automated monitoring tools in the CIS. The former, however, tends to underestimate the true incidence of patient safety incidents, whereas automated ADE detection tends to be associated with a high false-positive rate.

Once a medication error has been identified, it is helpful to classify it according to severity of patient harm (Chapter 1, page 11). More details are available at NCC MERP's Web site.[41]

Monitoring medication and CDS effects is explored further in Chapter 7.

WORKSHEETS

Worksheet 4-1

CIS inventory

In the first column of this worksheet, list the name and system type (from Table 4-1) for all the CIS components that you have identified in your survey of IS pertinent to your CDS efforts (see discussion in chapter). Consider subdividing the list by IS type. If there are many available systems, you might initially focus on those that appear most relevant and powerful for achieving your priority clinical objectives related to medication management. Keep in mind that the more comprehensively you outline your infrastructure, the easier it will be to identify potential CDS intervention options that are available in your environment.

In the second column, begin noting which of the CDS intervention types from Table 1-1, page 5, that each system can deliver or facilitate. You might need to refine this section as you get into more intervention development details in the next chapter.

This book emphasizes that coded data are important in certain CDS interventions. In the third column, document the information types the system handles and any coding schemes used. Again, pay particular attention to key items, such as laboratory test names, drug names, and patients' clinical problems.

The fourth column is for documenting the system user types and how well the system is penetrated into that user population. The notes column can be used to document other key system features, such as any knowledge bases it contains and its interoperability with other key systems.

System Name/ Type	CDS-related Functionality	Information Types (Coding System)	System Users and Usage	Notes
Ordering				
See clinical records, next				
Clinical records and patient management				
Better Care Inc./ Inpatient EMR and CPOE	• Order sets • Documentation templates • Relevant data display • Alerts	• Diagnosis information (ICD-10) • Order information (CPT) • Lab results (LOINC) • Imaging results (home-grown scheme)	Nurses, doctors, and pharmacists; 50% of physicians are currently using	Uses drug knowledge base from XYZ Corp for drug interaction and allergy alerting
Outpatient Computer Corp.	• Order sets • Documentation templates • Relevant data display • Alerts	• Visit diagnosis (ICD-10) • Problem lists (ICD-10) • Medication lists (National Drug Code [NDC]) • Visit notes (text)	25% of outpatient clinics, mostly primary care	Not yet exchanging data well with inpatient system
Given Meds Corp.	• Alerts • Documentation templates • Relevant data display	• Date/time for medication administration • Medications (NDC) • Dose administered	100% of nurses at two hospitals	Linked to hand-held devices

Worksheet 4-1 *continued*

System Name/ Type	CDS-related Functionality	Information Types (Coding System)	System Users and Usage	Notes
Departmental data management				
Get Your Labs Inc.	• Relevant data display • Alerts	• Lab results (LOINC) • Anatomic pathology results (text)	Doctors, nurses, pharmacists all use it frequently	
Clinical content				
Know-it-all Reference	• Disease and drug reference — infobutton capability	• Disease management info (ICD-9) • Drug reference info (NDC)	Doctors, nurses, pharmacists all use it frequently	Linked to hand-held devices

Worksheet 4-2

Linking Systems and Objectives

In the next chapter we explore in more detail CDS-enabled strategies for addressing specific objectives. Reading this chapter and filling out Worksheet 4-1, meanwhile, will help trigger some initial thoughts about how your available CIS and CDS assets can be applied toward addressing the priority objectives you identified in Chapter 2. Drawing on the information in Worksheet 4-1, this worksheet can help document those notes.

In the first column, list your priority medication management objective(s) from Worksheet 2-3, page 56. In the second column, list some potential ideas for CDS interventions that could help address that objective, drawing from information of the sort presented in this chapter. In the next three columns, bring forward information from Worksheet 4-1. In the last two columns, record information about whether and how the currently available systems can enable the desired CDS functionality and clinical outcomes.

Medication Management Objective	CDS Intervention	System Name/ Type/Vendor	Information Type	System User and Usage	Adequacy to Complete Intervention (Good, Need Upgrade, Need Replacement)	Note
Prevent prescription of medication to allergic patients	Prescription allergy alert window	Better Care CPOE	Medication list (NDC), allergy list, XYZ Corp Drug Database	Physicians	Need upgrade — Alert functionality needs to be modified to trigger at moment of order submission; medication list user interface needs to be friendlier	Accurate medication list is critical; need to discuss alert trigger rules — consult clinical IT advisory committee
Prevent prescription of medication to allergic patients	Pharmacy med check	Safe Drugs Pharmacy System	XYZ Corp Drug Database, drug formulary, allergy list	Pharmacist	Need upgrade — EMR and drug database interfaces need to be built, pharmacist alert feature needs to be built	Allergy content — consult Clinical IT advisory committee for vetting

CONCLUDING COMMENT

Healthcare delivery organizations—including hospitals, physician practices, and others—are increasingly making substantial investments in CISs to enhance care quality, safety, and efficiency. Successfully implementing these systems requires significant time, money, and organizational attention and usually entails significant workflow and process re-engineering.

These efforts and systems therefore provide important context and tools for CDS-enabled enhancements to medication management. Although it's critical to keep a strong focus on addressing top-priority organizational goals (as outlined in Chapters 2 and 5), it is likewise important to fully capitalize on the momentum that major CIS implementations can bring to corresponding CDS efforts. As we have noted, it is largely through such CDS functionality that the value of the major CIS investments is fully realized.

REFERENCES

1   The Certification Commission for Health Information Technology (CCHIT). http://www.cchit.org, accessed 10/2/08.

2   American Society of Health-System Pharmacists. *Survey Investigates Role of Pharmacy in Technology Use in Hospitals.* http://www.ashp.org/s_ashp/article_press.asp?CID=167&DID=2024&id=24262, accessed 10/2/08.

3   National Center for Health Statistics. *Classifications of Diseases and Functioning & Disability.* http://www.cdc.gov/nchs/about/otheract/icd9/abticd9.htm, accessed 10/2/08.

4   As of this writing, U.S. Department of Health and Human Services has proposed October 2011 as the date for transition to ICD-10 CM/PCS coding system. See CMS Web site: http://www.cms.hhs.gov/ICD10/04_Statute_Regulations_Program_Instructions.asp#TopOfPage. Updated 25 Aug 2008.

5   American Medical Association. CPT (*Current Procedural Terminology*). http://www.ama-assn.org/ama/pub/category/3113.html, accessed 10/2/08.

6   U.S. National Library of Medicine. *RxNorm.* http://www.nlm.nih.gov/research/umls/rxnorm/, accessed 10/2/08.

7   Regenstrief Institute, Inc. *Logical Observations Identifiers Names and Codes (LOINC).* http://loinc.org/, accessed 10/2/08.

8   U.S. National Library of Medicine. *SNOMED Clinical Terms (SNOMED CT).* http://www.nlm.nih.gov/research/umls/Snomed/snomed_main.html, accessed 10/2/08.

9   The University of Iowa College of Nursing. *Center for Nursing Classification & Clinical Effectiveness.* http://www.nursing.uiowa.edu/excellence/nursing_knowledge/clinical_effectiveness/index.htm, accessed 10/2/08.

10 Ash JS, Berg M, Coiera E. Some unintended consequences of information technology in health care: the nature of patient care information system-related errors. *J Am Med Inform Assoc.* 2004; 11(2):104-112. http://www.pubmedcentral.nih.gov/articlerender.fcgi?artid=353015, accessed 10/2/08.

11 See, for example, Kotter JP, Cohen DS. *The Heart of Change: Real Life Stories of How People Change Their Organizations.* Boston: Harvard Business Press; 2002. Excerpts available at: http://books.google.com/books?id=YBf3S1X8ItsC, accessed 10/2/08.

12 Kuperman GJ, Reichley RM, Bailey TC. Using commercial knowledge bases for clinical decision support: opportunities, hurdles, and recommendations. *J Am Med Inform Assoc.* 2006; 13(4):369-371.

13 See, for example, the Certification Commission for Healthcare Information Technology (CCHIT) certification test scripts such as: http://www.cchit.org/files/comment/2008/round05/CCHITTestScriptENTERPRISE08ProposedFINAL.pdf, accessed 10/2/08.

14 The Joint Commission 2009 National Patient Safety Goals Hospital Program. http://www.jointcommission.org/PatientSafety/NationalPatientSafetyGoals/09_hap_npsgs.htm, accessed 12/13/08. In Chapter Manual, see "Goal 8—Accurately and completely reconcile medications across the continuum of care."

15 For example, the merger of RxHub and SureScripts, see http://www.surescriptsrxhub.com/, accessed 10/2/08.

16 Teich JM, Merchia PR, Schmiz JL, et al. Effects of computerized physician order entry on prescribing practices. *Arch Intern Med.* 2000; 160(18):2741-2747.

17 Background on infobuttons and the version of the HL7 standard approved in May 2008 can be found here: http://www.hl7.org/v3ballot2008may/html/domains/uvds/uvds_Context-awareInformationRetrieval (Infobutton).htm#REDS_DO010001UV-Infobutton-ic, accessed 12/13/08.

18 Kuperman GJ, Bobb A, Payne TH, et al. Medication-related clinical decision support in computerized provider order entry systems: a review. *J Am Med Inform Assoc.* 2007; 14(1):29-40. http://www.jamia.org/cgi/content/abstract/14/1/29, accessed 10/2/08.

19 Miller RA, Waitman LR, Chen S, et al. The anatomy of decision support during inpatient care provider order entry (CPOE): empirical observations from a decade of CPOE experience at Vanderbilt. *J Biomed Inform.* 2005; 38(6):469-485.

20 Metzger JB, Welebob E, Turisco F, et al. Effective use of medication-related decision support in CPOE. *Patient Safety and Quality Healthcare.* September/October 2008. http://www.psqh.com/sepoct08/cpoe.html, accessed 10/2/08.

21 Institute for Safe Medication Practices. *ISMP's List of High-Alert Medications.* http://www.ismp.org/Tools/highalertmedications.pdf, accessed 10/2/08.

22 See, for example, U.S. Food and Drug Administration. *Name Differentiation Project.* http://www.fda.gov/CDER/Drug/MedErrors/nameDiff.htm. 04 Sept 2008.

23 Institute for Safe Medication Practices. *ISMP's List of Confused Drug Names.* http://www.ismp.org/tools/confused-drugnames.pdf, accessed 10/2/08.

24 The Joint Commission. *National Patient Safety Goal: Identify and, at a minimum, annually review a list of look-alike/sound-alike drugs used in the organization, and take action to prevent errors involving the interchange of these drugs.* http://www.jointcommission.org/NR/rdonlyres/C92AAB3F-A9BD-431C-8628-11DD2D1D53CC/0/LASA.pdf, accessed 10/2/08.

25 Institute for Safe Medication Practices. *ISMP's List of Error-Prone Abbreviations, Symbols, and Dose Designations.* http://www.ismp.org/tools/errorproneabbreviations.pdf, accessed 10/2/08.

26 The Joint Commission. *The Official "Do Not Use" List.* http://www.jointcommission.org/PatientSafety/DoNotUseList, accessed 10/2/08.

27 STEPSTools is a multi-stakeholder initiative to address this dose rounding challenge in small children. See Vanderbilt University Medical Center. *STEPSTools.* http://www.pedstep.org, accessed 10/2/08.

28 The Joint Commission. *Performance Measurement Initiatives.* http://www.jointcommission.org/PerformanceMeasurement/PerformanceMeasurement/, accessed 10/2/08.

29 Kamal J, Rogers P, Saltz J, et al. Information warehouse as a tool to analyze Computerized Physician Order Entry order set utilization: opportunities for improvement. *AMIA Annu Symp Proc.* 2003; 336-340.

30 Starmer J, Lorenzi N, Pinson CW. The Vanderbilt EvidenceWeb – developing tools to monitor and improve compliance with evidence-based order sets. *AMIA Annu Symp Proc.* 2006:749-753.

31 Payne TH, Hoey PJ, Nichol P, et al. Preparation and use of preconstructed orders, order sets, and order menus in a computerized provider order entry system. *J Am Med Inform Assoc.* 2003 Jul-Aug; 10(4):322-329.

32 Institute for Safe Medication Practices. *Effective Approaches to Standardization and Implementation of Smart Pump Technology, A Continuing Education Program for Pharmacists and Nurses.* http://www.ismp.org/profdevelopment/SmartPumpTechnologyforwebce.pdf, accessed 10/2/08.

33 Institute for Healthcare Improvement. *Reduce Adverse Drug Events (ADEs) Involving Intravenous Medications: Implement Smart Infusion Pumps.* http://www.ihi.org/IHI/Topics/PatientSafety/MedicationSystems/Changes/IndividualChanges/ImplementSmartInfusionPumps.htm, accessed 10/3/08.

34 Fanikos J, Fiumara K, Baroletti S, et al. Impact of smart infusion technology on administration of anticoagulants (unfractionated Heparin, Argatroban, Lepirudin, and Bivalirudin). *Am J Cardiol.* 2007 Apr 1; 99(7):1002-1005.

35 FDA. *A Guide to Drug Safety Terms at FDA;* see "Boxed Warning." http://www.fda.gov/consumer/updates/drugterms041108.html, accessed 12/13/08. See also Wikipedia. *Black Box Warning.* http://en.wikipedia.org/wiki/Black_box_warning, accessed 10/3/08.

36 USA Today. *9 Steps You Can Take to Prevent Pharmacy Errors* 14 Feb 2008. http://www.usatoday.com/money/industries/health/2008-02-13-pharmacy-tips_n.htm?loc=interstitialskip, assessed 12/13/08.

37 Hospital Care Quality Information from the Consumer Perspective. *CAHPS ® Hospital Survey.* http://www.hcahpsonline.org/, accessed 10/3/08.

38 Kaushal R, Goldmann DA, Keohane CA, et al. Adverse drug events in pediatric outpatients. *Ambul Pediatr.* 2007 Sep-Oct; 7(5):383-389.

39 Institute for Healthcare Improvement. *Trigger Tool for Measuring ADEs.* http://www.ihi.org/ihi/workspace/tools/trigger/, accessed 10/3/08.

40 Institute for Healthcare Improvement. *IHI Global Trigger Tool for Measuring Adverse Events.* http://www.ihi.org/IHI/Topics/PatientSafety/SafetyGeneral/Tools/IHIGlobalTriggerToolforMeasuringAEs.htm, accessed 10/3/08.

41 National Coordinating Council for Medication Error Reporting and Prevention. http://www.nccmerp.org/, accessed 10/3/08.

Chapter 5
Configure CDS Interventions to Address Specific Targets

TASKS

- Plan and develop CDS interventions that focus on specific processes and outcomes related to medication use. Focus particularly on top-priority targets identified in Chapter 2, but also keep in mind basic and other important medication management CDS objectives.
- Consider user needs and workflows, available CDS and CIS infrastructure, and the CDS Five Rights in this work.
- Use the suggestions contained in this chapter as a starting point for further exploration with pertinent clinical experts and stakeholders in your organization; however, be aware that the CDS recommendations are NOT intended as clinical guidance.

KEY LESSONS

- Alerts should be used gingerly; try to optimize "upstream" CDS support so that medication decisions and use are appropriate at the outset, with alerts only used as a last-resort safety net.
- Meticulous attention to workflow is critical; focus on supporting and enhancing this as much as possible so CDS becomes an aid to care processes and decision making, rather than a hindrance.
- Pertinent research literature, colleagues, vendors, and other external information sources can be helpful for developing and optimizing CDS to address specific targets.

DISCUSSION

Chapter 4 provides guidance on improving medication use from the perspective of the different CISs through which CDS can be delivered at various stages of the medication-use cycle. This approach is helpful for ensuring that the substantial investment in these systems yields appropriate returns for enhancing medication use. In this chapter, we explore a complementary perspective. We turn our attention to how CDS, and the full range of available CISs, can be harnessed to address many of the medication-related objectives you may have selected in Chapter 2. Following are some considerations to keep in mind as you review this guidance and begin tackling specific objectives:

- This is a guidebook on CDS, not a clinical medicine textbook. As such, the recommendations that address specific targets are intended as a starting point for further discussions with pertinent clinical stakeholders and experts in your organization and NOT as clinical guidance.

- As we noted in Chapter 4, key capabilities in CIS and CDS systems are only just beginning to become standardized, so not all the suggestions outlined in the chapter will be easily implemented in every system. Engaging with your vendor, as well as broader efforts toward functionality standardization, can help accelerate progress in areas of greatest need and importance. Widely supported certification criteria for health IT products include safe and effective medication use as a key objective, and stakeholder participation in these evolving criteria are welcomed.[1]

- Because CPOE and complete EMRs are such powerful CDS channels, their use underpins many recommendations in this chapter. For organizations that do not have these systems fully implemented, consider whether/how these recommendations could be addressed in your currently available systems and workflows.

- Consider how your institution is currently using CDS to optimize each component of medication utilization; develop mechanisms to optimize each,

focusing initially/especially on targets identified as top-priority in Chapter 2, page 31.

- Even when considering more advanced decision support, recognize when care can be improved by optimizing basic CIS components, such as order sentences and order sets in CPOE (see Chapter 4, page 96) or by simplifying the process before adding the decision support.

- CDS interventions are *part* of the overall plan for improving medication management, not the only solution; it is therefore important to seek and cultivate synergies between your CDS efforts focused on organizational priorities (such as core measures) and related efforts by other parts of the organization (for example, the quality department).

- Your CDS program should anticipate user needs (those that CDS recipients may recognize, as well as those they may not) and provide critical decision support at the time it will be most helpful (see discussions of CDS Five Rights in Chapter 1, page 2 and Chapter 3, page 60).

- Interruptive alerts should generally not be approached as the primary tool for guiding end-user behavior, since this often leads to overalerting and frustration for all parties. Ideally, interruptive alerts should primarily serve as a safety net to prevent serious errors when other less intrusive methods don't produce the desired action.

- As you select and build interventions to address targets, revisit the "CDS 10 Commandments" (see Chapter 3, page 83) to increase your likelihood of success.

- Special populations, such as children or the elderly, can be considered in the greater context of a target, such as dosing, or may be defined as their own target. Later in this chapter we provide some initial considerations for medication CDS related to pediatric and elderly patients.

Many CDS interventions (and CIS through which they are delivered) are relatively early in their life cycle and therefore do not have clearly established "best implementation practices." In addition, much of the published literature on using CDS to address specific topics is based on homegrown CISs and CDS.[2] Therefore, in general, guidance on optimizing CDS to address specific targets (using the systems that readers typically have available) is an art, or at least an inexact science.

The recommendations in this chapter are based on the experiences and insights that the editors, contributors, and reviewers bring to this guide, as well as an opportunistic (rather than a comprehensive and systematic) literature sampling. We attempt to outline what useful intervention strategies to address specific targets might look like, as well as limitations and other factors to consider—all offered as a starting point for further exploration with your team, colleagues in other organizations, and the literature. As discussed in this guide's preface, we hope to leverage collaborative technologies to broaden the input into this guidance and produce an evolving resource of increasingly effective and valuable best practices for addressing key targets.

Several forms are presented in the Worksheet section of this chapter to help you document ideas and discussions with stakeholders about translating the guidance offered here into specific intervention design features. The forms address intervention design features, probing for potential causes of intervention failure, and documenting final design sign-off by pertinent stakeholders. You might consider glancing at them now and using them as appropriate.

This chapter covers many potential CDS targets, which we have divided into two groups: (1) those related to basic medication safety and formulary issues (such as drug-allergy problems and DDIs); and (2) other key issues (such as proper use of medications as reflected in core performance measures for regulatory and payment programs). These topics and their page number are listed for your reference:

Basic Medication Safety and Formulary Targets

- Decrease Errors Related to Abbreviations (page 115)
- Decrease Errors from LASA Drug Names (page 117)
- Optimize Formulary Compliance (page 120)

- Minimize Allergic Reactions to Drugs (page 122)
- Minimize DDIs (page 125)

Other Key Medication Management Targets

- Ensure Proper Dosing (page 133)
- Ensure that Patients Do Not Receive Contraindicated Medications (page 148)
- Eliminate Inappropriate Drug/Therapeutic Duplication (page 149)
- Optimize Laboratory Monitoring and Follow-up (page 150)
- Minimize Problems with Medications Used in Radiologic Procedures (page 151)
- Minimize ADEs Associated with Specific Drugs/Classes (page 152)
- Optimize Medication Use Associated with Regulatory/Payments/Transparency-related Targets (page 155)

Basic Medication Safety and Formulary Targets

Decrease Errors Related to Abbreviations

Abbreviations in general, and related to medications in particular, are commonly used in care delivery settings. However, they can be a source of ambiguity and confusion and thereby can increase the chance for error, which makes managing their use important for medication safety; this is an area in which CDS (as we have broadly defined it in Chapter 1) can be helpful.

Abbreviations are addressed by The Joint Commission in Patient Safety Goal 2B,[3] the "Do Not Use" list, which includes a standardized list of abbreviations, acronyms, symbols, and dose designations that are not to be used throughout the organization. This patient safety goal stipulates that abbreviated drug names are not allowed on orders or on any medication-related documentation that is handwritten (including free-text computer entry) or on preprinted forms.

Under consideration by The Joint Commission—though not proscribed as of this writing—is to eliminate the use of Do Not Use abbreviations in medication-related CIS, such as CPOE, EMR clinical documentation and medication recon-

Abbreviation Highlights

- Avoid "Do not use" abbreviations in all coded fields used for medication ordering.
- Consider all areas of the record in which medications are to be found in efforts to address dangerous abbreviations: these include orders, eMAR, medication reconciliation list, notes, and others.
- Carefully consider whether/how to minimize abbreviation use when their inclusion creates confusion or errors; never allow abbreviated drug names to be used on orders or on any medication-related documentation that is handwritten (including free-text computer entry) or on preprinted forms.
- Discourage use of free-text fields for medications in orders and notes; instead use structured pick lists or tools to insert ordered medications into notes, when possible.
- Make sure instructions for patients use patient-friendly terms, including minimizing abbreviations that might not be recognizable.

ciliation applications, and eMARs. They currently do recommend that organizations strive to eliminate Do Not Use abbreviations from these applications. Some CDS-enabled approaches for managing dangerous abbreviations are outlined next.

- Abbreviations specified on The Joint Commission "Do Not Use" list, as well as those on your organization-specific list, should be avoided by allowing only discrete entries in fields such as medication frequency or dose ("Daily" or "Qday" instead of "QD," "Units" instead of "u"), or by allowing orders with "QD," for example, to be accepted and programming the computer to convert the final order to say "QDay." Values with long names, such as "international units," will pose a challenge to fields with character limits, but these challenges can be addressed.

- Minimize free-text entry, which encourages use of inappropriate abbreviations, in orders and any medication lists, such as those in medication reconciliation forms or clinician progress notes. Provide pick lists or carry over previously documented electronic medication information when possible. For example, when building clinician-note templates, you should provide the ability to "pull in" the codified home medication list or current orders.

- Use rules to identify user-entered medication names that contain dangerous abbreviations (for example, in free-text physician notes and other applications). Suggest/implement appropriate changes (for example, change "insulin 100 u/mL" to "insulin 100 units/mL").

- When printing out forms or instructions for patients, spell out all terms in patient-friendly language. For example, "BID" is an acceptable abbreviation when communicating among healthcare workers about how often a medication should be taken but should be written out as "twice daily" or "two times a day" for the patient. Or consider recommending specific times to further decrease ambiguity and confusion, such as 6:00 a.m. and 6:00 p.m.

- Although drug names should not be abbreviated in many situations such as in pick lists, order sets, and the eMAR, there is benefit in some cases to allowing searches by abbreviation, particularly if the physician typically thinks in terms of the abbreviation. For example, many physicians are familiar with the abbreviation "ppd," but might not know to search by "purified protein derivative." Searches by abbreviation should call up the full drug name that is then used for the order or other purpose in the EMR, CPOE, or other application.

Decrease Errors from Look-alike/ Sound-alike Drug Names

Drug names that can be confused with each other, in either written or verbal communications, continue to be a common source of harmful medication errors. Although poor legibility of handwritten prescriptions is an often-cited culprit, errors from look-alike/sound-alike (LASA) drug names still pose significant risks in electronic systems.

The following citations identify sources of information about commonly confused drug names, and can be a resource for CDS-related efforts to minimize errors.

- ISMP's current list of confused drug names includes nearly 200 pairs of names.[4]
- The 8th annual national MEDMARX® Data Report released January 2008 by USP[5] reveals that more than 1,400 commonly used drugs are involved in errors linked to drug names that look alike or sound alike. USP has also released a free "Drug Error Finder" that allows users to search drug names associated with these LASA errors and provides information about error severity.[6]
- One study found that pairs of names that are similar (based on automated, quantitative measures) were between 25 and 523 times more likely to be involved in medication errors than pairs that do not have similar names.[7]
- The Joint Commission addresses LASA errors with National Patient Safety Goal (NPSG) 3C: Identify and, at a minimum, annually review a list of LASA drugs used by the organization, and take action to prevent errors involving the interchange of these drugs.[8]
- In 2001, the U.S. Food and Drug Administration (FDA) Office of Generic Drugs requested manufacturers of 16 look-alike name pairs to voluntarily revise the appearance of their established names to minimize medication errors resulting from look-alike confusion. The letters encouraged manufacturers to supplement their applications with revised labels and labeling that visually differentiated their established names with the use of

LASA Highlights

- Keep generic and trade names linked in the CPOE search function and throughout communication to pharmacy and eMAR systems.
- Use TALLman letters for drug pairs that are commonly confused.
- Encourage prescribers to link medication orders to a clinical problem in the patient problem list during prescribing; this action can help clarify why the medication is being used and decrease the chance for confusion with unrelated medications that may look or sound similar.
- Use alerts to warn about LASA drugs gingerly and only in the medication-management cycle phase and workflow point where dangerous confusion commonly occurs.
- Consider the role for medication barcoding at dispensing and at administration as a strategy for reducing LASA drug errors.

"TALLman" letters. Table 5-1 lists the established names involved and the recommended revisions.[9]

Although the systems reduce or eliminate handwritten information, LASA issues persist in CPOE and the EMR. Confusion may be an issue particularly for medications that are unfamiliar to a clinician, such as a new drug or one they rarely use. LASA problems can also arise when the formulary has one drug in the frequently-confused pair but not the one the prescriber is considering. When prescribers see the one available, they may incorrectly assume it is the one they wish to select (or carry over from a from a patient's home medication list during medication reconciliation). Verbal orders

Table 5-1: FDA Recommendations on Differentiating Selected LASA Drug Names

Established Name	Recommended Name
Acetohexamide	AcetoHEXAMIDE
Acetazolamide	AcetaZOLAMIDE
Bupropion	BuPROPion
Buspirone	BusPIRone
Chlorpromazine	ChlorproMAZINE
Chlorpropamide	ChlorproPAMIDE
Clomiphene	ClomiPHENE
Clomipramine	ClomiPRAMINE
Cyclosporine	CycloSPORINE
Cycloserine	CycloSERINE
Daunorubicin	DAUNOrubicin
Doxorubicin	DOXOrubicin
Dimenhydrinate	DimenhyDRINATE
Diphenhydramine	DiphenhydrAMINE
Dobutamine	DOBUTamine
Dopamine	DOPamine
Glipizide	GlipiZIDE
Glyburide	GlyBURIDE
Hydralazine	HydrALAZINE
Hydroxyzine	HydrOXYzine
Medroxyprogesterone	MedroxyPROGESTERone
Methylprednisolone	MethylPREDNISolone
Methyltestosterone	MethylTESTOSTERone
Nicardipine	NiCARdipine
Nifedipine	NIFEdipine
Prednisone	PredniSONE
Prednisolone	PrednisoLONE
Sulfadiazine	SulfADIAZINE
Sulfisoxazole	SulfiSOXAZOLE
Tolazamide	TOLAZamide
Tolbutamide	TOLBUTamide
Vinblastine	VinBLAStine
Vincristine	VinCRIStine

Source: FDA/Center for Drug Evaluation and Research. *Name Differentiation Project*. http://www.fda.gov/cder/drug/MedErrors/nameDiff.htm. Updated May 8, 2002.

are another potential source of sound-alike errors in organizations that have CPOE, as well as those that do not.

Studies have shown that similarity in both spelling and sound increases the probability that pharmacists (and college students as a control group) will make false recognition errors when trying to remember drug names.[10,11] This is a particular problem with different forms of the same drug, such as new liposomal dose forms that carry very similar names but are typically dosed differently.

Many liposomal drugs remain on The Joint Commission-required LASA list because errors are common. An example is an error in a CPOE environment that resulted from confusing conventional amphotericin B and AmBisome® (liposomal amphotericin B formulation). A consult service recommended AmBisome 5 mg/kg in the consult note and verbally on the phone; when placing the order, however, the primary service selected conventional amphotericin B (both were available) and ordered a 5 mg/kg dose, which is five to ten times greater than the recommended dose of conventional amphotericin B.

Strategies for reducing the risk of LASA errors include the following:

- Include both trade and generic names in the searchable drug name so that if the drug is searched generically (amphotericin), all formulations will be in view (for example, both the conventional and liposomal forms of amphotericin), and the liposomal form will also include the generic component (for example, amphotericin B liposomal [AmBisome]). Searcher confusion may still persist, so ready access to dosing information (such as via infobuttons linked to drug names) or more proactive support through alerting about possible overdosing (see Dosing section later in this chapter) can enhance safety. For cases in which drug formulations can be easily confused and thereby lead to dangerous consequences, consider also whether it might be useful to remove one or more of the problematic agents from the formulary and/or CPOE.

- Use TALLman letters for certain drug pairs throughout the medication-use cycle—for example, in CPOE, pharmacy information, and medication-administration systems. Confirm with your CIS and/or CDS vendor that this lettering is available for pertinent systems. Some survey research suggests that the TALLman lettering approach is gaining widespread acceptance and that those who adopt it find it helpful.[12]

- ISMP recommends that the medication indication be included on the order or prescription to help pharmacists correctly interpret the order.[13] There is room to more efficiently support the workflow for this indication-linking task in many CPOE systems; customer feedback to vendors about this can help accelerate these improvements. A useful approach is for the prescriber to link the medication to a problem on the problem list. In this way, all clinicians involved in the medication use process, including pharmacists and nurses, can see why the drug is being used, which may help reduce LASA errors. The challenge is producing an up-to-date and reconciled problem list. Even this linking approach may not address errors related to different dose forms or products—such as long- versus short-acting formulations—based on the same active ingredient. For example, insulins are commonly involved in LASA errors, and an indication is not likely to help prevent this error. Other CDS approaches for such dosing and other medication safety concerns as outlined in this chapter should be considered for addressing LASA issues found to be problematic in your organization.

- ISMP recommends alerts for common LASA drugs.[13] This use should be balanced with an overall approach to alerts that minimizes the risk that excessive workflow intrusions will result in users ignoring all alerts. If you do use alerts, think about the points in the process where the errors originate. Consider whether the alert should be at ordering (CPOE), dispensing (pharmacy system), administration (eMAR), or at each stage if the error is common throughout the medication use cycle. For example, don't put an alert in CPOE if the problem is one of similar packaging; put it in the pharmacy system and the eMAR. As an option, you can use alerts in an automated dispensing cabinet (ADC), but note that this approach will not likely add any benefit if you stock only one drug per drawer.

- Using bar codes for selecting drugs in the pharmacy and when loading the ADC provides the most reliable means for preventing LASA errors at the dispensing phase. Bar codes at the point of care offer the best intervention to prevent errors at the administration phase, as well.

- Keep both trade and generic name linked through to the eMAR, since many LASA errors occur at the administration phase. Your eMAR display should match as closely as possible the description on the drug package so the nurse can easily identify the correct drug formulation, thereby minimizing LASA administration errors. This is particularly important with different dose forms of the same drug that may be ordered in similar strengths (oxycodone versus OxyContin®).

Optimize Formulary Compliance

A drug formulary is a list of drugs available for use in a particular organization. Formularies can be "tiered," by requiring, for example, lower co-payments for generic and "preferred" medications than for brand name and non-preferred drugs. Formularies are used to control medication cost and utilization and should also take into consideration drug safety, effectiveness, and clinical outcomes—individually and in relation to other drugs.[14] CDS can facilitate getting appropriate clinical knowledge and pertinent data to individuals and groups that develop the formularies (such as P&T committees), as well as to those who order/prescribe specific medications.

Typically P&T committees establish the basic policies and procedures for formulary management, which then serve as the foundation for CDS efforts to help prescribers use medications accordingly. Because CPOE mediates drug ordering, it presents

Formulary Highlights

- Consider the pros and cons of having non-formulary items available for ordering in CPOE
- Require for both free-text medication or non-formulary entries, a reason that will feed to the pharmacist and that can be audited retrospectively.
- Include only formulary or preferred drugs in order sets.
- Allow users to select the new order directly from the alert when using alerts to suggest a formulary replacement.
- Retain the link between non-formulary home medications and inpatient orders to facilitate discharge reconciliation.
- Communicate with clinicians about formulary details and rationale prior to launching CDS interventions to improve formulary compliance; this can increase intervention acceptance by end users and value to the organization.

a powerful opportunity to guide awareness of, and adherence to, the formulary. Likewise, medication reconciliation on inpatient admission and discharge are important steps in which formulary issues come into play. Next we present some considerations for applying CDS to formulary compliance, focusing on CPOE/ordering, medication reconciliation and general issues.

CPOE/Ordering

- A key consideration is whether non-formulary medications will be available in CPOE. One approach is to allow only formulary medications to be searched and ordered. This strategy can provide an effective roadblock to non-formulary ordering, but can also lead clinicians to enter their orders in a free-text medication field not subject to any CDS built into your system (for example, checking for allergies, improper dosing, DDIs.) Prescribers may also become frustrated by being unable to find the medication, which could foster pushback against the CPOE system and the implementation team. If a free-text medication order is placed, the system might be configured to prompt the clinician to specify why that particular drug is being ordered—to assist with downstream efforts by pharmacy staff and others to address formulary and other CDS issues about the specific order. This feedback can also provide broader insights into non-formulary drug ordering. Beware, however, that additional data collection from prescribers will slow workflow and can potentially create frustration (see Chapter 6, page 188, for tips on optimizing user acceptance and creating user feedback channels).

- Order sets should only list formulary medications and, ideally, the drug of choice per the P&T committee or appropriate medical staff committee.
- If you choose to keep non-formulary medications available to order in CPOE, you can use alerts to notify the clinician about this status and offer an option to order the formulary—or preferred— medication directly from the alert. Research has shown that this approach can be an effective way to change practice because it introduces the change directly into physician workflow. For example, at one hospital, an alert prompting the prescriber to switch to the preferred H2-blocker showed a 97% compliance with the drug of choice, sustained during a two-year follow-up.[15] A less intrusive strategy may be to indicate formulary status on the medication selection list (if this capability is available in your system) or within the order sentences that you localize for your organization and formulary.
- Your organization may want to restrict use of certain medications to experts, such as dermatologists or infectious diseases specialists. CDS can

facilitate this strategy by restricting the ability to order those agents (such as via CPOE) only to those physicians. This requires that the ordering system classifies each user by pertinent categories, such as medical specialty, rather than identifying and treating all prescribers in a homogenous way.

Medication Reconciliation

- Ideally, clinicians should be able to search for any medication when building the "home medication list" during computer-facilitated admission reconciliation, since it is important to accurately document what the patient is actually taking. When converting home medications to inpatient orders, any non-formulary medication should point the user to the organization's formulary medication of choice. The system should retain the link between the non-formulary home medication and the corresponding inpatient drug order to facilitate medication reconciliation upon discharge. Not doing so is a common source of medication error because it risks the patient going home taking two medications for the same indication—that is, the substitute used in the hospital, as well as the original home medication.

General Issues

- You should always try to couple CDS with educational outreach about the formulary and new CDS to prepare physicians for the guidance and prompting they will receive during ordering; for example, to switch to a preferred medication. Ideally this outreach should be done before new formulary-focused CDS interventions are launched, so that the medical staff is aware of the formulary medications, the reasons for selection, and the process for recommending changes. This pre-implementation work will also help surface legitimate prescriber considerations related to non-formulary ordering, which can be incorporated into formulary CDS design.
- Using CDS to limit use of a particular drug may fail when physician buy-in or agreement to the practice change is insufficient. The phenomenon

of "gaming the system to fulfill the requirements of an alert" is well-illustrated in one hospital's experience with human growth hormone[16] and speaks to the fact that CDS is not effective for changing physicians' minds about something for which they have strong opinions. Again, educational outreach and dialog are the appropriate tools in these circumstances.

Minimize Allergic Reactions to Drugs

ADE research indicates that some errors causing the most severe outcomes are related to drug allergies.[17] Although the ideal system to prevent avoidable allergic reactions may seem simple in concept, many challenges arise in practice related to workflow and data accuracy. We next outline key elements for a desirable approach, and then flesh out practical challenges and suggestions for working through them.

The following are considerations and suggestions—divided into several subtopics—for CDS to minimize allergic reactions. Again, local policies and practices, as well as CIS/CDS functionality, may influence the extent to which you can apply specific recommendations.

Recording Allergies: Who, What, Where, When, How?

- All licensed clinicians (such as physicians, nurses, pharmacists) should be able to enter allergy information. The risk of incomplete allergy information may outweigh the risk of having input "too many allergies that may not be true allergies." Keep in mind that inaccurate allergy data are a risk no matter who enters the information.[18]
- Patients will increasingly be documenting drug allergy and intolerance information themselves via tools such as personal health records (PHRs). This change can both support and complicate efforts to provide automated and other supports for avoiding problematic drugs. Organizations should consider educational programs, policies, and the like to help ensure that allergy information from all pertinent sources is documented and handled in a manner that optimizes safety.

Allergy Highlights

- Physician, pharmacist, and nurse workflow should facilitate patient allergy documentation and verification in **one,** single place in the CIS environment, which has been established for this purpose.
- Ensure that allergies are documented for a patient before CPOE accepts medication orders.
- Only allow substances to which the patient is allergic to be entered in coded form. Require also that the allergic reaction be documented in a codified format; this can help differentiate mild and severe allergies, as well as adverse drug reactions and intolerances.
- Require a reason for overriding an allergy alert.
- Work with your CIS and CDS vendors and local stakeholders *before launch* to ensure that allergy alerts presented to users are appropriate and helpful and don't contribute to alert fatigue.
- When clinicians record an alert override reason, such as "patient tolerates medication," provide an easy mechanism (such as via a link from the alert) for the prescriber to access the allergy field and remove the allergy from the list.
- Prompt clinicians to add new allergies if it can be inferred that the patient experienced an allergic reaction.

- Capture patient allergies as coded data elements that are integrated in all clinical-IS modules. That way they are presented during ordering, pharmacist verification, medication administration, and writing discharge prescriptions. Users should be able to enter discrete allergies by either drug name or drug class; you can build common allergies into system-wide folders to facilitate easier entry. Most commercial databases are extensive and regularly updated with new medications, so there is minimal need for free-text allergy entry.

- Document all allergies in the same section of the record—a "single source of truth"— regardless of who enters the information. This consistency avoids having different entries about patient allergies (such as in physician and nursing documentation), which may create conflicts and hinder ready access to this key information. Both nursing allergy documentation within forms and physician documentation within notes should be linked directly to the single source of truth allergy list.

- Maintain allergies from admission to admission and make available the full allergy documentation history to all users. The idea is to build upon this single source of truth rather than recreate it at each healthcare episode.

- Because order transmission is instantaneous in a CIS, orders can potentially be executed quickly. Therefore, you should try to ensure that allergies are documented before medications are ordered or during conversion of home medications to orders. This task can be prompted with an alert directly linked to a blank shared allergy field, or, better yet, making the need and opportunity to enter allergy information very prominent in clinician workflow to minimize the need for alerting. For example, in the case of physicians, orders are typically written before the history and physical examination is documented, so making clear the need for them or others to complete missing allergy information at the beginning of (or prior to) the ordering workflow is ideal.

- Upon admission to the hospital or visit to the outpatient doctor, the CIS and/or CDS system should support clinicians in reviewing documented allergy information to ensure that it is current and complete. Workflow friendly approaches, such as relevant data display, should be emphasized over intrusive alerting.

- An allergy CDS intervention should be capable of conducting a "reverse allergy check." That is, providing notification, in an appropriate time and format, that the patient is already receiving an offending medication without apparent harm. This notification can help clinicians reassess whether the medication should be removed from the allergy list.

More How's: Free Text, and No Known Allergies versus Allergy Not Documented

- Documenting allergies as free-text should be avoided if possible. This is because CDS rules cannot easily and reliably check against allergies recorded as free-text. If clinicians become accustomed to, and expect to receive, an alert when ordering a medication in error, this false expectation that there is an allergy safety net during ordering might increase the error risk at this stage. If allergy documentation is available in both structured and free-text formats, it is difficult to train users on circumstances for which it is appropriate to enter a free-text allergy (see discussion that follows in this chapter). If free-text allergy documentation is permitted, some organizations send a printed list of allergies documented in this format to the pharmacy and have pharmacists help investigate and update the record with an appropriate coded entry when this is possible.

- We recommend using No Known Allergies (which is often abbreviated NKA) rather than No Known Drug Allergies (NKDA). In a comprehensive EMR you should document food and environmental allergies in the same place as medication allergies, as each can arise during care delivery and have severe consequences. As noted in the previous section on abbreviations, consider in the various places where the term is used whether fully spelling it out is more appropriate than using the "NKA" shorthand.

- Consider what should be documented when a patient cannot give an allergy history. When NKA or NKDA is documented, then clinicians may assume (incorrectly) that this important history has been obtained. If there is a standard way to document that allergy information has been sought and is not currently available, then CDS approaches, such as relevant data display and alerts, can be used to help ensure that this information is documented as soon as it's available. For example, Northwestern Memorial Hospital in Chicago has a rule that prompts physicians to document allergies before any medications can be signed. If an allergy history cannot be obtained, the rule facilitates a notation linked to the ordered medication that a history is not available, which serves as a communication to the pharmacist. The rule is then suppressed until 24 hours later when it will prompt the physician again to enter allergy information if it has not been updated in the interim.

Alerting and Allergy Data Integrity

Some studies have shown that 80%+ of allergy alerts result in an override.[19,20] This high override frequency is due to causes such as non-exact matches between documented patient allergies and offending drugs. For example, the ordered drug and medication to which the patient has a documented allergy have similar structures or are in the same class but are not identical. Reasons physicians commonly give for overriding allergy alerts include that the patient is not allergic to the medication (for example, because of a non-exact match) or that they are aware of the allergy and are monitoring for problems. Of note, when physicians report in response to an alert that the patient is not allergic to the medication, they often do not remove the drug from the allergy list.[19] This is a missed opportunity for reducing alert overrides during subsequent prescribing. The following are recommendations for optimizing alert triggering and the data upon which this triggering is based.

- Leverage capabilities available in your CISs for allowing users to document whether a medication

reaction is an allergy or an intolerance/side effect and the type of reaction the patient experienced, such as nausea or hives.[21] This information is useful in many ways for clarifying communications and ensuring safe medication use. For example, it can help pharmacists who receive an allergy alert and must decide whether the reaction represents a true contraindication for the drug, as opposed to an intolerance that might not prevent using a medication similar in structure or in the same drug class. In addition, reaction information can be helpful at the ordering stage in customizing alerts or in preventing alerts from being triggered by entries that do not represent a contraindication (such as a mild intolerance). The lack of widely used standards for documenting this type of information can be problematic, but increasing attention to these types of issues within national HIT interoperability initiatives should help reduce these challenges over time.[22]

- Note that requiring clinicians to document reactions along with offending agents can increase documentation time and may require some training to ensure they understand the need for this documentation and can do it properly. This decision should be made by a multidisciplinary group in charge of medication safety and has implications similar to prohibiting free-text allergy entry. For example, will your physicians tolerate being forced to enter a reaction? Many patients may not remember what their reaction was, so an "unknown" option will be necessary. The discussions on governance and policies in Chapter 2, page 28, and Chapter 8, page 246, might be helpful in addressing these issues.

- Look into your allergy database capabilities to see if it handles "inactive ingredient allergies." If not, you may need to individually add these to the system. Note that data on which products contain inactive ingredients are not fully developed and reside at the National Drug Code (NDC)[23] code level. This checking can be further complicated when the system doing the check does not have information about the NDC code for the drug being dispensed. Latex allergies fall into this category, for example, since the list of injectable medications that contain latex in their packaging is constantly changing. Because latex is not a recognized allergen from its drug content vendor, Northwestern Memorial Hospital has created an alert to fire on "chart open" in the pharmacy system as a reminder to prepare any IV medication "latex-free" for patients whose allergy list includes latex.

- Consider how capturing the allergy or adverse reaction in a discrete fashion might be useful for local and national research efforts. Access to this coded information can also create advantages in the long term for electronic adverse drug reaction surveillance for widely used and newer medications on the market.

- In summary, the following recommendations, reported in a chart review study on a sample of overridden allergy alerts,[19] can be helpful for improving allergy data integrity and decreasing clinically unhelpful alerts.

  - Reaction data should be coded. Subsequent allergy alerts should specify the previously noted reaction and indicate whether it was a sensitivity/intolerance or a true allergic reaction.

  - Display interruptive alerts only for true allergic reactions, and make warnings about high dangers (such as anaphylaxis) easily identifiable.

  - For narcotics, generate an interruptive alert only for exact match allergies. For non-exact matches, a non-interruptive alert can be displayed and may recommend increased monitoring or premedications, when necessary.

  - You should display no alert (or a non-interruptive notification within the CIS user interface) for prescription of a "sulfonamide non-antibiotic" in the context of a sulfa allergy.

  - To facilitate data analysis and updating patient allergies, users should be able to select override reasons from a menu of choices rather than having to enter them as free-text.

  - Selecting an override reason such as "patient does not have allergy/tolerates" or "patient taking already" should automatically bring the clinician to a screen that allows the user to remove the drug allergy from the allergy list, when appropriate.

  - Overrides should be audited on a regular basis to identify alerts that are not useful. (See Chapter 7, page 207, for further discussion on evaluating and responding to alert overrides.)

  - You should prompt clinicians to enter new allergies if it can be inferred that an allergic reaction may have occurred. You can accomplish this when a medication is discontinued (likely most useful in the outpatient setting as medications change frequently in the inpatient setting) or when a new order for diphenhydramine (which may be used to treat allergic reactions) is written.

The sidebar on the next page illustrates steps one organization took to improve their allergy CDS by preventing free-text allergy entry.

Minimize Drug-drug Interactions

As with allergies, no simple success formula exists for implementing CDS for DDIs to optimize patient safety and user acceptance. Many pertinent CDS and CIS tools still lack desired functionality, and no consensus exists on which DDI alerts should interrupt physicians or other clinicians. The information provided in the sidebar on page 128 offers some high-level suggestions, followed by more detailed ideas for improved DDI decision support delivery.

Research shows that many DDI warnings are overridden. For example, a study of five adult primary-care practices found that 89.4% of high-severity DDI alerts were overridden.[20] Physician reviewers judged that 41% of these alerts were inappropriate. Such findings suggest two significant and complementary problems with alerting: many DDI alerts are inappropriate and thus hinder workflow, while at the same time, potentially important alerts go unheeded. "Alert fatigue" caused by the former

Coded Allergy versus Free-text Allergy at Memorial Hermann

Houston-based Memorial Hermann Healthcare System initially allowed staff to enter allergies in either coded form or as free-text within their CISs. It used a systematic approach to identifying the key issues and problems with free-text allergy entry:

- Analysis revealed that approximately 3% to 5% of all drug-allergy entries were recorded as free text.
- Numerous instances were found in which documented allergies were overlooked during prescribing, partly because allergies were stored as free-text; as a result, CDS allergy alerts did not work.
- To address this problem, clinical staff was given additional education on the importance of entering coded allergies.
- Post-education data showed a drop in the percentage of free-text allergy entries; however, after two months, free-text allergy entry rose again.
- In response, the organization revisited its plans to completely turn off enterprise-wide the option for free-text allergy entry. Several steps were taken to increase this strategy's success before it was implemented:
  - Re-educate staff on the importance of allergy documentation.
  - Create an enterprise-wide favorites folder covering the top allergies documented in the system to make it easier for users to select common allergies (Table 5-2).
  - Create easy-to-recognize synonyms for some common allergies (Table 5-3).
  - Create a process for documenting unverified allergies.

Table 5-2: Top 10 Coded Allergies (May 2006)

Penicillins	504
Codeine	472
Sulfa drugs	413
Penicillin	350
Morphine	186
Aspirin	122
Demerol	95
Iodine topical	94
Vicodin	84
Erythromycin	74

Table 5-3: Common Allergy Synonyms

Coded Allergy	Synonym
Angiotensin converting enzyme inhibitor	ACE inhibitors
Angiotensin II inhibitors	ARB's, ARBs, ARB
Adhesive	Adhesive tape, band-aids, surgical tape, paper tape, medical tape, plastic tape

Memorial Hermann created a coded term, "Allergy unverified," to be used as a flag to indicate that a patient's allergy information is unverified. It also printed a daily report to inform pharmacy staff about new admissions with unverified allergies. Pharmacy could then work with nursing to verify the allergy and update the patient's allergy profile.

After completing these preparatory steps, Memorial Hermann broadcast a message to the entire health system that it was disabling the field for free-text allergy entry. To allow users to adjust to the new workflow, there was a 45-day period between this message and the date that the field was disabled.

The conversion was uneventful and generated substantial positive user feedback. In summary, the organization recommends a three-fold strategy for handling allergy entry CISs: (1) provide education on the importance of avoiding free text entry, and disable this capability after preparing clinicians; (2) ensure an easy procedure to enter coded allergies; and (3) develop a process to deal with unverified allergies.

Source: Memorial Hermann Healthcare System, Houston, TX. Used with permission.

issue is considered to be a contributor to the latter problem.

CDS to minimize important DDIs is a challenge for a number of reasons:

- DDIs manifest differently in different patients.
- Evidence that a DDI exists may be weak, that is, documented in only a few cases.
- Content vendors have different systems for grading DDIs. These generally include severity and documentation filters but may or may not include a reliability or evidence rating. However, since there are not widely adopted standards for indicating interaction severity and associated clinical evidence, these ratings may vary considerably across vendors. Each may apply their own standards, and most are conservative, due to

liability concerns. As an example, content vendors may assign a DDI severity based on a "class effect" that may present a theoretic DDI based on similar drug structure, but without clinical evidence or experience that specifically documents the particular interaction or severity.

- It is not clear at what DDI severity level (and other parameters, such as strength of evidence) different clinicians should be alerted in order to optimize both workflow and safety.

To Interrupt or Not to Interrupt

Implementers often initially approach CDS for DDIs with interruptive alerts delivered either at order entry through CPOE or at order transcription into the pharmacy system. For drugs that should

DDI Highlights

- Contraindicated drug pairs should trigger an alert that is difficult to override.
- For situations where orders include "usually avoid combinations," or pairs in which one drug needs a dose change, it may be appropriate to provide workflow-interrupting alerts and require that a reason be documented for an override.
- Consider showing highest level alerts (for example, DDI is most severe and best documented) to physicians and a broader range of somewhat less urgent but still important alerts to pharmacists; consider suppressing alerts for drug combinations that the patient is known to tolerate.
- Locally customizing intrusive alerting based on characteristics such as the danger severity level for specific drug pairs may be helpful to balance safety with clinician workflow, but optimal tools for doing so might not be available.
- Good governance and consensus processes are vital for managing implementation issues such as determining which clinicians will see DDIs at each severity level and whether/how individual pairs of interacting drugs will be handled in a customized manner.
- Providers and CIS/CDS vendors should collaborate on better strategies to minimize unnecessary reliance on interruptive alerts and enhance use of unobtrusive information presentation (for example, rounds report, on-screen data display) for potentially important interactions of lesser severity.

never be used together (Category A) or for drugs that require a dose adjustment for one of the agents (Category B), an interruptive alert at these stages may be the appropriate time and delivery method. Other DDIs may require monitoring lab tests or the patient for clinical symptoms after the patient has received the two drugs concomitantly (Category C). Although all categories are clinically important, an interruptive alert in CPOE may not be the best delivery method for Category C, as action may not be necessary at this stage. Corollary orders (for important labs to follow) or documentation tools linked to appropriate action reminders (to help with follow-up for clinical symptoms suggesting a DDI) might be more workflow-friendly and helpful CDS interventions in this case.

There are data that examine physician and pharmacist reaction to DDI alerts and their suggestions for improvement.[24] Investigators in this study found less negative reaction to the alerts as one might expect from the data about alert overrides. Suggestions from prescribers emphasized adding management options to the alert, and pharmacists recommended making it more difficult to override lethal interactions. In the primary care alert override study cited previously,[20] nearly all of the overrides were considered valid (in many cases because the patient had tolerated the offending combination), leading those investigators to suggest that such tolerated combinations should not trigger alerts for medication renewals in ambulatory CPOE.

Most DDI rule bases from vendors are extensive, for example, including tens of thousands of drug pairs. This number is clearly too large to be effective, if the only method for notifying clinicians about a potential interaction is through a workflow-interrupting alert triggered in an unfiltered way from the rule base. Many vendor databases allow filtering by such factors as reaction severity and documentation supporting the interaction (for example, case reports versus larger studies). However, even when these filters are used (so that only interactions with high severity and good documentation are flagged), the number of alerts that can be shown to prescribers at order entry can have a low signal-to-noise ratio.

Another challenge with DDIs, especially in the outpatient setting, is due to an inaccurate medication list that has old or outdated medications. For example, a patient may have taken an antibiotic for 10 days then discontinued its use, but if it still appears on the medication list, it may be flagged as interacting with other new medications. These problems can be avoided by ensuring that there is a single accurate source for documenting and reviewing patient medications across care settings when possible (see Chapter 4, page 41 [reconciliation step]) and that the list is updated before new prescriptions are written.

CDS vendors are aware of these challenges, but progress toward solutions has been slow. Close collaboration among provider organizations, CIS vendors, CDS suppliers, standards organizations, and others should be fostered to accelerate approaches for optimizing DDI notification usefulness. National efforts, such as those by the American Health Information Community (AHIC) ad hoc CDS Workgroup and related entities, are moving to establish forums for such communication and collaboration and explore national CDS content repositories.[25] Such repositories could potentially include the most dangerous Category A interactions strongly supported by evidence. In a step toward this goal, efforts have identified clinically important DDIs likely to be encountered in community and ambulatory pharmacy settings and detected by computerized systems.[26]

Customizing DDI Information Presentation
If your CIS vendor(s) for systems such as CPOE and pharmacy management provide tools to customize DDI rules and alerts at the local level, a number of options are available for handling these notifications:

- Turn off DDI alerting completely.
- Turn on alerts for a certain DDI severity.
- Change the severity of individual drug pairs to improve the signal-to-noise ratio. That is, identify a subset of the most severe and clinically important of the severe DDIs to trigger alerting.

These options should be considered for inpatient and outpatient settings, as is pertinent to your efforts. Some organizations define a highest DDI alert level to show physicians and a second level of important, but somewhat less critical, DDI alerts to show pharmacists. Even without CPOE, organizations can consider which DDIs are most highly problematic locally and nationally and undertake educational outreach to minimize prescriptions for these combinations.

Configuring DDI alerts locally requires a CDS governance structure (see Chapter 2, page 28 and Chapter 8, page 246). Consensus on decisions as to what alert level to show physicians versus pharmacists may be relatively straightforward for an entire DDI category (for example, based on severity levels). However, changing levels for individual drug pairs is significantly more challenging due to the number of drug pairs that must be considered to increase the signal-to-noise ratio and potential disagreement between members about individual decisions. Implementing a governance process to address such fine details on a large scale is important but labor intensive and not widely implemented across organizations. Chapter 8 provides recommendations for setting up such processes.

Interruptive alerts are just one approach for ensuring that clinicians are aware of potentially dangerous DDIs. You should consider the full range of options for reducing this preventable medication error. Again, it is helpful to start with educational outreach and dialog with prescribers and pharmacists to facilitate consensus prior to CDS interventions about how best to handle various DDI situations. Online sources, such as those provided by the FDA, can be used to educate clinicians about DDIs.[27] CDS interventions to consider include the following, among others:

- Notify prescribers up front about drugs your organization has deemed to cause the highest safety risk when combined or "Category A" DDIs (concomitant use contraindicated), and use an interruptive alert at order entry that is difficult to override if these combinations are prescribed; some alerts for the most dangerous combinations could be nearly impossible to override. Only a handful of drug pairs will be addressed in this way.

- Handle Category B DDIs with interruptive alerts that are easier to override; require prescribers to provide a codified reason why they overrode the alert to assist with clinician education and to use for further fine-tuning of that alert. This category should include drugs for which the clinical recommendation is to "usually avoid combination" or combinations in which one of the drug doses may need to be adjusted because of the DDI. Show alerts that physicians override to the pharmacist, along with the override reason, to assist with safety verification for the specific patient and to reduce false-positive alerting more generally.

- Provide, for Category C DDIs, non-interruptive notification at some point in user workflow, for example, on the side of a pertinent prescriber and/or pharmacist data management screen, with a link to more information about the interaction, if desired. Because Category C DDIs include interactions for which monitoring the patient for any adverse effects is adequate, immediate action by physicians is not required and mandatory workflow disruption should be avoided. In the inpatient setting, interactions in this category may also be presented as a tickler on a rounds report to prompt clinician review for any untoward effects during daily patient rounds. If your EMR doesn't accommodate such reports, you may be able to use the pharmacy IS or related tools to provide pharmacists with information about such DDIs that require monitoring (for example, through an aggregate report or by providing this information directly on a pharmacist rounds report, so they can be addressed verbally with the prescriber).

If your environment includes both inpatient and outpatient settings, you should consider whether the balance between intrusive alerting and other forms of information display (especially for Category C) should be the same in both settings. The inpatient environment, which is characterized by continual patient monitoring through frequent daily clinician interactions, may have less need for interruptive alerts about interacting drug pairs for which the patient needs monitoring. In the outpatient environment, where opportunities to monitor possible interaction effects are much less frequent, more aggressive notification may be warranted. As always, the signal-to-noise ratio of delivered information should be carefully considered.

Ideally, information contained within the patient record should be used when appropriate to filter DDI notification, though such highly patient-specific alert triggering capabilities may not be widely available. When practical, this approach could help address the common complaint and override reason from prescribers that they receive alerts for an intentional action or for a risk they had already considered. For example, on admission to the hospital, a patient may be on interacting drugs (such digoxin and amiodarone, or warfarin and synthroid), but the interaction is stabilized because necessary monitoring and adjustments have been done. In these cases, there may be no need for an interruptive alert if no additional action is necessary, so suppressing alert firing under these circumstances might be helpful.

Similarly, it would be ideal for the alert to be suppressed (or only presented in an unobtrusive passive manner) if the interacting drugs exist together on the "ongoing home meds list" or when the drug pair is entered in the same ordering episode. This functionality could potentially decrease nuisance alerts for "well-known" and "well-managed" drug interactions, while still triggering an alert when an interacting drug is added to an existing drug. It should be kept in mind, however, that adverse interaction consequences that are not recognized as such may occur in these types of situations for which alert suppression is considered.

Table 5-4: Prescriber DDI Notification

Level of DDI Alert	Number of Rules	Percent of Rules	Percent of Alerts Fired	Percent of Orders Which Resulted in Alert	Percent Compliance with Alert
1 (Hard Stop)	101	4.6	0.2	0.02	100
2 (Interruptive)	1,093	49.9	28.4	1.4	29
3 (Non-interruptive)	995	45.5	71.4	3.2	9 (extrapolated from sister hospital)

Source: Partners HealthCare, Inc., Boston, MA. Used with permission.

Optimally, all DDI levels for a particular patient should be accessible with the "click of a button" when so desired by the clinician. For example, on daily rounds, a patient may have a new complaint or a lab abnormality. If the patient is on 10 medications—and especially when some of the medications are new—the clinician should be able to evaluate all medications for possible DDIs that may be contributing to the change. This functionality may not be readily available in CISs as yet, but such on-demand evaluation would be very useful clinically.

Which DDIs Should Be Presented?

At this point there are not clear best practices regarding which specific DDI alerts are best to show prescribers and/or pharmacists. Hopefully this important guidance will soon be available, for example, from collaborative processes for identifying success strategies, such as those used to create this book, together with research of the sort cited earlier.[26] The following are examples of how some organizations that contributed to this book handle DDI alerting:

- Partners Healthcare uses three primary approaches for notifying prescribers about potential DDIs that could be clinically significant: a "hard stop" that does not allow the combination to be prescribed, an interruptive alert that cautions prescribers about the DDI but allows the combination to be ordered when they provide an override reason, and a non-interruptive notification through on-screen display that the user can heed (and/or seek further information through an infobutton) or ignore. These rules about potentially dangerous DDI combinations, and their assignment to the various notification categories, were developed through the Partners' CDS governance processes. Table 5-4 presents an overview of Partners' DDI prescriber notification approach and results from more than 1.6 million inpatient medication orders over a recent one-year period at one of their hospitals. Partners' informatics experts anticipate that these results would be consistent across time and across their inpatient and outpatient settings and other facilities.

- Approximately 3,500 drug pairs are programmed to interrupt physicians at Northwestern Memorial Hospital (highest level), but actual opportunities for alerts are far fewer because many drug pairs contain at least one drug not included on the formulary. About 8,000 drug pairs interrupt NMH pharmacists, who report anecdotally that some of the interruptions are useful, but signal-to-noise ratio is too low.

- Memorial Hermann also found many paired drugs in the highest category and took efforts to decrease the number of drug pairs that resulted in an interruptive alert. They developed a working list of only high-risk medications to bring the number of DDI pairs that trigger interruptive alerting to approximately 300. Even using this relatively concise list, they still found the need to turn off additional DDI pairs from this set, based on common clinical practice. Examples of DDIs that needed to be excluded from triggering alerts include drug pairs that contain benzodiazepines and opioid analgesics; these combinations are routinely prescribed by anesthesiologists and other physicians, and are a part of their evidence-based CPOE order sets. The following are some observations and recommendations based on their experience:

  – Consider keeping all the contraindicated drug pairs active for alert triggering.

  – Consider keeping all the drug pairs with at least ONE high-risk medication active (high-risk as defined by your organization).

  – Ensure that all drug pairs that may be given by a route that does not cause an interaction (topical, shampoo, etc.) are excluded from triggering alerts. Note that this approach depends on your system's ability to customize individual DDI pairs.

  – Monitor alerts continuously for abnormal spikes in firing frequency, which may suggest a recent change in prescribing behavior. You may consider turning off drug pairs that commonly cause interruptive alerts but do not lead to a change in clinician behavior. If these ignored

DDI warnings are genuinely problematic clinically, than educational outreach to clinicians is needed.

Personalizing DDI Alerting

Because "overalerting" can pose a significant challenge to effective and well-received CDS, some have suggested that physicians be allowed to select which drug pair alerts they see, or to develop different alerts for different physician groups. For example, one can envision physicians requesting that they never receive alerts for DDIs about which they are fully aware, such as the interaction between ACEIs and potassium supplements. In addition, some may further argue that more seasoned clinicians might not need the same prescribing guardrails as those more junior. It should be noted, however, that increased experience may not decrease prescribing error frequency. In one study, the error rate for attending physicians was better than first-year residents, but worse than second- and third-year residents and fourth-year fellows.[28] In addition, with patients increasingly receiving multiple drugs from various providers in both inpatient and outpatient settings, there is increasing risk that medications prescribed by different prescribers will have a dangerous interaction.

Although customizing alerting for individual clinicians is a provocative idea, the extent to which current systems allow this ability is unclear. Even when user-specific customization is technically feasible, the decision to allow it should be informed by the organization's approach to balancing standardization to foster safety and reliability with individual autonomy. This question, similar to allowing "personal" order sets, can be addressed by the medication management oversight committee and other stakeholders. Quality/patient safety/risk management will want input regardless and, at the very least, locally reported errors should be reviewed for any relationship to the requested change. (Note that DDIs are rarely voluntarily reported, as they may not be recognized as such.) Critically reviewing overridden alerts over time should help organizations refine clinically valid alerts. This is a good topic for further research.

Alert Overrides

When a physician is presented with a DDI alert and overrides it, your system should be configured such that the same alert and the reason for the prescriber override are sent to the pharmacist for review. Pharmacists then have the difficult job of deciding when to contact the physician. (For example, a pharmacist may question whether the override was merely an inadvertent busy-clinician bypass or a thoughtful decision to proceed despite the interaction.) Good communication channels and well-functioning working relationships between prescribers and pharmacists (which can be facilitated through the CDS team's efforts to establish consensus around how DDI and related information will be handled) are important for optimizing how these situations are addressed.

When entering verbal orders, nurses should see the same DDI alerts that physicians would see upon entering the orders directly. When administering a medication, nurses should see information about any DDIs (including override reasons from physician and/or pharmacist) as relevant information (for example, in an eMAR), not in the form of an alert. If both physician and pharmacist overrode the alert, the nurse needs to be aware of these actions. However, nurses will generally not take action on the DDI information in these cases (that is, they will administer the interacting medications as prescribed), unless there is concern that the interaction notification should be addressed otherwise.

Other Key Medication Management Targets
Ensuring Proper Dosing

Incorrect dosing is a common and important medication error type that commonly causes preventable ADEs. Basic dosing guidance can and should be provided with appropriate order sentences and order sets. Researchers have decreased serious dosing errors by 55% and decreased doses exceeding the maxi-

---

> ## Dosing Highlights
>
> - Prioritize drug dosing CDS in your program in a manner that reflects its high importance based on medication safety research, taking into consideration other local medication priorities.
> - Start with default doses in order sentences and order sets as the foundation for your dosing CDS efforts.
> - Consider starting with a small set of priority drugs for dose limit checking if you are custom developing these checks. However, if the tool/content is provided by your CDS vendor, consider activating dose limits for all drugs after reviewing this material for consistency with local standards and practice.
> - Focus on the administration phase for alerts regarding drugs given "PRN" (that is, "as needed").
> - See related subheadings that follow for other specific CDS recommendations related to dosing in special populations, such as patients with decreased kidney function, very old or young patients, and others.

---

mum from 2.1% to 0.6% by using standard defaults for medication doses and frequencies. Advanced decision support for dosing should have the capability to address each of following, as appropriate for specific medications and patients: indication for the drug, and patient characteristics such as age, weight, height, physiologic status, comorbidities, and concomitant medications.[29]

Order sentences and order sets, covered more thoroughly in Chapter 4, page 96, form an important base for the more advanced dosing support discussed in this section. Additional dosing guidance can be embedded in order sentences and order sets, as well as in other pertinent applications in the prescribing and verification workflow, complementing basic approaches for presenting prescribers with standard dosing options. For example, reference information with situation-specific dosing information can be displayed in various tools, such as CPOE, pharmacy systems, and others—potentially including paper order sets as well. It is desirable to make this support context-sensitive and readily available, instead of requiring the physician or pharmacist to leave the ordering or verification process to manually search for the information in a separate place, such as a reference book or a Web site. This embedded or linked information might include care plans for certain indications, in which the plan contains defaulted dose information and/or detailed options. For example, at Texas Health Resources, antibiotic dosing for neonates can be easily adjusted for both postmenstrual and postnatal newborn age (PMA, PNA, respectively) because this information is included directly within pertinent order sets (see Figure 5-1, page 147).

A medication safety initiative by the National Health Service in the United Kingdom[30] included developing recommendations for dosing decision support, focusing on medications for which dosing errors can be particularly problematic. These recommendations, summarized in Table 5-5, can be used to stimulate thinking about dosing guidance in your organization.

Some CIS and CDS systems offer an extensive predefined rule set—and the capability to develop custom rules—that can be applied as a safety net to help detect improper drug dosing, along the lines outlined in the Table 5-5. These rules can address pertinent medication factors such as dose limits and indication-based dosing, and patient factors such as weight, kidney function, liver function, age, and others. In the subsections that follow, we consider how rules and other CDS approaches can help ensure proper dosing in light of these factors.

Dose-range Checking: Single, Daily and Cumulative Doses

Medications, like any substance introduced into the body, are dangerous in excessive amounts. For some drugs, the harm caused by even relatively small overdoses can be great. Toxicity can result from a single medication dose or from multiple doses received over the course of a day or longer. As illustrated in Table 5-5, there are also circumstances in which it might be helpful to detect drug underdosing. Automated dose range checking in applications such as CPOE and pharmacy systems can help ensure that medications prescribed and dispensed do not reflect excessive or inadequate dosing. The following are some considerations for setting up automated dose range checking.

Basic dose limits should screen both single dose and daily dose. Keep in mind that many drugs will need different dose ranges for different routes of administration, such as oral and intravenous. For some medications, such as chemotherapy or IV ketorolac, checking the cumulative dose received over a few days or over the patient's lifetime may be necessary (see next section).

PRN medications can be a challenge for daily-dose CDS at the ordering stage. Many medications can be administered frequently, but there is a maximum daily dose. Order examples for which this is important include: acetaminophen 650 mg by mouth every four hours as needed (with a maximum dose of 4 grams in 24 hours), or labetalol 20 mg intravenously every 20 minutes as needed for elevated blood pressure. The intent is not to administer at every interval for 24 hours; however, the daily dose check may interpret the order that way and flag an excessive daily dose. Ideas to consider for PRN dose checking, together with available capabilities of your CIS, include the following:

- Use alerts at the administration phase instead of at order entry—checking carefully for all medications that may include the specific drug. For example, acetaminophen is a drug that is highly toxic when given in excessive doses and is contained in a variety of combination medication

Table 5-5: Suggested Key Decision Support for Dosing Problems

Drug Group	Dosing problem						
	Dosing by Indication	10-fold dosing errors	Default Dosing	Total Daily Dosing	Frequency/ administration rate	Ingredient doubling/ Therapeutic duplication	Underdosing
Anti-thrombotics							
Aspirin (low dose)	Recommend 75 mg dose if prescribed as antiplatelet — need to link to diagnoses of stroke, diabetes, MI, etc.		Default to aspirin 75 mg each morning with or after food		Alert if prescribed more than once daily	Alert if more than one aspirin-containing preparation prescribed	
Heparin/LMWH*	Recommend doses appropriate for prophylaxis or treatment depending on indication and patient's weight	Prevent prescription if heparin infusion dose exceeds 15 units/kg/hr by a factor of 10	Default to appropriate dose depending on indication and patient's weight		Alert if dosing interval is inappropriate (12 or 24 hours depending on indication)		Alert if LMWH dose too low for patient's weight
Warfarin			Default to appropriate dose based on INR/recommended loading regimen		Alert if prescribed more than once daily		
Cardiovascular							
Betablockers	Alert if new prescription and patient has computer recorded diagnosis of CCF and prescribed dose above that recommended for initiation		For new prescription, if patient has computer recorded diagnosis of CCF, recommend appropriate starting dose				
Digoxin		Prevent prescription if more than 10-fold greater than appropriate dose for weight		Alert if cumulative loading dose greater than 1 mg in 24 hours (or appropriate loading dose by weight in paediatrics)			
Potassium supplements					Alert if rate of administration rate exceeds 40mmol/hour	Alert if more than one potassium-containing preparation prescribed concurrently (e.g., oral & IV, IV & TPN)	

* Low-molecular-weight heparin

Table 5-5: *continued*

Drug Group	Dosing problem						
	Dosing by Indication	10-fold dosing errors	Default Dosing	Total Daily Dosing	Frequency/ administration rate	Ingredient doubling/ Therapeutic duplication	Underdosing
Endocrine							
Corticosteroids	Recommend dose based on indication			Recommend osteoporosis prophylaxis if high-risk dose of steroid prescribed for more than 3 months (e.g., prednisolone > 7.5 mg daily)		Alert if patient prescribed more than one preparation of corticosteroid	
Insulin (sliding scale)	Recommend appropriate sliding scale regimen*		Default to recommended sliding scale regimen*				
Central Nervous System							
Opiates	Alert if opioid dose exceeds recommended dose for post-surgical analgesia in patient who has undergone surgery	Prevent prescriptions if paediatric dose exceeds recommended dose for weight 10-fold			Alert if interval between administering opiate dose is shorter than that prescribed (e.g., for PCA)	Alert if 2 or more modified release or topical opiate preparations prescribed concurrently	Alert if p.m. dose of opioid is less than that recommended for regular dose (e.g., for morphine, less than 1/6 of the 24-hour cumulative regular dose)
Phenothiazines/ butysophenomes, etc.						Alert if more than one agent prescribed	
Phenytoin					Alert if IV administration rate exceeds that recommended		
Anti-inflammatories							
Methotrexate			Default to weekly dosing schedule		Alert if administration frequency exceeds weekly		
NSAIDs						Alert if more than one NSAID-containing preparation prescribed (including low-dose aspirin)	

---

* Sliding scale regimens should be agreed upon at a local level, but a national focus will be needed to enable implementation of these alerts.

Table 5-5: *continued*

Drug Group	Dosing problem						
	Dosing by Indication	10-fold dosing errors	Default Dosing	Total Daily Dosing	Frequency/ administration rate	Ingredient doubling/ Therapeutic duplication	Underdosing
Antimicrobial agents							
Vancomycin	Recommend dosing schedule based on weight and renal function for new prescriptions				Alert if administration rate exceeds that recommended		
Aminoglycosides	Recommend dosing schedule based on weight and renal function for new prescriptions				Alert if frequency of administration is inappropriate for dose prescribed		

Source: University of Nottingham, Nottingham, UK. Used with permission.

products. You might set up a rule to detect when the nurse has administered 3 grams of acetaminophen in 18 hours and trigger an alert via the eMAR or barcode-point of care (BPOC) system that the 24-hour dose is nearing the maximum. BPOC can be an effective CDS delivery channel because it processes data in real time at the point of medication administration. Manual documentation may follow administration, so a warning on nurse interaction with the eMAR may be too late.

- Have the physician identify the maximum daily dose in addition to the frequency at the point of order entry, and configure dose-checking software to evaluate both variables. More proactively in CPOE, the maximum dose can be specified as part of the default in a predefined order sentence. Specifying maximum doses in these ways may be appropriate for some PRN medications that can be prescribed and administered on a short frequency interval but for which there is a well-

referenced maximum dose. For example, labetalol may be given every 10 minutes as needed for perioperative hypertension, up to a total dose of 300 mg. An appropriate order may be 20 mg intravenously every 10 minutes PRN hypertension. When the dose-checking software is configured to alert at a daily maximum of 300 mg, this order may produce an alert if the system extrapolates to a total 24-hour dose (when administered every 10 minutes) of 2,880 mg. However, the intent of this order is for labetalol to be used as needed in the immediate postoperative period. If the order details included a maximum dose of 300 mg, the nurse would be notified of this maximum, and the dose-checking software could evaluate the both the 10-minute interval and the prescribed maximum dose. This example addresses decision support at the prescribing phase; considerations for checking/alerting at the administration phase is also very useful—as outlined earlier for acetaminophen.

Dose-range checking for some medication classes will be challenging. For example, no specific predefined maximum dose for opioids exists; a dose that is acceptable for a cancer patient who has developed tolerance to the drugs may easily be fatal to an opioid naive patient. Dosing such medications should account for various patient parameters that may not be available as discrete coded data in an EMR, so it is difficult to write dose limit rules. For example, in dosing opioids, prescribers should consider the indication, whether the patient is currently on chronic opioid therapy (and if so, at what dose), and previous patient experience with opioid therapy. Although preconfigured order sentences and proactive dose checking might not be possible or appropriate in this case, CDS in the form of context-sensitive infobutton links to information about opioid dosing and dose equivalents, provided within the ordering workflow, may be useful.

There are relatively few medications that require checking for cumulative doses delivered over extended time periods, but for some cancer chemotherapy agents and other drugs, it is an important requirement. A starter list may include daunorubicin, doxorubicin, doxorubicin liposomal, amphoteracin B, mitomycin C, epirubicin, and bleomycin.

Automating long-term cumulative dose checks can be a challenge when all the patient's care is not carried out in the same facility or managed using the same EMR. For example, many oncology patients receive most drug treatment cycles as an outpatient but may also receive care within an inpatient facility. It can be helpful in this case, and for other purposes, to use CDS to facilitate documentation and flagging somewhere in the EMR (and/or other CISs) that the patient is currently receiving (or has received in the past) one of these drugs, together with dosing details. This information can be used to remind clinicians about the need for cumulative dose monitoring and/or support the calculation when the data are available.

Ensuring Correct Dosing Based on Indication

Certain drugs are dosed differently based on the indication for which they are being used. For example, the drug desmopressin (also known as DDAVP) is used in different doses for diabetes insipidus versus nocturnal enuresis versus bleeding prophylaxis. Likewise, certain antimicrobial and antiviral medication doses vary widely depending on the indication. For example, the recommended IV acyclovir dose for central nervous system herpes simplex or varicella zoster infection is double the dose indicated for other localized infections, such as genital or cutaneous herpes simplex. CDS can be used to provide prescribers with this dosing information in various ways, such as through reference information, documentation tools, order creation facilitators, rules for proactive suggestions and alerting, and the like.

To proactively suggest indication-specific dosing, data in the CIS about patient problems or diagnoses must be associated with corresponding drug dosing information. This linking requires that an up-to-date, coded and complete problem list is available before orders are generated (documentation tools can help with this) and that these codes match the medication indications. The Joint Commission encourages links between indication and drug, but automated linking for proactive dose suggestions may be a challenge for now. Similar considerations apply to safety net rules for checking appropriate indication-based dosing after orders are entered.

In CPOE, a simpler way to address indication-specific dosing is to create multiple instances of orderables (for example, "desmopressin for diabetes insipidus" and "desmopressin for nocturnal enuresis") and then offer the corresponding appropriate doses. Or, you can put all the different indications in a special order set focused on the drug, with suggestions for dosing per each different indication. Of course order sets (in CPOE, Web portals, or paper) focused on a particular condition should have the drug doses that are relevant to that condition.

When prescribers or pharmacists have questions about indication-specific dosing today, they often consult reference sources. Using tools such as infobuttons to bring this information in a context-sensitive way into workflow—for example, by linking directly from the drug name in a CIS to dosing information—can be a relatively high-value, low-cost CDS approach.

Weight-based Dosing

CPOE systems should allow clinicians to order a weight-based dose and should automatically calculate a total dose to be administered, based on the most recent weight entered into the system. The following are some CDS-related considerations for setting this up.

- The formula should generally round to the nearest acceptable whole dose that can readily be dispensed and administered. For example, in a 67 kg patient, an order for enoxaparin 1 mg/kg BID might round to 70 mg BID, instead of 67 mg BID when such a dose might need further adjustment by a pharmacist or be difficult for the nurse to accurately administer. CDS approaches related to rounding like this can be vetted through pertinent CDS/medication management governance bodies discussed in Chapter 2, page 28.
- In the pediatric population, weight-based dosing systems should not round but instead should calculate the closest dispensable doses based on "rounding increments" (which are determined based on drug and age bracket). Research is underway to determine optimal rounding strategies for pediatric medications and make this information available for clinical decision support.[31]
- Your CIS should allow the prescriber to alter the "dosing weight" if so desired. There are a number of situations (based on drug and patient clinical parameters) for which the clinician may choose to use a "dry weight" or a "birth weight" in the calculation, rather than the patient's current weight. Similarly, in some cases an estimated weight may be entered, or a patient's clinical situation may

cause the weight to change significantly over time. Ideally a mechanism should be in place to indicate which of these many potential weights are being used (or should be used) for dose calculations.

- It is critical for both the ordered mg/kg dose and total dose to be visible to all users (such as the pharmacist and nurse) throughout the medication-use process. Displaying dosing information in both formats conveys the order intent and allows for a double check, which is especially critical in the pediatric population.

Ensuring Safe Dosing in Patients with Renal Impairment

An estimated 3% of Americans have varying degrees of chronic renal insufficiency.[32] Since many drugs are eliminated by the kidney and/or can cause kidney and other damage when blood levels are excessive, kidney function is a critical issue in safe drug dosing. CDS plays an important role in helping ensure that prescribers are aware and respond appropriately when patients have kidney dysfunction that must be considered in drug selection and dosing decisions—or when changes in kidney function may be caused by current medications.

Various books and articles are available that offer guidance on safe medication dosing in patients with kidney disease.[33,34] Pertinent clinical experts and CDS implementers in your organization might find current versions of such references useful for informing CDS interventions in this arena. Once again, the full spectrum of CDS interventions, together with the CDS Five Rights, should be considered in your approach to this important target.

In the subsections that follow, we consider three situations in which CDS can be applied to help promote safe medication use in patients with renal insufficiency:

- Initial medication dosing in a patient with acute or chronic renal insufficiency
- Patient on a medication that is nephrotoxic and has worsening creatinine clearance

Renal Dosing Highlights

- Choose a formula to calculate estimated creatinine clearance (if the formula is not provided by the CDS vendor).
- Use rules at order initiation to screen for drugs that need to be dose adjusted for renal function, and recommend appropriate dosing.
- Incorporate rules to evaluate changes in laboratory values that reflect worsening or improving renal function during therapy with medications that require renal dosing, and notify prescribers about the possible need to re-adjust dosing accordingly.
- When possible, present user with the recommended adjusted dose (and the opportunity to enter that order), rather than just alerting that the dose may be inappropriate.
- Notify the clinician (such as via an alert, report to pharmacist, or page) when the patient is on a nephrotoxic drug (that is, one that can worsen renal function) and lab values indicate declining renal function.

- Patient on a medication that needs to be dose adjusted in renal insufficiency and has lab evidence of worsening renal function.

Renal Dosing at Order Entry

Knowledge bases from commercial CDS content vendors generally have renal dosing guidelines for initial doses; however, this guidance tends to be conservative. Although they provide a good place to start, the content may need to be reviewed and adjusted based on local practice and expert opinion

in areas for which compelling evidence to guide dosing is absent.

If you are writing your own rules to trigger notification about the possible need for renal dose adjustment, a number of things should be considered in determining how renal dysfunction will be quantified. Kidney function is often expressed in terms of "creatinine clearance," the rate at which the kidneys clear a particular chemical from the body. Creatinine clearance is a key parameter for adjusting drug dosing for kidney dysfunction and can be estimated in various ways using factors such as patient height, weight, and blood test results. CDS can help ensure that these data are current and available for needed calculations, and can assist with determining the creatinine clearance and recommending dosage modifications accordingly.

Keep in mind that different creatinine clearance formulas may be appropriate in different circumstances. These are discussed in sources such as the National Kidney Foundation guideline on estimation of glomerular filtration rate (GFR).[35] You should also consider how the data needed for the calculations will be obtained. Following are further details on creatinine clearance and its CDS implications.

- Creatinine clearance formulas differ in their accuracy and the number of parameters they require. For example, some organizations use the Cockcroft-Gault formula, which is relatively simple, requiring patient age, gender, height, and weight in the calculation. Other formulas may be more accurate but are also more complex (for example, requiring additional variables such as body surface area [BSA] and race).
- It may be fine to use a simple but "accurate enough" formula; the goal is to be practical rather than perfect (without compromising safety). Consultation and consensus between the CDS team and local experts (such as from pharmacy, nursing, and medical staff) can help determine an optimal local strategy.
- In selecting a formula for your rules, consider which parameters are readily available electroni-

cally, without the need to unnecessarily burden prescribers to provide missing data. The extra information may not add much value anyway due to diminishing returns in creatinine clearance accuracy. In addition, some pioneering organizations in this area have found that clinicians typically do not provide data, such as height and weight, for these calculations when prompted at order entry.

- It is best to incorporate height and weight documentation within workflow steps before any medications are ordered. For example, gathering this information can be reinforced within nursing workflow at admission; prompts can be used if the data are not recorded at this time.
- For the pediatric patient, a current height and weight should be mandated when possible, since it is necessary for an accurate creatinine clearance calculation.
- When height and weight are not available during an ordering session for a drug that requires renal dosing, consider prompting for the data but giving physicians the option to not enter it. For cases in which gross approximations wouldn't present a potential safety hazard, you might have the system assume a default height and weight—say, 60 kg man; 50-55 kg woman. If you take this approach, consider notifying the prescriber that specific defaults, rather than actual parameters, have been used in generating the dosing recommendation. Alternatively, use a formula for which the missing data is not an element.
- Once you have the renal insufficiency level estimated by the creatinine clearance, the actual dosage adjustment may be determined from a commercial database obtained from a CDS vendor or through locally developed rules.

If your CIS (such as CPOE, pharmacy system) and/or CDS vendor is supplying drug safety rules and dosage adjustments as an integrated offering, the renal insufficiency calculation will typically be included within the package. Nonetheless, the considerations previously discussed regarding access to key patient data will still be important. For example,

if the vendor-supplied decision support uses a formula that requires a weight (such as Cockcroft-Gault), it is vital to have this information available for use by that CDS application.

It can be most desirable in CPOE to automatically detect when patients have renal insufficiency based on creatinine clearance and automatically provide recommended adjusted doses for ordered medications that are covered by the renal dosing rules you have deployed. That is, the displayed order sentences from which the prescriber selects should contain doses that have already been adjusted for that particular patient's renal function and have been noted as such. Querying the user whether they want the dose adjustment calculation, or only supplying it in response to a user request, may be less effective for ensuring that dosing is appropriate for kidney function.[36] Functionality to readily accomplish proactive dose recommendations may not be widely available, but with increasing attention to medication safety in health IT certification standards,[1] important capabilities such as this one will hopefully become more widespread.

If your CIS does not support the proactive approach described earlier, consider alerting as a safety net to notify the prescriber when the single or total daily dose of an ordered medication is excessive for the patient's kidney function. Such alerts should include options for the prescriber to easily modify the order so that the dose falls within the appropriate dose range (which should likewise be explicit in the alert).

See also Chapter 3, page 62, for a discussion and sample workflow map (Figure 3-4) addressing how renal function determination can be incorporated into workflow associated with a particular drug that requires renal dosing.

Medications Contraindicated in Renal Failure
For medications that should not be used in a patient whose estimated creatinine clearance is below the medication's minimum safe clearance, CDS interventions should help the prescriber substitute a more appropriate medication rather than recommending a dose adjustment. One study[37] showed a significant

Table 5-6: Safe Creatinine Clearance Levels for Specific Medications Used in a CDS Study

Safe Estimated Creatinine Clearance	Medications
> 10 mL/min	acetazolamide, ifosfamide, methotrexate, pancuronium, gold sodium thiomalate, spironolactone
> 30 mL/min	alendronate, choline magnesium salicylate, demeclocycline, diflofenac, ibuprofen, indomethacin, ketorolac, naproxen, salsalate, tolmetin
> 40 mL/min	sotalol
> 50 mL/min	chloral hydrate, chlorpropamide, metformin, nitrofurantoin, penicillamine, phenazopyridine, probenecid, ribavirin
> 80 mL/min	auronofin

Source: Galanter WL, Didomenico RJ, Polikaitis A. A trial of automated decision support alerts for contraindicated medications using computerized physician order entry. *J Am Med Inform Assoc.* 2005; 12(3):269-274. Used with permission.

decrease in the likelihood that the patient received a contraindicated medication by using alerts at order entry. The cut-off creatinine clearance ranges and medications used in that study are in Table 5-6 and represent a good starting data set for further consideration by your organization.

Patient Is on a Medication and Renal Function Is Changing

Even when patients are started on a medication that is dosed appropriately for their kidney function, further adjustments may be needed if this function changes over time (which is not rare in either inpatient and ambulatory settings for certain patient types). The following two scenarios are important to consider:

1. Medications that are toxic to the kidneys and may need to be discontinued when creatinine clearance worsens. Triggers that this may be an issue include a newly posted, increased serum creatinine result (which may indicate worsening creatinine clearance) together with data that the patient is taking a potentially offending drug. It can be helpful to measure both change from last posted creatinine and change from the patient's

known baseline. An alert can be used to notify responsible clinicians to consider discontinuing the nephrotoxic medication or adjusting its dose (see next point).

2. Drugs that need to be dose-adjusted based on worsening or improving renal function. You can use the same medication set covered by your rule that screens on order entry, but the trigger here is the changed creatinine clearance value rather than the ordered medication. This represents more advanced decision support that may not be widely available. Alternatively, you can create a list in pharmacy of all patients with changing renal function who are also receiving medications that either need to be dose adjusted or are contraindicated, given each patient's current kidney function.

One special circumstance to consider in deploying such CDS is patients with end-stage renal disease on dialysis. Patients may need decreased doses for many medications, but the changes in their serum creatinine level typically indicate a recent dialysis session rather than a change in kidney function requiring drug or dose changes. It is helpful to identify patients on dialysis and the method used (hemodialysis, peritoneal dialysis, or continuous arteriovenous hemofiltration) in your EMR, preferably in the problem list. This information can then be used in your renal function rules, for example, to ensure that the initial medication dose is appropriate for a dialysis patient. These same patients may be excluded from the rules that address changing renal function. Kidney function rules can also use this dialysis information, since some medications that are contraindicated due to kidney toxicity in patients with milder forms of renal dysfunction may be acceptable in patients on dialysis.

Ensuring Safe Dosing in Patients with Hepatic Impairment

Approximately 2.5 million people suffer from liver disease in the United States, roughly 1.4% of the population.[38] Although the liver plays an important role in processing certain drugs, dose adjustments for liver dysfunction are not as commonly made as renal-dose adjustments. Generally, clinicians consider clinical problems associated with chronic or acute liver disease, or look at liver function and other related tests, to assess the need for dosage adjustment or alternative medication selection. Prescribing recommendations may refer to more specific disorders such as hepatitis and cirrhosis when addressing patient dosing and cautions.

CDS to guide dosing in hepatic dysfunction is not as mature as that for renal dosing for a variety of reasons, including the less frequent need for such adjustment and the relatively scarce evidence to guide these modifications.

In relation to other targets, developing drug/disease CDS capabilities in your medication management program just for hepatic dose adjustments may not be a priority for your organization. Exceptions might include settings that treat many patients with acute and chronic liver disease (for example, a liver transplant center) or that have experienced a sentinel event in this area.

If you do want to address this issue in your medication CDS program, the Child-Pugh classification system for alcoholic cirrhosis and portal hypertension

Elderly Use Highlights

- Ensure appropriate initial dosing via suggestions based on age, or use an alert for out-of-range dosing.
- Use order sets and other upstream interventions, with alerts as a safety net, to prevent prescribing potentially inappropriate medications in elderly patients.
- When using an alert, make sure it describes the patient risk and allows alternative medications or dosing to be prescribed directly from the alert.
- Consider producing and addressing a periodic follow-up list of elderly patients on inappropriate medications as a complement or alternative approach to alerting.

is the clinical tool that is most often used to assess hepatic function in relation to medication dosage adjustments. Using package-insert review, pharmacists developed a list of 23 agents with specific dosage recommendations based on Child-Pugh scores.[39] This list may not be complete because pharmaceutical companies are only required to perform pharmacokinetic studies in liver disease when more than half of the drug is eliminated by the liver. However, this relatively small list is a good place to start.

Ensuring Safe Medication Use and Dosing in the Elderly Population

Due to physiologic and other changes that accompany aging, elderly patients often respond differently to medications. In addition, adverse drug effects have significant medical and safety consequences for older adults. As a result, certain drugs should not be used in this population or should be prescribed differently—such as with lower starting and maintenance doses.

CDS content vendors that supply commonly used knowledge bases to support drug interaction checking and the like, often provide age-based dosing guidelines as well. The recommendations in these sources tend to be conservative.

When using separate rule sets to support renal and age-based dosing, there are several potential ways to configure the system to respond when both a patient's age and kidney function trigger dose adjustment notifications. The system might use the most conservative recommended dose, usually the one based on renal function. Alternatively, it might display some notification flag along with the respective dosing recommendations and require the user to specify a dose based on this information. Another approach—when pertinent, solid clinical evidence is available—is to provide individual rules that address both age and renal function dimensions and present one appropriate dose or range. Close collaboration between the medication safety and CDS experts in your organization can be helpful in developing and executing a strategy for dealing with dosing CDS that addresses both age and kidney function, if this is a priority for your organization.

For drugs that should be avoided altogether in the elderly population, the Beers criteria and the Canadian criteria[40,41,42,43] are commonly referenced. In addition, warfarin, insulin, and digoxin are drugs commonly used in the elderly population and may require dose adjustment and careful monitoring. These drugs may cause many more ED visits in elderly patients than Beers criteria drugs.[44] Inappropriate medication use in older adults may be at least as problematic in inpatient as in outpatient settings[45] and a potentially important intervention target.[46]

The following are points to consider in developing CDS to avoid potentially inappropriate medication use in elderly patients.

- As always, consider alerts as a safety net, and try to use CDS delivered "upstream" to support correct prescribing decisions. For example, condition management information available at the medication selection stage—for example, via infobut-

tons—can offer guidance regarding appropriate drug selection and dosing in the elderly population. Similarly, order sets can include such imbedded or linked guidance.

- When alerts are used and triggered on order entry, they should suggest an appropriate alternative that can be directly ordered from the alert. Construct the alert so the "reason to avoid use" is prominent. For example, "Caution in older patients: Has a long half-life in the elderly, producing prolonged sedation and increasing the risk for falls and fractures. Alternative medications are preferred; [list of medications with option to order directly]."

- An alternative "downstream" method to alerts in the inpatient setting is producing a report listing patients who are receiving potentially contraindicated medications; this list can then be reviewed by pharmacists or a geriatrics consult service. Analogous reports, handled through appropriate channels, may be of value in outpatient settings as well.

A study examining CDS effects in reducing prescriptions for potentially contraindicated drugs in elderly outpatients found alerts to be effective.[47] The study focused on a relatively few contraindicated medications and offered an alternative medication in the alert, as listed in Table 5-7.

Although the alerts were not entirely successful in eliminating prescriptions for these medications in elderly patients, a trend toward decreased prescribing was evident. Because the Beers criteria list is extensive, it may be advisable to start with a few contraindicated drugs that are prescribed relatively frequently. This approach may make it easier to provide alternatives in the alert, which may have been a significant factor in the success of the study just discussed—that is, by making it easy for the prescriber to take the appropriate action.

Another study focusing on similar medications that may provide useful background for local efforts to decrease inappropriate drug prescribing in ambulatory elderly patients[48] showed modest reductions by using a computerized pharmacy alerting system

Table 5-7: Medications Triggering Alerts in Elderly Patients and Suggested Alternatives, in a CDS Study[47]

Medications Triggering Alerts	Suggested Alternatives
Long-acting Benzodiazepines Diazepam Flurazepam Triazolam Chlordiazepoxide	**Shorter acting Benzodiazepines** Oxazepam Temazepam
Tertiary Amine Tricyclic Antidepressants Imipramine Amitriptyline Doxepin	**Secondary Amine Tricyclic Antidepressants or others** Nortiptyline Desipramine Buspirone Trazadone Paroxetine

in conjunction with collaboration between physicians and pharmacists.

Ensuring Safe Dosing in Children and Neonates

Calculating neonatal and pediatric drug doses is typically based on patient weight. CPOE and pharmacy systems should therefore generally use a patient's most current available weight for this calculation. Once again, ensuring an accurate and recent weight is vital for this population.

As mentioned earlier, a key issue is rounding to a dispensable unit. This issue arises, for example, when the weight-based dose calculation suggests 72.31 mg, but medication is only available in 70 mg and 75 mg doses. One option is to create rounding rules to automatically adjust the dose and present the recommendation before the prescriber signs the order. Alternatively, rounding can be left to the prescriber, perhaps supported by links to pertinent reference information. As previously noted, a national initiative is underway to synthesize guidance on this issue that can be incorporated into CDS systems.[31]

The sidebar on the next page outlines a pioneering organization's experience with pediatric CPOE and CDS.

Neonates have additional factors that need to be considered for appropriate dosing CDS:

• Postnatal age and postmenstrual age: these parameters can directly drive CDS that calculates recommended doses or can be used to present pertinent options for the prescriber in a paper or electronic order set. Figure 5-1 on page 147 is an example of the latter.

• Birth weight versus current weight versus dry weight: the appropriate one to use may vary depending on the medication. It is ideal when all these weights are recorded, and the CDS rule can use the appropriate weight based on the drug; at the least, physicians should be able to select which weight to use in the calculation.

Ensuring Safe Drug Use in Pregnancy

Currently, CDS to support safe medication use in pregnant patients is typically based on the FDA categories for drug use in pregnancy, which indicate the

Experience with Pediatric Dosing CDS at Vanderbilt University

In 2004, faculty in the division of Biomedical Informatics at Vanderbilt University, Nashville, TN, published a prospective trial that involved pediatric patients admitted to the Pediatric Critical Care Unit in the tertiary-care children's hospital before and after CPOE implementation. The implementation resulted in significantly reduced medication prescribing errors and potential ADEs.[49]

Several years after implementing CPOE, Vanderbilt added patient-specific decision support, which included the following:

- Weight- and age-specific dosing information delivered during ordering
- Menu dose options provided in mg/kg or mg, depending upon weight of patient
- Calculations performed by the computer
- Only presenting to the prescriber intervals and doses appropriate for a particular patient
- Dose rounded to standardized values
- Dose check warnings provided for single doses

By adding patient-specific decision support to their basic CPOE, they were able to further reduce potential ADEs involving inappropriate medication dose or interval in a pediatric population.

availability and implications of research data concerning this use (see Table 5-8). As of this writing, though, FDA is considering major changes to how it presents medication risks associated with pregnancy and lactation.[50] CDS implementers addressing medication use in pregnancy should track these developments; yet another example of the essential role for careful attention to knowledge management, as addressed in Chapter 8. Outlined next are CDS recommendations based on the FDA categories in place as of this writing.

A useful starting point is to focus on pregnancy Category X drugs, for example, by considering how the CDS Five Rights can be used to ensure that women who are (or who could become) pregnant do not receive these medications. For certain medications, such as isotretinoin, the most proactive decision support is warranted because the consequences are so severe and the regulations surrounding dispensing are quite strict. Creative approaches to facilitate this alerting have been tried with success. For example, entering pregnancy or breast-feeding as "allergies" into the allergy field of pertinent CISs in order trigger alerts for Category X drugs; these "allergies" are then removed when the conditions no longer apply. Ideally, more standardized approaches for handling important information such as pregnancy and breastfeeding status will render such workarounds unnecessary.

The CDS Five Rights framework can also be used to make sure that information concerning Category A drugs is readily available when needed. For example, considering prescriber workflow for those who treat women who are (or could become) pregnant might suggest placing infobutton links at helpful places within CPOE or EMR applications to information about drugs that are safe to use in these patients. Likewise, you can consider when, where, and how to provide such women with access to information about Category A and X medications, as appropriate (for example, within their PHRs).

A difficulty that arises when considering proactive, interruptive, pregnancy-related CDS is clearly defining the patient subset for whom the medication

Figure 5-1: CDS for Neonatal Dosing

NEONATAL ANTIBIOTICS

Tobramycin

Select dose and frequency depending on postmenstrual age (PMA) and postnatal age (PNA)

Tobramycin 4 mg/kg every 24 hours
PMA greater than or equal to 35 weeks
PMA equals 30 to 34 weeks and PNA greater than 7 days
PMA less than or equal to 29 weeks and PNA greater than or equal to 29 days
☐ tobramycin (NEBCIN) neonatal injection   4 mg/kg, IV PIGGYBACK, EVERY 24 HOURS

> Inline guideline to assist with dosing at order entry

Tobramycin 4.5 mg/kg every 38 hours
PMA equals 30 to 34 weeks and PNA equals 0 to 7 days
PMA less than or equal to 29 weeks and PNA equals 8 to 28 days
☐ tobramycin (NEBCIN) neonatal injection   4.5 mg/kg, IV PIGGYBACK, EVERY 36 HOURS

Tobramycin 5 mg/kg every 48 hours
PMA less than or equal to 29 weeks and PNA equals 0 to 7 days
☐ tobramycin (NEBCIN) neonatal injection   5 mg/kg, IV PIGGYBACK, EVERY 48 HOURS

Source: Texas Health Resources, Arlington, TX. Used with permission.

Table 5-8: 2008 FDA Categories for Drug Use in Pregnancy

Category	Description
A	Adequate, well-controlled studies in pregnant women have not shown an increased risk of fetal abnormalities.
B	Animal studies have revealed no evidence of harm to the fetus; however, there are no adequate, well-controlled studies in pregnant women. *or* Animal studies have shown an adverse effect, but adequate, well-controlled studies in pregnant women have failed to demonstrate a risk to the fetus.
C	Animal studies have shown an adverse effect and there are no adequate, well-controlled studies in pregnant women. *or* No animal studies have been conducted and there are no adequate, well-controlled studies in pregnant women.
D	Studies—adequate, well-controlled, or observational—in pregnant women have demonstrated a risk to the fetus. However, the benefits of therapy may outweigh the potential risk.
X	Studies—adequate, well-controlled, or observational—in animals or pregnant women have demonstrated positive evidence of fetal abnormalities. The use of the product is contraindicated in women who are, or may become, pregnant.

Source: US Food and Drug Administration. *Pregnancy and the Drug Dilemma.* http://www.fda.gov/fdac/features/2001/301_preg.html#categories. Accessed 9/17/08.

alert is appropriate (such as those who are currently pregnant or will become so during a pertinent time interval). It might be ideal if all EMRs permitted (and clinical workflows supported) users in consistently and explicitly documenting critical variables such as whether a patient is known to be pregnant, might be pregnant, or is lactating. However, this is typically not the case.

One approach is to provide warnings for all women of child-bearing age when Category X drugs are used, though this may be associated with a very low signal-to-noise ratio depending on the population (for example, most alerts will fire for women who are not pregnant or won't be soon). As we've discussed, these situations can lead to prescribers routinely dismissing such alerts without due attention and may result in a critical contraindicated situation being overlooked despite an appropriate alert.

The situation can be improved somewhat by modifying the alert not to fire when hysterectomy or tubal ligation is in the problem list, though for this to be effective, these conditions must be faithfully documented in a coded fashion. Even so, false-positive alerting is likely to be frequent. An alerting strategy should first try to ensure that relevant data and knowledge flows prevent patients currently known to be pregnant from being prescribed, or from receiving, Category X drugs. Beyond that, a thoughtful strategy based on the CDS Five Rights that balances the potential harm from the drug, the patient population characteristic, the risks for "alert fatigue" from many false-positive alerts, and similar considerations, is prudent.

The considerations just discussed apply to both inpatient and ambulatory settings, but for inpatients, the time scale is short enough and the use of toxic medications frequent enough that every effort should be made (such as by nurse and/or physician) to carefully document pregnancy status on *all* female patients who potentially could be pregnant. This information may be added to assessment forms, pertinent display screens and the like and, as with other such data used for CDS, should be coded when possible.

Of course, one must consider the reliability of information obtained about pregnancy status or risk by patient report; for example, patients may be in early pregnancy stages and unaware. Therefore, pregnancy testing may be needed in some situations. In addition to its importance for medication prescribing, this information can also be highly important for services such as radiology and surgery. In the inpatient setting, it may be reasonable to consider some form of alerting (such as interruptive vs. non-interruptive) on *all* female patients who might be pregnant when drugs with the greatest risk for causing birth defects or fetal harm are ordered.[51]

Sampling the details from available studies[51] and reviews[29] on the topic can serve as a starting point for further exploration into opportunities and challenges using CDS for safer prescribing in pregnancy.

Ensuring That Patients Do Not Receive Contraindicated Medications

In preceding sections, we have discussed strategies for safely prescribing medications that should never be used for populations, such as elderly patients or those with renal disease. There are other situations in which medications are contraindicated, and similar considerations for preventing dangerous prescribing apply. For example, interruptive alerting that ideally is triggered by circumstances very specific to the contraindication can be a cornerstone but requires careful attention to gathering the pertinent clinical data. Strategies for delivering information about the contraindication that complement alerting, such as thoughtfully placed infobuttons and annotations to order sets, should be considered as well.

Besides pregnancy, age, and renal/hepatic function as previously discussed, lactation/breastfeeding is another relatively common condition for which certain drugs are inappropriate, and an intrusive alerting strategy is worth considering. Rarer examples that might warrant this type of attention include G6PD deficiency,[52] porphyria,[53] and drugs that lower seizure threshold in patients with a history of seizures.[54] But again, providing coded access to the CDS logic that the patient has these conditions can be problematic, so careful attention to ensuring that these data have been gathered and are available in the system is necessary. Once the data are available, commercial CDS knowledge bases or locally developed rules can supply the alerting logic and enable CISs to return pertinent warnings. Because the problems are much rarer, false-positive alerting may be less of a problem.

Eliminating Inappropriate Drug/ Therapeutic Duplication

Most commercial CDS applications with proactive alerting capabilities can trigger alerts on drug duplication or therapeutic duplication in both CPOE and pharmacy systems. Alerts are typically a primary method for delivering information to clinicians about potential duplications but can be problematic in this situation. The challenge, particularly with inpatients, is that many patients are on duplicate therapy intentionally, such as scenarios involving numerous post-op PRN anti-emetics or stool softener/laxatives. Also, when a patient is on two different doses of the same medication—such as metformin 500 mg with breakfast and 850 mg with dinner—there may be two separate orders entered, potentially resulting in a duplication alert even though the dual orders are intentional and appropriate.

Frequent alerts about situations that are not clinically important (to which false-positive duplication notifications contribute) can increase the risk that clinicians may ignore all alerts, including the important ones. Studies examining pharmacist interventions before and after CPOE activation with duplicate alert-checking software showed an increase in pharmacist interventions for inadvertent duplications.[55,56] Careful attention is needed to ensure that clinically important duplications are identified and appropriately addressed, while at the same time, minimizing false-positive alerting; some organizations disable duplicate checking to avoid false-positives.

Acetaminophen prescribing illustrated the challenges with duplication alerts—echoing issues and opportunities raised earlier about dose checking for PRN medications. This drug can be ordered by itself for pain or fever and is also used in combination with many drugs such as oxycodone, propoxyphene, and hydrocodone. A patient may have orders for acetaminophen PRN for mild pain and acetaminophen/hydrocodone 10 mg/325 mg PRN for moderate pain. This is a very common approach in the post-op/post-procedure population enabling therapy customized to specific patient needs. The nurse and the patient make the decision about which PRN drug to use at the point of administration (using the pain scale and previous patient experience). CDS rules may inappropriately flag these as duplicates, even though the orders are intentional and reasonable. Nonetheless, overdoses of acetaminophen can be highly toxic.

Approaches to consider for minimizing false-positive duplication alerts include:

- Only trigger alerts on new orders added to an existing list (do not alert on concomitant orders placed during one ordering session, such as a post-op order set, but *do* alert when those orders duplicate drugs already active for the patient).
- Focus alerting on select "high-risk" therapies such as anticoagulants, in which inadvertent therapeutic duplication between low-molecular-weight heparin (such as enoxaparin) and unfractionated heparin have led to deaths.[57]
- Consider flagging opioid duplication only when one of the agents is ordered "around-the-clock" instead of PRN or when one agent is added to a regimen that already contains another opioid. This is one approach to addressing the fact that, despite using alerts, errors with opioid duplications continue to occur (for example, as a result of alerts being ignored due to alert fatigue) and can lead to patient harm.
- Perform dose range checking at the administration phase. For example, explore the eMAR or bar-code system's ability to add up the dose administered for all the medications that contain acetaminophen and alert when the maximum 3 to 4 gram dose is approached within 24 hours.

- Consider using non-interruptive notifications in various workflow systems to help make clinicians (and possibly ambulatory patients) aware of potential duplications in a less intrusive fashion.

Optimizing Laboratory Monitoring and Follow-up

CDS interventions can help ensure that clinicians appropriately monitor and address laboratory studies that are related in important ways to particular medications. For example, they can verify that a patient is on an appropriate antibiotic based on laboratory evaluation of the bacteria responsible for the infection. When the organism and its antibiotic sensitivities are posted from the microbiology lab to a patient's record, a CDS rule can determine whether the organism causing the infection is susceptible to the antibiotics that the patient is taking. When this is not the case, a CDS rule can recommend switching to an appropriate antibiotic based on the culture results. This type of CDS intervention requires interfacing and communication between the laboratory system and the EMR and its rules engine. Although possibly complex to deploy (for example, because of the communication issues between systems and getting coded access to actionable, microbiology results), this type of intervention can potentially increase the speed with which adjustments to the regimen in critical situations are made and thereby improve care quality and outcomes.

Another opportunity for using CDS rules to monitor lab data is to identify, and help clinicians quickly and appropriately respond to, serum drug levels or other laboratory markers that may indicate a potential problem (such as an ADE or subtherapeutic drug level). This may be due to overdosing, underdosing, or other patient-specific factors affecting response to the medication. Anytime a "critical" lab result (such as one dangerously outside the normal range) is posted to the patient's record, and the patient is on a drug that could potentially be causing that critical value, an alert could be sent to both the physician and the pharmacist (redundancy in a critical alert is good in this case). Here are a few examples for which such monitoring and alerting may be appropriate:

- **Hypokalemia and Hyperkalemia:** The patient's illness and/or various medications can cause hyperkalemia or hypokalemia (elevated or low levels of serum potassium, respectively). Both conditions can be dangerous themselves and can also make toxic effects from other drugs much more serious. CDS rules can monitor for these conditions (as well as potentially offending or complicating drugs) and recommend a medication change; they can also provide the clinician with guidance on managing these potassium abnormalities.[58]

- **Metformin-induced Lactic Acidosis:** According to the boxed warning on the FDA labeling, metformin causes this potentially dangerous acid-base blood disturbance in approximately 0.03 cases/1,000 patient years with approximately 50% fatality (0.015 cases/1,000 years).[59] This is more common in patients with diabetes who also have renal disease and/or congestive heart failure (CHF), and are therefore are at greater risk for decreased blood supply to the body tissues. (A systematic review from several years ago[60] found, however, no increase in lactic acidosis in clinical trials with patients taking metformin under study conditions.) CDS can prospectively identify patients at risk for serious complications by identifying those with decreased renal function or CHF in the problem list. As noted in earlier discussions, an alternative to an interruptive alert presented to the inpatient prescriber is to prepare a printed or electronic report for pharmacy or care management staff listing patients who might be at risk for a serious ADE. This information can then be reviewed with the prescriber(s). Such a "batch" approach could be useful in non-urgent clinical situations such as the "CHF-metformin" scenario, but might not be appropriate for more urgent situations, such as one involving dangerous levels of hypokalemia.

Minimizing Problems with Medications Used in Radiologic Procedures

Intravenous agents used in radiologic procedures (for example, radiocontrast and MRI contrast) are treated for drug safety purposes as medications by The Joint Commission. You should likewise consider them in your efforts to use CDS for decreasing adverse drug reactions. The following are items to keep in mind in this regard:

- The risk of lactic acidosis (see previous discussion) is elevated in patients receiving metformin who undergo radiologic evaluation with iodinated contrast media. Consider triggering an alert about this risk in patients receiving metformin when a radiology study with contrast is placed in the CPOE system.

- Some patients with impaired renal function, or other risk factors, can undergo radiologic evaluation with iodinated contrast media more safely if they are premedicated with IV saline, sodium bicarbonate, or oral acetylceistine before the procedure. CDS can help identify these patients and support appropriate action. For example, options and recommendations for this premedication can be presented within an order set for a procedure with elevated risk from a large contrast volume, such as cardiac catheterization. Reference information, provided via infobuttons in pertinent CIS, can likewise provide helpful guidance on premedication. A "downstream" safety net approach might be an alert at order entry for those patients at higher risk for radiocontrast-induced kidney damage. This approach requires that the specific risk factors are clearly defined and the pertinent data are available in a format that can be processed as alert triggers.[61]

- Gadolinium-based contrast media used in some MRI studies have been associated with nephrogenic systemic fibrosis/nephrogenic fibrosing dermopathy (NSF/NFD), a rare multisystem fibrosing disorder that principally affects the skin but may affect other organs in patients with renal insufficiency. Several factors, including previous exposure to gadolinium-based contrast and degree of renal dysfunction, may increase a patient's risk for this disorder. CDS rules can be used to evaluate the risk factors present in the record and notify the ordering prescriber or radiologist about increased risk so that appropriate action can be taken.[62]

There are additional challenges and limitations to consider in deploying CDS to improve safe radiology agent use. First, radiocontrast should be addressed along with all nephrotoxic medications (see earlier sections on renal dosing). However, this may present a challenge to organizations that don't use ISs to manage these drugs in the same way as other medications.

For example, in some cases contrast may not be directly ordered through CPOE (that is, when the test itself is ordered), since the contrast type and volume may be decided by the radiologist and documented in a separate radiology IS. This system may not contain the patient's medication profile, which is needed for drug-interaction checking (such as between metformin and iodinated contrast). Similarly, applying CDS may be complicated because these special contrast media may not be dispensed through the pharmacy IS, and administration may not be documented on the eMAR, which makes it difficult to check interactions in those systems. For those wishing to use commercial drug interaction databases, it is necessary to ensure that interactions with these agents are covered. In addition, pertinent data about radiologic agents used, and relevant patient information, must be available to send to the database for checking.

These issues tie back to the discussion in Chapter 4, page 86, regarding the important role for cataloging available systems needed for CDS and the data interplay between them. A glance at that material in this context might be useful for applying CDS to this target, for which such data interplay can be a critical issue.

Minimizing Adverse Events Associated with Specific Drugs/Classes

Although errors and ADEs can arise when using any medication, there are relatively few specific drugs and drug classes that are most commonly associated with preventable patient harm in outpatient and inpatient settings.

The sidebar in Chapter 2, page 36, lists medications *used by outpatients* that were found in a systematic literature review to be most commonly associated with preventable hospital admissions; note that the top four categories were responsible for more than half of the preventable admissions.[63] The study further examined drug groups associated with ADEs and over-treatment, under-treatment, and patient adherence problems. Underlying causes for the admissions included problems with prescribing, monitoring, and patient adherence—all ripe candidates for CDS. Also in this sidebar, a table lists medications commonly causing preventable ADEs in the *inpatient setting* that were identified by a literature review.[64]

A UK workgroup examined the medications that are most commonly associated with patient harm according to these studies and considered underlying causes and support opportunities. The checkmarks in Table 5-9 indicate areas in which the workgroup suggested CDS rules and alerts could help improve medication safety. This grid can help inform your CDS efforts regarding these drug groups.

Although many CDS approaches described earlier in this and other chapters address considerations for safely using specific medications or drug classes, it may be useful to approach certain medication classes as a target for special focus. This is particularly true when you have evidence of patient harm from these agents—and/or PI initiatives focused on them—within your organization. The following suggestions for a few drug categories build on the recommendations in Table 5-9. They are not intended to comprehensively list categories or interventions, but rather provide ideas to further stimulate conversation with your team about possible approaches and implementation strategies for important drug

categories. As reiterated throughout this book, you should consider all points in the medication use process, as well as the CDS Five Rights, to fully harness CDS in preventing errors with these drugs from occurring or reaching the patient.

General CDS Strategies to Consider for "High Alert" Medications

- Create standard pathways that inform and remind prescribers about potential problems/errors, and guide them away from such problems.
- Identify patients at highest risk for known errors (for example, using surveillance and relevant data display).
- Use standard IV concentrations and doses.[65] (CDS rules and other interventions can help to ensure that only standard concentrations and doses can be ordered.)
- Support nursing during medication administration, for example, by emphasizing high-alert drugs in bold within the eMAR and by displaying administration information that spells out infusion instructions, a reminder to check lab value before administering, and the like.
- Set and use standard monitoring parameters. (CDS interventions such as corollary orders can support physicians in ordering appropriate follow-up specific to a medication.)
- Use protocols to administer reversal agents/antidotes. (CDS interventions such as order sets can help implement these protocols.)

Anticoagulants

The Joint Commission National Patient Safety Goal 3E requires organizations to "…reduce the likelihood of patient harm associated with use of anticoagulant therapy."[66] Table 5-10 contains suggestions for applying CDS at various points in the medication use process to several important drugs in this class; it can serve as a starting point for further consideration with your team.

The CDS Five Rights model, and recommendations throughout this guide and in Table 5-10, emphasize that effectively engaging patients in CDS

Table 5-9: Summary from a UK Workgroup of Suggested Alert Requirements for Specific Drug Groups

Drug group	Dosing problem							Patient characteristic	Renal failure		Co-morbidities		Monitoring problem		Interaction	Duration	Form/route of administration			Prophylaxis
	Dosing by Indication (1)	10-Fold dosing errors (2)	Default Dosing	Total daily Dosing	Frequency / administration rate	Therapeutic duplication / Ingredient doubling	Under dosing	Demographic (age / sex / ethnicity)	Renal Dosing (Creatinine)	Renal Dosing (eGFR) (3)	Disease Contraindication	Disease Contraindication by proxy (4)	Lab Interaction (initiation)	Lab Interaction (5) (continuation)	Drug-drug interaction	Rapid withdrawal	Brand not stated	Infusion preparation	Inappropriate route of administration	Not prescribing prophylactic medication
Antithrombotics																				
Aspirin (low dose)	✓	✓	✓		✓	✓							✓		✓					
Heparin & LMWH	✓	✓	✓	✓	✓			✓	✓	✓	✓		✓	✓	✓					
Warfarin		✓	✓	✓	✓				✓	✓	✓		✓	✓	✓					
Cardiovascular																				
Betablockers	✓		✓					✓	✓	✓	✓	✓	✓	✓	✓	✓				
Digoxin		✓		✓	✓			✓		✓	✓		✓	✓	✓					
Diuretics													✓	✓	✓					
IV / oral potassium				✓	✓	✓			✓	✓	✓		✓	✓	✓					
Endocrine																				
Corticosteroids	✓			✓		✓					✓					✓				✓
Insulin (sliding scale)			✓						✓	✓			✓	✓						
Oral antidiabetics						✓		✓	✓	✓	✓		✓		✓					
Central Nervous System																				
Lithium				✓			✓		✓	✓	✓		✓	✓			✓			
Opiates	✓	✓		✓		✓		✓			✓	✓								✓
Phenothiazines/ butyrophenones etc.							✓													
Phenytoin					✓		✓							✓	✓			✓		
Anti-inflammatories																				
Methotrexate					✓	✓			✓	✓	✓		✓	✓						
NSAIDs								✓	✓	✓	✓		✓	✓	✓			✓		
Anti-microbial agents																				
Aminoglycosides				✓	✓			✓	✓	✓	✓		✓	✓	✓					
Vancomycin			✓		✓				✓	✓	✓		✓	✓				✓		
Other																				
Vinca alkaloids																			✓	

Source: The University of Nottingham, Nottingham, UK. Used with permission.

Table 5-10: Examples of CDS Interventions to Enhance Safe Anticoagulant Use

Drug	Ordering	Dispensing	Administration	Education	Monitoring
Heparin	Order set, weight-based protocol, baseline platelets, trigger to include order for PTTs, alert upon entry of heparin for patients with history of Idiopathic Thrombocytopenic Purpura (ITP), duplicate therapy checks for low-molecular-weight heparin (LMWH) given in previous 12–24 hours	Standard concentration, bar-code verify before dispense	Smart pump with guardrails	Patient education and engagement materials to support their understanding of underlying condition and role for medication	Automatic ordering of PTT; PTT outside of range notifies nurse or physician; alert for falling platelets in patients on heparin
Low-molecular-weight heparins (enoxaparin, dalteparin)	Order set, weight-based and indication-based ordering, adjust initial dose in renal failure, prompt for appropriate DVT prophylaxis	Bar-code verify before dispense	Bar-code at point of care	Same as above; includes guidance on self-administration if patient going home	Dose changes necessary for worsening or improving renal function, patient education
Warfarin	Standardized protocols for initiation and maintenance, INR visible in ordering screen, alerts for the many important DDIs	Bar-code verify before dispense, all protocols and alerts seen by physician are reviewed by pharmacist	Bar-code at point of care, INR visible in eMAR, or elevated INR alert in bar code to prevent warfarin administration	Same as for heparin; emphasize details on self-monitoring interactions and bleeding	Alert notification for high INR, Pharmaco-surveillance for phytonadione as a reversal agent

efforts is important for optimizing outcomes. In the case of anticoagulants, for example, a recent study demonstrated that patients who reported that they had received medication instructions from a physician or nurse and a pharmacist had significantly fewer hospitalizations for warfarin-related bleeding than those who did not.[67]

Chemotherapy and Other Drug Classes
In addition to the medication classes described earlier, there are less frequently used drugs that have a high harm risk when used inappropriately. You can address some risks with the decision support approaches discussed in Chapter 4 and earlier in this chapter (for example, alerts, order sets, infobuttons,

etc., to minimize dosing errors and contraindications), while others will need specific attention based on the risk. The following are some examples:

Approaches for chemotherapy in general:

- Safe prescribing requires protocol template support. The full protocol is defaulted for daily and therapy dose, and the weight is plugged in for autocalculation. With the many standard and research chemotherapy regimens available, protocol templates are very important for safe dose ordering, checking, and administration.

- Protocols should include all appropriate pre-medications to avoid omissions that can lead to preventable adverse events.

- Protocol-specific dose alerts should be presented in both CPOE and the pharmacy system.

- Two nurse co-signature verification should be required on the eMAR.

Doxorubicin: provide CDS related to cumulative dose.

- Drug-induced cardiomyopathy and CHF incidence rises to unacceptably high levels when the cumulative dose of the drug exceeds 550 mg per square meter of BSA.[68] As discussed earlier in this chapter, CDS interventions can help track cumulative dose and notify clinicians about general and patient-specific dose-related toxicity risks.

Vincristine: provide CDS related to contraindicated route.

- The drug is fatal when given intrathecally.[69] CDS alerts and other interventions can be used to help prevent vincristine from ever being ordered or administered via a route other than intravenous.

Indomethacin and Neoprofen: provide CDS related to contraindications.

- These drugs are used to medically treat congenital heart defects, such as patent ductus arteriosus. They are contraindicated in neonates with thrombocytopenia or renal insufficiency; CDS interventions such as alerts can be used to detect these contraindications and notify clinicians when they are present. Reference information delivered via infobuttons and other routes may also be helpful.

Drotrecogin Alfa: provide CDS regarding numerous contraindications.

- This drug is contraindicated in the following instances: active internal bleeding, intracranial neoplasm or evidence of cerebral herniation or mass lesion, known hypersensitivity to drotrecogin alfa, recent hemorrhagic stroke (within three months), recent intracranial or intraspinal surgery, severe head trauma (within two months), presence of an epidural catheter, or trauma with an increased risk of life-threatening bleeding.[70] CDS can be used to detect these contraindications and notify clinicians when they are present; infobutton-delivered reference information may also be helpful.

Optimizing Medication Use Associated with Regulatory/Payment/Transparency-related Targets

As discussed in Chapter 2, healthcare providers face an increasing number of mandatory initiatives from external entities, such as payers and regulators. These often include improving and/or publicly reporting data related to medication use and outcomes as requirements for payment and accreditation. Such transparency and incentives are key components in the four cornerstones of value-driven healthcare that are being widely adopted by the public and private sectors.[71] There are robust opportunities to apply CDS to address these targets. The following are initial ideas to stimulate exploration by your team. This topic is so rich and important that the group that developed this guide has begun a follow-on initiative that delves much more deeply into best practices for applying CDS in this domain.

Ensure Appropriate Use of Venous Thromboembolism Chemoprophylaxis

VTE, which includes both PEs and DVTs, is a major cause of preventable morbidity and mortality. Although there are effective therapies for preventing VTE, and detailed European and North American consensus guidelines on applying these therapies, appropriate VTE prophylaxis remains underutilized.[72,73,74]

Following are CDS strategies for improving VTE prophylaxis use that have been reported in the literature. They might trigger ideas about approaches useful in your organization:

- CDS interventions are accessible via terminals located outside each operating room. After surgery, the clinician enters data describing the case and orders treatment. The computer critiques the plan based on guidelines, and the clinician is notified immediately if additional therapeutic suggestions apply.[75]

- The computer screens all patients at risk for VTE and identifies those who are not receiving appropriate prophylaxis. Computer-generated alerts are sent to the clinician responsible for that patient. The clinician can decide to override the alert or order appropriate prophylaxis directly from the alert screen.[72]

- The computer searches the patient database three times a day for patients about to undergo one of 224 surgical procedures identified as requiring VTE prophylaxis. A reminder (DVT) appears next to each eligible patient on both the online and printed operating room schedule. Surgical staff has modified work patterns to ensure that all designated patients receive appropriate anticoagulation or sequential compression devices (an effective non-drug approach to VTE prevention) prior to surgery.[76]

- CDS application calculates appropriate anticoagulant medication dosage based on the patient's body weight. If heparin infusion is discontinued, but the monitoring test specific to the infusion (PTT) is not, a warning message is displayed.[77]

Next we consider implementation factors to keep in mind as you develop CDS interventions to optimize VTE prophylaxis and outcomes in your organization.

Selecting high-risk patients to target for CDS interventions that increase appropriate VTE prophylaxis can be a complex process if these patients are not already flagged within your CIS. There are sev-

eral DVT risk-assessment tools readily available that can be applied to *all* patients at time of admission to identify these high-risk patients. For example, see the risk assessment tools listed in the Society of Hospital Medicine (SHM) VTE Resource Room.[78]

Some organizations make this DVT assessment a required task for nursing to complete at admission to the hospital. If these patients are high risk, the DVT assessment score can be saved to the patient profile. For example, Advocate Health Care has built a VTE prophylaxis alert to help ensure that nursing assesses all admitted patients for VTE risk. If the completed risk profile is positive, the alert requires the nurse to contact the physician for further VTE prophylaxis orders. When using such an approach, the clinician group responsible for conducting the risk assessment (for example, nursing) should receive appropriate training on the tool and workflow support for using it to ensure that the assessment is conducted consistently and appropriately.

Once the CIS contains information about patients at risk for VTE, it can be used to support CDS for ensuring that the physician is aware of this risk and responds accordingly. This notification can be accomplished through various workflows depending on the CIS infrastructure. In pre-CPOE environments, the nursing staff can communicate the elevated risk and recommendation to the physician—and perhaps take a verbal order for the prophylaxis. With EMRs and CPOE, order sets, relevant data display, alerts, infobuttons, and the like can help ensure that the prophylaxis is ordered as indicated (see Chapter 4).

For patients who are not high-risk on admission but require DVT prophylaxis at time of surgery, it is useful to imbed the prophylaxis orders within surgical order sets. If any DVT prophylaxis components are missing from a patient's orders, the system could display a reminder for the surgeon to include all the indicated elements. If prescribers decide not to provide any DVT prophylaxis, they may choose to do so and document the reason why within the alert (see Chapter 7, page 207, for discussion of alert override reasons).

Ultimately, with a fully integrated EMR using robust codified data, the CDS intervention could collect all the necessary information related to risk, perform the screen, and present appropriate prophylaxis interventions for ordering.[72] These recommendations ideally should be fully tuned to the specific patient, for example, by taking into consideration all pertinent risk factors, together with patient weight and lab parameters (such creatinine clearance), in suggesting specific medications and doses.

Note that SHM provides a very broad and deep online resource to support performance improvement around VTE prophylaxis; it contains a very helpful implementation guide, as well as ideas, references, and tools that could be useful in your efforts.[78] AHRQ has also published online a detailed guide for quality improvement around hospital-acquired VTE.[79] Various other Web-based resources might be worth reviewing as well. For example, the IHI Web site offers stories of organizations' efforts to improve in this area,[80] and the Illinois Hospital Association (IHA) has published online a quality improvement article on VTE prophylaxis and treatment in surgical patients.[81]

Make Sure Patients Are Receiving Drugs Indicated per National Quality Measures

There is increasing movement toward national consensus on healthcare quality measures pertinent to a variety of settings.[82] Organizations such as NQF play a leading role in developing this consensus,[83] and payers, regulators, and accrediting bodies (such as The Joint Commission[84] and CMS[85,86]) are using these measures as the basis for accreditation, pay-for-performance, and pay-for-reporting initiatives.

Many ambulatory and inpatient quality measures assess how often patients are given indicated medications for common and important conditions, such as acute myocardial infarction, heart failure, and pneumonia, as well as preventive medications, such as immunizations. The stakes can be high (accreditation, public perception of provider quality, reimbursement, etc.) so as we discussed in Chapter 2, these targets are a natural focus for CDS-supported improvements.

The approaches outlined throughout this chapter and Chapter 4 come into play here as well. To start, identify specific measures on which to focus your CDS efforts. These might include items covered in pay-for-performance programs and/or publicly reported measures for which there are substantial improvement opportunities in your organization. You can then explore CDS approaches to help prescribers comply with the measure. For example, consider opportunities to foster regular use of order sets for the pertinent conditions, with the drugs indicated by quality measures clearly called out—or perhaps "default checked" in CPOE or paper-based systems.

Immunizations, which can be administered in inpatient and outpatient settings, present important opportunities and challenges. For example, if vaccines have been administered and documented in the outpatient setting in an outpatient paper record or an EMR not linked to the inpatient EMR, an inpatient assessment is needed to determine vaccination status and eligibility. When nurses perform this assessment and document it online, systems can be set up to generate automatic vaccine orders based on committee-approved standing orders.[87,88]

Because all patients can benefit from seasonal influenza vaccination, nurses at Northwestern Memorial Hospital screen ALL patients for vaccination status on admission, with a rule generating the influenza vaccine based on the screening criteria. Similarly, all patients older than 65 years are screened for pneumococcal vaccination. This approach expands the number of patients receiving vaccinations to prevent disease and bypasses the need to prospectively identify the "appropriate population" based on the core measure requirements, which had been a particular challenge within the organization.

Partners HealthCare has a robust process for applying CDS to optimize performance on national performance measures; see Table 5-11 for a sampling of its approach to some specific core measures.

Figure 5-2 presents two screens from a PI CDS tool from Partners HealthCare. Such relevant data

Table 5-11: Sample Data Sources and Interventions to Support CDS for Specific Core Measures

Core Measures Description	Measurement Data Sources	Clinical Knowledge for Decision Support — Examples
Discharge instructions for congestive heart failure (CHF) patients	1. Discharge orders for review of medication list, recommended activity level, recommended diet, recommended weight monitoring, follow-up, and management of worsening symptoms 2. Documented tasks that the above items were reviewed 3. Audit trail that education materials, discharge instructions, medication list, etc. were printed is connected to above tasks as relevant	1. CHF discharge order set with orders for performing discharge tasks including medication list review, activity level review, follow-up appointment review, diet review, weight monitoring review, and management of worsening symptoms instructions 2. Discharge tasks that are populated by nursing care plan or orders to capture completion of the discharge tasks 3. Printable materials for education, medication list, etc. as HTML links associated with above tasks that log when materials were printed for a given patient
Evaluation of left ventricular systolic dysfunction (LVSD)	1. Admission, pathway, or discharge orders for echocardiogram 2. Intra-admission echocardiogram result posted to clinical data repository	1. Admission, pathway, or discharge orders for echocardiogram as component of CHF management order sets and pathways 2. Discharge clinical documentation checklist or task list that ensures cardiac echo is scheduled at discharge if not completed during admission 3. Decision support rules that check for the presence of completed echocardiogram during admission and post task to nursing discharge task list if not performed
Angiotensin converting enzyme inhibitor (ACEI) or Angiotensin II Receptor Blocker (ARB) for left ventricular systolic dysfunction	1. For ACEI, electronic medication administration record 2. For patient contraindications, clinical documentation, allergies, laboratory data, problem list 3. For LVSD, echo report has discrete field that indicates LVEF< 40%	1. Discharge order set with ACEI on discharge order if LVSD present 2. Rules that cause ACEI order to be defaulted if echo report or problem list include LVSD 3. Documentation template in echo report with coded field for EF < 40% 4. Documentation template for ACEI contraindication capture
Smoking cessation advice/counseling for CHF patients	1. Nursing and/or physician documentation template	1. Congestive heart failure admission order set containing smoking cessation counseling order 2. Documentation template for smoking cessation counseling

Source: Partners HealthCare System, Inc., Boston, MA. Used with permission.

Figure 5-2: Coronary Artery Disease Quality Dashboard Example

Screen A: Report on aggregate performance on quality measures for an individual physician

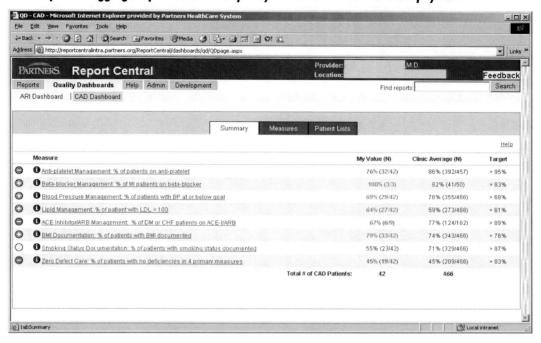

Screen B: Drill down to lists of this physician's patients that meet specific criteria (used to support further follow-up and intervention)

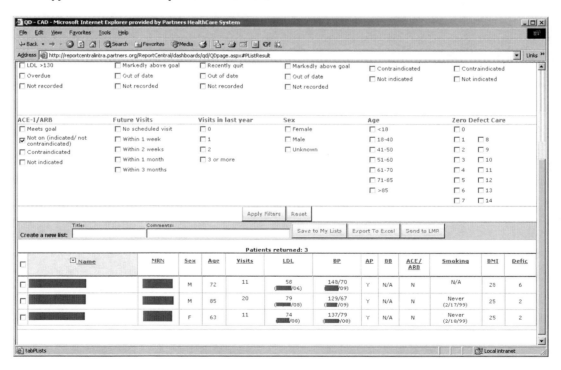

Source: Partners HealthCare System, Inc., Boston, MA. Used with permission.

display in the form of clinician dashboards can help highlight patients not receiving medications as indicated by core measures and foster corrective action.

In CPOE environments, to supplement dashboards such as those just illustrated, consider alerting the prescriber when indicated drugs are not prescribed at the close of the order session. These alerts should allow providers to indicate patient exclusions as appropriate (see sidebar on next page). Some such explicit documentation by the physician is required to ensure that patients ineligible for the intervention are not included in the measure denominator and therefore do not count against the organization in aggregate performance on the measure. Another way to document this information is to push the exclusion criteria data, which could be in the form of an alert override, to a physician note that is part of the physician documentation. Veterans Administration (VA) hospitals use this method.

Finally, it can be helpful to use documentation templates, prompts, and other tools to support physicians and other care team members in ensuring that data about the exclusion criteria for specific measures are added to other structured areas of the EMR, as appropriate. For example, if a beta-blocker indicated by a core measure for cardiac disease is not being used due to a contraindication based on the patient's asthma, the physician could be prompted to add this "contraindication" condition to the problem list if it is not already there (in addition to the documentation that this condition is the reason why the beta-blocker was not given).

Minimize Medication-related Contributions to Hospital-acquired Conditions

As of October 2008, Medicare is no longer reimbursing hospitals for the additional expenses associated with certain preventable hospital-acquired conditions (HACs).[89] The list of HACs addressed in such payment policies is growing, and other payers are following suit. A full description of these conditions and the related CDS possibilities is beyond the scope of this book, but a few opportunities are highlighted in the following sections. Note that the

DVT/PE following certain surgeries is on this HAC list, so earlier comments about using CDS for these conditions apply in this context as well.

Patient falls. Since falls may be associated with inappropriate medication use or monitoring (with sedatives, for example), it is important to consider CDS for minimizing these contributory factors. An initial step is identifying patients at increased risk for falls. Various fall risk assessment tools[90] can be used, in conjunction with information about drugs that may further increase this risk,[91] in planning a CDS approach. CDS interventions, such as infobuttons and documentation tools, can help ensure that clinicians are aware of these assessment tools and risks, and use them appropriately and efficiently. For example, they can assist in gathering risk data, performing the calculation, and providing information about appropriate interventions based on the score. Alerts (either interruptive or non-intrusive, depending on the risk) and relevant data display can be considered to help ensure that clinicians are aware of specific medications that may exacerbate high risk in a particular patient.

Healthcare-associated infections. These include surgical and catheter-associated infections, as well as infections with certain multidrug-resistant organisms. CDS can be useful in supporting appropriate antimicrobial selection and careful monitoring. For example, relevant data display can be used within surveillance systems to monitor patients at risk for certain infections (for example, due to their medications or underlying conditions) and help ensure that clinicians respond accordingly. In addition, relevant data display interventions can help track local infection patterns and antibiotic susceptibility profiles, which can be used in turn as input for CDS on empiric antibiotic selection. Putting the appropriate antibiotics into order sets, with the appropriate limit on post-op doses defaulted into the order sentence, can be very effective for promoting compliance with drug choice and duration for surgical prophylaxis. Similarly, rules and relevant data display to track patients with multidrug-resistant organisms can help ensure they receive appropriate

Addressing Contraindications to Prescribing Beta-blocker Therapy at THR

Texas Health Resources (THR) has deployed a successful approach to addressing contraindications to prescribing beta-blocker therapy for patients with heart failure.

The THR CDS strategy for drugs addressed by quality measures includes appropriate medication orders in the CPOE order set for the specific condition (for example, beta-blockers for heart failure; see Figure 5-3). The beta-blocker subsection within the order set is configured to require order selection as a forcing function; that is, at least one option must be selected. Included in this subsection is a non-medication order that can be selected to document the reason for not prescribing beta-blocker therapy. The prescriber is forced, therefore, to either select an indicated drug or the option that indicates that all the available drugs are contraindicated; see Figure 5-4. The specific contraindication(s) selected by the prescriber is then captured as documentation that justifies excluding the heart failure patient from the denominator of the pertinent indicator. To further support the prescriber in understanding and complying with the measure, the order set subsection is highlighted as being a "performance measure" and provides an evidence link for clinicians who are interested in accessing a synthesis of the supporting literature.

Figure 5-3: Beta-blockers Noted as a Performance Measure in a Heart Failure Order Set

Beta Blockers – PERFORMANCE MEASURE
Evidence Link

O SPECIFY REASON BETA BLOCKER NOT ORDERED
O carvedilol (COREG) tablet
O metoprolol XL (TOPROL XL) tablet
O . . .

Figure 5-4: Documenting Reason for Not Prescribing Beta-blocker Therapy with Order Set

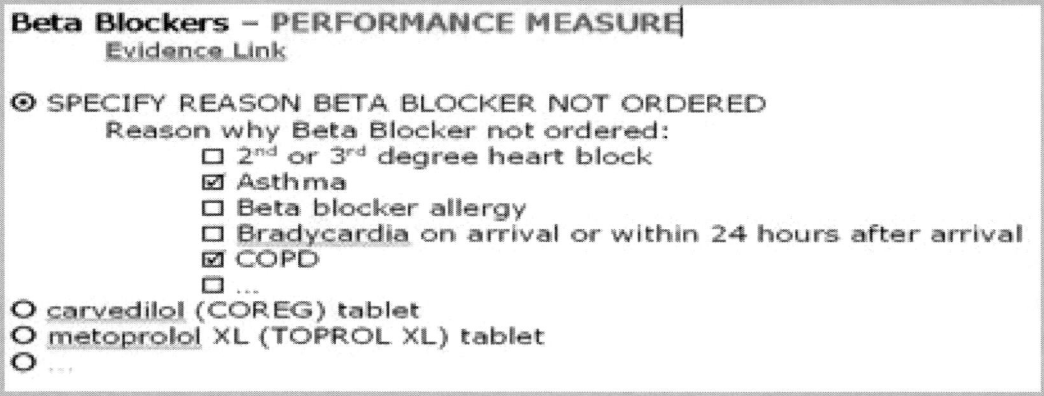

Beta Blockers – PERFORMANCE MEASURE
Evidence Link

⊙ SPECIFY REASON BETA BLOCKER NOT ORDERED
     Reason why Beta Blocker not ordered:
          ☐ 2nd or 3rd degree heart block
          ☑ Asthma
          ☐ Beta blocker allergy
          ☐ Bradycardia on arrival or within 24 hours after arrival
          ☑ COPD
          ☐ ...
O carvedilol (COREG) tablet
O metoprolol XL (TOPROL XL) tablet
O ...

Source: Texas Health Resources, Arlington, TX. Used with permission.

treatment and are managed with appropriate precautions against spreading the infection to others.

Never Events.[92] These refer to a list of conditions identified by NQF as serious reportable adverse events that are of major concern to stakeholders and that are potentially preventable. For some Never Events, CDS (including its focus on medication use) may play an important role in your organization's overall prevention strategy. For example, included in this list is "patient death or serious disability related to a medication error," so many targets and strategies addressed in this chapter contribute to this overall goal. Likewise, "patient death or serious disability associated with hypoglycemia, the onset of which occurs while the patient is being cared for in a healthcare facility" is another explicit Never Event that may be addressed with the strategies outlined in this chapter and in Chapter 4. For example, the approaches to ensure proper insulin dosing and use can reduce occurrence of this Never Event, since insulin overdoses are a primary cause for hypoglycemia.

Support Medication Reconciliation

A full discussion of the medication reconciliation requirements and strategies pertinent to The Joint Commission's National Patient Safety Goals[66] (see Goal 8) is outside the scope of this book, but there are several opportunities within a medication reconciliation program for CDS enhancement. The following list can serve as a starting point for your further consideration.

- Reference tools that help identify at admission the medications that a patient is taking as an outpatient (for example, based on pill characteristics, when the prescription bottles aren't available)

- Automated screening and reference information to help identify drug duplication, interactions, etc. during discharge reconciliation (see earlier in this chapter for details of CDS interventions to address these objectives)

- Triggers within the record to support efficient reconciliation documentation and validation at each hospital transition phase (admission, transfer, and discharge); in addition to triggers, the medication reconciliation system should have CDS functionality to track clinician reconciliation compliance at each step.

- CIS/CDS functionality that supports converting the "patient home medication list" to inpatient orders. The reverse should be supported at discharge, that is, converting inpatient orders to an updated "home medication list" and electronic discharge prescriptions. For example, home medications converted to a formulary medication for inpatient administration will require significant reconciliation efforts at discharge. Fully automated CDS that links these conversions to the inpatient setting and then again to the outpatient needs may not exist yet, but these conversions are vital for the transition at discharge. Consider relevant data display, reference information, and other CDS approaches to support the process.

- External transfer reconciliation is an important step in medication reconciliation and offers another opportunity for CDS. Your CDS approach should incorporate medication reconciliation records obtained from transferring hospitals. This helps ensure, for example, that a neonate does not get an extra dose or earlier dose of an antibiotic at the receiving hospital, because clinicians there didn't realize that the dose was given before transfer. If this cannot be done automatically, a warning alert for new babies being transferred can be triggered to ask, "Did the patient already receive this antibiotic from transferring hospital?"

Useful implementation suggestions for medication reconciliation in paper and electronic format are available as a toolkit[93] developed by Northwestern Memorial Hospital, with support from AHRQ.

WORKSHEETS

Worksheet 5-1

Intervention Specification Form

The guidance in this chapter, which builds on information in previous chapters, has hopefully prepared your organization to specify in detail how you will provide CDS interventions that address specific priority targets. The intervention specification form that follows can help document key intervention features. Such explicit documentation can guide developers and facilitate discussion with key stakeholders during the intervention development process. It also provides a useful record for reference and future enhancement efforts after it is finalized.

A separate specification form should be completed for each intervention you plan to build. In the following example, the specifications most pertinent for validation with stakeholders and development by technical staff have been divided into separate worksheets that illustrate how related versions of the form might look for these two purposes. Depending on your style, organizational needs, and specific interventions addressed, you can either combine these two forms into a single document for intervention validation and development for each intervention or keep them as separate forms.

The first several rows in the validation version carry data over from Worksheet 3-2, page 79, (such as intervention name, medication management objective, target action). This information provides context for intervention reviewers and developers. Baseline performance and desired outcomes for the interventions are drawn from Worksheet 2-3, page 56. The PI targets may have evolved in the vetting process up to this point, but now is the time when key stakeholders will sign off on delivering against these targets. It might not be practical to assign hard quantitative targets for every single intervention. Nonetheless, the more aggressive you are about defining and cultivating measurable benefits, the more likely you are to reap tangible and meaningful improvements from your efforts (see Chapter 7).

More than one intervention might be focused on achieving the target. These interdependencies can be noted in the fifth row in the worksheet "Associated interventions focused on objective."

The remaining items on this validation form reflect the various specifications that result from your dialog, analysis, and vetting of issues and questions outlined earlier in this and previous chapters. The items on the developer's specification form that follows also come from these explorations.

Checkbox	Intervention Feature	Details
Intervention name: Prescription allergy alert window		
Version for Intervention Validation		
❏	**Clinical medication management objective:**	Prevent prescription of medications to allergic patients
❏	**Target actions:**	Inform prescriber of patient's penicillin allergy at point of medication ordering
❏	**Baseline performance:**	3% of penicillin prescriptions are to patients allergic to penicillin

Worksheet 5-1 *continued*

Checkbox	Intervention Feature	Details
❑	**Desired outcome:**	0% of penicillin prescriptions are to patients allergic to penicillin
❑	**Associated interventions focused on objective:**	Educate staff on allergy incidence and prevention efforts; review/update organizational policies and workflows around documenting patient allergies with staff; training for all involved based on updates
❑	**Workflow step:**	Standard medication and allergy reconciliation procedure for each patient by medical staff
❑	**CDS intervention and pertinent CIS applications:**	Prescription allergy alert window
❑	**Approach:**	Proper initial medication and allergy list reconciliation; enter into CPOE system; alerts are triggered during medication order submission; prescriber must sign if choosing to proceed
❑	**Clinical background:**	Medication and allergy lists need to be updated and used by the CPOE system to check for allergies and DDI interactions; prescription errors in this regard are unacceptable
❑	**Selection criteria:**	Alert triggering rules will be determined by Clinical IT advisory committee
❑	**Exclusion criteria:**	Alert triggering rules will be determined by Clinical IT advisory committee
❑	**Target population for intervention:**	All patients
❑	**User interface:**	CPOE system
❑	**Monitoring:**	CPOE-user interaction reporting; in-house electronic adverse event reporting system
❑	**Evaluation:**	Quality improvement committee will work with adverse event reporting database of the hospital to track allergy related prescription errors; IT will assist with obtaining pertinent CPOE logs
❑	**Primary stakeholders:**	CQO, CMO, P&T Committee
❑	**Clinical champion for this project:**	James E. (CQO)

Worksheet 5-1 *continued*

Checkbox	Intervention Feature	Details
❏	Urgency/required delivery time:	Six months
❏	Jobs to be affected by this project:	Prescribers, nurses, IT database developers
❏	Adverse consequences of implementing this project:	Slow workflow down; inaccurate medication and allergy lists lead to improper false-positive or false negative alerting
Version for Developers		
❏	Description:	Trigger alert window in CPOE when the order is being submitted; requiring prescriber signature override for order to proceed
❏	CIS application affected:	CPOE
❏	Intervention type:	Triggered Alert window; interruption of order submission process
❏	Workflow step:	Medication ordering
❏	Intervention triggered by:	New medication order entered into CPOE triggers allergy check (using allergy databases as intermediary) to determine if this new medication can cause allergic reaction given patient's documented allergies
❏	Presentation type:	Alert window with proper warning text
❏	What (information presented):	Medication information and reason for the trigger; suggestion on alternative agent, and option to order
❏	Alerting:	Yes
❏	Who (user):	Prescriber
❏	Action items:	Prescriber must choose to terminate medication submission or proceed by stating a reason and signing it; alternative choices are suggested with option to order
❏	Feedback channels and plan:	Utilize existing communication mechanisms for medical staff and Clinical IT advisory committee; place CDS team e-mail address on alert. Will establish a subcommittee on alert management

Adapted from: Abookire SA, Teich JM, Bates DW. An institution-based process to ensure clinical software quality. *Proc AMIA Symp.* 1999:461-466.

Worksheet 5-2

FMEA Drill Down

This worksheet is intended to help with anticipating potential problem areas for the proposed CDS intervention(s) so they can be addressed prior to launch. It takes the user through a modified Failure Mode and Effects Analysis[94] that spans the medication-management process. This analysis should be conducted before the intervention specification (as in Worksheet 5-1) is complete, so that the final design addresses potential intervention failure modes.

Traditionally, the occurrence, detection, and severity score used in the analysis is a numerical value of 1–10, with 10 being the most frequent, less detectable, and harmful, respectively. A simplified version uses a three-point scale (1–3).

For severity, 1 = no patient harm, not a quality issue, 2 = NCC MERP Index A-D (error, no harm), 3 = NCC MERP Index E-I (harm). (See Chapter 1.)

For occurrence, 1 = limited # of patients, less than 25%, 2 = moderate # of patients, 25%–50%, 3 = affects almost all patients.

For detection, 1 = at time of occurrence, 2 = by memory or surveillance, 3 = by chance.

Typically, the scores are subjectively determined. Since in the intervention, "prescription allergy alert window" happens during ordering in the medication management cycle, we will focus on the five scenarios that would cause this intervention to fail (for example, when the medication that the patient is allergic to is ordered). RPN is the product of values across the three parameters. The failure mode with the highest RPN is likely to give the best return if the failure mode can be remedied. The scores can be revised once data are collected (for example, regarding actual alert override rates), providing a dynamic picture of priority opportunities to address potential intervention problems.

Medication Management Node	Failure Mode	Causes	Effects	Occurrence Score	Detection Score	Severity Score	RPN	Action
Medication-management objective: Prevent prescription of medications to allergic patients								
Intervention name and ID: Prescription allergy alert window								
Order	Wrong patient selected and alert window not triggered	Mis-clicked	Medication ordered	1	2	3	6	Verify correct patient identifier

Worksheet 5-2 *continued*

Medication Management Node	Failure Mode	Causes	Effects	Occurrence Score	Detection Score	Severity Score	RPN	Action
	Alert window not triggered	Penicillin allergy not known	Medication ordered	2	2	3	12	Ensure accurate updating of patient allergy list
	Alert window not triggered	Trigger rules not specific	Medication ordered	1	1	3	3	Revise trigger rules
	MD "clicked through" alert	MD in a hurry to order	Medication ordered	1	3	3	9	Place hard stops in ordering process that requires override signatures
	MD override alert	MD with inaccurate allergy information	Medication ordered	1	2	3	6	Ensure accurate updating of allergy list for patient
Dispensing	N/A	N/A	N/A					
	N/A	N/A	N/A					
Administration	N/A	N/A	N/A					
Education	N/A	N/A	N/A					
Monitoring	N/A	N/A	N/A					
Dx/Selection	N/A	N/A	N/A					

Worksheet 5-3

Intervention Approval Form

Having thoughtfully chosen CDS targets and developed and vetted specific interventions with key stake-holders, it can be useful to formally obtain "sign-off" from pertinent parties before proceeding to launch.

Worksheet 5-3 can be used to document your discussions with various stakeholders about the completed intervention specification forms. If you are seeking validation/approval for relatively few interventions (for a single corresponding objective), you can put them all on one form; otherwise it might be better to have a separate form covering interventions for each objective, or even for each individual intervention.

You can use this form to document all your validation discussions with the many different stakeholders to help track the various comments, or use it only to document final sign-off by the approvers. Similarly, you can record discussions and comments from individuals, committees, or both.

Clinical Medication Management Objective	Intervention Name and ID	Reviewer	Date Presented	Comment	Date Approved	Project Owner
Prevent prescription of medication to allergic patients	Prescription allergy alert window	John S. (chief of medical staff)	4/1/2008	Too many alerts — slows the MD down — would like to discuss possible changes to trigger rules	Pending discussion	Betty P. (CMIO)
		James E. (CQO)	4/2/2008	Need rapid implementation and measure outcomes	4/3/2008	
		Nathan W. (CMO)	4/2/2008	Proponent; eager for additional medication CDS for core measures	4/8/2008	
		Kari R. (CNO)	3/25/2008	Proponent	4/5/2008	

Worksheet 5-3 *continued*

Clinical Medication Management Objective	Intervention Name and ID	Reviewer	Date Presented	Comment	Date Approved	Project Owner
		John S. (chief of medical staff)	4/4/2008	Alerts appropriate now, alert management committee established for ongoing review	4/10/2008	

CONCLUDING COMMENTS

This chapter discusses CDS approaches for a broad range of specific medication-management targets. Despite the fact that medication CDS is receiving substantial energy and attention in local and national efforts, many gaps in research, CIS and CDS tools, and best implementation practices still exist. Available evidence comes from relatively few organizations that in many cases use homegrown CIS and/or CDS systems. As a result, many comments provided in this chapter are based on anecdotal experience and extrapolations or best guesses based on that experience.

Lack of standardized and optimized functionality in CIS and CDS systems—together with the relatively "early stage" knowledge about optimal CDS workflow—will be factors in successfully applying the guidance provided here. As previously noted, increasing attention to health IT certification standards, together with collaborative approaches to developing best implementation practices, should accelerate progress toward more useful tools and strategies.

Hopefully you have found useful information in this chapter for addressing specific organizational improvement priorities that you identified in Chapter 2. Work toward each target may start as a focused and time-limited implementation project, but in many cases it will (and should) evolve into an iterative improvement process. As technology and related workflows mature to become more seamlessly intertwined, richer information exchange between people and systems should give rise to fewer challenges and increasing CDS benefit.

In the next two chapters we discuss, respectively, how to successfully launch the interventions you have developed and measure—and continually improve—their results.

REFERENCES

1   Certification Commission for Healthcare Information Technology. CCHIT Home Page. http://cchit.org/, accessed 9/17/08.

2   Wolfstadt JI, Gurwitz JH, Field TS, et al. The effect of computerized physician order entry with clinical decision support on the rates of adverse drug events: a systematic review. *J Gen Intern Med.* 2008; 23(4):451-458.

3   The Joint Commission. *The Official "Do Not Use" List.* http://www.jointcommission.org/PatientSafety/ DoNotUseList/, accessed 10/3/08.

4   Institute for Safe Medication Practices. *ISMP's List of Confused Drug Names.* http://www.ismp.org/Tools/ confuseddrugnames.pdf, accessed 10/3/08.

5   U.S. Pharmacopeia. *U.S. Pharmacopeia 8th Annual MEDMARX Report Indicates Look-alike/Sound-alike Drugs Lead to Thousands of Medication Errors Nationwide.* http://vocuspr.vocus.com/vocuspr30/Newsroom/Query. aspx?SiteName=uspharm&Entity=PRAsset&SF_PRAsset_ PRAssetID_EQ=105435&XSL=PressRelease&Cache=), accessed 10/3/08.

6   U.S. Pharmacopeia. *Findings of Look-alike and/or Sound-alike Drug Errors.* http://www.usp.org/hqi/similarProducts/ choosy.html, accessed 10/8/08.

7   Lambert BL. Predicting look-alike and sound-alike medication errors. *Am J Health Syst Pharm.* 1997; 54(10):1161-1171.

8   The Joint Commission. *National Patient Safety Goal 3C.* http://www.jointcommission.org/NR/rdonlyres/ C92AAB3F-A9BD-431C-8628-11DD2D1D53CC/0/ LASA.pdf, accessed 10/3/08.

9   U.S. Food and Drug Administration, Center for Drug Evaluation and Research. Medication Errors. *Name Differentiation Project.* http://www.fda.gov/cder/drug/ MedErrors/nameDiff.htm, asscessed 12/13/08.

10   Lambert BL, Chang KY, Lin SJ. Effect of orthographic and phonological similarity on false recognition of drug names. *Soc Sci Med.* 2001; 52(12):1843-57.

11   Lambert BL, Chang KY, Lin SJ. Immediate free recall of drug names: effects of similarity and availability. *Am J Health Syst Pharm.* 2003; 60(2):156-68.

12   Institute for Safe Medication Practices. *Use of Tall Man Letters is Gaining Wide Acceptance.* http://www.ismp.org/ Newsletters/acutecare/articles/20080731.asp. 31 July 2008.

13   Institute for Safe Medication Practices. *Progress with Preventing Name Confusion Errors.* http://www.ismp.org/ Newsletters/acutecare/articles/20070809.asp, accessed 9/17/08.

14   U.S. Pharmacist. *Principles of a Sound Drug Formulary System.* http://www.uspharmacist.com/oldformat.asp?url= newlook/files/Feat/sound.html&pub_id=8&article_id=652, accessed 10/3/08.

15   Teich JM, Merchia PR, Schmiz JL, et al. Effects of computerized physician order entry on prescribing practices. *Arch Intern Med.* 2000; 160(18):2741-2747.

16   Bates DW, Kuperman GJ, Wang S, et al. Ten commandments for effective clinical decision support: making the practice of evidence-based medicine a reality. *J Am Med Inform Assoc.* 2003; 10(6):523-530.

17   Bates DW, Cullen DJ, Laird N, et al. Incidence of adverse drug events and potential adverse drug events. Implications for prevention. ADE Prevention Study Group. *JAMA.* 1995; 274(1):29-34.

18   Kuperman GJ, Gandhi TK, Bates DW. Effective drug-allergy checking: methodological and operational issues. *J Biomed Inform.* 2003; 36(1-2):70-79.

19   Hsieh TC, Kuperman GJ, Jaggi T, et al. Characteristics and consequences of drug allergy alert overrides in a computerized physician order entry system. *J Am Med Inform Assoc.* 2004; 11(6):482-491.

20   Weingart SN, Toth M, Sands DZ, et al. Physicians' decisions to override computerized drug alerts in primary care. *Arch Intern Med.* 2003; 163(21):2625-2631.

21   See, for example, the Certification Commission for Healthcare Information Technology (CCHIT) certification requirements for this functionality in its inpatient system test scripts: www.cchit.org/files/certification/08/Inpatient/ CCHITTestScriptENTERPRISE08FINAL.pdf, accessed 10/3/08.

22   See, for example, the Healthcare Information Technology Standards Panel (HITSP) medication management interoperability specification: http://www.hitsp.org/ConstructSet_ Details.aspx?&PrefixAlpha=1&PrefixNumeric=07, accessed 10/3/08.

23   U.S. Food and Drug Administration. The National Drug Code Directory. http://www.fda.gov/cder/ndc/. 03 Sep 2008.

24   Ko Y, Abarca J, Malone DC, et al. Practitioners' views on computerized drug-drug interaction alerts in the VA system. *J Am Med Inform Assoc.* 2007 Jan-Feb; 14(1):56-64.

25   American Health Information Community. *AHIC April 2008 Meeting: Clinical Decision Support Recommendation Letter.* http://www.hhs.gov/healthit/documents/ m20080422/6.2_cds_recs.html. 22 Apr 2008.

26 Malone DC, Abarca J, Hansten PD. Identification of serious drug-drug interactions: results of the partnership to prevent drug-drug interactions. *J Am Pharm Assoc.* 2004; 44(2):142-151.

27 U.S. Food and Drug Administration. *Preventable Adverse Drug Reactions: A Focus on Drug Interactions.* http://www.fda.gov/CDER/DRUG/drugReactions/default.htm. 31 July 2002.

28 Lesar TS, Briceland LL, Delcoure K, et al. Medication prescribing errors in a teaching hospital. *JAMA.* 1990; 263(17):2329-2334.

29 Kuperman GJ, Bobb A, Payne TH, et al. Medication-related clinical decision support in computerized provider order entry systems: a review. *J Am Med Inform Assoc.* 2007; 14(1):29-40.

30 Avery AJ, Howard R, Barber N, Bates DW, Coleman J, Fernando B, Ferner R, Jacklin A. Report for NHS Connecting for Health on the production of a draft design specification for NHS IT systems aimed at reducing risk of harm to patients from medications (2006). Report available at: http://www.connectingforhealth.nhs.uk/systemsandservices/eprescribing/news/averyreport.pdf, accessed 12/12/08

31 Vanderbilt University Medical Center. *STEPSTools.* http://www.pedstep.org. 04 Oct 2007.

32 Coresh J, Wei GL, McQuillan G, et al. Prevalence of high blood pressure and elevated serum creatinine level in the United States: findings from the third National Health and Nutrition Examination Survey (1988-1994). *Arch Intern Med.* 2001; 161(9):1207-1216.

33 Brier ME, Aronoff GR, eds. *Drug Prescribing in Renal Failure, 5th ed.* Philadelphia: ACP Press; 2007.

34 Munar MY, Singh H. Drug dosing adjustments in patients with chronic kidney disease. *Am Fam Physician.* 2007; 75(10):1487-1496. http://www.aafp.org/afp/20070515/1487.html, accessed 10/3/08.

35 National Kidney Foundation. *GFR.* http://www.kidney.org/professionals/KLS/gfr.cfm, accessed 10/3/08.

36 Chertow GM, Lee J, Kuperman GJ, et al. Guided medication dosing for inpatients with renal insufficiency. *JAMA.* 2001; 286(22):2839-2844.

37 Galanter WL, Didomenico RJ, Polikaitis A. A trial of automated decision support alerts for contraindicated medications using computerized physician order entry. *J Am Med Inform Assoc.* 2005; 12(3):269-274.

38 Pleis JR, Lethbridge-Cejku M. Summary health statistics for U.S. adults: National Health Interview Survey, 2006. *Vital Health Stat 10.* 2007; (235):1-153.

39 Spray JW, Willett K, Chase D, et al. Dosage adjustment for hepatic dysfunction based on Child-Pugh scores. *Am J Health Syst Pharm.* 2007; 64(7):690-693.

40 Beers MH, Ouslander JG, Rollingher I, et al. Explicit criteria for determining inappropriate medication use in nursing home residents. UCLA Division of Geriatric Medicine. *Arch Intern Med.* 1991; 151(9):1825-1832.

41 Beers MH. Explicit criteria for determining potentially inappropriate medication use by the elderly. An update. *Arch Intern Med.* 1997; 157(14):1531-1536.

42 McLeod PJ, Huang AR, Tamblyn RM, et al. Defining inappropriate practices in prescribing for elderly people: a national consensus panel. *CMAJ.* 1997; 156(3):385-391.

43 Fick DM, Cooper JW, Wade WE, et al. Updating the Beers criteria for potentially inappropriate medication use in older adults: results of a U.S. consensus panel of experts. *Arch Intern Med.* 2003; 163(22):2716-2724.

44 Budnitz DS, Shehab N, Kegler SR, et al. Medication use leading to emergency department visits for adverse drug events in older adults. *Ann Intern Med.* 2007 Dec 4; 147(11):755-765.

45 Rothberg MB, Pekow PS, Liu F, et al. Potentially inappropriate medication use in hospitalized elders. *J Hosp Med.* 2008; 3(2):91-102.

46 Budnitz DS. Inappropriate medication use in hospitalized older adults—is it time for interventions? *J Hosp Med.* 2008; 3 (2):87-90.

47 Smith DH, Perrin N, Feldstein A, et al. The impact of prescribing safety alerts for elderly persons in an electronic medical record: an interrupted time series evaluation. *Arch Intern Med.* 2006; 166(10):1098-1104.

48 Raebel MA, Charles J, Dugan J, et al. Randomized trial to improve prescribing safety in ambulatory elderly patients. *J Am Geriatr Soc.* 2007; 55(7):977-985.

49 Potts AL, Barr FE, Gregory DF, et al. Computerized physician order entry and medication errors in a pediatric critical care unit. *Pediatrics.* 2004; 113(1 Pt 1):59-63.

50 U.S. Food and Drug Administration. *Pregnancy and Lactation Labeling.* http://www.fda.gov/cder/regulatory/pregnancy_labeling/default.htm . Updated 11 Jun 2008.

51 Raebel MA, Carroll NM, Kelleher JA, et al. Randomized trial to improve prescribing safety during pregnancy. *J Am Med Inform Assoc.* 2007; 14(4):440-450. Epub 2007 Apr 25.

52 For more information about this condition, see Associazione Italiana Favismo—Deficit Di G6PD. *What is G6PD Deficiency (and its severe case called Favism).* http://www.g6pd.org/favism/english/index.mv?pgid=intro, accessed 10/3/08.

53 For information about drugs that are safe and unsafe in patients with porphyria, see American Porphyria Foundation. *Porphyria Overview.* http://www .porphyriafoundation.com/about_por/overview/overview03. html, accessed 10/3/08.

54 For information on some drugs that may lower seizure threshold, see Epilepsy.com/Professionals. *Drugs That May Lower Seizure Threshold.* http://professionals.epilepsy.com/ page/table_seniors_drugs.html, accessed 10/3/08.

55 Fair MA, Pane F. Pharmacist interventions in electronic drug orders entered by prescribers. *Am J Health Syst Pharm.* 2004; 61(12):1286-1288.

56 Senholzi C, Gottlieb J. Pharmacist interventions after implementation of computerized prescriber order entry. *Am J Health Syst Pharm.* 2003; 60(18):1880-1882.

57 The Institute for Safe Medication Practices. *Hazard Alert! Action Needed to Avert Fatal Errors from Concomitant Use of Heparin Products.* http://www.ismp.org/hazardalerts/ HeparinAlert.asp, accessed 10/3/08.

58 Galanter WL, Polikaitis A, Di Domenico RJ. A trial of automated safety alerts for inpatient digoxin use with computerized physician order entry. *J Am Med Inform Assoc.* 2004; 11(4):270-277.

59 U.S. National Library of Medicine. Daily Med – Current Medication Information. See FDA prescribing information for metformin on NLM DailyMed Web site: http:// dailymed.nlm.nih.gov/dailymed/drugInfo.cfm?id=1173. Revised Apr 2006.

60 The Cochrane Collaboration. Risk of Fatal and Nonfatal Lactic Acidosis with Metformin Use in Type 2 Diabetes Mellitus. http://www.cochrane.org/reviews/en/ab002967 .html. Updated 16 Nov 2006.

61 Goldenberg I, Matetzky S. Nephropathy induced by contrast media: pathogenesis, risk factors and preventive strategies. *CMAJ.* 2005; 172(11):1461-1471.

62 Broome DR, Girguis MS, Baron PW, et al. Gadodiamide-associated nephrogenic systemic fibrosis: why radiologists should be concerned. *AJR Am J Roentgenol.* 2007; 188(2):586-592.

63 Howard RL, Avery AJ, Slavenburg S, et al. Which drugs cause preventable admissions to hospital? A systematic review. *Br J Clin Pharmacol.* 2007; 63(2):136-147.

64 Kanjanarat P, Winterstein AG, Johns TE, et al. Nature of preventable adverse drug events in hospitals: a literature review. *Am J Health Syst Pharm.* 2003; 60(17):1750-1759.

65 See for example, San Diego Patient Safety Consortium. *Safe Administration of High-Risk IV Medications, Intra- and Inter-Hospital Standardization: Drug Concentrations and Dosage Units—How-to Guide.* http://www.chca.com/mm/ pdf/Appendix%20D%20-%20San%20Diego%20Patient% 20Safety%20Consortium.pdf, accessed 10/3/08.

66 The Joint Commission. *National Patient Safety Goals.* http://www.jointcommission.org/PatientSafety/ NationalPatientSafetyGoals/08_hap_npsgs.htm, accessed 10/3/08.

67 Metlay JP, Hennessy S, Localio AR, et al. Patient reported receipt of medication instructions for warfarin is associated with reduced risk of serious bleeding events. *J Gen Intern Med.* 2008; 23(10):1589-1594.

68 Singal PK, Iliskovic N. Doxorubicin-induced cardiomyopathy. *N Engl J Med.* 1998; 339(13):900-905.

69 U.S. National Library of Medicine. Daily Med – Current Medication Information. See FDA prescribing information for vincristine on NLM DailyMed Web site: http:// dailymed.nlm.nih.gov/dailymed/drugInfo.cfm?id=6735, accessed 12/14/08.

70 Contraindications and warnings in product label, *Drotrecogin alfa (activated).* http://www.fda.gov/cder/foi/ label/2001/droteli112101LB.pdf, accessed 12/14/08.

71 See 23 Aug 2007 HHS press release on progress regarding executive order on four cornerstones of healthcare performance improvement: U.S. Department of Health & Human Services. *Executive Order is Helping "Change the Culture" in Health Care to Achieve Better Quality, Value, and Affordability.* http://www.hhs.gov/news/press/2007pres/08/ 20070823a.html, accessed 12/14/08.

72 Kucher N, Koo S, Quiroz R, et al. Electronic alerts to prevent venous thromboembolism among hospitalized patients. *N Engl J Med.* 2005; 352(10):969-977.

73 Havig O. Deep vein thrombosis and pulmonary embolism. An autopsy study with multiple regression analysis of possible risk factors. *Acta Chir Scand Suppl.* 1977; 478:1-120.

74 Cohen AT, Tapson VF, Bergmann JF, et al. Venous thromboembolism risk and prophylaxis in the acute hospital care setting (ENDORSE study): a multinational cross-sectional study. *Lancet.* 2008; 371(9610):387-394.

75 Durieux P, Nizard R, Ravaud P, et al. A clinical decision support system for prevention of venous thromboembolism: effect on physician behavior. *JAMA.* 2000 Jun 7;283(21):2816-21.

76 Mosen D, Elliott CG, Egger MJ, et al. The effect of a computerized reminder system on the prevention of postoperative venous thromboembolism. *Chest.* 2004; 125(5):1635-1641.

77 Starmer JM, Talbert DA, Miller RA. Experience using a programmable rules engine to implement a complex medical protocol during order entry. *Proc AMIA Symp.* 2000:829-832.

78 Society of Hospital Medicine. *Venous Thromboembolism Resource Room* http://www.hospitalmedicine.org/ ResourceRoomRedesign/RR_VTE/VTE_Home.cfm; see also page in Resource Room on Risk Assessment: http:// www.hospitalmedicine.org/ResourceRoomRedesign/ RR_VTE/html_VTE/12ClinicalTools/06_Risk.cfm, accessed 10/3/08.

79 AHRQ. Preventing Hospital-Acquired Venous Thromboembolism; A Guide for Effective Quality Improvement http://www.ahrq.gov/qual/vtguide/. Aug 2008, accessesd 12/14/08.

80 Institute for Healthcare Improvement. *SCIP: Best Safety Practices to Prevent Post Operation Myocardial Infarction and Venous Thromboembolism.* http://www.ihi.org/IHI/Topics/ PatientSafety/SafetyGeneral/ImprovementStories/ SCIPBestSafetyPracticestoPreventPostOperation MyocardialInfarctionandVenousThromboembolism.htm, accessed 10/3/08.

81 Illinois Hospital Association. *Venous Thromboembolism Prophylaxis and Treatment for Surgical Patients—Achieving the Standard of Care.* http://www.ihatoday.org/issues/ quality/venous.pdf. 19 Jan 2007, accessesd 12/14/08.

82 Quality Measures Management Information System. *Measure Care Setting.* https://www.qualitynet.org/qmis/ browseMeasuresMore.htm?id=20, accessed 10/3/08. For more information about this CMS initiative, see https:// www.qualitynet.org/qmis/about.jsp, accessed 10/3/08.

83 See National Quality Forum. *NQF National Priorities Partnership.* http://www.qualityforum.org/about/NPP/, accessed 10/3/08.

84 The Joint Commission. *Facts about ORYX ® for Hospitals, Core Measures and Hospital Core Measures.* http://www. jointcommission.org/AccreditationPrograms/Hospitals/ ORYX/oryx_facts.htm, accessed 10/3/08.

85 CMS/Centers for Medicare & Medicaid Services. *Overview.* http://www.cms.hhs.gov/pqri/. Updated 16 Sept 2008, accessed 12/14/08.

86 CMS/Centers for Medicare & Medicaid Services. *Hospital Compare.* http://www.cms.hhs.gov/ HospitalQualityInits/11_HospitalCompare.asp#TopOfPage. Updated 01 Oct 2008, accessed 12/14/08.

87 Dexter PR, Perkins SM, Maharry KS, et al. Inpatient computer-based standing orders vs physician reminders to increase influenza and pneumococcal vaccination rates: a randomized trial. *JAMA.* 2004; 292(19):2366-2371. http:// jama.ama-assn.org/cgi/content/abstract/292/19/2366, accessed 10/3/08.

88 Tavakoli F. Using work flow analysis and technology assessment to improve performance on quality measures. *Jt Comm J Qual Patient Saf.* 2008; 34(5):297-303, 245.

89 CMS/Centers for Medicare & Medicaid Services. *Hospital-Acquired Conditions (HAC) in Acute Inpatient Prospective Payment System (IPPS) Hospitals.* http://www.cms.hhs.gov/ HospitalAcqCond/Downloads/hac_fact_sheet.pdf, accessed 10/3/08.

90 Minnesota Falls Prevention Initiative. *Keep Minnesotans Right Side Up.* http://www.mnfallsprevention.org/ professional/assessmenttools.html, accessed 9/17/08.

91 See research results on drugs that are associated with falls, such as a recent report from University of North Carolina researchers. *Some Drugs Increase Risk of Falling: UNC Researchers.* http://uncnews.unc.edu/news/health-and-medicine/some-drugs-increase-risk-of-falling-unc-researchers.html. 09 July 2008, accessed 12/14/08.

92 CMS/Centers for Medicare & Medicaid Services. *Details for: Incorporating Selected National Quality Forum and Never Events into Medicare's List of Hospital-Acquired Conditions.* http://www.cms.hhs.gov/apps/media/press/factsheet .asp?Counter=3043. 14 Apr 2007. See also subsequent update, *CMS Improves Patient Safety for Medicare and Medicaid by Addressing Never Events.* http://www.cms.hhs .gov/apps/media/press/factsheet.asp?Counter=3224. 04 Aug 2008.

93 Northwestern Memorial Hospital. *Medications at Transitions and Clinical Handoffs (MATCH) Initiative.* http://www .medrec.nmh.org, accessed 10/3/08.

94 See, for example, FMEA information and tools on the IHI Web site. *Institute for Healthcare Improvement. Failure Mode and Effects Analysis Tool.* http://www.ihi.org/ihi/workspace/ tools/fmea/, accessed 10/3/08.

Chapter 6

Deploy CDS Interventions to Optimize Acceptance and Value

TASKS

- Approach deployment with the end goal in mind, and maintain persistent focus on the desired outcomes and expected benefits; the CDS interventions are a means to these ends, not ends in themselves.
- Attend carefully and fully to change management issues.
- Test interventions within workflow prior to go-live with at least the typical end users and workflows; consider all pertinent intervention recipients (for example, various clinicians and/or patients). Be prepared to receive feedback from testers and to address the input as appropriate, either before go-live or in post-launch refinement.
- Give careful thought to the rollout plan; ensure that launch details are well-communicated, end-user champions are fully utilized, users are appropriately trained and supported, and ample mechanisms for user feedback with timely responses are in place.
- Be vigilant after rollout for signs that the interventions (especially intrusive alerting) might be alienating users, and respond accordingly.

KEY LESSONS

- Deploying CDS is done *with* clinicians and other end users—not *to* them. Make them partners in ensuring that anticipated benefits (including the ones they are supposed to directly experience) are realized.

- Change-management issues are critically important. Organizations and end users have a limited capacity to effectively absorb change, so proceed accordingly. For example, give end users an opportunity to become comfortable with CPOE before introducing intrusive CDS interventions that may have significant false-positive rates.

- Problematic situations that weren't accounted for during the design and testing phase typically arise as a result of CDS rollout. Accept and plan for this fundamental CDS implementation tenet (for example, by paying careful attention to user feedback and other intervention effects—see Chapter 7).

DISCUSSION

Launching CDS interventions—particularly those with significant effects on workflow—can be trying for both implementers and end users. Close collaboration among these groups around CDS purpose and methods, as outlined in previous chapters, can help decrease tension and risk and increase chances for success. Key activities and considerations associated with three major areas of the rollout itself are addressed in this chapter: change management; prelaunch testing; and rollout logistics, such as phasing, training, and communication.

Change Management

Because it involves altering work processes and decision-flows, deploying CDS interventions in clinical practice is, in essence, a change management exercise. Many CDS implementers find it invaluable to consult resources on how to effectively lead organizational change. John Kotter and other change management thought leaders have written excellent general guides on this topic,[1] which has also been addressed from a CDS-specific perspective in other sources.[2]

Do CDS with Affected Stakeholders, Not to Them

A central theme that will be emphasized throughout this chapter (building on recommendations made previously in this guide) is that launching CDS interventions shouldn't be the first time that the CDS team reaches out to end users and related stakeholders. Rather, the launch phase should be more like the tip of an iceberg, with extensive joint work as outlined in previous chapters beneath the surface (that is, preceding the launch). This foundational work includes building a shared appreciation for the critical medication-related challenges adversely affecting care delivery (Chapter 2), conducting a detailed analysis of pertinent end-user workflow (Chapter 3), and preparing potential CDS interventions that address targeted improvement opportunities (Chapters 1, 3, 4, and 5).

Ideally, those affected by new CDS interventions should enthusiastically await (and help prepare for) their launch as an opportunity to test the shared hypothesis that the new processes will drive enhancements mutually desired by all parties. Role-playing modified workflows throughout the design process can help instill confidence in a positive outcome by answering questions such as: How will tasks, data, and knowledge flow, and will these changes drive desired outcomes? It may be difficult to have *all* users eager to receive each specific new intervention due to limited time and other resources necessary for building this level of engagement. There may also be potentially irreconcilable conflicts between the needs and constraints of the various stakeholders. Nonetheless, setting as a guidepost the goal of widespread commitment and excitement about the CDS interventions before launch can be a useful approach for optimizing launch-related efforts.

As you prepare to roll out new CDS interventions, keep in mind all the roles and processes that will be affected. These include all the links in the chain required to deliver the intervention's targeted end result. The workflow analysis (and role plays) should have flushed out many of these important links. For example, if the goal is to substantially increase the proportion of patients that receive a particular immunization as indicated, will an adequate vaccine supply be available to accommodate this goal? Is there adequate storage in the pertinent settings? Will the added time required to deliver the immunization (and perform related documentation tasks) adversely affect workflow and staffing needs? When we refer to "intervention stakeholders" in the remainder of this chapter, keep in mind not only the CDS recipients directly affected but also all these other links in the chain to the desired outcome.

Assess the "Change" Environment

To the extent that there has been prior dialog with the intervention stakeholders, the CDS team will appreciate the obstacles and facilitators for the workflow and cultural changes that the new interventions will require. In order to understand exactly where these stakeholders are currently on the path to this change, you should conduct a formal readiness assessment before launch. This can involve the following activities:

- Determine the extent to which end users buy-in to achieving the targets on which the CDS interventions are focused.

- Assess their preconceived notions and experiences with the CDS types you will be using (for example, alerts, documentation tools, and infobuttons) and for the underlying CISs (such as EMRs and CPOE) that will be delivering the CDS.

- Identify end-user expectations about the specific interventions that will be launched (response times, length/components of information delivered, etc.) and potential obstacles to success.

- Expose a wider spectrum of users to the new intervention(s) prelaunch than might have been engaged at earlier stages (see Testing section later in the chapter); listen carefully to their feedback and its implications for the workflow and other changes that will be needed after launch.

- Consider how well intervention stakeholders other than recipients—and the key related processes these stakeholders perform—are prepared to provide a strong link in the chain to success.

As just noted, an ideal situation is to have all stakeholders interests (for example, the care delivery organization; its leadership, medical and other staff, CDS recipients and stakeholders; and the patient) aligned behind the CDS intervention by launch time. To the extent that these are misaligned, there may be problems at rollout or soon thereafter. For example, if a hospital deploys an alert to change physician ordering behavior, and the physician doesn't agree with the recommended practice, then the desired change is unlikely. This disconnect may be due to the physician's informed disagreement or to an educational gap. In either case, general receptivity to interventions should be assessed and addressed prior to launch.

Similarly, senior management support for interventions and their intended outcome should ideally be lined up well before launch (see Chapter 2, page 27). This support includes that of both administrative officials and clinically active leadership (such as clinicians representing pharmacy, nursing, and physicians). If these stakeholders aren't well engaged, then it is less likely that resources will be available to ensure intervention success. Resources will be needed for various key tasks, including assessing intervention effectiveness and addressing subsequent enhancements to the CDS intervention—or CIS infrastructure—that may be required to further improve intervention effectiveness. It may be prudent to reaffirm this support prior to launch when questions remain.

End-user satisfaction is a critical quantity that the CDS interventions should either preserve or enhance; degrading it is one of the key factors in deployment failure. The readiness assessment should establish a baseline for this satisfaction with the pertinent systems, workflows, etc. Both quantitative and qualitative data are useful, but resources and organizational support may limit what can be gathered. When satisfaction is high at the start, care should be taken to ensure that the new processes add perceived value and do not undermine satisfaction. If workflows or interactions with underlying ISs are already problematic, it is unlikely that the CDS interventions layered on top will be optimally successful until these are addressed. Hopefully by this point you will have addressed opportunities for interventions to enhance workflow, for example by making it more convenient to access needed information (such as via infobuttons or patient data flow sheets) or complete specific tasks (through order sets or documentation tools).

End-user expectations and receptivity regarding CDS in general, and the planned CDS interventions in particular, are important factors to consider. They help determine the organization's capacity for absorbing the changes that may be required to work flows, policies, and responsibilities. What do the targeted clinicians (or patients) see as the value from CDS in addressing their priorities? To what extent do they consider interruptive alerts in general to be helpful versus inappropriate intrusions or nuisance?

What is their tolerance for false-positives in specific types of alerts (for example, related to drug allergies or interactions)?

These receptivity questions are particularly essential for physicians affiliated with hospitals, but not employed by them. If these physicians feel burdened or annoyed by CDS interventions, it cannot only threaten the intervention success but can potentially add further strain to the delicate symbiotic relationship with the hospital. Alignment around goals and a climate of collaboration beginning early in the process (see earlier discussion and Chapter 2) can help minimize conflict during the launch phase. For example, physicians may tolerate some false-positive alerting when they are fully committed to the objective that the alert is supporting and have had input into optimizing its deployment and value.

The prelaunch assessment process and results can further deepen collaboration between the implementation team and end users. For example, the former can gain insights into acceptable alerting thresholds, and the latter can gain an appreciation for the factors required to optimize value, such as availability of clinician-entered data to support more relevant alerting.

Many seasoned implementers recommend a "start low and go slow" approach. This strategy focuses initially on launching interventions that address the highest priority outcomes and for which organizational receptivity and success are likely. Subsequent deployment efforts can advance the program incrementally by building on early wins, thereby fostering stakeholder engagement and goodwill. Proceeding at a pace that overwhelms individual and organizational capacity to absorb change decreases the chance for success, and can trigger negative stakeholder sentiment toward not only the specific intervention but potentially toward the entire improvement effort and CDS team. Pertinent attitudes can be examined as part of a readiness assessment and used to guide rollout sequencing and pace.

In assessing end-user population readiness, consider both the "typical" intervention users as well as other key constituencies that may not have opportunity to use the intervention as often or in the same way. These might include pediatric, perioperative, ED, and outpatient surgery areas. Medication use is clearly critical in these areas, so hopefully their particular needs and constraints have been addressed throughout the CDS development process, and this attention will continue during the rollout phase and beyond. Successful CDS implementation across diverse settings involves a balance between addressing local needs (which can become unmanageable in the extreme) and having a one-size-fits-all approach (which can impede acceptance and value). To the extent possible, standardization based on a consensus-building model should be strongly encouraged. The readiness assessment can help determine an optimal balance.

If you have a newly implemented EMR or CPOE, ensure there is some user comfort and satisfaction with these systems before introducing too many interruptive CDS elements. Determine the extent to which clinicians are using the existing clinical system, and find ways to optimize use of the components most critically needed for CDS intervention success. For example, ensure that allergy information is consistently and appropriately entered in the clinical systems before launching allergy alerts in CPOE (see Chapter 5, page 122).

It can be very helpful to encourage users to actually see the intervention in action (for example, in test systems) prior to implementation (see Testing Prior to Go-Live, later in this chapter). If they haven't seen the system, then the anticipated alterations in workflow, value from the delivered information, and other parameters remain theoretical—they may sound good, but in reality may prove impractical. Having end users (especially champions) directly observe CDS capabilities and limitations will help bring into sharp focus critical issues that may affect rollout success—at a time when they may be addressed before creating problems. Conversely, to the extent that the CDS team has "gotten it right" based on a thorough and systematic approach to the development process, the end-user preview can drive enthusiasm and support that will help ensure success.

Involve the Right People

The CDS governance and management processes outlined in Chapter 2, including the charter for the CDS program and its medication-management component, provide the framework for intervention launch. That is, they define the "who, what, where, when, why, and how." As you get closer to rollout, different stakeholders in the processes and outcomes related to the interventions will assume specific roles in ensuring success. The readiness assessment helps prepare these stakeholders, and the interventions, for this step.

For example, it can be very helpful for administrative and clinical leadership to demonstrate understanding and meaningful commitment to the high-level goals (for example "we strive to eliminate preventable harm from medication use") and to the corresponding CDS as a means to these ends (such as "we are investing heavily in systems and processes to achieve this goal in concert with our CDS strategy"). More detailed objectives and tactics related to the interventions should likewise be supported by clinical managers (such as heads of nursing, pharmacy, clinical departments) and informatics team leads (such as the CMIO).

Strategies for making this executive support meaningful include involving these leaders in the feedback loop around launch time and demonstrating the CDS team's responsiveness to major concerns that surface. As emphasized repeatedly throughout this guide, thoroughly monitoring CDS intervention benefits and unintended consequences should be "baked" into the program from the outset. This can involve the CMIO, super users or various direct, paper and electronic channels (such as surveys, bulletin boards, mailboxes for the support team, CDS team walk rounds, and others). In any case, interest demonstrated by the CMIO and clinical, quality, and other leaders in this feedback can reinforce for end users that CDS and PI are a collaborative effort. The CMIO (or person in a similar position) should remain in close contact with other clinical leaders, always available for feedback.

Perhaps even more important than "support from above," however, is strong engagement and modeling of desired end-user responses by champions, who are peers of targeted users.[3] As discussed in Chapter 1, champions are CDS program stakeholders who play a critical role in its success. These individuals are respected members of the constituencies that will be receiving the CDS (for example, nurses, pharmacists, patients and physicians), who fully understand and support the CDS efforts, goals, and strategies and can serve as ambassadors for successful use by their peers.

Ideally these champions will have been significantly engaged throughout the CDS intervention lifecycle and will already be serving as a rich, bi-directional information conduit between their peers and the CDS team. At launch then, they should be enthusiastic intervention consumers and a wellspring of encouraging anecdotes that stimulate similar successes by their colleagues. These anecdotes will hopefully include anticipated benefits, such as time saved, errors avoided, increased professional satisfaction through better access to information for answering questions and guiding decisions, and the like.

Around launch time, if not earlier, liability questions and related legal considerations regarding CDS interventions are frequently raised. For example, will alert triggers, messages delivered, user response and the like become part of the record and be retained in an archive and/or log? Is this discoverable in legal proceedings? What are the implications for individual clinicians and the organization? Of course faulty CDS itself can lead to harm and liability, and testing is key to risk management. The upshot is that legal issues around CDS are complex and in flux. Engaging your organization's legal counsel and consulting peers in other organizations (for example, through listservs) and literature about such issues may be very helpful in crafting your approach to legal matters surrounding CDS deployment. Appendix B: Some Medico-legal Considerations provides some additional comments and resources.

Last but not least, the CDS team responsible for deploying the interventions (see Chapter 2, page 25) has a critical role in managing *all* the tasks outlined in this chapter. Clearly this team should be highly multidisciplinary with representatives or input from pharmacists, nurses, physicians, IT, quality/safety, and others.

For example, the CDS team should carefully monitor, along with intervention results during the period surrounding launch, the needs and concerns of all key intervention stakeholders. These include end users from pertinent clinical areas, subject matter experts, and other links in the outcome chain. This broad focus is important even when an intervention is seen as only directly affecting one user type (such as nurse or pharmacist). This is because the care team's inter-dependent nature will likely result in some intervention effects for other stakeholders; hopefully these interconnects will have been made explicit through workflow mapping as outlined in Chapter 3, page 60. If not, these maps can be created or modified by the implementation team at this time for use in subsequent enhancement rounds.

Move to Consensus and Support

A powerful change management tool is helping those involved in the change to see what things are changing so that they can feel excited about and committed to the change and take action to help achieve desired results.[4] In the launch communication section that follows, we suggest the use of tools such as brochures that emphasize the rationale behind new interventions, screen shots of what the intervention will look like, and a listing of user-specific benefits. Such material is a good step in the right direction.

An example of a further innovative step is using video to graphically illustrate what the "future state" will look like and the benefits it will bring. Such material can be developed in-house with an inexpensive video camera and local staff doing the production. The video can depict the new workflows throughout the processes affected by the intervention, as well as real benefits that accrue to specific stakeholders (for example, efficiency gains for clinicians and care safety and quality for the patient).

To the extent that the appropriate groundwork for the intervention has been laid, scripting such a video should be straightforward. We have heard anecdotal reports that this demonstration technique worked effectively to solidify consensus and support around needed change. Although an illustration this elaborate won't be practical for most interventions, and possibly not at all, it's worth keeping in mind as a model for the see-feel-change paradigm for process improvement and may stimulate similar creative approaches in your organization.

Implement with Anticipated Benefits in Mind

Hopefully you have laid a strong foundation for your intervention launch by carefully assessing your organization's priority opportunities for improving medication management, selecting realistic improvement goals based on local conditions and national benchmarks, and preparing CDS interventions that will help achieve those goals. The fundamental challenge for intervention rollout is to ensure that when the CDS is available to users, it produces the anticipated benefits and desired outcomes (as outlined in Worksheet 2-3, page 56, and Worksheet 5-1, page 163).

A benefits sentence that succinctly and quantitatively captures what the implementation effort is all about can help keep all stakeholders working synergistically toward the goal. (This assumes, of course, that they've all committed to the objective.) Depending on implementation scope, benefits may be high-level, such as "We will reduce over the following 12 months the rate of preventable harm from medication use by 20%, from Y% to X%; the specific harms include ..." Or they could be more granular, such as substituting "medication use" with "avoidable allergic reactions." In practice, the higher-level statement will often be comprised of several more specific targets and statements.

It may be difficult to gather all the quantifiable data needed to make such a detailed statement, but it's an important goal. These statements can serve as guideposts for all the various launch activities outlined later in this chapter. For example, they can be emphasized in rollout communications to help keep the objective top-of-mind for all stakeholders. A clear, consensus-driven picture of a priority target can help keep everyone attuned to the key question underlying success in rollout and beyond, which is "What can we do to help ensure that we achieve the desired outcome?" Although this may seem (and be) an overly optimistic expectation for typical end users, the closer this ideal can be approximated, the more likely ultimate success will be.

Tracking progress in an accurate and quantifiable way may be challenging due to problems with data availability, formats, and interchange across systems but is nonetheless important. The benefits statement can help inform the data gathering strategy discussed in previous and upcoming chapters. Although difficult, quantifying progress toward stated goals is one of the most powerful tools for driving improvement.

The following is an overview of key benefits-driven system implementation[5] components. This work is deeply rooted in the key tasks outlined in earlier chapters and "meets the road" during intervention launch.

- The *benefits framework* drives everything else— it outlines the strategic outcome(s) anticipated from the CDS interventions and typically does not include the tactical details. The framework uses "benefit sentences," previously mentioned, to ensure that everyone is clear on specific goals addressed by one or more interventions.
- *Forecasts* are developed for each item on the benefits framework to serve as targets and motivation. The process of developing the targets adds to a shared understanding of how the benefits are realized with the CDS tools.
- *Metrics,* based on each forecast, measure whether the forecast has been met; monthly or quarterly operational reports are produced to monitor progress and guide quick interventions when desired results are not realized.
- *Benefit requirements* are developed, in detail, for each expected benefit. These are detailed technical "specs" that describe process, technology and cultural changes required for the benefit

to be realized. The benefit requirements drive changes in the models (forecasts) because they reveal shortcomings in the existing tools that will lead to benefits *not* being realized. The benefit requirements are then used to modify the implementation work plan, add hardware, and change software design and processes to ensure that these elements meet the benefit requirements.

Measurement and continuous improvement are discussed further in the next chapter.

Testing Prior to Go-Live

Details of appropriate testing depend to some degree on the specific intervention type being launched. For example, there will be slightly different issues to assess for documentation templates, order sets, alerts, etc. Relatively little testing will be needed for straightforward infobutton links to content on a local intranet site, whereas interruptive alerts that are triggered by several patient-specific data elements coming from different CISs will require more extensive testing.

General issues to formally assess include items such as whether the interventions make sense to end users, fit into their workflow, deliver useful information, and address intended business and clinical objectives. Technical issues include whether the intervention performs as expected, has access to the needed data, works appropriately with related systems, and the like.

Hopefully there will have been substantial user input and iterative assessment as emphasized in earlier chapters so no major surprises from a use or usability perspective will pop up at this stage. The goal here is to flush out unexpected show-stoppers that may have been overlooked. The most preferred scenario is that attention is focused on validating that the interventions perform as designed and anticipating the implementation nuances that can be addressed to ensure optimal user satisfaction and intervention success—for example, because of enhanced rather than impeded value and workflow.

A question may arise at this point about how to get busy clinicians, particularly non-employed physicians in community hospital settings, to devote significant time for the evaluation and feedback activities outlined in this section (and earlier chapters). We believe the answer ties back to the governance and prioritization tasks outlined in Chapter 2. Key committees and other pertinent management structures should have been used to create a shared urgency among pertinent stakeholders about the targeted performance improvements and a collaborative approach to driving this change. Difficulty getting clinicians' attention around new intervention testing and launch may be a warning sign about user receptivity to the intervention and may indicate the need for more work on the foundational issues—that is, doing CDS *with* key stakeholders, not *to* them.

The basic steps in a standard quality assurance (QA) approach are outlined next. They can be adapted as needed to address your implementation's specific requirements. Various resources are available with additional details on QA procedures if you need more information on this topic.[6]

Use Cases and Testing Scenarios

The use cases that you developed in Chapter 3, page 68, are now used to test your completed interventions. If significant time elapses between when the scenarios were vetted and this testing stage, you should ensure that they remain valid and appropriate according to clinical users and subject matter experts, including those users who were not necessarily involved in their development. All validated use cases should be included in the final software requirements documentation.

Typically, one or two basic use cases will be developed that relate to the intervention's primary objective. For example, the use case for a drug-allergy alert might include the user placing a drug order for a patient with a documented allergy to the drug. With further thought, many special cases and unusual situations can be envisioned. For example, these scenarios might include: when a drug is ordered from a drug family that is cross-allergenic to the patient's documented allergy; a drug is ordered to which the patient is allergic, but the alert has been overrid-

den in the past; the person viewing the alert is not authorized to make a final decision on whether it is safe to give the drug; and other variations. The basic use cases should derive from business needs, such as eliminating preventable allergic reactions to drugs. The more sophisticated variants result from taking a hard look at the basic case in light of rich clinical knowledge and practice experience. Stakeholders can provide helpful input here. Use case variants are an important way to catch needed design changes before launch and deserve careful consideration.

You should develop the narrative use cases into formal testing scenarios. These scenarios describe exactly how the user will interact with the intervention and the results from that interaction. Any changes necessitated by testing, and made to either the scenarios or the system design, should be reflected in the corresponding documentation. These testing scenarios will be used both by developers and end users in the testing steps outlined next.

Unit Testing

Software developers perform this testing to ensure that the pertinent application will deliver the CDS intervention as it has been built and that it functions as designed, independent of other CIS components. It involves applying the testing scenarios to ensure that valid inputs produce valid and appropriate outputs. Various invalid inputs that might occur in practice should also be tested to ensure that they are handled appropriately.

For technically straightforward interventions, such as links to reference material or documentation templates, this testing will be relatively simple. For more complex interventions, such as alerts that process a lot of patient-specific data, all logical branches and internal program flow should be validated. Unit testing for these more complex applications may involve special software for debugging and testing. This testing is typically handled by application developers, not the software QA staff. If staffing levels permit, developers not directly involved in creating the intervention should do unit testing. Include clinicians in testing at this stage and the next to help ensure that clinically inappropriate performance hasn't crept into the intervention.

Bear in mind that most CIS vendors will test the programming that underlies CDS interventions they support (such as rules engines for alerting), but that any local customizations may require additional testing. Similarly, verify that any processing done to incorporate clinical knowledge into the CDS intervention has not changed its clinical meaning or effect.

Integration Testing

Once each individual intervention component is working as designed, the next step is integration or functional testing. Here, system developers and administrative staff ensure that every individually developed system component works appropriately (for example, as called for in the use cases) when integrated with the existing CIS infrastructure. For example, integration testing verifies that the CIS response time is adequate at both peak and steady-state use levels after the new interventions have been added. Regression (verification) testing might also be necessary when the new intervention involves significant modification to the underlying CIS. This selective testing ensures that all new software is working as expected and that no new bugs have been introduced that cause previously working functions to fail.

User Acceptance Testing

This final prelaunch testing is performed by clinical end users to ensure that the system works for users as intended and meets all of the planned business and clinical requirements. User accounts are set up in a non-production environment to allow physicians, pharmacists, nurses, and other end users—together with IT staff—to simulate receiving and responding to CDS interventions during patient care activities. This helps identify *during a testing cycle* glitches in system design both from a workflow and an IS perspective, without potentially harming real patients.

This user evaluation often begins with testing scenarios that have been developed from the use cases. After the system has been shown to handle these successfully, users can be asked to go through several "real-life" situations or scenarios that they provide. Carefully selecting end users to perform this testing is critical to ensure that the results accurately reflect the broader user experience with the intervention that may occur after launch. Representatives from all the pertinent user groups should be included, as emphasized in discussions about working with intervention stakeholders presented earlier in this book.

Be particularly attentive to user testing results; they can help assess widespread user readiness for the interventions and identify the need for additional education, support, or incentives to ensure successful adoption. This testing also can uncover difficulties, such as unexpected or counterproductive side effects, workflow implications, or costs associated with the intervention. Potential remedies that can be instituted before launch may emerge from these evaluations. However, the careful analysis and validation steps already accomplished should significantly reduce surprises at this late stage.

If you have not done so already, test the user feedback channels. Make sure that e-mail links, calls to help desk and pager numbers, and the like are routed and responded to appropriately.

As we discussed in Chapter 5, CPOE is a rich medium for deploying CDS interventions to improve medication safety. Consider using the Leapfrog CPOE test (see Chapter 7, page 216) to validate that the CDS functionality will perform as required by the test prior to launch.

Beta Testing/Pilot Launch

After the CDS intervention has successfully passed all the testing phases above, it is ready to be moved to the live CIS and the patient care environment. When a new intervention does not disrupt workflow very much and is not controversial (such as straightforward links to reference material), it is often appropriate to release the intervention to all clinical users at the same time. For very complex or intrusive interventions (such as multistep protocols or workflow-interrupting alerts), it can be helpful to release the intervention initially to a few selected clinical users, such as a single practice or inpatient unit.

During this pilot or beta-testing period, supplying an easy and convenient method for users to provide feedback to the intervention deployment and development teams is particularly important. You should make sure you have adequate staff to seek out and respond to this input to help ensure success during the subsequent full-scale rollout.

As a double check on intrusive alert behavior, consider configuring these alerts to fire "behind the scenes" in the production environment. In other words, allow alerts to be triggered by clinical events in the production system, but do not display the resulting messages to clinical users during testing. This approach is particularly important with CISs that do not allow robust simulation of "real world use" in preproduction environments. The CDS team can review a log of the alerts, in collaboration with pertinent experts and users, to assess their appropriateness. Alerting criteria and other details can then be fine-tuned as needed prior to "turning on" the alert for clinical end users. Keep in mind the following points about this testing strategy:

- It can provide an estimate of how frequently alerts will fire, and this information can be used in preparing users, for example, through communications as outlined later in this chapter.
- Some manual chart review may still be needed to validate that triggers are correct.
- Monitoring alert firing "behind the scenes" can reveal possible incorrect triggers and the like but will not identify those patients for whom an alert should have been triggered but was not. This case will require supplementary analysis besides reviewing alert firing logs.
- You should develop a timeline that allows adding alerts over a defined period. Adding alerts just for the sake of alerts, of course, is not advisable, whereas the ability to add alerts depending on need has value. You may build into your timeline a several-week period to evaluate new alerts, followed by an additional few weeks to make needed

revisions. In any case, have a plan for when you will take alerts live after testing to ensure they move smoothly toward production (see Rollout Logistics, next).

- For alerts that fire "behind the scenes" during this testing, consider the clinical implications of important alerts that may fire (for example, if an actual patient danger is identified) and provide mechanisms for making sure these situations are appropriately addressed.

Full-live Evaluation

Once the intervention has proven successful during limited use, it is ready to be released to all intended users. The feedback channels will serve as the means whereby the implementation team can assess user response to the system. We will discuss ongoing evaluation in greater detail in Chapter 7.

Not all CDS interventions will require an extensive testing procedure. Nonetheless, a thoughtful testing approach can help prevent surprises from derailing the positive results expected from CDS program planning and intervention development. It can also help engender confidence in the program and individual interventions from both leadership and end users.

Worksheet 6-1 can be used to document prelaunch testing for each intervention.

Rollout Logistics: Phasing, Communication, Training, and Other Tasks

Next we consider several key steps associated with releasing your tested interventions to their intended end users.

Establish Rollout Phasing

Since organizations have limited capacity to develop interventions and absorb the resulting change, your medication management CDS program will be rolled out incrementally. Factors driving this phasing include the relative benefits expected from the interventions, end users' receptivity toward them, ease with which they can be deployed, and related variables.

In an instructive example, one organization turned on all medication alerts initially in its CPOE system, anticipating that this strategy would accelerate its realizing the CDS benefits. Their experience, which echoes that of many other organizations, is that this strategy was too much, too soon. Alert fatigue developed and, as a result, physicians and pharmacists ended up ignoring almost all alerts. This situation forced a cutback on alerts and reconsidering which ones were the most important.

In contrast, Texas Health Resources uses a staged approach to introducing medication-related alerts over time, initially launching alerts consisting of drug-allergy interaction warnings. These alerts are working well (for example, they are accepted by end users and support desired outcomes). The organization is building on this strong foundation by introducing additional interaction alerts incrementally—such as drug-drug, drug-pregnancy, drug-laboratory, duplicate drug. This phasing will be based on data and feedback from a clinician pilot group using a production environment and should help to ensure that these new interventions can each be successfully "absorbed" by target recipients.

The lesson illustrated by these examples is that carefully planned, incremental rollouts allow users to accept each successive layer of CDS and allow the CDS team time for appropriate design, testing, and early aggressive monitoring for each new intervention. By prioritizing rollout sequence and managing the pace of releases, you can better accommodate organization and end users' ability to absorb change.

Similar considerations apply to rolling out interventions across facilities in a multihospital system. Some organizations prefer to focus on a single facility and "get all the kinks worked out" before moving to other sites. Other organizations prefer what some call a "big bang" approach in which CDS functionality is launched simultaneously (perhaps along with major CIS components, such as CPOE) across multiple facilities. There are examples of these big bang rollouts working successfully, but clearly tremendous preparation and attention to all the user

and organizational issues emphasized throughout this book is critical.

Communicate Launch Details

It is imperative that you design and execute a well thought-out plan to communicate pertinent information about new or significantly modified interventions to *all* stakeholders (including patients, clinicians, perhaps the community, and others). This messaging helps reinforce everyone's understanding and enthusiasm about the goals that are being addressed, the changes to workflow and processes that will be taking place, the benefits different stakeholders can expect, the channels that are available for feedback, and the like.

When all the preliminary steps leading up to launch have been carefully addressed, these communications solidify the foundational work. To the extent that the environment hasn't been fully prepared, the information may be new to some stakeholders, so conveying it thoroughly and carefully is especially critical. Insufficient communication is an important contributor to failed CIS and CDS implementations.[7,8]

You should fully leverage all available communication channels and resources, such as any internal public relations (PR)/communications staff and processes. It is likely that previous IT implementations at your facility—for example, EMR components or CPOE—have spawned formal communication tools and meeting protocols with the various stakeholder communities that may be used for the CDS intervention rollout. Be sure to include these in your planning, keeping in mind that undercommunicating is a much greater risk than overcommunicating.

Advocate Health Care uses a homegrown "8 × 8 communication strategy" to help ensure that stakeholders are aware of important system changes. See Table 6-1 for an example of what this might look like. You can consider this approach—conveying key information eight times in eight different ways—as you develop your communication plans. Again, launch should be the tip of the iceberg, so many

Table 6-1: 8 x 8 Communication Example

Event to Be Communicated	Method	Message	Start Date	End Date	Responsible Party
Launch of new interruptive alerting about dangerous DDIs in CPOE system	E-mail — 2 instances	An updated CPOE version with new alerting for the most high-risk drug interactions will be in production on 1 June. Extensive work with end users and the CIS/CDS vendors has taken place to minimize nuisance alerting. It won't be perfect at launch, and the CDS team is committed to continually optimizing the value of these alerts. Several channels for feedback are available and will be monitored closely. [Click here to send message to CDS team]	1 April	15 May	Kerry Fieldcrest
	Notices on launch day — via various electronic and paper channels	Same as above	Same as above	1 June	Same as above
	Brochures — distributed in workplaces of each intervention stakeholder and electronically on intranet	See mock-up — includes summary of interactions to be targeted, rationale for selection, benefits expected, highlights from e-mail message	Same as above	Until supplies run out after launch	Luke Smith
	Bulletin boards in pertinent gathering places (such as medical staff lounge)	Same as above	Same as above	1 July	Luke Smith
	EMR notice	New high-risk drug interactions will be in production on June 1; click here for details [link to brochure on intranet]	1 May	31 May	Jim Wann

Table 6-1: *continued*

Event to Be Communicated	Method	Message	Start Date	End Date	Responsible Party
	Web notice to departmental intranet sites (such as nursing, pharmacy, radiology, etc.)	Same as brochure	Same as above	Same as above	Rhonda Jones— intranet; John Fisher— conference
	Presentation at medical and other staff meetings, prior to launch	Combination of all the above and below	15 May	15 May	David Wells, MD, CMIO
	Positive buzz created by physician and pharmacy champions with colleagues	"There is close collaboration between the medical staff, pharmacy staff, CDS implementation team and others on these alerts; they're not perfect but they work well. In realistic testing scenarios, we've seen how they really will make a significant difference in patient safety."	1 May	Ongoing	Julie Patel, MD, medical staff; Sam Knight, RPh, clinical pharmacist

instances of these communications should ideally happen well before rollout.

These launch communications should be two-way, building on the dialog that was established early in intervention development and continued through the readiness assessment. The CDS team should ensure that the messages are reaching the intended audience and be attentive to their feedback at this final prelaunch stage. Use both formal (such as surveys) and informal mechanisms (such as chatting with stakeholders on walk rounds) for gathering feedback.

Any last major concerns that surface during these rollout exchanges should be addressed through subsequent communications using the appropriate channels previously discussed and through changes to the intervention and rollout as well, if possible.

The CDS team must be careful to avoid being defensive about any identified shortcomings and remain open to opportunities for improvement. Even when major concerns cannot be addressed right away, reassurances that the CDS team is listening and taking issues seriously can help build trust in the CDS program and implementation staff.

An important issue to keep in mind for communication and planning purposes is whether/how CIS/CDS/computer system outages might affect interventions and users. Your organization may already have experience addressing these "downtime" issues with CISs already deployed. In any case, you should consider how such downtime may affect the CDS interventions you are launching, such as infobuttons, alerts, order sets, documentation tools and the like. In many cases, there may be potentially straightforward workarounds, such as using alternative channels (paper, Internet) for providing users with the needed information that the intervention normally delivers. You should consider though, implications from key safety net interventions (such as certain critical, interruptive alerts) not being available. Planning during intervention development and/or testing should address these issues, which can be included as appropriate in user communications.

Just as good communication with intervention stakeholders starts well before launch, it continues indefinitely after rollout. This continuous improvement cycle is discussed further in Chapter 7.

Provide Convenient Training, Support, and Feedback Mechanisms

Communication and training/education should be viewed as two distinct activities. For example, notification via multiple avenues may be sufficient "communication" to notify users that drug-allergy alerts will be activated in the system, *if* they are in agreement with the alert recommendations. However, an intervention designed to change clinician behavior in an area in which they may have important knowledge gaps (such as concerning a new test or treatment) should be more successful when coupled with "education or training."[9] A case in point: a recent study at Northwestern Memorial Hospital to increase gastroprotection among NSAID users showed that the combination of an alert with education was superior to either education or alert alone.[10]

Depending on the intervention type, varying degrees of training may be needed to ensure that users appropriately respond to the intervention. For example, intuitive interventions such as infobuttons (which use well-accepted interface paradigms, such as hyperlinks that implicitly convey to users "click here to get more information") may require little or no training. This was the experience at the Brigham and Women's Hospital of Partners HealthCare when infobutton links were embedded with drug names in their eMAR application to provide nurses with quick access to summary information on patient

medications. Widespread use of these infobutton links picked up quickly, despite minimal or no nurse training.

Interventions that are more complex or that require more nuanced user action may require training. This might include ensuring that physicians understand the opportunities and steps to properly access and complete order sets in an electronic environment, such as within a CPOE application. Of course, deep end-user involvement throughout all the earlier developmental stages should help make the interventions as intuitive as possible and therefore minimize training needs.

Consider also whether your CDS intervention will require skills, such as typing, in which all end users may not be proficient. Strategies such as advanced training on these skills, alternative data entry, or other workaround might be helpful.

Strategies to enhance your training efforts include the following:

- Explore pertinent training resources available from your CIS and CDS vendors; ask about printed materials, Web sites and other computer-based offerings, as well as live training programs.
- Adopt "train the trainer" approaches that include cultivating super users who understand the intervention mechanics well and can serve as a resource to their colleagues.
- Ensure that key representatives from the various departments (for example, expected heavy intervention users) are trained early to minimize bumps after rollout. Offer training at convenient times (including non-business hours) to ensure ample opportunity for interested users.
- Tailor training duration and intensity to user needs and constraints; make training resources available prior to formal training sessions to optimize use of training time.
- Leverage existing formal training mechanisms and venues that may be available for nursing, pharmacy, and other clinical staff.
- Provide shorter, more focused training as necessary; for example, physicians often require a more informal and ad hoc process. Training and

cultivating super users may be very helpful here as well.

- Pay very careful attention to expressed concerns and non-verbal communication during training, especially from those who were not "friends of the project" during earlier stages. These can provide clues to potential problems that may arise after launch.
- Remember that most "training" will occur on-the-job after launch, so make sure there is adequate CDS staff (or others they have trained) available to support end users. This may include staff potentially "at their shoulder" during early launch phases with more intrusive or complex interventions, and readily available via phone or e-mail as needed in all cases.

For both training and support, outreach by the CDS project's clinical informatics leadership (for example, CMIO) directly to physicians and other influential clinicians can be helpful in ensuring that the these groups' needs and concerns are adequately addressed for interventions in which they play a central role (such as intrusive alerts in CPOE). These clinicians typically fit into different categories, each of which may benefit from a tailored approach:

- Early technology adopters—those who are likely to explore the intervention soon after launch, or who might be early users of the underlying CIS through which the CDS will be delivered (for example, CPOE)
- Clinical thought leaders—for example, clinicians whose patient care expertise is respected by colleagues and whose response to the CDS will be particularly noteworthy to peers
- Clinicians closely connected with management—for example, chief quality/safety officer, who may play influential roles in CDS governance and may, therefore, be particularly sensitive to how the interventions work
- Super users—who understand intervention mechanics well and can help other users solve problems
- Champions—who can model intervention and how successful intervention use can drive value for their peers and patients

Critical elements for supporting end users during launch include super users and champions, ready access to feedback channels to the CDS team for reporting concerns and questions, and timely responsiveness by the team to user needs and feedback. Organizations typically lack good processes for handling such feedback, so there may not be a strong foundation on which to build for the CDS interventions. Nonetheless, this deserves careful attention within the CDS program.

One example of a CDS intervention feedback channel is incorporating a "feedback button" similar to the ones online retailers use on Web sites to give customers an option to complete an online customer survey. Texas Health Resources adapted this feedback button approach for its drug alerts. The override form within these alerts allows users to provide feedback on alert utility and presents coded choices for specific override reasons—one of which is labeled "Inappropriate alert." CDS staff monitor the coded override reasons and free-text feedback to identify patterns suggesting opportunities to enhance alert usefulness.

Similarly, Advocate Health Care uses an electronic feedback button in its CIS. By clicking this button, users can enter a change or enhancement request that is forwarded to the implementation team via the organizational intranet. Feedback ranges from new synonym requests for items in search lists, to requests that flawed CDS alerts receive attention from the CDS team. This information gets logged in a relational database that is widely available to internal stakeholders and is updated regularly by the implementation team with status about how the feedback is being addressed. Feedback initiators are automatically sent monthly updates with this information. This "closed loop" approach to feedback management has effectively eliminated what frustrates users and implementers in some organizations as the "black hole of 'what happened to my request?'"

Other organizations invite user feedback by including within alert messages the e-mail address for the clinician responsible for the alert. In any case, make sure that by the time any interventions are launched, ongoing routines to monitor and support their content and delivery mechanics are already in place. This will be discussed in greater detail in the next two chapters, but the initial plan should be developed and put into place at this stage. The plan should include the party responsible for the intervention and an initial monitoring frequency.

Feedback from users that is gathered through these channels (as well as proactively through surveys and walk round by CDS project team members) forms an important part of the continuous improvement cycle driving ongoing enhancement to the CDS intervention and its value. Chapter 7 provides more details on measurements that help drive this cycle.

Formalize and Execute the Launch Plan

The details of how your CDS program will address the communication, training, feedback, and other rollout elements should be documented in a formal launch plan. This will help ensure that all stakeholders (such as the CDS team and its sponsors, as well as other interested stakeholders) can all have a shared picture of the path to a successful launch.

This explicit documentation and sharing can also make it easier to gain broader input into plan details and thereby help anticipate and address potential challenges and opportunities. The worksheet samples presented in the next section of this chapter can trigger ideas for how you might handle rollout documentation.

You can use Worksheet 6-2 as a model to develop your own tool for documenting the plan to notify the affected community about the upcoming launch, train them on effectively using the intervention, gather their feedback after implementation, and assign responsibility and timetables for intervention maintenance.

Similarly, you can use Worksheet 6-3 to track in detail how the rollout phasing is progressing. It is especially useful when more than a few interventions will be launched in this cycle or when individual interventions will be launched in several stages. Besides overall project tracking, it can serve other specific needs, including planning and allocating personnel for intervention testing, training, and support. Worksheet 6-4 is a model for logging user feedback about interventions, and their disposition.

WORKSHEETS

Worksheet 6-1

Prelaunch Testing

This worksheet can be used to document prelaunch testing and results. For some intervention types, professionals in your information services division or a consulting company assisting with intervention development may complete this worksheet. It is organized by intervention, since that is generally how the testing will be conducted. In the second column, list the medication objective targeted by the intervention; this can help reinforce this key connection for those completing and reviewing this worksheet. You can carry this information forward from one of the earlier worksheets (for example, Worksheet 5-1, page 163).

In the third column, identify the owner, or champion, for this intervention. Columns four and five document the test type and scenario. Testing type includes unit testing, user verification testing, integration testing, pilot testing and the like. The last three columns are used to document when and by whom the testing was done, the results, and other pertinent notes that the testers wish to convey back to the implementation team.

Intervention Name	Medication Management Objective	Owner	Test type	Test Scenario	Date/ Tester	Results	Note
Prescription allergy alert window	Reduce preventable ADEs	James E. CQO	User simulation	Prescriber given medication orders to enter, with some triggering alerts — user timed and surveyed	4-10-08/ Dr. Tai	User interface intuitive; ordering process minimally perturbed	

Worksheet 6-2

Intervention Launch Plan

This worksheet can be used to document your plan to notify the affected community about the upcoming launch, train them on effectively using the intervention, gather their feedback after implementation, and assign responsibility and timetables for intervention maintenance. Documenting this information can be used to build a clear and shared picture about plan details for the implementation team and also to gather input from selected stakeholders to help optimize the plan.

This sample worksheet is organized by the individual CDS interventions (followed by the corresponding objective) listed in the first and second columns and brought forward from earlier worksheets (such as Worksheet 6-1). Depending on the number and types of interventions you are launching at this stage and how the components of your plan interrelate, you might want to organize it differently (for example, by the clinical objective you are addressing). Similarly, if there are several major components to your launch, you might want to create a separate worksheet for each component.

In the third column, list the individual responsible for the intervention, and in the fourth list the IS that will be used to deliver it. These first four columns provide context for the details in the next three columns regarding the communication, training, and intervention plans. You might want to break one or more of these columns out into a separate table. For example, you might create a table as in Table 6-1 to document your communication plan. You can use the last column to document notes for the project team or plan reviewers.

Intervention Name	Clinical Medication Management Objective	Owner	Clinical IS	Communication Plan	Training Plan	Intervention Maintenance Plan	Note
Prescription allergy alert window	Reduce preventable ADEs	James E. CQO	Better Care CPOE	E-mail, Clinical IT advisory committee	Individual training on site	PI committee to report regularly on outcome metrics in Worksheets 7-2 and 7-3	We will watch response to this very closely, as it is first interruptive alert in CPOE.

Worksheet 6-3

Implementation Status

This worksheet is a working document that provides a snapshot of the interventions you are rolling out, individually and collectively. Once again, the set of interventions being rolled out can be organized in a variety of ways; in this sample, it is organized by individual intervention. The first four columns can be brought forward from earlier worksheets, such as Worksheet 6-2. Documenting intervention users in the fifth column can help with tracking intervention types that are deployed for different end-user types. The testing completed date in the sixth column identifies when the intervention has completed the pre-rollout evaluation. This information can help alert you to interventions that might be stuck at this stage. The seventh column specifies the target date for initially launching each intervention. Seeing all these dates together can be helpful for sequencing and appropriately spacing out the individual intervention launches and modifying the schedule as needed. The actual launch dates and locations in the eighth and ninth columns track your rollout progress. This can be helpful both for reporting progress to other stakeholders and for tracking the pace at which the organization can successfully deliver and absorb new interventions.

Intervention Name and ID	Medication Management Objective	Owner	Clinical IS System	Implementation Clinical Users	Date Testing Completed	Planned Launch Date	Actual Launch Date	Launch Location	Notes
Prescription allergy alert window	Reduce preventable ADEs	James E. CQO	Better Care CPOE	Physicians	4/2/2008	4/6/2008	4/7/2008	5 south	Anticipate proceeding to DDI alerts after allergy alerts have stabilized

Worksheet 6-4

Feedback and Resolution

Each intervention you are launching should be listed in this worksheet; again, the first two columns can be carried forward from others in this chapter. In the third column, list the feedback strategy details, such as the use of online feedback, surveys, polls, etc. As discussed earlier in this chapter, these should include feedback mechanisms that are both user-initiated (such as e-mail links within interventions) and implementation-team initiated (such as surveys and interviews), as appropriate. Record all the substantive feedback you receive for each intervention through the various channels in the fifth column, indicating the date and source for the feedback in the fourth column.

Although the details might not be immediately apparent, a plan for addressing each substantive issue should be documented at some point in the sixth column. When the issue is resolved, that can be noted in this column as well; the seventh column can be used to indicate the target or actual date for resolution, as appropriate. Use the last column to indicate the priority for addressing the issue (for example, low, medium, high).

Intervention Name and ID	Clinical Medication Management Objective	Feedback Strategy	Feedback Date and User	Feedback	Plan/Resolution	Target Date/ Actual Date	Priority
Prescription allergy alert window	Reduce preventable ADEs	Survey	4-21-08/ Dr. Brown	Took too much time to override alerts	Analyze/improve override process	5-15-08/	High

CONCLUDING COMMENTS

This launch phase marks both an end and a beginning. The complex planning and development stages culminate in delivering knowledge interventions to clinicians and patients. This in turn begins the process of (hopefully) enhancing decisions and actions to measurably improve medication use and outcomes.

Once again, this process is more of a change management challenge than a technological one. Success will depend on the extent to which barriers have been anticipated and addressed in the earlier phases. Similarly, a launch that smoothly and effectively addresses communication, training, and rollout phasing creates the foundation that will help lead to realizing expected benefits. Creating short-term wins with CDS interventions in areas that are important to key stakeholders will help demonstrate the CDS program value, diffuse skepticism, and build momentum.

Even before any CDS intervention delivers knowledge to an end user, it is likely that your organization will have reaped significant benefits from intensified focus on the medication management cycle, related workflows, and CDS opportunities, as outlined so far in this guide. For example, work to identify and prioritize ways to improve medication use with CDS will likely have beneficial effects on related process- and outcome-improvement activities beyond the specific interventions now being launched. Hopefully, these CDS interventions themselves also will generate substantial returns, but it is worth considering these related side effects so you can cultivate these additional benefits.

The next step in the PI cycle is ensuring that the launched interventions achieve their desired results and are continually maintained and improved. Chapters 7 and 8 explore this challenge in detail.

REFERENCES

1 Kotter JP. *Leading Change.* Boston: Harvard Business Press; 1996.

2 See, for example, Ash JS. Organizational and cultural change considerations in Greenes RA, editor. *Clinical Decision Support: The Road Ahead.* London: Elsevier; 2007; 385-402.

3 Krall MA. Clinician champions and leaders for electronic medical record innovations. *The Permanente Journal.* 2001; 5(1):40-45. http://xnet.kp.org/permanentejournal/winter01/HSchamp.html, accessed 9/17/08.

4 For example, as outlined in the See-Feel-Change approach outlined in Kotter JP, Cohen DS. *The Heart of Change.* Boston: Harvard Business School Press; 2002.

5 See Thompson D, Johnston P. A benefits-driven approach to system implementation. *Hospital and Health Networks Magazine.* Spring 2008. Available on line at: http://www.hhnmag.com/hhnmag_app/jsp/articledisplay.jsp?dcrpath=HHNMOSTWIRED/Article/data/Spring2008/080709MW_Online_Thompson&domain=HHNMOSTWIRED. 02 July 2008, accessed 12/14/08.

6 See, for example, Galin D. *Software Quality Assurance: From Theory to Implementation.* Boston: Addison-Wesley; 2003.

7 Massaro TA. Introducing physician order entry at a major academic medical center: I. Impact on organizational culture and behavior. *Acad Med.* 1993; 68(1):20-25.

8 Dykstra R. Computerized physician order entry and communication: reciprocal impacts. *Proc AMIA Symp.* 2002; 230-234.

9 See, for example, Osheroff JA, Plenary Presentation at Medbiquitous Consortium 2007 Annual Conference: http://www.medbiq.org/events/conferences/annual_conference/2007/presentations/OsheroffJ_Plenary.pps, accessed 9/17/08.

10 Coté GA, Rice JP, Bulsiewicz W, et al. Use of physician education and computer alert to improve targeted use of gastroprotection among NSAID users. *Am J Gastroenterol,* 2008; 103(5):1097-1103.

Chapter 7

Measure Results
and
Refine the Program

TASKS

- Develop a systematic approach to assessing the value that your CDS interventions bring to improving medication management; consider the key questions related to setting up a measurement strategy (who, what, when…).
- Examine key structure, process, and outcome metrics to determine CDS intervention effects, especially the extent to which CDS interventions are helping achieve targeted goals; look for unintended consequences (positive and negative).
- Apply what you learn from evaluation to continually improving your CDS interventions and results.
- Prioritize your measurement activities to derive the greatest value from these efforts.

KEY LESSONS

- The more that executive stakeholders are accountable for outcomes targeted by CDS interventions, the easier it will be to obtain organizational attention and resources for measuring and improving CDS results; seek and cultivate these connections.

- The richer your baseline measurements prior to CDS implementation, the more detail you will be able to capture in assessments about intervention effects; this is particularly important regarding targeted outcomes.

- The measurement process is an ongoing activity that begins well before implementation (see Chapter 3), so you should plan and budget accordingly.

DISCUSSION

The first six chapters of this book outline key steps and considerations for developing and deploying CDS interventions. Now we focus on the critical task of evaluating the results that these efforts have on targeted objectives and other important processes and outcomes. This evaluation work includes developing an appropriate measurement strategy, performing ongoing measurement and effectively communicating results, and refining the CDS program to address evolving experience and organizational needs. It is important to appreciate from the outset that doing this effectively will require considerable effort and resources across the medication management/CDS program. Creating CDS interventions typically receives much greater attention, but their maintenance and monitoring extends over a significantly longer timeframe and usually requires greater resources than most organizations initially anticipate.

This chapter presents detailed considerations related to evaluating your medication-management CDS program, which are also applicable to a more comprehensive CDS evaluation plan. We appreciate that few organizations will be able to address all the issues and recommendations covered and therefore suggest that readers skim the information presented and delve more deeply into the elements that are most pertinent to local needs and priorities. To facilitate your further research, we provide references to literature that illustrate how the some approaches that are outlined can be successfully applied.

Readers jumping ahead from earlier chapters can likewise skim the information presented here to become familiar with some detailed issues that need to be considered from the earliest stages of developing the CDS intervention program.

Successful organizations typically adopt one of two strategies for dealing with the complexities of developing and executing a CDS evaluation plan. The first is recruiting and hiring individuals with significant experience in this area (for example, from academic institutions, CIS vendors, or other hospitals that have successfully implemented CDS measurement strategies). When this strategy is not possible or timely enough, organizations may access the needed expertise by engaging temporary consultants and having them lead key evaluation tasks—training the organization's employees in the process. Before setting down either path, it is important to thoroughly evaluate your organization's staff and skill set pertinent to the tasks outlined in this chapter to determine the best way to fill any evaluation knowledge or skill gaps.

We offer guidance on evaluating CDS effects by addressing several key questions, which provide the high-level outline for this chapter:
- Why measure?
- What to measure?
- Who will measure?
- How to measure?
- When to measure?
- What to do with the results?

The first section of this chapter contains background information that reinforces the motivations for careful measurement. The remaining sections address the "how to" by providing practical steps and more details for actually setting up the CDS evaluation program, or enhancing a broader CDS assessment initiative that may already be in place.

Why We Measure

Major reasons to measure include:
- Ensuring that the CDS tools provided to clinicians and patients are helping improve care
- Determining whether the interventions are working as expected and not disrupting workflow or negatively affecting care
- Learning continually from end-user experience and feedback, and using these insights to refine the interventions and their value in addressing priority targets
- Determining whether the interventions are cost effective, and communicating that information to organizational business leaders—justifying the CDS investments to CEO, CFO, and board, for example
- Creating new knowledge about best implementation practices and publishing the results so others can learn from our efforts

A plan to measure effects and respond accordingly should be built into the core of every process design and redesign—no less for CDS deployment. Although this chapter focuses on assessing an intervention once it's live, you should begin considering evaluation issues at the earliest CDS planning stages (see Chapter 3). For example, how will you know what effects the intervention has had, especially regarding targeted objectives? As new interventions are developed, associated data collection procedures and measures should be prepared in conjunction with them. Because improvement can and should be an ongoing process, evaluation efforts are never finished; project planning and resource allocation need to account for this critical component.

The following are some background points about evaluation to keep in mind:

- Measuring and reporting errors in diagnosis and treatment is not new, and this history provides a conceptual foundation for the topic at hand. For example, in Boston in 1911, Ernest Codman developed the "End Result Hospital." Within this hospital "all errors in diagnosis and treatment were recorded for every patient."[1] In addition, all patients were followed for many years after discharge to evaluate the final results of their care.[2]

- Donabedian's work on measurement and quality improvement has been influential in more recent efforts, including his improvement definition: The systematic measurement and evaluation of predetermined outcomes of a process, and the subsequent use of that information to improve the process based on customer expectations.[3]

- Present day healthcare thought leaders continue to emphasize the importance of driving measurable PI. For example, Don Berwick, President and CEO of the Institute for Healthcare Improvement (IHI), has commented that healthcare's single most important issue to address is its inability to improve.[4] As noted through references to its campaigns and resources in earlier chapters of this guide, IHI has been an important force in healthcare quality improvement. Careful attention to measurement and the full performance improvement cycle are important components of IHI's work.

- The National Quality Forum (NQF) is a leading public-private partnership "created to develop and implement a national strategy for healthcare quality measurement and reporting."[5] To complement its role as the national standard-setting organization for performance measures, NQF has recently formed the National Priorities Partnership "to establish national priorities and goals for performance measurement and public reporting."[6] This development will further increase the importance of NQF's work to measurement activities in provider organizations, for example, by influencing the performance dimensions that providers will need to assess and improve.

- It should be noted that there may in some cases be a close relationship between quality measurement and improvement activities carried out strictly to improve care and for the purposes of research and reporting in the literature. For the latter, there are strict requirements surrounding the need for a local Institutional Review Board (IRB) to approve the research protocol. Failure to obtain proper approval can trigger intervention by federal authorities.[7] Organizations can consult their legal counsel and IRB if questions arise about whether local measurement and improvement efforts would require such approval.

What to Measure
Measurement Philosophy

You should examine in some way the results from every CDS alert or other intervention you implement. An acronym that might serve as a helpful guidepost for your evaluation efforts is METRIC; Measure Everything That Really Impacts Customers.[8] For our purposes, "customers" includes all CDS intervention stakeholders—for example, the organization overall, clinicians, other key pertinent roles, and most especially, patients. Although this ideal may not always be attainable, the acronym helps focus attention on measurement priorities.

Since you cannot fully determine progress if you have not established your starting point, you should capture pre-intervention baseline data (Chapter 2, page 45) and document workflows (Chapter 3, page 60) pertinent to the intervention. Data capture can be difficult, especially in a paper-driven clinical environment, so you should fully leverage available processes and systems to obtain the most accurate baseline and follow-up measurements possible.

In determining what to measure, it is critical to avoid selecting measurements in a vacuum; make sure the proposed measurements (just as the interventions) align with the existing and planned organizational improvement initiatives. Consider how the medication-management CDS intervention objectives relate to other pertinent organizational activities for which measurement targets and processes may be in place. For example, if the interventions address targets that are the focus of reporting or reimbursement requirements (such as core measures from The Joint Commission and CMS—see Chapter 2, page 32), there may already be commitment and processes for capturing key data related to CDS interventions addressing these targets. More broadly, measurements needed to examine CDS effects may currently be captured by the organization for various purposes, so synergies between the CDS measurement needs and these efforts should be sought and cultivated.

Having emphasized how important it is to carefully evaluate any and all interventions, and to do so in light of related organizational activities, we now turn to specific metrics. Chapter 3, page 73, introduced four metric types, and we now consider these in more detail. A growing literature also examines evaluation targets for CIS and CDS applications, as indicated by the many evaluation studies cited in this and other chapters in the guide.

Four Types of Metrics

Discussions about healthcare quality measurement typically refer to structure, process, and outcome metrics and are rooted in Donabedian's work.[9] Next we consider issues pertinent to CDS intervention assessment in each of these categories—though we may

have used these categories somewhat differently than readers deeply steeped in them might expect. We also discuss system response time as a separate measure.

System Response Time Measurement

A basic system-oriented CDS intervention feature is how quickly the CIS/CDS system processes any triggering data from end users (or various other ISs) and displays the intervention—that is, the system response time. This system performance measure should be kept at a minimum because users typically consider waiting for an intervention more than one or two seconds as "taking forever" and therefore an unwelcome workflow intrusion. In Chapter 6, page 181, we discussed various types of prelaunch testing and noted the importance of considering system response times. We now provide some additional details about this measure, which can be periodically reassessed in ongoing evaluation of users' experiences with the deployed CDS portfolio.

When examining system response times, it is helpful to explicitly consider the start and stop events that surround the measurement and whether these events are system or user initiated. For example, when a clinician enters a drug name into a CPOE system (the start event), how long does it take for the system to display a pertinent alert (the stop event), such as a warning about a potential DDI or patient allergy? The user experience and workflow intrusion will be influenced by both the *system response time* and the time it takes for users to access, process, and address the CDS information presented—that is, the *user response time*. We consider user response times next under process metrics.

Some CDS and CISs can automatically assess and report certain system and user response times. The sidebar on the facing page presents such a system response time report, along with additional comments on interpreting and applying this information.

Structure Measurements

To appropriately interpret the effects that your CDS interventions are having, it is necessary to develop a clear picture of how these interventions are deployed. Structure measures characterize this available infrastructure and the forces that are helping drive observed changes. For example, structure indicators for a DDI alert might indicate any differences in how these alerts are configured to fire between nursing floors or between physician and patient types. This difference might be pertinent if otherwise dangerous combinations are permissible in the alert logic on certain clinical services, such as cardiology or oncology. As we discussed in Chapters 4 and 5, these situation-specific deployment capabilities must be available in the CIS; the question for structure measurement is how these capabilities are used to achieve the desired CDS objective.

System Response Time Measurement: An Example from Memorial Hermann Healthcare System

Figure 7-1 is an example of a system-generated system response time report. It shows the time it takes from when a medication order (that meets alert triggering criteria) is entered into the CPOE system until the pertinent alerts are displayed. In this application, the alerting is designed to occur when the user initially selects the order (causing it to be entered into a system workspace in which alert conditions are evaluated) but before the order is signed and transmitted for execution.

The script that enters the data to trigger alerts for system response time testing is designed to run at various times throughout the day. Each data point indicates the average time it took from trigger data entry until alert display for nine test transactions. These same transactions were tested at the times indicated on the x-axis in Figure 7-1, so the response time variation reflects how other system demands affect alert processing. The curves with the lowest two initial average response times reflect system response times for alerts on DDIs and dose range violations (as indicated, at the bottom of the graph). Further summary statistics on these alert response times are presented in the chart that follows the graph. The other lines on the system-generated graph represent other system response times related to selecting the patient profile, opening the pharmacy verification screen, processing signed orders, and the like.

This report is run daily and gives an idea of the system processing times that users experience with these particular CDS interventions. Any unexpected or excessive delays in system response are investigated and addressed. Such delays can be caused by a variety of factors, including intervention calculation complexity, hardware speed and memory, and other hardware/software processing demands. For example, when Memorial Hermann implemented a complex logic template with 290 processing steps, the time from alert trigger to user data presentation was unacceptable at nearly twelve seconds. Modifying server settings brought the delay down to four seconds, and adding additional system memory is being considered to further reduce this wait time. Similarly, software approaches (such as improving the use of indexed data to speed information retrieval) can help reduce system delays. These examples illustrate the importance of close collaboration with technology staff in addressing system performance issues.

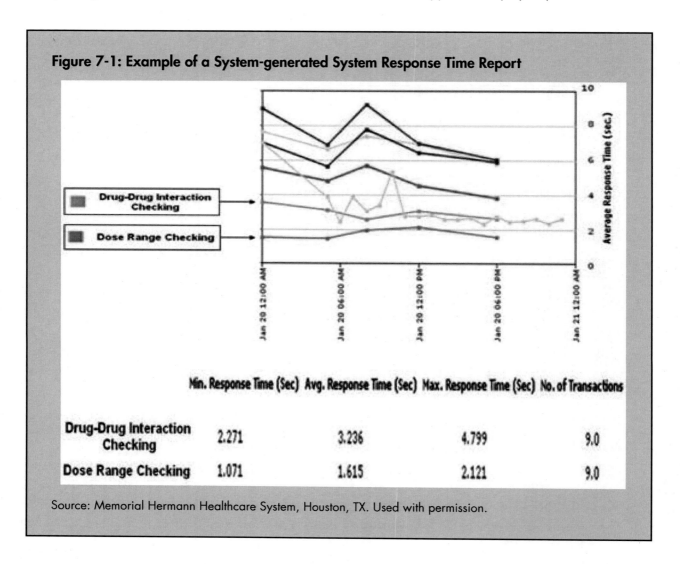

Figure 7-1: Example of a System-generated System Response Time Report

	Min. Response Time (Sec)	Avg. Response Time (Sec)	Max. Response Time (Sec)	No. of Transactions
Drug-Drug Interaction Checking	2.271	3.236	4.799	9.0
Dose Range Checking	1.071	1.615	2.121	9.0

Source: Memorial Hermann Healthcare System, Houston, TX. Used with permission.

Specific structure measures that relate to CDS interventions themselves include (among many others):

- Number and nature of interruptive alerts deployed, including systems in which these are displayed, such as CPOE, EMR, automatic dispensing cabinets, and smart pumps
- Number and nature of non-interruptive notices/ alerts deployed, such as information about patient allergies or decreased kidney function that may be available on various user displays within CISs, such as pharmacy systems or CPOE
- Number of alerts deployed by recipient role (nurse, provider, pharmacist, patient, other) and whether specific alerts are configured to not fire for certain roles, locations, patients and the like

- Whether and how end users can override alerts and document override reasons; how individual override reasons are handled—free text or coded
- Number of order sets deployed and the topics they cover
- Where and how infobuttons, documentation tools, relevant data displays, and the like are deployed

Related factors to consider are whether the CDS components are working as expected and usage data are available. For example, are alerts firing when and where you expected them to and being presented to appropriate end users in the correct medication management phase? The monitoring and feedback mechanisms that have been established to help answer these and related questions (as discussed in

Chapter 6) are an important infrastructure component that should be assessed through structure measures as well (for example, see Worksheet 5-1, page 163, the Feedback Channels and Plan row in which such information may have been documented).

In addition to characterizing the deployed CDS interventions themselves, it is likewise important to understand how use of underlying CISs will affect opportunities for CDS (see Chapter 4). For example:

- Is the CIS environment "mixed" in that some clinicians are using a particular application such as CPOE while others are not?
- Are prescribing providers using CPOE to place orders themselves, or are they relying heavily upon verbal or telephone orders?
- If verbal and telephone orders are used, are the providers staying on the phone for complete verbal read back, and are those taking the orders reviewing each alert?
- Are end users entering information as codified options rather than as free text options (such as allergies and medication orders)?

All these structural considerations provide the foundation for understanding how the deployed CDS interventions affect medication management processes and outcomes, which we discuss in the following two sections.

Process Indicators

Since the ultimate CDS intervention goals include positively influencing care processes and outcomes, this as well as the next metric categories are very important for your CDS program and its continual refinement. They can also be more complex than system performance and structural metrics, and therefore require special attention to measure and monitor appropriately.

Process indicators answer questions such as, *how are the CDS interventions affecting end users—and their decisions and work activities—at each stage of the medication-management cycle.* By characterizing whether and how CDS interventions are actually affecting care processes and flow, these metrics help determine how well users accept and value these interventions. There are many important process indicators; in the following sections, we highlight some considerations around assessing intervention use, their effects on workflow in the medication-management cycle, and their effects on users' time and satisfaction.

Intervention Use

It is often the case that CDS interventions such as infobuttons, order sets and the like are not used in practice as often as implementers expected or hoped. Careful attention to the prelaunch details can help minimize this mismatch, but in any case it's important to determine how often interventions are actually being used. Some pertinent use dimensions to assess include:

- How many order sets or order sentences are *utilized* (as opposed to deployed)? (See Process Indicator Report sidebar, page 205, for an example of how one organization answers questions such as this one.) Are these interventions being accepted and adopted as expected?
- When, how, where, and why are interventions such as infobuttons, flowsheets, or documentation tools being used? What can be gleaned about missed opportunities for effective use from these patterns?
- How often do various alerts *actually fire* across all ISs, and how do end users respond? Process measures related to altering and overrides are considered in more detail in a sidebar later in this section.
- Who is using the interventions, and what does the adoption curve look like? Pertinent adoption characteristics include:
  - **Adoption rate.** How many total users are accessing the interventions over time? A shallow adoption rate, indicating low usage and slow growth, can delay the time until full intervention value is realized and decrease momentum on progress toward improvement goals.
  - **Adoption audience demographics.** What characteristics differentiate users with different adoption rates? You may want to review

how both provider and patient characteristics can influence how well users accept and respond appropriately to CDS alerts and other interventions.[10] These nuances can help you refine interventions, as well as your training and communication process, to support more effective uptake. For example, you might tailor CDS training to emphasize how different clinician types can optimally use the intervention. Pertinent clinician characteristics include age, gender, training, experience with computers, clinical role and experience, relationship to the hospital (employed or affiliated), exposure time to pertinent IS per day, and comments and opinions regarding the system expressed during feedback sessions.[11] Pertinent patient characteristics include age, gender, diagnosis, and comorbidities.

- More specifically for prescribers, does role (such as physician, nurse practitioner, physician assistant, resident, or fellow) affect use? You might track and record, for example, information about prescriber role (accessible via CPOE sign on information and logs) and relate this information to alerts triggered and resulting action. This can potentially help with fine tuning alert triggers, suggesting the need for modified role-based training, and the like.

- Likewise for the medication administration step, information about the intervention recipient (such as the nurse administering the drug) can be retrieved from the pertinent system, such as eMAR, bar-code point of care system, or smart pump and used in similar ways.

- **CDS use in CPOE.** Pertinent statistics to consider over time include:

  - Percent medication orders entered into computer by physicians—sometimes referred to as "percent CPOE" for medication orders

  - Number of clicks on infobuttons in CPOE linking out to reference information

- Number of alerts in CPOE that are fired, accepted, and overridden (see sidebar, page 207)

- Time saved by using automated weight-based dosing instead of manual dose calculation[12]

- Turn-around time from order entry to medication administration[13]

To further explore the relationship between user characteristics and why a CDS intervention is or is not being used, you might consider conducting a culture survey. This can help determine users' beliefs, attitudes, and skills regarding the use of CISs and related hardware at different times in the implementation—before training, after training, after implementation. This information is useful since these systems typically provide the channel through which the CDS is delivered, so user interactions with them may influence their responses to the CDS interventions. The survey could also assess user perceptions about how easy and valuable it is to access and use the CDS tools themselves.[14] For example, user perceptions about tolerable system and user response times can help shed light on strategies for managing these times to optimize CDS acceptance and use (see Effects on Users' Time and Satisfaction on page 206).

Effects on Workflow in the Medication-Management Cycle

CDS intervention effects on medication-related outcomes are mediated through influencing decisions and actions within the medication-management cycle. Assessing in some detail what exactly these influences are in practice can therefore be very helpful in determining whether the interventions are having the desired effects and in identifying opportunities to further enhance their value.

The workflow mapping described in Chapter 3, page 60, helps identify "what was" and "what should be" in terms of pertinent medication management processes. Mapping should be revisited to answer "what is" happening now that the CDS interventions

Process Indicator Report Example from Memorial Hermann Healthcare System

Table 7-1 presents a snapshot of how often specific CDS interventions, in this case care plans and order sets, are used in two different healthcare facilities at Memorial Hermann over a one-week period.

This report helps the CDS team understand how use varies among interventions over time and between different facilities. Such reports should ideally be automated to run on a regular basis and monitored closely to identify any gaps or trends in how often specific CDS interventions are used. Such changes might indicate some problem with the intervention itself or changing care delivery circumstances that might alter intervention use or usefulness.

Table 7-1: Use of Specific Care Plans and Order Sets in Two Facilities over One Week

Person Location - Facility (From)	Plan Name	# care plans
Hospital #1	OB/GYN Vaginal Delivery Multiphase MPP	70
	Admission Common Orders - Adult (Direct Admit) MPP	37
	Admission Common Orders (Post EC) MPP	29
	Pain, Acute	28
	Respiratory, Impaired Gas Exchange	27
	ESP, Anxiety/Fear/Hopelessness	19
	OB/GYN Cesarean Delivery Multiphase MPP	18
	Admission Common Orders - Adult ICU MPP	10
	Neonatal Admission Common Orders Nursery Level 1 MPP	10
	Cardiac, Chest Pain	9
Person Location - Facility (From)	**Plan Name**	**# care plans**
Hospital #2	Pain, Acute	54
	Cardiac, Tissue Perfusion	23
	Cardiac, Chest Pain	18
	Infection, Actual	16
	Neuro/Muscular/Safety, Impaired Physical Mobility	15
	Cardiac, Fluid Volume Deficit	12
	Respiratory, Impaired Gas Exchange	10
	PT, Ambulation Deficits	9
	Neuro/Muscular/Safety, Risk for Injury	8
	Respiratory, Ineffective Breathing Pattern	8

Source: Memorial Hermann Healthcare System, Houston, TX. Used with permission.

have been deployed. Even with the careful planning we have advocated, you should expect that the new workflow realities will not exactly match the models. These deviations can be important sources for shared learning among the CDS implementation team and intervention end users.

Effects on Users' Time and Satisfaction

An important use and usability process measure is how long it takes users to interact with the intervention once it has been presented. The user experience with the intervention will include both this *user* response time as well as the *system* response time discussed earlier. Time pressures pushing out non-essential care processes is a major reason why clinicians (physicians especially) may not use certain CDS interventions. It is therefore helpful to carefully assess user response times. Some specific issues to consider, among others, are the following:

- Is the speed and ease with which users can complete a specific task after the CDS has been added better or worse? In some cases processes may take longer (for example, CDS-enabled electronic prescribing in some studies),[15] and it must then be determined if this delay is acceptable. Answering this acceptability question requires that both the evaluator and end user consider the broader intervention effects, such as prescriber time saved in avoiding pharmacy calls and having to correct medication orders.

- For interruptive alerting, how long does it take from the time the alert is displayed until the end user acts on it? This is the time, for example, from the point at which a duplicate therapy or drug interaction alert fires to when the triggering condition is addressed by the user (such as by changing the prescription[15]) or the alert is dismissed.

- For non-interruptive alerting (such as relevant data display of a patient's allergy listing in the patient header, or pertinent patient lab values in the order detail for certain medications), what is the length of time taken until this information is recognized and acted on? For example, how much time elapses from when information about

impaired kidney function is available onscreen until an appropriate manual dosage adjustment is entered (or at least until the user notices the pertinent information)?

- Similarly for other interventions, what is the length of time from the point at which the intervention is displayed to when the user notices it and completes the interaction? For example, do users notice that order sets might be available for a given condition (in paper or electronic environments)? How long does it take them to find the pertinent order set or determine that none is available? How long does it take to complete an order set once it has been accessed? For infobutton links to Internet/intranet information sources, how long do users spend reviewing retrieved information? Likewise for data flowsheets or data entry forms?

Pertinent end-user workflows and time constraints—together with intervention "user friendliness"—influence these user response times and users' impressions about these times. The workflow mapping approaches outlined in Chapter 3, page 60, provide a foundation for evaluating this dimension. Not all systems will be able to automatically report all these details, and it will likely be necessary to perform some manual, onsite workflow evaluations and time and motion studies. For example, you may want to measure how long it takes the average end user to notice a system-initiated warning or informative message that does not require user intervention (or ask whether the information is noticed at all).

This manual analysis might include the evaluator documenting factors related to task completion, such as whether the user experienced difficulty or delays dealing with (or noticing) the intervention or was multitasking. These observations can augment and help with interpreting system-generated response time data (for example, by answering, "What was taking so long?"). Directly observing intervention use can also suggest intervention enhancements, such as by better supporting important multitasking activities that users may typically do in association with the intervention. Remember to consider both the system and user response time components (as applicable) to fully appreciate the workflow delays that users may experience with various interventions.

It is important to keep in mind that specific process effects on users, such as time required to interact with interventions, workflow changes, usefulness of information provided and others, combine to influence users' satisfaction with specific CDS interventions and with the CDS program more broadly. This satisfaction level is worth assessing since it can be an important factor in building the collaborative relationship that we have emphasized is a key to program success. More recommendations about assessing user satisfaction—which can apply to clinicians, patients, and others—are presented in the "How to Measure" section, page 221.

A Deeper Dive into Alerting and Overrides

Since intrusive alerts and how users respond to them are such an important and often problematic issue in CDS deployment, we provide more detailed considerations on pertinent process indicators for this intervention type.

To continually improve the alerts' value and the clinical practices alerts are intended to support, you should carefully monitor how these interventions affect work processes. Because intrusions into clinical workflow can be both irritating and potentially dangerous for patients, it is important to evaluate which alerts are being overridden, by whom, from which locations, and why.[16,17]

Many organizations are shocked by the surprisingly high alert override rate (which may be greater than 99%) when they first turn on a new medication-related alert. Often implementers will respond by inserting a pop-up form requiring that clinicians enter the reason they are overriding the alert before they can continue using the system. This form may contain both a coded list of likely override reasons (such as, "patient currently on medications and tolerating well," or "will monitor patient closely") along with a free text field in which the user can enter unstructured comments.

In managing excessive alert overrides, the goal is not necessarily to eliminate all alert overrides but rather to reduce them to a more reasonable level. CDS developers hypothesize that if they understood why clinicians were overriding the alerts, they could refine their alert logic and reduce many false-positive events.[18] Organizations must be very careful when introducing mandatory pop-up forms in an attempt to collect these data. For one thing, clinicians may already be annoyed that they received the alert, and further displeased that they are now being asked to enter one more piece of data that provides them with no direct value. Therefore, they may be inclined to select the first item from the list as the reason, just to get past the pop-up and move on. Obviously, such spurious override data are of little or no use to the CDS implementer.[19] In addition, a recent report[20] found that in a small but clinically significant number of instances, clinicians tried to use the free text override field to "communicate" important information to other clinicians. Since these alert override reasons are processed by the CDS team and not routinely displayed to any other users on the patient's care team, this communication failed.

If you are experiencing high alert override rates, consider using mandatory override reason forms judiciously. In this situation, you might turn on these forms for a short time (such as a few weeks), review the override data, and make any appropriate changes to the alert logic. You can then test, implement the changes, and review the new override rate and reasons. Some tips can help increase clinician acceptance of override reason documentation screens. For example, if prescribers override an allergy alert and give "not a true allergy" as a reason, consider offering the capability to easily modify the allergy documentation to reflect this information. In any case, once the high false-positive alerting problem has been resolved, consider removing the mandatory override reason screen. If the problem has not been solved, then consider removing the alert until you develop a suitable plan to reduce false-positive alerting.

To the extent that CDS deployment (including intrusive alerting) is approached as a joint effort among stakeholders (see Chapter 6, page 176), end users may better appreciate why it is important to document reasons for not accepting an alert's recommendation. Responsiveness from the CDS team, as reflected by alert refinements based on feedback from override reasons, can further enlist user support in supplying this information when it is most needed.

The following are detailed alert-related indicators to assess, along with how this information can be used:

- What alerts are *actually firing* for various users (as opposed to *just deployed* within the CIS) at each phase of the medication management cycle and in various ISs? This metric indicates how the programmed alert triggers are translating into delivered messages. Is this actual information delivery appropriate (within the CDS Five Rights framework) for addressing the objective that the alert is designed to support? The frequency with which the alert triggers occur can be useful in subsequent efforts to decrease false-positive alerting by fine-tuning the triggers. Keep in mind that rules and alerts designed to prevent very rare events that should never occur may rarely fire or never fire, yet can still be useful. The prioritization process discussed in Chapter 2, page 41, can help determine when such rules might be valuable.

- How often is each alert overridden? Can you measure by specific end user to determine whether there is a pattern by individuals, or whether there is a more global issue with the intervention? Override data provide feedback to the CDS team about how helpful users (individually and collectively) find the alert to be. If users are overriding alerts that demand attention, then appropriate action should be taken to address the cause. For example, when disagreement exists about the alert recommendations (which will hopefully be infrequent if the earlier steps in this guide are followed) then end-user education/dialog about the underlying clinical issues—through pertinent clinical oversight bodies—might be helpful. When there is agreement with the recommendations, and "alert fatigue" caused by excessive false-positive alerting is the culprit, then efforts to increase overall alert appropriateness should be undertaken.

- Which of the coded reasons offered by the CIS are users selecting for each override? This information will help determine, when supplemented with further investigation as needed, whether coded override reasons are only chosen based on their placement on the list (for example, when the first choice is the most often selected choice whether or not it is pertinent) or if they accurately reflect a thoughtful user response. This metric and investigation also helps to determine if the override reasons available for the user to select are appropriate and sufficiently specific (for example, if they are considered clinically relevant). To the extent that there are many overrides that are appropriate (that is, for false-positive alerts), the CDS team should explore potential refinements to specific triggering data, alerting logic, and other approaches (such as revisiting the CDS Five Rights) that could be used to reduce these nuisance alerts.
- Is there a specific physical location or provider type—surgery suite or oncology unit—that is experiencing an abnormally high override rate? Again, this could indicate a specific type of false-positive alerting that might potentially be addressed by refining alert triggers or display rules. A study examining DDI alert overrides found that although many recipients want to turn off specific DDI alerts, recipients agreed that no frequently overridden alert could be safely turned off hospital-wide.[21] These results reinforce the premise that tuning alerts to recipients might be a fruitful avenue to explore.

Although we have recommended judicious use of mandatory forms for documenting override reasons, these forms do serve useful purposes, such as in diagnosing highly excessive alerting. Close collaboration with end users and thoughtful deployment can help decrease the nuisance caused by this tool. For example, presenting users with pre-defined/coded override reasons in a drop-down list (as opposed to requesting free text entry) is one useful approach for speeding the process for users and gathering data that are easier to analyze and act on.

As previously noted, care and some additional investigation may be required when interpreting the override reason data, since users may simply select the first choice on the list for expediency. If the list is so long that a vertical scroll bar is necessary, those reasons at the end of the list will never get used. Our recommendation is to keep the list of reasons short, simple, and relevant to the specific alert that has been displayed; when possible, make the first item on the list the most likely reason in most cases.

Below are override reasons that have been used for different alert types within several leading organizations. Remember, the override reason list should be carefully constructed, ideally with a different list at least for every different alert type (such as DDI or drug-allergy). Note that some CISs do not allow implementers to provide different override reasons for different alert types. This can lead to inappropriate override reasons appearing for some alerts if the reasons aren't determined globally with this constraint in mind.

The override reasons listed next reinforce points made earlier about key alert message components (for example, being explicit about the trigger for the alert and its rationale, and providing a specific recommended action and shortcut for executing that action). You might use this list to seed discussions with your CDS team and intended alert recipients about appropriate override reasons for alerts you will be deploying. Remember to carefully tune and limit the override reasons that are presented for each alert type you are implementing. Consider also the possibility of making user entry of alert override reasons voluntary instead of mandatory (if your systems provide this functionality).

Override reasons:

- Patient is (or "is not"...depending on alert recommendation) allergic to the drug. (When possible, the alert should display the reported allergic reaction and data source. This will help clinicians differentiate between a patient-reported intolerance to penicillin that caused abdominal discomfort from an anaphylactic reaction reported by an intensive care unit nurse).
- Patient does not have the condition that triggered the alert.
- New patient data are available that indicate the alert is no longer valid (for example, an alert indicating that according to clinical guidelines the patient is not eligible for a transfusion, may not "be aware" that the patient is actively bleeding).
- New scientific evidence is available that invalidates the alert (for example, a new clinical guideline is available that contradicts the previous guideline that formed the basis for the alert).
- Alert is incorrect (for reasons encompassing, or other than, those previously listed).
- Patient is currently taking the medication for which the alert is recommending against (for example, because the patient has a listed allergy to it or because it interacts with another drug) and is clinically stable.
- Patient has taken and tolerated the medication in the past.
- Benefit of medication outweighs the risk to the patient.
- The dose has been adjusted accordingly (for example, a physician may intentionally and carefully order two medications in the same class for a particular clinical purpose, so a duplicate therapy warning would not need to be heeded).
- Decline suggestion. Reasons might include other comorbidities, treatment cost, patient refusal, or other reason (option for user to enter free text information here).
- Defer alert for: (specify or allow user to enter period, such as days, weeks, or months, depending on alert type and IS capabilities).
- I acknowledge the risk and am planning/monitoring accordingly.
- Contraindicated order will be discontinued.
- Other: please enter text below. (This option can be problematic. If inputting text is not required, the request can easily be ignored. If it is required, users may simply enter a nonsensical response; for example, space, period, or any character, and move on. Either way, evaluating these disparate free text reasons for any length of time is difficult and time consuming.)

Outcome Measures

The indicators we have considered so far (system performance, structural measures reflecting what interventions are deployed, and process measures indicating how they affect users and workflows) illuminate key features of the deployed CDS portfolio.

They are essential tools for enhancing CDS use and usability. An ultimate purpose for which the interventions are used, however, is to influence important care delivery results. These include safer and more effective medication use and resulting increases in patient health and decreases in preventable mortality and harm. Outcome measures demonstrate the extent to which these and related objectives are being achieved.

Properly interpreting outcome measures depends on results from the other measure categories. For example, if you see a change in outcomes (length of hospital stay, drug utilization, patient disease parameters, and the like) but have no data to demonstrate that clinicians are using as anticipated the CDS interventions that are focused on these targets, then it may be difficult to convince stakeholders that the interventions are driving the changes.

Questions that CDS outcome measures are designed to answer include:

- Did an order get changed as the result of an alert and thereby help avoid an ADE?
  - If it was not changed, did an ADE develop because the alert was ignored?
  - Were there any unplanned medical or surgical interventions that were required to address the resulting preventable ADE?
- Has there been a measurable positive effect from an order set (or other CDS interventions) on patient care outcomes?
  - Is there a reduction in ALOS for conditions in which order sets are being used?
  - Have medication costs decreased because prescribers are selecting less expensive, equally efficacious drugs?
  - Are drug-resistant organisms less prevalent as a result of more appropriate antibiotic selection and therapy duration?
  - Is there an improved medication turnaround time from reduced need for pharmacy to clarify orders during the verification process?

As these examples illustrate, CDS may influence various patient and organizational outcomes, including care efficiency, safety, quality, and cost. Because the factors that determine these results are often numerous and complex, definitively sorting the specific contribution from the CDS intervention(s) can be difficult. The following are approaches for teasing out CDS effects and considerations for using each:

- Comparing variables before CDS intervention versus after intervention.[22] Before/after studies can be difficult to interpret because introducing certain interventions (for example, when potentially harmful conditions trigger alerting) often sheds light on previously unrecognized medication use problems, which can make it falsely appear that the new system is causing more errors.
  - Before/after conditions can also be affected by other initiatives the organization may have simultaneously undertaken. Similarly, results can be affected by seasonal variations (for example, new class of residents and interns or increase in expected alert activity—such as at the beginning of influenza season for flu immunization alerts).
- Prospective, randomized trial in which some clinicians, units, or patients have the intervention and some do not.[23]
  - These studies can be expensive and difficult to carry out. It may be difficult to get administrators to allow you to "withhold" CDS from some patients or clinicians (on ethical grounds, even though proof of intervention's effectiveness does not exist). Note the point earlier in this chapter about obtaining IRB approval for such research studies.
  - It may be difficult to keep all other conditions constant during the trial. Often many CIS infrastructure elements are changing in significant ways that aren't anticipated at the trial outset.
- Rolling or staggered implementation with repeated measures in which different parts of the organization (such as nursing units within a hospital) are sequentially implemented.[24]
  - This allows units on which the intervention is deployed to later serve as controls for the initial units implemented.

- If you observe similar changes (such as in magnitude and direction) on multiple units, then it is more likely that the observed changes are related to the intervention and are not merely artifacts.

- Although these methods are more susceptible to selection bias and other limitations than prospective randomized, controlled trials, they can be very helpful in identifying and isolating program-wide effects.

Other issues to keep in mind when developing and applying metrics to assess outcomes include:

- Are the needed data generally available in a consistent, codified form appropriate for analysis and, if so, will they be reliably available in each patient-specific instance?

- Can the outcome "numerator" and "denominator" be determined in a widely accepted and unambiguous way? For example, if the outcome of interest is reducing drug overdoses, does consensus exist on a clear, computable definition for what is meant by "drug overdose," (the measure numerator) as well on what comprises the population in which this outcome will be assessed (the denominator)?

- Are the data submitted voluntarily or are they automatically captured from ISs? Since voluntary submission typically underestimates occurrence to a significant degree[25] and may, therefore, be inaccurate, automated means are preferred for quantification when possible. Voluntary data, however, may provide useful occurrence details and identify areas missed by automated methods. When submitted and collected appropriately, these data can supplement data collected through automated means. Consider approaches that balance the strengths and limitations of various ADE and outcome detection methods.[26]

Even though it can be difficult to create an indisputable cause-and-effect link between a CDS intervention and a clinical outcome, it is important to thoughtfully gather and interpret data to get a sense of what, if any, relationship exists. Based on this analysis, together with guidance provided by easier-to-measure process indicators, you can strengthen the CDS value in improving outcomes in a data-driven manner.

We now outline in more detail several key clinical outcome types that you will want to carefully consider in setting up and evaluating outcome metrics for your CDS program—safety, quality, and financial. Keep in mind that in research studies, as well as in your own efforts, several of these may be considered together within a single evaluation initiative.

Safety

A central goal in applying CDS to medication management is to reduce preventable patient harm. Several interrelated terms and concepts are pertinent here, since they underpin medication safety assessments. An article entitled "Clarifying Adverse Drug Events: A Clinician's Guide to Terminology, Documentation, and Reporting" provides a helpful overview of these terms and their implications for clinicians.[27]

This review describes an *adverse drug reaction* as harm directly caused by a drug at normal doses, an *adverse drug event* as harm caused by drug use (including inappropriate use), *medication error* as inappropriate drug use that may or may not result in harm, and *side effect* as a usually predictable or dose-dependent drug effect that is not the principal effect for which the drug was chosen. Also pertinent are the NCC-MERP error categories[28] (listed in Chapter 1, page 11) that reflect the extent of patient harm associated with an error. An important point for understanding, measuring, and reporting CDS effects on medication use is that not all medication errors cause harm. Likewise, there are circumstances in which a patient might experience harm from a medication without an associated error (for example, when the patient experiences an adverse drug reaction that couldn't be prevented based on current knowledge).[29]

Typically, what we would most like to measure and improve regarding CDS and medication safety is the role that CDS interventions play in addressing errors that lead to ADEs that cause significant and preventable patient harm (for example, NCC MERP categories E-I). To the extent that you measure errors or ADEs to understand CDS effects, you will need to consider harm and preventability as well. Analyzing these in detail may be prohibitively complex in many cases, but keeping these issues in mind can help ensure effective and practical data gathering and interpretation. Also consider in your assessment and improvement efforts the role for CDS in helping to ensure that clinicians and patients understand medication side effects (which may be neither preventable nor due to an error), and anticipate and respond to them appropriately.

In designing and using metrics to assess CDS effects on medication safety, you should also consider the following:

- How you will identify error reduction within each step in the medication-management cycle and within pertinent systems at each step (for example, CPOE—prescribing; bar coding, eMAR, smart pumps—administration).
- How you will evaluate error reduction in NCC-MERP categories (B-I), individually and collectively, since they are interrelated. For example, catching errors in the prescribing step using CPOE alerts may cause an increase in documented Category B errors (those caught before reaching patients), compared with pre-intervention baselines. Though the total number of errors may appear to have increased due to CDS, you must consider that the intervention may be surfacing errors that might not otherwise have been recognized and documented—and therefore not amenable to correction prior to intervention deployment.
- How you will assess the specific errors you have targeted (for example, as outlined in Chapter 2 and Chapter 5), such as drug-allergy and drug-drug interactions, drug overdoses, and the like. Published research studies can provide ideas for measuring how CDS interventions affect specific targets. These include studies that examine alert effects on prescribing contraindicated medications

in patients older than 65 years of age[30] and many others cited in the Chapter 5 reference list, page 170.

ADE rates, both before and after applying targeted CDS, can be assessed by looking in CISs for signals suggesting possible drug-related incidents, such as sudden medication stop orders, antidote ordering, and certain abnormal laboratory values.[31] IHI built on earlier research in developing a broadly applicable tool for estimating ADE rates. This Trigger Tool for Measuring ADEs consists of "triggers" that suggest a likely ADE. Triggers include administration of diphenhydramine (commonly used to treat allergic reactions to medications) or naloxone (used to reverse narcotic overdoses); Table 7-2 provides a more complete list of triggers and the ADE-related process that may be associated with each.[32] The triggers do not confirm an ADE, but they suggest situations that may warrant further investigation to determine whether an ADE has occurred. In addition to a trigger list, IHI also provides a Web-based tool for tracking and investigating trigger events, tools for estimating event rates per admission and per 1,000 drug administrations, and benchmark data which hospitals can use to compare their performance with other institutions.[33]

As noted in the process metrics discussion, you should look for ADEs that result when the recipient overrides an alert that could have prevented the error if it was addressed appropriately. When you find these, you should investigate causes for the missed CDS opportunities (for example, alert fatigue as suggested by a high ratio of overrides/total number of alerts).

Another safety-related issue (related to a process metric) to examine on a periodic basis is the number and percent of medication orders entered as free text in CPOE systems.[34] CDS interventions, such as order sets and order sentences, should minimize the orders entered in this fashion since they may be more prone to error and not subject to CDS safety checks.

It is important to remember that CDS cannot only help reduce patient harm, but it can also inad-

Table 7-2: IHI Trigger Tool: List of Triggers Suggesting Possible ADEs

Trigger	Process Identified
T1: Diphenhydramine	Hypersensitivity reaction or drug effect
T2: Vitamin K	Over-anticoagulation with warfarin
T3: Flumazenil	Oversedation with benzodiazepine
T4: Droperidol	Nausea/emesis related to drug use
T5: Naloxone	Oversedation with narcotic
T6: Antidiarrheals	Adverse drug event
T7: Sodium polystryene	Hyperkalemia related to renal impairment or drug effect
T8: PTT > 100 seconds	Over-anticoagulation with heparin
T9: INR > 6	Over-anticoagulation with warfarin
T10: WBC < 3000 × 10⁶/μl	Neutropenia related to drug or disease
T11: Serum glucose < 50 mg/dl	Hypoglycemia related to insulin use
T12: Rising serum creatinine	Renal insufficiency related to drug use
T13: *Clostridium difficile* positive stool	Exposure to antibiotics
T14: Digoxin level > 2 ng/ml	Toxic digoxin level
T15: Lidocaine level > 5 ng/ml	Toxic lidocaine level
T16: Gentamicin or tobramycin levels peak > 10μg/ml	Toxic levels of antibiotics
T17: Amikacin levels peak > 30 μg/ml, trough > 10 μg/ml	Toxic levels of antibiotics
T18: Vancomycin level > 26 μg/ml	Toxic levels of antibiotics
T19: Theophylline level > 20 μg/ml	Toxic levels of drug
T20: Oversedation, lethargy, falls	Related to overuse of medication
T21: Rash	Drug related/adverse drug event
T22: Abrupt medication stop	Adverse drug event
T23: Transfer to higher level of care	Adverse drug event
T24: Customized to individual institution	Adverse event

Source: Rozich JD, Haraden CR, Resar RK. Adverse drug event trigger tool: a practical methodology for measuring medication related harm. *Qual Saf Health Care.* 2003; 12(3):194-200. Used with permission.

vertently cause it, or lead to other unintended consequences. e-Iatrogenesis is a recently coined term referring to patient harm caused, at least in part, by IT. It is, therefore, essential to remain vigilant for these potential complications from your CDS efforts.[35] e-Iatrogenesis from CDS might arise in a various ways, including errors in logic or knowledge underlying the intervention, or in users' response

to information presented, as well as other related problems that lead to inappropriate treatment. These complications should be minimized through careful attention to development and testing as outlined in earlier chapters. As discussed earlier, excessive false-positive alerting can also distract clinicians from important clinical details and thus cause CDS-facilitated problems. Real or imagined e-Iatrogenesis can undermine confidence and support for the CDS interventions and should be carefully assessed and addressed.

Quality
IOM defines healthcare quality as: "The degree to which health services for individuals and populations increase the likelihood of desired health outcomes and are consistent with current professional knowledge."[36] Safety metrics, as just discussed, examine whether CDS is helping to avoid "undesirable health outcomes"; quality metrics look more broadly at whether CDS is supporting "desirable health outcomes" (such as patients living longer or being less burdened by disease).

As with safety, this link can be very difficult to firmly establish. Again, though, evaluating pertinent CDS structure and process metrics, together with outcomes more directly associated with care quality, can help assess the relationship between CDS and quality measurements and enhance it over time.

The quality outcomes supported by CDS may take a long time to manifest and may cross care settings. For example, CDS interventions targeted to increase appropriate inpatient medication use after a heart attack might not be expected to fully deliver outcome benefits until long after the patient is discharged. In these cases, proxy measures that examine processes (for example, the extent to which evidence-based services are ordered and delivered) and intermediate outcomes (such as length of hospitalization, disease-severity indicators, such as HbA1c in diabetics, readmissions, and short-term mortality) can shed light on the role of CDS in supporting desirable quality outcomes.

Guides are available for calculating some statistics pertinent to healthcare quality measurement, such as ALOS, mortality, and morbidities.[37] It is important to use, to the greatest extent possible, industry standard metrics that are most appropriate to the issue at hand. This helps establish credibility in evaluation results; as with any measurement effort, there is a tendency for those who disagree with the results to argue with methods.

For example, there are at least two methods that can be used to calculate ALOS:
• Method 1: (total discharge days/total discharges) = ALOS (in days)
• Method 2: (total inpatient days of care/total admissions) = ALOS (in days)

Because different data items are used in these calculations, they may produce different results in some circumstances. For example, if there are a large percentage of long-stay patients that are in the facility for longer than the measurement interval, Method 2 will not fully account for those inpatient days.[38] This example illustrates the importance of carefully choosing the metric most appropriate for the circumstance.

Because medication orders are an important component of "health services likely to increase desired health outcomes," you should measure CDS effects on the number, class, and type of medications ordered and the situations in which they are used. The literature sampling on outcomes outlined in the following bullets, and mentioned with the quality-related targets discussed in Chapter 5, page 157, may help augment your approach to quality-related outcome measures:
• Percent of patients treated with recommended drugs for specific conditions[39]
  – CDS in the form of guidelines and recommended options delivered via CPOE improve appropriate prescribing.
• Percent of patients requiring VTE prophylaxis that actually received it and effects on VTE events[40]
  – Alerts increased prophylaxis rates and markedly reduced VTE events (deep vein thrombosis and pulmonary embolism) in high-risk hospitalized patients.
• Percent appropriate antimicrobial prescribing and effects on mortality and drug resistance[41]
  – Local clinician-driven guidelines embedded in computer decision support program reduced mortality, ADEs, and cost per treated patient with no increased antimicrobial resistance.

- Improvement in symptoms and quality of life for patients in primary care practice with upper GI complaints[42]
  - Evaluation with (cases) and without (control) intervention using CDS tool for complaint diagnosis/treatment; tool improved symptom severity and quality of life. Physician visits, medication costs, and diagnostics tests were all significantly reduced among cases. The average cost for six months' treatment and follow-up was $199 for cases, compared with an average of $336 in the control group.

Financial

As studies cited earlier in this chapter and book indicate, CDS can have favorable effects on the costs associated with medication use, while simultaneously improving quality and/or safety. As financial pressures on the health system escalate overall, and for providers and consumers specifically, quantifying and optimizing these effects will become increasingly important. There are many potential financially-related metrics to consider, while also being vigilant for related quality and safety effects. Keep in mind the financial implications for all stakeholders as pertinent (for example, hospital or practice, as well as patient, and others). The following small sampling of categories will hopefully help stimulate ideas for specific financial metrics to track within your CDS program.

- Percent of all medication orders for preferred formulary drugs; CDS intervention (for example, order sets, alerts, etc.) effects on this number; financial implications from resulting increased formulary compliance
- Number of medication orders switched from an IV to oral (PO) route (for example, triggered by order sets or alerts) and resulting effects on inpatient ALOS and costs
- Financial implications of CDS targeted toward increasing quality and safety (for example, from decreasing additional costs and ALOS related to ADEs or VTEs); see report from AHRQ, *Reducing and Preventing Adverse Drug Events To Decrease Hospital Costs*[43]

- Costs and returns associated with CDS itself (for example, for use in cost/benefit analysis and optimization)
  - Has automating specific processes with CDS (for example, replacing manual chart reviews to identify medication management improvement opportunities with surveillance based on CDS rules) freed up staff resources that can be deployed in other ways? Can the amount and value of this additional resource availability be quantified?
  - What are the costs associated with deploying the CDS interventions, and can they be further optimized? For example, excessive false-positive alerting or poor user acceptance of CDS interventions may require additional technical and clinical personnel time to remedy and address user concerns. What are the costs associated with this, and how can these be minimized (for example, through alert trigger tuning, user education, etc.) for this intervention? Can the learning from this experience be applied to increase the cost-effectiveness of subsequent intervention efforts?

External Standardized CDS Evaluation Tools

As healthcare payers exert increasing pressure on providers to ensure that they are buying safe and effective care, these payers are turning greater attention to the role that CDS plays in supporting these outcomes. An excellent example is the Leapfrog CPOE Evaluation Tool,[44] which was developed by this employer organization to promote successful development and deployment in hospitals of specific CDS functionality to improve patient safety and clinical quality.

PI pressures may lead to increased development and use of such standardized CDS evaluations over the next several years. Comparing assessment results from these tools, along with implementation strategies and lessons learned, could accelerate the pace with which the potential value from CDS in medication management is fully realized.[45,46]

For now, acute care hospitals can use the Leapfrog CPOE Evaluation Tool for credit toward the Leapfrog Group's CPOE standard[47] and to help drive enhanced value from their CPOE/CDS efforts.

Briefly, the Leapfrog evaluation tool works by simulating several different clinical scenarios that should evoke CDS responses. Organizations taking the test create mock patients based on the scenarios within their production CPOE system. The evaluation examines how the system responds when the user enters various unsafe or otherwise problematic medication orders from the scenarios for these test patients. Table 7-3 describes the various CDS categories that are evaluated by the Leapfrog tool. Organizations that participated in preliminary tool evaluations demonstrated substantial opportunities for improving their CDS performance. For example, none of the six test sites had a portfolio of CDS interventions in place that covered all CDS areas evaluated by the tool.[48]

Who Will Measure

As we previously emphasized, the evaluation plan for your medication management CDS interventions should be developed early, after determining which organizational roles will be responsible for creating and executing the plan. In assigning these tasks, you should consider whether the individuals have the appropriate skills and training to succeed in these efforts and from what source(s) you will obtain the resources to fund the evaluation.[49]

Leveraging Available Resources

To help address these issues, you can begin by assessing evaluation processes and responsibilities in place within your organization. Questions to consider include:

• Who currently performs measurements related to the broader CDS program, and to structure, process, and outcomes related to other aspects of medication management and care delivery? Are nurse managers measuring near-misses or actual events? How are they capturing information? More than likely, your organization is already per-

forming some pertinent measurements. Therefore, it is critical that you thoroughly document and evaluate these efforts in light of the CDS-related needs discussed in this chapter. Also, ensure that the individuals or groups currently conducting the measurements will be able to continue to do so once new CDS-related technology and processes are implemented—and ideally, enhance their efforts to address additional CDS-related needs.

• What tools, such as analytical applications and databases with pertinent information needed for the metrics, are currently in place to support needed measurements? Who has access to them, and what processes are they currently using to collect and analyze information? Are there synergies that can be cultivated between these current efforts and new CDS interventions and related measurement activities? Reducing the total time and staff it takes to gather and analyze data needed for CDS and other priorities—for example, through better leveraging an EMR, data warehouse, or similar data gathering and analysis application—can have a significant ROI.

Next, identify additional resources that could potentially assist with evaluation efforts. These might include:

• Motivated and engaged end users such as nurses, pharmacists, and physicians. For example, hospitalists are increasingly playing important roles in such PI activities.

• Managers, including unit/department and specialty managers

• Existing committees and departments, especially pharmacy department and pharmacy and therapeutics committee, quality assurance, and of course the CDS team.

Table 7-4 presents a skeletal outline of some key roles that might assist with evaluation activities, the types of issues for which these roles might be helpful, and why this support might be useful. This material is intended to serve as a trigger for broader and deeper thinking about pertinent roles and activities in your organization.

Table 7-3: CDS Categories Assessed by the Leapfrog CPOE Evaluation Tool

Category	Description
Therapeutic duplication	Therapeutic overlap with another new or active order; may be same drug, same drug class, or components of combination products
Single and cumulative dose limits	Specified dose that exceeds recommended dose ranges; will result in a cumulative dose that exceeds recommended range; can also include dose limits for each component of a combination product
Allergies and cross allergies	Allergy has been documented or allergy to other drug in same category exists
Contraindicated route of administration	Order specifying a route of administration that is not appropriate for the identified medication
Drug-drug and drug-food interactions	Results in known dangerous interaction when administered together with a different medication or results in an interaction in combination with a drug or food group
Contraindications/dose limits based on patient diagnosis	Contraindication based on patient diagnosis or diagnosis affects recommended dosing
Contraindications/dose limits based on patient weight	Contraindication based on age or weight
Contraindications/dose limits based on laboratory studies	Contraindication based on laboratory studies or for which laboratory studies must be considered for dosing
Contraindications/dose limits based on radiology studies	Contraindication for this patient based on interaction with contrast medium (in ordered radiology study)
Corollary	Intervention that requires an associated or secondary order to meet the standard of care (prompt to order drug levels during medication ordering)
Cost of care	Test that duplicates a service within a time frame in which there is typically minimal benefit from repeating the test
Nuisance	Order with such a slight or inconsequential interaction that clinicians typically ignore the advice or prompt

Source: Kilbridge PM, Welebob EM, Classen DC. Development of the Leapfrog methodology for evaluating hospital implemented inpatient computerized physician order entry systems. *Qual Saf Health Care*. 2006; 15(2):81-84. Used with permission.

Other important considerations include:

- Determining who wants to—versus who should—measure; some managers will want to measure for their own purposes, such as to evaluate personnel or departments.
- Coordinating all evaluation efforts to limit inefficiency or duplication, ensuring that all goals are being met (organizational, departmental,

individual), and leveraging available resources appropriately to address evaluation needs. A well-documented and vetted evaluation plan can help.

Whether you select centralized versus local data collection depends on whether your organization is a single hospital or a multifacility integrated delivery network (IDN). The goal in either case is to maximize resources and allow for appropriate autonomy.

Table 7-4: Skeletal Outline of Different Stakeholders and Their Potential Evaluation Role

Who	What	Why
End users		
Physicians	Order sets for specific diseases	Determine usefulness of the order sets and the use patterns for each.
Nurses	User feedback—what's working and what's not	Understanding from a user standpoint how the CDS affects workflow is key.
Pharmacists	Medication errors Medication turnaround time	Pharmacists are central figures in the medication management process.
Managers		
Unit/department	Departmental usage statistics	Has the system been adequately customized for this department?
Specialty	Usage statistics Override rates	Has the system been adequately customized for this specialty; has the right content been developed?
Quality Team		
Core team members	Core quality measures Patient safety measures	Is the CDS system helping the hospital achieve the desired quality and safety goals?
CDS Team		
Core team members	Entire evaluation program	Well positioned between clinical and IS to gather performance, structure and process metrics, and coordinate efforts on outcome metrics.

Some local departments or facilities may want to do their own collection and measurement rather than rely on a central team from larger multifacility organization. Either way, it is extremely beneficial when you can agree on measure details and definitions (see "What to Measure" section, page 199). Once consensus has been achieved, measures can be compared across locations and/or interpreted correctly within an individual facility. Without this explicit consensus, there may be subsequent disagreement about what the measurements mean and what should be done about them.

Whatever team is responsible for setting and reporting on the CDS performance measures for medication management, it must be clearly and tightly connected to appropriate governance mechanisms within your organization (see Chapter 2, page 25). For example, the evaluation effort should be linked to new or existing structures responsible for CDS and for medication management. This connection is necessary to coordinate pertinent internal communication, external reporting, and refinements aimed at the CDS interventions and/or broader medication management activities.

Responsibility for CDS measurement activities will depend on how your organization manages the various components of its CDS program overall and the medication management components specifically. For example, some use one team that manages all CDS aspects, including implementation, development, training, communication, process redesign, and system evaluation. Others separate the work and have very specific measurement duties performed by a select few who do not have other responsibilities in the process. Several approaches, which are not mutually exclusive, include:

- **Option 1:** CDS implementation team performs measurement.
- **Option 2:** A separate "CIS benefits realization team" is established to perform measurement. This group may be part of the formal EMR/CIS project structure but separate and independent from the CDS implementation team.
- **Option 3:** The organization's PI or quality group, which has organization-wide responsibility for quality/safety outcomes measurement and analysis, performs the measurement.

Ensuring Access to Needed Evaluation Skills

You might not find all of the skills required to evaluate CDS performance metrics in your organization's current staff, and at least some skills typically must be brought in from outside. Pertinent skill sets to inventory and seek include:

- **Technical:** At a minimum, the person(s) who performs the measurement will have the technical skills to run reports from several different systems, such as the EMR, CPOE, pharmacy system, data warehouse, business intelligence systems, and other such tools your organization has developed or acquired from vendors. Ideally, they'll also know how to build and configure those reports and be able to identify potential problems and create solutions for improved reporting capabilities. These technical staff may or may not be the same as those who configure and maximize the CDS interventions within the CIS infrastructure.

- **Clinical:** At a minimum, the evaluation team must understand all pertinent clinical workflows and potential CDS effects on each medication management phase. This familiarity is necessary to address the clinical complexity and nuances that will inevitably arise from developing and evaluating the performance metrics. Ideally, the team should therefore include clinicians (pharmacists, physicians, and/or nurses and others) who together are sensitive to these issues and can work well with each type of clinical end user throughout the evaluation process.

- **Data analysis and presentation:** Besides pertinent clinical expertise, rich analytical skills are required to deal appropriately with the metric complexities, statistical considerations, and the like. Individuals with expertise in multiple quantitative and qualitative data collection techniques, data and statistical analysis, and interpretation skills should be included on the team, or at least be readily available to it. Similarly, conveying CDS interventions effects in a clear and credible way to all pertinent stakeholders (leadership, end users, clinical and technical implementation staff, etc.) is essential to help the organization understand and enhance results from the program. Individuals with the communication skills and credibility to accomplish this should also be included on the team.

- **Cross-functional:** The tasks previously outlined do not occur in isolation; they are highly interdependent. As a result, team members must not only have adequate competency in the respective functions but also have appreciation for the needs and challenges associated with other evaluation program components. Good collaboration skills, and ability to work with others who have complementary expertise and responsibilities, are key. Increasingly, team members with formal clinical informatics training will be a part of this mix.[50]

Securing Funding for Evaluation

Before leaving this "who" section, we consider briefly who will financially support evaluation activities.

Many organizations do not allocate adequate funding at the CDS program outset for ongoing maintenance and (especially) for evaluating CDS interventions after their initial deployment. This is often true more broadly for IT-enabled process changes. Strategies to avoid this problem were outlined in Chapter 2 and several key points are reiterated next:

- Create and present both the quality/safety and financial business case to pertinent executives within the organization (CMO, CFO, CEO, and board, if necessary) at the beginning of the process, and formalize the CDS efforts in a broad and/or medication-specific charter.

- Document baseline measurements to provide comparison points for each alert and other interventions and to reinforce that the goal is measurable improvement in these priority targets.

- Ensure that each evaluation team member has sufficient dedicated time to perform his or her pertinent duties. These activities should be core position responsibilities and not merely "add-on tasks as time allows," since the targets being evaluated should include organizational priorities.

- Outline expected resource needs from the very beginning, knowing that CDS interventions will likely require as many resources, if not more, to maintain and evaluate as they did to implement. Resources may include headcount and their time, funds to acquire additional needed expertise as outlined earlier, and analytic software tools and databases, among many others.

- Communicate to all appropriate executives that driving improved outcomes with CDS is not a "once and done" effort but is a process that continues throughout the organization's lifetime.

How to Measure

How to measure is inextricably linked to *what* you measure. This section builds on the previous "what" discussion, and other suggestions in this chapter, by providing additional details on gathering needed data and managing the measurement process.

As we have mentioned, it is important to develop an explicit, formal evaluation plan in early opportunity assessment and intervention development project stages. This plan can evolve as needed and should ideally address all the major issues outlined in this chapter that are pertinent to your efforts. The following are some tasks that you might keep in mind in formulating and executing your approach to evaluating the effects that your CDS interventions have on medication management. Worksheets 7-1 through 7-4 might also help your team think through and document these tasks.

Create an Intervention Inventory

The number and complexity of CDS interventions you deploy to improve medication management will likely increase over time, so an important starting point for measurement is cataloging the objectives you are targeting and the CDS interventions you are using to address them. If you have been using the worksheets in previous chapters, you may find information you have documented in Worksheet 3-2: Selecting Interventions, page 79, and Worksheet 5-1: Intervention Specification Form, page 163, useful for creating the catalog. In Chapter 8, page 242, we will further discuss such an inventory in the context of knowledge management.

Develop a Generic Protocol for Intervention Assessment

Driven by regulatory and accreditation requirements, most healthcare organizations today will have at least some mechanisms in place for evaluating medication (and related CDS) issues addressed by these drivers; these can serve as the plan foundation. For example, nearly all acute care facilities are reporting to CMS "core measure" performance information, such as the percentage of patients receiving specific drugs indicated for particular diseases. Infrastructure currently used for measuring, reporting, and improving performance might also serve related CDS program evaluation needs. Additional resources and interest engendered by medication management-related CDS efforts can be leveraged to augment these core activities with additional efforts and infrastructure to address the specific needs outlined in this chapter.

For example, business intelligence or data analysis tools that are increasingly available may already be in place and supporting PI, or might be acquired as needed.

A framework for leveraging available infrastructure to address the evaluation program needs might contain the following elements:

- Document how you are capturing pertinent evaluation information today—for example, time and resources required, collection method, impact on end users (if any), timing (during or pre/post clinical encounter).
- Review measurement options for each intervention.
  - Does the new CDS intervention enable enhanced means for gathering needed evaluation information?
  - Can a report be created to automatically capture the desired information from available ISs? Determine when that report will run and confirm that information will be captured in the system, preferably in a codified manner.
  - Do you need to augment the information capture with other methods, such as chart review or end-user shadowing?
- Finalize method for capturing information (see next section).
- Educate end users on their role (such as expectations, communications, follow-up plans).
- Begin measurement process and apply to each intervention deployed.

Keep the following considerations in mind when analyzing CDS performance data:

- Be careful that the data you collect mean what you think they mean. Always check with some end users to make sure that you are collecting data that reflects what is really going on in the clinical setting.
- Strive for data that are practical to gather, relevant, actionable, credible, valid, accurate, and reliable. Data that are not believable or are inaccurate may not be useful—or worse.
- Consider practical significance in addition to statistical significance.

- Use highly readable scorecards to organize data for analysis and presentation. For example, summary graphs and red/yellow/green "stoplight" analyses, with drilldown to fuller details, can be more useful for many purposes than massive spreadsheets packed with numbers.
- Remember that you may need to cleanse the information (that is, delete irrelevant data) and use risk adjustment to facilitate appropriate comparisons.
- Remember, "Not everything that counts can be counted, and not everything that can be counted counts."[51]

In the sections that follow, we outline more specific approaches for fleshing out the generic assessment protocol.

Consider and Select Data Collection Methods

Where data needed for analysis reside and how you will obtain them are two important and sometimes challenging questions. Reports from the systems serving up the CDS interventions (such as CPOE, EMR, and other CIS/CDS applications) will be a core component in determining how you measure your CDS interventions. Most CIS/CDS vendor systems come with some standard reports, but in most cases you will want to develop custom reports to address your specific needs. You should think about this issue early in the process to maximize the reports' value and better shape how the intervention and associated measurement capabilities are built.

You can extract medication-error data from your facility's medication-error analysis and reporting system. Ideally this system will be an electronic source, such as from homegrown or commercial tools that look at administrative and/or clinical data; this information can be augmented with data from online or paper forms for clinician error reporting, if available and needed. It may be useful to follow a structured data scheme, such as NCC-MERP taxonomy of medication errors, that allows for merging and comparing data across facilities *in your organization.* Note that ISMP and NCC-MERP have expressed that "Use of medication error rates to compare health care organizations is of no value."[52] This is due to differences across organizations in factors such as culture, error definitions, reporting systems, patient populations that affect reporting, and underlying error incidence. You should consider these issues carefully if you plan to compare facilities within your organization.

It is also important to keep in mind that the data available for analysis in voluntary reporting systems will be representative of actual errors only to the extent that these errors are recognized and entered into the system. Culture comes into play here, and voluntary error reporting generally isn't as rich in healthcare as in other high-risk activities such as aviation. Near-misses can be important sources for improvement pearls, so consider addressing culture and complete reporting as part of the governance and management work outlined in Chapter 2.

CDS usage data can be obtained from various sources, including CIS/CDS system-generated log files; electronic surveys deployed close to the time of intervention use; and direct observation by, or in-person feedback sessions to, the evaluation team members.

Table 7-5 illustrates an example of how these sources facilitate data gathering to assess CDS use and effects. For each data collection method, consider the available and desirable balance between free text versus structured information. Free text can be more expressive, while structured information is generally much easier to aggregate and analyze. Some methods such as incident reports, documentation forms completed during user shadowing, and surveys can include both free text and structured elements; you can adapt the data format to best address specific needs and constraints.

Additional ideas on strategies to gather outcome information can be gleaned from the discussion and literature references in the Safety and Quality sections under "What to Measure."

Once informed about data collection methods available in your organization and ISs generally, you can begin to develop more detailed protocols for evaluating use and effects for each deployed CDS

intervention and for applying this information to drive continuous improvements.

Assess Intervention Use

The foundations for this evaluation were presented earlier in the sections on response time, structure, and process metrics. The data collection methods and other elements presented in Table 7-5 can be used as a starting point for a plan to answer key questions about intervention use. For example, who is using the intervention? Why (or why not)? When? Where? How?

In general, basic usage measurement (such as for each question just mentioned, except for "why") should be performed as much as possible via automated or custom reports whose output is objective. Some data gathering may still require patient chart review and/or end-user interaction in person or electronically (for example, to answer "why").

Table 7-6 is an example of a protocol for evaluating order set use, both in paper-based and CPOE environments, and applying the results.

Assess End-User Impact, Satisfaction, and Workflow

Again, the foundations for these measurements can be found in the earlier discussion on response time, structure, and process metrics. Some effects on users are suggested by response time data (how much time do users spend waiting for CDS or responding to the intervention?) and process data (what can be inferred about user frustration based on alert override data?).

These objective clues are supplemented by more subjective measurements based on eliciting feedback from each end-users group. Their satisfaction with the value and usability of CDS interventions can be determined using data collection methods such as those outlined in Table 7-5. Also consider the following approaches:

- Assessments pre- and post-intervention launch and periodically thereafter
- Scheduled interviews and focus groups, as well as ad hoc interactions from evaluation team walk rounds, to elicit feedback

Table 7-5: Methods for Gathering CDS Use and Effects Data as Applied to Inpatient Order Sets (Focusing on Medication Use Components)

Data Collection Method	Assessments/Goals	Timing	Data Gathering Resources (to Supplement Evaluation Team)
Chart review (electronic [semi-automated vs. manual] vs. paper)	Review appropriateness and outcomes related to medication ordering for specific diseases	Post-discharge	Clinicians
End user shadowing	Reasons for using/not using order sets Workflow impact End user satisfaction/issues	Real time	Qualitative researchers
System-generated reports (CPOE)	Overall utilization by diagnosis and physician Specific medication utilization for each order set Modifications to default medication selections	During hospitalization	Data analysts to extract data or run reports
Incident reporting	Identify specific CDS-related problem areas; self-reported, ad hoc	During hospitalization or post-discharge	Clinicians involved in patient care
Qualitative end user surveys	End user satisfaction	Post-discharge	Individuals experienced in data interpretation

- An online forum for user feedback, including specific e-mail channels or an intranet blog

Intervention effects on workflow are important factors in user satisfaction, productivity, and efficiency. Key questions here include:

- How many steps and how much time is needed to use an intervention (for example, order set, documentation tool, infobutton), and how does this compare with alternative approaches for users to perform the underlying tasks?
- For alerts, how many steps and how much time is needed to accept an alert and its suggestions, or to override it?

- How much variation is there from the "accepted" workflow? Many times, individuals don't use recommended workflows because they are following prior habits or because they have found an easier or better way than the recommended approach to accomplish the same task. Analyzing variation should not be looked at as a search for those who are breaking the rules but instead an evaluation of what really works for front-line end users.

As with user satisfaction, some of this workflow information can be gleaned from system reports on response times, but subjective information is useful to flesh out user perceptions. More objective data

Table 7-6: Measuring Order Set Utilization

Paper Order Sets

- Method - chart review, user feedback
- Steps
  - Choose a manageable number of priority order sets for initial evaluation (such as those that address conditions covered by core measures).
  - Make sure all order sets are available in all areas in which ordering takes place (for example, ED, all units, ambulatory offices, online).
  - After discharge, run a report for all patients discharged with those same diagnoses (for example, those pertinent to the core measures under study).
  - Perform chart pulls (for a random subset, if necessary, of discharges covering all pertinent physicians/specialties and locations), and determine whether order set was utilized.
  - Review medication section of the order set.
    - Capture which medications were used.
    - When a specific medication (such as aspirin for heart attack) was not used, determine if reason was captured in chart and catalog it.
  - Interview/survey a subset of physicians (especially those who did not use the order set at all or did not use drugs as called for by core measures) to assess reasons for non-compliance, or (in those who did respond as desired) feedback on order set use.
- Reports
  - Create report of order set utilization by physician and determine if there is a difference by:
    - Specialty
    - Ordering location (ED, floor, office, other)
  - Create report of which medications were:
    - Ordered (including user feedback on the intervention)
    - Not ordered when expected (catalog reasons documented in chart and conveyed personally by prescriber)
- Goals
  - These reports should be used to drive enhancements, such as:
    - Increased ease with which order sets are accessed
    - Continual refinement of the order sets, the medications on them, and how they are presented (for example, explanatory text, default order selections)
    - Updated communications to the end users; for example, about order set value

Electronic Order Sets with CPOE

- Method - electronic reporting with chart review as necessary; user feedback
- Steps
  - Choose a manageable number of priority order sets for initial evaluation (such as those that address conditions covered by core measures).
  - Make sure all order sets under study are available online through the system.
  - Run a report by diagnosis and physician to determine whether an order set was utilized (many CPOE systems provide this functionality).

Table 7-6: *continued*

- Create a report to show whether medications indicated by core measure were ordered (you may need to perform chart reviews to determine this).
- Create a report to show reason documented by prescriber for not ordering indicated medications (for example, if alerts/reminders are fired and include opportunity for prescriber to document override reason). Ideally, you will have set up the CPOE system to accept coded reasons and deployed it in such a way that users are properly documenting reasons; some manual review (ideally through an electronic system) may be needed to determine why an indicated drug was not ordered.
- Interview/survey a subset of physicians (especially those who did not use the order set at all or did not use drugs as called for by core measures) to assess reasons for non-compliance, or (in those who did respond as desired) feedback on order set use.
- Reports and Goals (same as above for paper order sets, plus the following item)
  - Improve end-user training, as needed, on underlying CPOE system and order set "tips and tricks" to increase use and usefulness.

can be obtained by shadowing users on a periodic basis and documenting a brief time and motion study.[53]

Assess Patient Impact

Approaches for evaluating CDS effects that are most important to patients (such as improvements in care safety and quality) are considered earlier in the discussion on outcomes. These effects may include:

- Avoiding harmful medication errors
- Appropriately using prophylactic medications to prevent avoidable complications and conditions (such as VTE and vaccine-preventable illness)
- Appropriately using drugs that minimize morbidity and mortality from acute and chronic disease
- Patients understanding their conditions and medications better, resulting in their increased satisfaction, engagement, adherence, and health status
- Patient financial benefits resulting from prescribers selecting cost-effective drug treatments

Although clinicians typically are the primary focus as CDS recipients, as noted throughout this book, patients themselves are increasingly important CDS intervention users. More widespread use of PHRs and related tools is accelerating this trend. As

a result, the "end user" assessments presented earlier regarding utilization, workflow, and satisfaction will apply to patients, as well, when they are the end user.

Assess Financial Impact to the Organization

The metric types discussed earlier under "Financial" in the "Outcome Measures" section (page 210) can be used to quantify the effects that one or more interventions have on departmental and organizational finances. Data for these assessments will typically come from a combination of chart review (ideally electronic and semiautomated) and system-generated reports (for example, from administrative and financial systems).

For metrics such as formulary adherence, ALOS, and cost per case, available ISs can typically produce needed reports. In cases for which it is necessary to correlate data from disparate clinical and financial systems, the analysis can be problematic because these systems may use different coding schemes and definitions for key terms. Patience, perseverance, and close collaboration with pertinent individuals in finance, IT, and other departments may be needed to appropriately assess financial effects from CDS interventions. This effort can be useful though, especially in an organization for which such ROI data influences resource allocation to projects. As cited earlier in this guide, there are examples of well-executed ROI studies that might trigger ideas for your evaluations.[54,55]

When to Measure

Overall, deciding when to measure is tied to the lifecycle stage for the intervention (such as design, testing, launch, and the like), what you are measuring, how quickly the underlying outcomes and processes are likely to change, and how you will use the evaluation results. For example, the measurements may drive intervention enhancement, public reporting, and/or incentive-based staff compensation—each of which may have implications for assessment timing. Ideally, you should only release interventions if you can devote at least some attention to evaluating effects, so any deployed intervention should be subject to at least some analysis at key lifecycle stages as outlined in this and prior chapters.

Early after initially deploying alerts and other CDS interventions, you should conduct an evaluation of response time, as well as structural and process metrics to ensure proper functioning, and look for negative unanticipated consequences as discussed ealier in this chapter. Outcome measures (such as quality, safety, financial) should be assessed at the earliest time you would expect to see a change, or sooner if the other metrics suggest that something about the CDS interventions might be moving things in the wrong direction. Once the evaluation team has a sense of how much and how fast key post-launch metrics are changing, the measurement scope, detail, and frequency can be adjusted accordingly.

The reality is that most organizations do not have enough resources or time to measure every intervention, with the detail just described, and as often as they would like. Therefore, organizations must prioritize their measurement activities, focusing at least on ensuring that there are no major problems with any of the interventions and getting at least a gross sense of their value. Beyond that, use governance structures (as discussed in Chapter 2)

to prioritize measurement efforts across interventions, and the lifecycle for each, in a manner that optimally supports the medication management charter.

What to Do With the Results

Overall evaluation goals include determining the extent to which the deployed CDS interventions are achieving the targeted objectives, the nature of any unintended consequences, and lessons that can be applied to continually enhancing the value that the CDS interventions bring to improving care delivery and outcomes. Key activities related to these goals include communicating the evaluation results and their implications to stakeholders, and using the results as input to subsequent rounds of the PI cycle outlined in this guide.

Many organizations devote substantial resources to deploying CISs and associated CDS functionality, yet underplay evaluation and, therefore, fail to fully engage in effective PI. Those that heed the guidance to plan for measurement beginning in early project phases, and execute a thoughtful evaluation approach throughout the intervention lifecycle, are well-positioned to use this feedback loop to close the gap between desired and actual clinical and CDS performance.

If the data about CDS results are accurate, actionable, and credible (see Develop a Generic Protocol for Intervention Assessment under How to Measure, page 221), then they should document for the evaluation team the issues about intervention value outlined in the first sentence of this section. The task then is to convey these messages to other stakeholders in the organization so they can respond appropriately, including supporting subsequent improvement rounds.

As noted in the *who* section of this chapter, one or more individuals on the evaluation team (or working closely with it), should clearly and credibly articulate the evaluation results and implications to others. The objective is to have the recipients understand and believe the information and to prepare and motivate them to take action appropriate for their role (for example, as outlined in governance figures in Chapter 2, pages 25–28).

The following are some considerations for this critical communication function:

- Why should evaluation results be communicated?
  - To the extent that the CDS-supported medication management goals are driven by senior organizational leadership, the evaluation results will be very important to them and others. For example, when compensation plans and other powerful drivers are tied to results, then scrutiny over their accuracy (particularly if unfavorable) may be intense. Methodologic rigor, transparency, and close stakeholder engagement throughout the evaluation process can be helpful here.
  - Besides such high-stakes implications, each of the "who" stakeholders plays a role in enhancing the CDS program. Tasks associated with these roles may include, among others: revising targets and priorities and allocating resources (executives); designing and launching CDS interventions to address current or revised targets (the CDS team and collaborators); and helping make interventions practical and useful and successfully adopting them (end users). Information about what has been done so far and the result is key to addressing each one of these tasks.
- Who should receive this information? (See Chapter 2 for stakeholders, page 24.)
  - Consider assessing each "customer type" who needs communication about the evaluation results; create a strategy and tracking tool to determine what communication they need, how often they need it, and who will deliver it. The following bullets outline several such "customers" who will likely appear on your list.
    - Quality and performance improvement teams, as well as the pertinent CISs team (such as EMR, CPOE, PHR)
    - Project and organizational leadership
    - End users; usually at a department level at a minimum and, in many cases, at an individual level

- Patients and community (the improvement in quality patient care can be a great differentiator in the healthcare marketplace)
- CIS and CDS vendors (to continually improve the systems and their capabilities)
- How can the information be conveyed? (See Chapter 6, Communications, page 185.)
  - Dashboards
    - Many analytical and business intelligence applications can create dashboards for review and presentation. Consider different dashboards for different audiences, outlined earlier, to address specific perspectives and needs for this overview information.
  - Scorecards
    - Like dashboards, scorecards can be created via automated systems or manually from available data and generic applications such as spreadsheets; these are often used with departments and individual clinicians for feedback on performance.
  - Department Meetings
    - Representatives from the CDS team, quality department, or PI team present evaluation results at regular department meetings with a focus on continual improvement and patient safety. Over time, representatives from the specific departments should present the data and manage the communication to their departments.
  - Marketing
    - In collaboration with the marketing department and others within the organization, develop and execute a communication plan to convey pertinent messages about the program results, as appropriate, to the community, other internal stakeholders, and other organizations (for example, via journal publications and conference presentations). Recall the caution noted earlier in this chapter about IRB approval if you are considering publishing evaluation results.
- When should evaluation results be presented?

– Develop a schedule that is appropriate for each stakeholders' group and each intervention type. Keep in mind the pace at which metrics are likely to change and the role that each stakeholder plays in responding to the results.

Once again, if the evaluation has been conducted thoughtfully, and corresponding care is applied to the communication tasks just outlined, then the results will hopefully speak clearly to recipients about what they mean and what should be done about them. When powered by this data, subsequent iterations through the steps outlined in this guide should become more efficient and effective. The worksheets that follow can facilitate this process.

WORKSHEETS

Worksheet 7-1

Metric Selection and Use

This worksheet is anchored by a list of example metrics that are arranged into four outcome categories: efficiency, quality, safety, and cost. For each intervention, complete a separate checklist. Consider what specific metrics might be appropriate for assessing the intervention's role in addressing its corresponding objective. Note that interventions may address more than one clinical objective, and clinical objectives may be targeted by more than one intervention. The idea behind this worksheet is to help you brainstorm and make explicit how you will know the effects the intervention is having and how you will measure those effects. The last three columns are a scratchpad for thinking through the "who," "when," and "how" for using each metric that you select for the intervention.

Check Those That Apply	Metric	Metric Owner	Measurement Schedule	Collection Method
Medication Management Objective: Prevent Prescription of Medication to Allergic Patients				
Intervention Name: Prescription Allergy Alert Window				
	Efficiency			
☑	By how much has time taken to use system is increased or decreased?	PI coordinator	Weekly x 4	Silent observer, system logs
	How has efficiency been affected at the following medication management process nodes:			
☑	Prescribing	PI coordinator	Weekly x 4	Silent observer, system logs
❏	Transcribing			
❏	Dispensing			
❏	Administering			

Worksheet 7-1 *continued*

Check Those That Apply	Metric	Metric Owner	Measurement Schedule	Collection Method
	Quality			
✓	Mortality rate	PI coordinator	Monthly	Existing adverse event reporting process
✓	Morbidity rate (including adverse drug events and reactions)	PI coordinator	Monthly	Existing adverse event reporting process
✓	Length of stay changed?	Sam D. (medical records)	Monthly	Chart review — semi-automated
✓	NCC-MERP outcome metrics	Jean S. (pharmacist)	Monthly	Chart review
✓	Effects of CDS on number, class, and type of medications ordered	Jean S. (pharmacist)	Monthly	Existing pharmacy database
	Safety			
	Are number of errors reduced at each of the following medication management nodes:			
✓	Prescribing	PI coordinator	Monthly	Existing adverse event reporting process
❑	Transcribing			
✓	Dispensing	PI coordinator	Monthly	Existing adverse event reporting process
✓	Administering	PI coordinator	Monthly	Existing adverse event reporting process
✓	Are number of errors reduced at each NCC-MERP category (B to I)?	Jean S. (pharmacist)	Monthly	Existing adverse event reporting process
✓	Are there unintentional adverse effects?	James V. (CDS Team/evaluation)	Monthly x 6	Walk rounds, focus groups with clinicians to assess qualitative alert responses

Worksheet 7-1 *continued*

Check Those That Apply	Metric	Metric Owner	Measurement Schedule	Collection Method
	Cost			
☑	Resource management changes due to CDS implementation - cost/benefit ratios	Joan R. (billing)	Monthly	Query current billing system
☑	Change in cost of prescribed medication related to CDS interventions	Joan R. (billing)	Monthly	Query current billing system

Worksheet 7-2

Performance against Objectives

In this chapter, we have recommended many different metrics to assess intervention deployment and effects. Whatever data you do gather, you will need some mechanism for assembling and reviewing this information, with special attention to highlighting results for the primary targets the interventions are designed to address. The purpose for this sample worksheet is to help trigger your thinking about how you might approach this documentation task.

This sample worksheet is anchored in the first column by listing clinical objectives addressed by interventions launched within your CDS program. The first five columns can be carried over from the Intervention Specification Form, if you created one for each intervention using Worksheet 5-1. Note that a single clinical objective might be followed by several rows of interventions if a set was implemented to address the objective. When documenting baseline performance and desired and actual improvement, make sure you are clear on whether these pertain to the specific desired action targeted by the intervention or to the broader objective.

In the sixth column, record the measured progress toward the key target of interest, and in the seventh column indicate how performance on other pertinent metrics selected in Worksheet 7-1 have changed as a result of the intervention. In the last column, record any other pertinent intervention effects—both positive and negative.

Medication Management Objective	Intervention Name	Target Action	Baseline	Desired Outcome	Actual Performance	Effects on Specific Outcome Metrics	Other Positive and Negative Effects
Prevent prescription of medication to allergic patients	Prescription allergy alert window	Inform prescriber of patient's allergy at point of medication ordering	3% of prescriptions are to allergic patients	0% of prescriptions are to allergic patients	1% of prescriptions are to allergic patients	Pending	Slow down of ordering process for many users when alerts fired; returned to baseline within 2–3 weeks.

Worksheet 7-3

Measurement-Related Activity Timeline for Each Intervention

This worksheet is intended to make explicit how steps related to metric use overlay the intervention lifecycle for different measure types. Its focus is long-term intervention management. Note that there will be shorter cycles of measurement, analysis, and enhancement at various phases of intervention development, such as workflow mapping and prelaunch testing.

Echoing themes in this chapter, metric management is divided into six processes: (1) define collection venue and strategy, (2) prepare data supply and assign roles, (3) collect baseline metric values, (4) collect post-intervention metric data, (5) analyze results, and (6) report data analysis and address implications. You can use this worksheet to help estimate the timing for various measurement activities related to each intervention. In the first column, list the pertinent metrics from Worksheet 7-1. To the right of each metric, draw bars of various lengths that represent the six metric stages. The length of each bar estimates the duration of each stage across the various intervention lifecycle steps.

Intervention name: Prescription allergy alert window
Clinical Medication Management Objective: Prevent prescription to allergic patients

INTERVENTION LIFE CYCLE

METRIC	Birth	→ Test →	Implement	→	Modify
EFFICIENCY					
By how much has time taken to use system increased or decreased?	1, 2	3 3	4	5	6
How has prescription efficiency been affected?	1	2 3	4	5	6
QUALITY					
Mortality rate?	1, 2	3	4	5	6
Morbidity rate (including adverse drug events and reactions)	1, 2	3	4	5	6
Length of stay changed?	1, 2	3	4	5	6
NCC-MERP outcome metrics?	1, 2	3	4	5	6
Effects of CDS on number, class, and type of medications ordered?	1, 2	3	4	5	6
SAFETY					
Are number of errors reduced in the following nodes:	1, 2	3 3	4	5	6
Prescribing?					
Dispensing?					
Administering?					
Are number of errors reduced at each NCC-MERP category (B to I)?	1, 2	3 3	4	5	6
COST					
Resource management changes due to CDS implementation?	1, 2	3 3	4	5	6
Change in cost of prescribed medication related to CDS interventions?	1, 2	3 3	4	5	6

Worksheet 7-4

CDS Program Enhancement Plans

This worksheet is organized around the broad medication management goals you are addressing. Its goal is to help stimulate your thinking about how to ensure that your CDS program is optimally addressing these goals and adding new targets to the program as appropriate. You might develop a worksheet like this after you have interventions deployed, stabilized, and at the point of generating some value, and you begin considering some "next round" enhancements.

To fill in the first column, go back to Worksheet 2-1, page 50, and Worksheet 2-3, page 56, and copy (or infer) the high-level clinical goal(s) that you are addressing with deployed interventions. While you are revisiting the worksheets prepared from Chapter 2, be on the lookout for other CDS goals or high-level clinical objectives that might be appropriate to add now to the scope of your medication management CDS program. In fact, if and when your organization is ready to contemplate significant program enhancements, you can actually begin the next pass through all the steps in this book.

For now, copy the clinical objectives and intervention names from versions of Worksheet 5-1, page 163, that you completed for each intervention into the second and third columns. The effectiveness summary in the fourth column is a summary of the intervention effects synthesized from the last three columns of Worksheet 7-2. The issues and usability summary synthesizes the major issues and opportunities uncovered over time in Worksheet 6-4 on intervention feedback and resolution.

The last column is the punchline for this worksheet. It presents an overview of the next major steps in your CDS program. It should begin to outline a plan for improving intervention acceptance and use among recipients and effectiveness in achieving target objectives. You can also begin noting additional interventions that might help achieve objectives, as well as additional objectives and goals to tackle, based on ongoing dialog with other stakeholders and any capability enhancements to underlying CIS infrastructure.

High Level Medication Management Goal	Medication Management Objective	Intervention Name	Effectiveness Summary	Issues and Usability Summary	Enhancement Plan
Reduce preventable adverse drug events	Prevent prescription of medication to allergic patients	Prescription allergy alert window	Encouraging results from initial post-deployment phases	Override process too lengthy	Streamline override process; proceed to addressing additional medication management stages for allergy CDS; begin addressing CDS for drug-drug interactions more comprehensively

CONCLUDING COMMENTS

It can be challenging to evaluate results from your medication management CDS efforts in a manner that yields accurate and actionable results, but this work is absolutely essential. You can't expect to realize optimal CDS benefits and ROIs (and certainly not measurable progress toward priority goals) without a substantial commitment to measurement.

Besides motivating and informing efforts by diverse stakeholders to achieve shared goals, careful evaluation can help dispel wishful thinking by the CDS team and others that "everything is going well." Potential problems that must be flushed out early include adverse effects from CDS on clinicians and, especially, on patients.

It is wise for the CDS team and other stakeholders to have a healthy skepticism about how much value the organization's CDS efforts are actually bringing to important outcomes. If you dig beneath the surface at even organizations with "the best" CDS programs, you find plenty of room for improvement. Excellence is a journey driven by measurement-supported continuous improvement, not by any particular end state.

As with many other CDS program components, thoughtful prioritizing is a key for evaluation activities. This chapter outlines many different measurement-related considerations that will hopefully be useful in helping your organization select a subset for action that will yield the greatest returns for your program. Carefully monitoring at least some critical CDS intervention effects, followed by iterative refinements, should enable any organization to significantly improve their overall medication management processes and outcomes over time.

REFERENCES

1 Neuhauser D. Ernest Amory Codman, MD. *Qual Saf Health Care.* 2002; 11(1):104-105.

2 Codman EA. *A Study in Hospital Efficiency: As Demonstrated by the Case Report of the First Five Years of a Private Hospital.* 1st edition. Oakbrook, IL: Joint Commission on Accreditation of Healthcare Organizations Press; 1995 Dec.

3 Donabedian A. Quality of care: problems of measurement. II. Some issues in evaluating the quality of nursing care. *Am J Public Health Nations Health.* 1969; 59(10):1833-1836.

4 Berwick DM. Continuous improvement as an ideal in health care. *N Engl J Med.* 1989; 320(1):53-56.

5 National Quality Forum. *About Us.* http://www.qualityforum.org/about/, accessed 9/18/08.

6 National Quality Forum. *NQF National Priorities Partnership.* http://www.qualityforum.org/about/NPP/, accessed 9/18/08.

7 See, for example, news item from the Health and Human Services Office for Human Research Protections (OHRP) regarding its actions involving a state-wide performance improvement effort: http://www.hhs.gov/ohrp/news/recentnews.html#20080215, accessed 9/18/08.

8 We learned of this acronym from Mark Granville, Senior Vice President, Client Experience, Healthcare, Thomson Reuters.

9 See, for example, the "What types of measures can we use" section of the "Understanding Quality Measurement" document on the AHRQ website: http://www.ahrq.gov/CHToolBx/understn.htm#typesa, accessed 9/18/08.

10 Sittig DF, Krall MA, Dykstra RH, et al. A survey of factors affecting clinician acceptance of clinical decision support. *BMC Med Inform Decis Mak.* 2006; 6:6.

11 Lindenauer PK, Ling D, Pekow PS, et al. Physician characteristics, attitudes, and use of computerized order entry. *J Hosp Med.* 2006; 1(4):221-230.

12 Menachemi N, Ettel DL, Brooks RG, et al. Charting the use of electronic health records and other information technologies among child health providers. *BMC Pediatr.* 2006; 6:21.

13 Jensen J. The effects of Computerized Provider Order Entry on medication turn-around time: a time-to-first dose study at the Providence Portland Medical Center. *AMIA Annu Symp Proc.* 2006: 384-388.

14 Sittig DF, Kuperman GJ, Fiskio J. Evaluating physician satisfaction regarding user interactions with an electronic medical record system. *Proc AMIA Symp.* 1999; 400-404.

15 Overhage JM, Perkins S, Tierney WM, et al. Controlled trial of direct physician order entry: effects on physicians' time utilization in ambulatory primary care internal medicine practices. *J Am Med Inform Assoc.* 2001; 8(4):361-371.

16 Weingart SN, Toth M, Sands DZ, et al. Physicians' decisions to override computerized drug alerts in primary care. *Arch Intern Med.* 2003; 163(21):2625-2631.

17 Shah NR, Seger AC, Seger DL, et al. Improving acceptance of computerized prescribing alerts in ambulatory care. *J Am Med Inform Assoc.* 2006; 13(1):5-11.

18 East TD, Henderson S, Pace NL, et al. Knowledge engineering using retrospective review of data: a useful technique or merely data dredging? *Int J Clin Monit Comput.* 1991-1992; 8(4):259-262.

19 Lin CP, Payne TH, Nichol WP, et al. Evaluating clinical decision support systems: monitoring CPOE order check override rates in the Department of Veterans Affairs' computerized patient record system. *J Am Med Inform Assoc.* 2008; 15(5):620-626.

20 Chused A, Kuperman GJ, Stetson PD. Alert override reasons: a failure to communicate. *AMIA Annu Symp Proc.* 2008: 111-115.

21 van der Sijs H, Aarts J, van Gelder T, et al. Turning off frequently overridden drug alerts: limited opportunities for doing it safely. *J Am Med Inform Assoc.* 2008; 15:439-448. http://www.jamia.org/cgi/content/abstract/15/4/439, accessed 10/7/08.

22 Bates DW, Leape LL, Cullen DJ, et al. Effect of computerized physician order entry and a team intervention on prevention of serious medication errors. *JAMA.* 1998; 280(15):1311-1316.

23 Hicks LS, Sequist TD, Ayanian JZ, et al. Impact of computerized decision support on blood pressure management and control: a randomized controlled trial. *J Gen Intern Med.* 2008; 23(4):429-441.

24 Agency for Healthcare Research and Quality. *Monitoring and Evaluating Medicaid Fee-for-Service Care Management Programs: A User's Guide.* AHRQ Publication No. 08-0012. 2007 Nov. http://www.ahrq.gov/qual/medicaidffs/, accessed 9/18/08.

25 Nuckols TK, Bell DS, Liu H, et al. Rates and types of events reported to established incident reporting systems in two US hospitals. *Qual Saf Health Care.* 2007; 16(3):164-168. http://qshc.bmj.com/cgi/content/abstract/16/3/164, accessed 10/7/08.

26 Ferranti J, Horvath MM, Cozart H, et al. Reevaluating the safety profile of pediatrics: a comparison of computerized adverse drug event surveillance and voluntary reporting in the pediatric environment. *Pediatrics.* 2008; 121(5): e1201-1207.

27 Nebeker JR, Barach P, Samore MH. Clarifying adverse drug events: a clinician's guide to terminology, documentation, and reporting. *Ann Intern Med.* 2004; 140(10):795-801. http://www.annals.org/cgi/content/abstract/140/10/795, accessed 9/18/08.

28 National Coordinating Council for Medication Error Reporting and Prevention (NCC MERP). *NCC MERP Taxonomy of Medication Errors.* http://www.nccmerp.org/pdf/taxo2001-07-31.pdf, accessed 9/18/08.

29 The figure in reference 27 (Nebeker JR, Barach P, Samore MH. Clarifying adverse drug events: a clinician's guide to terminology, documentation, and reporting) is a nice graphical illustration of this point.

30 Smith DH, Perrin N, Feldstein A, et al. The impact of prescribing safety alerts for elderly persons in an electronic medical record: an interrupted time series evaluation. *Arch Intern Med.* 2006; 166(10):1098-1104.

31 Classen DC, Pestotnik SL, Evans RS, et al. Computerized surveillance of adverse drug events in hospital patients. *JAMA.* 1991; 266(20):2847-2851.

32 Rozich JD, Haraden CR, Resar RK. Adverse drug event trigger tool: a practical methodology for measuring medication related harm. *Qual Saf Health Care.* 2003; 12(3):194-200.

33 Institute for Healthcare Improvement. *Trigger Tool for Measuring ADEs.* http://www.ihi.org/ihi/workspace/tools/trigger/, accessed 9/18/08.

34 Sittig DF, Campbell EM, Guappone K, et al. Recommendations for monitoring and evaluation of inpatient Computer-based Provider Order Entry systems: results of a Delphi survey. *AMIA Annu Symp Proc.* 2007: 671-675.

35 Campbell EM, Sittig DF, Ash JS, et al. Types of unintended consequences related to computerized provider order entry. *J Am Med Inform Assoc.* 2006 Sep-Oct; 13(5):547-556.

36 Institute of Medicine. *Crossing the Quality Chasm: The IOM Health Care Quality Initiative.* http://www.iom.edu/CMS/8089.aspx, accessed 9/18/08.

37 See, for example, Horton LA. *Calculating and Reporting Healthcare Statistics, 2nd Edition.* Chicago: American Health Information Management Association; 2006.

38 See discussion in PA Department of Health's Health Statistics—Technical Assistance Tools of the Trade: http://www.health.state.pa.us/hpa/stats/techassist/avghospstay.htm, accessed 9/18/08.

39 Teich JM, Merchia PR, Schmiz JL, et al. Effects of computerized physician order entry on prescribing practices. *Arch Intern Med.* 2000; 160(18):2741-2747.

40 Kucher N, Koo S, Quiroz R, et al. Electronic alerts to prevent venous thromboembolism among hospitalized patients. *N Engl J Med.* 2005; 352(10):969-977.

41 Pestotnik SL, Classen DC, Evans RS, et al. Implementing antibiotic practice guidelines through computer-assisted decision support: clinical and financial outcomes. *Ann Intern Med.* 1996 May 15; 124(10):884-890.

42 Horowitz N, Moshkowitz M, Leshno M, et al. Clinical trial: evaluation of a clinical decision-support model for upper abdominal complaints in primary-care practice. *Aliment Pharmacol Ther.* 2007; 26(9):1277-1283.

43 Agency for Healthcare Research and Quality. *Reducing and Preventing Adverse Drug Events to Decrease Hospital Costs.* http://www.ahrq.gov/qual/aderia/aderia.htm, accessed 9/18/08.

44 The Leapfrog Group. *Leapfrog CPOE Evaluation Tool.* https://leapfrog.medstat.com/cpoe/, accessed 9/18/08.

45 Leonard KJ, Sittig DF. Improving information technology adoption and implementation through the identification of appropriate benefits: creating IMPROVE-IT. *J Med Internet Res.* 2007; 9(2):e9.

46 Osheroff JA, Teich JM, Middleton B, et al. A roadmap for national action on clinical decision support. *J Am Med Inform Assoc.* 2007; 14(2):141-145.

47 The Leapfrog Group. *Factsheet—Computerized Physician Order Entry.* http://www.leapfroggroup.org/media/file/Leapfrog-Computer_Physician_Order_Entry_Fact_Sheet.pdf, accessed 9/18/08.

48 Kilbridge PM, Welebob EM, Classen DC. Development of the Leapfrog methodology for evaluating hospital implemented inpatient computerized physician order entry systems. *Qual Saf Health Care.* 2006 Apr; 15(2):81-4. See also 10/14/08 Leapfrog press release: Leapfrog issues a caution that quality assurance necessary during implementation of computerized medication management systems. http://www.leapfroggroup.org/media/file/LF_News_Release_CPOE_Evaluation_Tool.pdf, accessed 12/14/08.

49 Thompson DI, Henry S, Lockwood L, et al. Benefits planning for advanced clinical information systems implementation at Allina hospitals and clinics. *J Healthc Inf Manag.* 2005; 19(1):54-62.

50 Educational programs such as those from AMIA seek to ensure an adequate workforce of appropriately trained individuals for these roles. See, for example AMIA 10 x 10™. http://www.amia.org/10x10/, accessed 9/18/08.

51 McKee M. Not everything that counts can be counted; not everything that can be counted counts. *BMJ.* 2004; 328(7432):153. http://www.bmj.com/cgi/content/short/328/7432/153, accessed 9/18/08.

52 The Institute for Safe Medication Practices. *Frequently Asked Questions (FAQ).* http://www.ismp.org/faq.asp#Question_6, accessed 9/18/08.

53 There are numerous studies in the literature reporting time and motion studies in healthcare that can trigger ideas about conducting these studies at your organization. They can be identified by searching on the Internet generally or in medical literature databases. Here is an example of one such study: http://www.rwjf.org/pr/product.jsp?id=31332, accessed 9/18/08.

54 Kaushal R, Jha AK, Franz C, et al. Return on investment for a computerized physician order entry system. *J Am Med Inform Assoc.* 2006; 13(3);365-367.

55 Massachusetts Technology Collaborative. *Saving Lives Saving Money: The Imperative for Computerized Physician Order Entry in Massachusetts Hospitals.* 2008 Feb. http://www.masstech.org/ehealth/cpoe/cpoe08release.html, accessed 9/18/08.

Chapter 8

Approach CDS Knowledge Management Systematically

TASKS

- Catalog your CDS knowledge assets that support medication management; develop an explicit plan to manage key asset features, such as currency, appropriateness, consistency, coding and vocabularies, and value to end users and the organization.
- Consider the people, infrastructure, and tools available for managing knowledge assets, and ensure they are deployed to greatest effect in addressing organizational needs.
- Put in place explicit mechanisms for managing processes and decisions related to both the knowledge assets themselves and the overall medication management CDS program.

KEY LESSONS

- KM for the medication CDS program should be treated as a component of the larger task of managing your organization's overall portfolio of CDS assets and processes.
- It is optimal to have in place necessary KM infrastructure before you begin any CDS rollout. This includes people, time and technical resources; pertinent governance structures and processes; plans for asset management, updating, and versioning; and the like.

DISCUSSION

Knowledge management (KM) can be viewed as a framework and toolkit of approaches for helping to further integrate several key tasks presented in previous chapters. These include:

- Establishing the CDS charter and program governance
- Setting improvement targets
- Documenting rollout plans
- Measuring and continually improving medication-related outcomes

In this chapter we provide a brief overview of KM and how it applies to an organization's CDS knowledge assets and related decisions and processes.

Knowledge Management Basics

The term "knowledge management"—widely used in business and other settings—is often interpreted differently depending on the circumstances and audience. Wikipedia, for example, defines KM as "a range of practices used by organizations to identify, create, represent, and distribute knowledge." It has a "focus on the management of knowledge as an asset and the development and cultivation of the channels through which knowledge, information, and signal flow."[1]

Within the realm of CDS, the field of KM is relatively new, and likewise broad. For example, pioneers in the topic have noted that, "Knowledge management can have diffuse boundaries— boundaries that encompass the entire organization."[2] These authors note that boundaries can be defined in several ways to make KM efforts meaningful and tractable, and point out three key functions for KM. These include applying clinical knowledge to patient care through specific interventions (for example, by addressing the CDS Five Rights), using formalized processes to discover new knowledge that can be used to improve the CDS program (as described in Chapter 7), and managing the knowledge incorporated in the CDS interventions (as we discuss in this chapter).

Successful KM approaches rest on a foundation of key personnel and robust ISs that remain scalable over time and organizational growth. To obtain the necessary resources for the KM effort, it is essential that the organization understand up front how KM supports its overall goals. Over time, the KM process should generate new knowledge about CDS value and publish these findings to stakeholders throughout the organization (especially those that control resources) to justify the ongoing investment in the activity (see Chapter 7, page 227).

Figure 8-1 contains questions that you can consider when setting up and/or refining your organization's KM approach. Some data to help answer these questions can be gleaned from discussions and worksheets in previous chapters; other issues are further outlined in this chapter.

The discussion in this chapter so far has probably reinforced the assertion that KM has "diffuse boundaries." To help provide focus and clarity, for the remainder of this chapter we focus on two key KM activities: managing CDS knowledge assets, and managing process and decisions related to ensuring that those assets deliver intended benefits to the organization.

Since this guidebook covers a subset of an organization's CDS and quality improvement efforts, the KM pertaining to CDS for medication management needs to be considered within these broader contexts. The following recommendations on managing CDS knowledge assets, and processes and decisions, will hopefully be useful for both medication-specific CDS activities and your CDS program more broadly.

Managing CDS Knowledge Assets

Although not approached this way in many institutions, it is helpful to consider your organization's CDS content assets as a single portfolio of knowledge resources. These assets might exist in several different forms, such as order sets, alerts, rules/reminders, reference information, and documentation templates (see Table 1-1, Clinical Decision Support Intervention Types, page 5). They may be standalone or integrated into CISs, such as CPOE and EMRs.

Figure 8-1: Questions to Consider about Organizational Knowledge Management

Goals

- What are the high-level goals and more specific objectives for the efforts to improve medication use with CDS?
- Is available CDS content optimally leveraged to meet CDS goals given available CIS infrastructure?
- What programs are in place to determine the extent to which targets are being met?
- What progress toward goals has been achieved to date?

CDS Assets

- What intervention types are deployed throughout the enterprise? (See Table 1-1, page 5, for a summary of intervention types.)
- How many of each type is deployed and what domains/topics are covered?
- What are the attributes for each intervention (for example, as outlined in Figure 8-2)?
- Are the clinical information and recommendations consistent across interventions?
- Is there an appropriate balance of content that is developed locally, shared, obtained from free sources, and purchased from commercial vendors (see Chapter 3, page 74)?

Processes

- How do subject matter experts, CDS implementation staff, and others collaborate on determining and implementing CDS interventions and workflow modifications, and then communicate about these with leadership and other stakeholders?
- How are individuals (such as subject matter experts) compensated for their role in developing and maintaining the knowledge assets (for example, since this may affect quality/quantity of available expert input and will affect total costs of the CDS program for medication management)?
- Is there an audit trail for the decisions that are made about the content assets, and why and how they are made? Who maintains this trail, and how is that done?
- What tools are being used by the organization to manage its content asset repository (for example, applications for content authoring, storing, updating, editing, and change tracking)? Who is responsible for these tools, and how are content versions managed?
- How is feedback from end users managed?

Assets may exist across multiple sites within a hospital or among hospitals in an IDN. In addition, virtually all organizations have both paper-based and electronic medical reference information available for clinicians and patients that also should be considered as portfolio components. This universe of deployed content assets may come from various sources, including internal content experts, CIS vendors (provided directly with the system or shared among their institutional users), governmental agencies and clearinghouses, other healthcare institutions, publicly accessible Web sites, and commercial CDS content vendors (that can include print reference publishers).

CDS KM activities related to these knowledge assets will include the mechanisms that you use to address the issues outlined in the subsections that follow.

Your CDS Portfolio: Maintaining an Inventory of Deployed Knowledge Assets

It is essential to have a systematic approach to managing all pertinent organizational knowledge assets from early in the CDS deployment. In fact, since all existing healthcare delivery facilities have some CDS knowledge assets in use (think reference books on shelves, bookmarked Internet medical reference sites, and the like) formalizing this approach can even precede developing any new interventions.

Although initially it may be possible to track interventions informally, this will eventually become impossible to do effectively as your deployed CDS asset portfolio increases in size and complexity. Loosely tracking and coordinating CDS content that is manually "hard coded" into systems (for example, specific links to Web-based resources or rules that are maintained locally) can be particularly challenging. Even with CIS and CDS vendor-supplied systems, the search and cataloging capabilities may not easily support collecting these data about what CDS is actually deployed.

At some point, successfully managing information about CDS interventions used in your environment will require special tools and a systematic approach. Although it might not be possible to have all the information desired, a coordinated and thorough approach to managing information about deployed assets is an important goal. Recognize that you have made substantial investments in your CDS interventions and much is at stake. The considerations outlined next, along with worksheets in this and previous chapters (such as Worksheet 8-1 [CDS Knowledge Asset Inventory]; Worksheet 5-1, page 163 [Intervention Specification Form]; Worksheet 6-3, page 193 [Implementation Status]; and Worksheet 7-2, page 232 [Performance against Objectives]) will help in implementing a successful approach to monitoring your CDS portfolio.

In most cases, the knowledge assets and processes related to CDS for medication management should be handled as components of a broader CDS activity portfolio. This is true even for drug-specific knowledge such as allergy and DDI alerts acquired from vendors, for example. Nonetheless, it may be important to track these KM elements, specifically as a subcomponent of the broader CDS efforts. This can be useful, for example, in garnering resources for medication-related CDS initiatives, since the targets are such an important part of organizational safety and quality efforts.

Pioneering organizations have described their approach to managing CDS assets.[3] For the knowledge assets you have deployed, consider tracking important attributes (including the CDS Five Rights and related maintenance issues) outlined in Figure 8-2.

As noted, some worksheets in earlier chapters, and Worksheet 8-1 in this chapter, can be used to gather and document this information.

For quality, efficiency, and cost reasons, it is useful to have a systematic approach to procuring and managing your CDS assets. This approach should address important interrelationships among content sets and intervention types. For example, similar content might be deployed in various CDS interventions (for example, alerts, reference materials, and order sets) for patient safety, disease management, and PI programs. An overarching perspective is necessary to ensure that there are optimal efficiencies, synergies, and consistency in selecting, obtaining, disseminating, monitoring, and maintaining this information.

CDS Knowledge Currency and Appropriateness

All CDS interventions need to be re-evaluated regularly to ensure that the clinical knowledge they convey is accurate, up-to-date, and delivered in a way that will achieve the desired outcome. Because the CIS infrastructure technical and content components can be complex, changes to these components in one part of the IS may require repeated testing to ensure that other interrelated parts of the system continue to behave as expected after implementing the change.

Similarly, because the evidence base and expert opinion on which best practices rest are continu-

Figure 8-2: Key Attributes to Track for Deployed CDS Interventions

- Source, versions, and acquisition and maintenance costs
- Process for vetting, localizing, and approval/adoption
- Maintenance: process for making changes to the asset, either locally or requesting from vendor
- Key dates: creation/review/update
- Intervention formats included (for example, order sets, alerts, and infobutton links to reference materials)
- Specific populations covered (for example, pediatric-specific assets/considerations)
- Specific practice locations affected (for example, alerts may be generally deployed but switched off in ED or ICU locations due to impact on time-critical workflows)
- Primary end-user targets for intervention/knowledge (such as patient, pharmacist, nurse, or physician)
- Systems through which knowledge/intervention are delivered (such as Web, EMR, CPOE, departmental system)
- Intervention effects on key processes and outcomes

ally shifting, it is essential to ensure that the content underlying the CDS interventions remains synchronized with this knowledge. Some organizations assign responsibility for the different content areas to respected individuals with domain expertise in each area. These experts review and periodically update content for which they are responsible and help address concerns that arise about this content. An ideal situation would be an integrated knowledge maintenance environment wherein a change need be made only once in one area, and then automatically cascaded to all appropriate content components throughout the system. Although this ideal may be difficult or impossible to achieve with current applications, using an overarching governance mechanism that helps coordinate review and updating across the CDS asset collection is nonetheless important.

Assigning an "expiration date" to the knowledge components of all CDS interventions can be a useful strategy to keep the knowledge base current. It is important to realize that reaching an expiration date does not mean the intervention ceases to function. Having an alert stop working when clinicians are used to seeing it can, in fact, be dangerous. Rather, this time period is set to force a regular review process. These time limits should correspond to the anticipated "shelf life" of the intervention's knowledge and trigger content review by an appropriate

domain expert after a predetermined time since the last review. As a general rule of thumb, most or all interventions should be reviewed at least annually.

You should also develop mechanisms for detecting practice-changing clinical information and modifying CDS content accordingly. This action-requiring information includes newly reported results from certain major clinical trials and research meta-analyses, drug withdrawals from the market, and other major changes in the knowledge base supporting clinical practice and CDS. Purchasing content from a third party CDS or CIS vendor can alleviate some updating issues, since these vendors typically provide content maintenance and updating for their offerings (see Buy versus Build versus Share in Chapter 3, page 74). In any case, there should be in place internal mechanisms for monitoring overall CDS portfolio currency.

To ensure that interventions, especially alerts, remain appropriate, you can keep a close eye on use and usability issues (see process metrics discussion in Chapter 7, page 203, and Worksheet 6-4, Feedback and Resolution, page 194), especially after changes to the hardware, software, or any related content. Dramatic changes in usage patterns (such as alert overrides or order sets use) can indicate that a content or system change may have affected applicability. Carefully and proactively evaluate alerts and rules each time new versions of underlying clinical information software are implemented. This should be completed before the updated applications are released into the live environment to ensure that they do not cause any unintended consequences. Because rules can be interrelated in complex ways, especially as their numbers increase, maintaining proper performance of the entire rule set as it evolves is challenging, but critical.

Just as the clinical knowledge base evolves, so do the vocabularies and coding schemes that are used to trigger and process the CDS interventions. As a result, it is important to ensure that changes to these schemas do not have adverse effects on CDS intervention behavior. For example, if rules are triggered by coded data (such as names of laboratory tests, drugs, patient clinical problems, and the like) and the codes describing these data change, alert triggering logic will need to be modified accordingly.

Knowledge Consistency across Interventions and Systems

The clinical guidance provided by CDS interventions should be consistent across different ISs (for example, CPOE, pharmacy system, PHR) and interventions (such as order sets, alerts, reference material). This is necessary to ensure that all clinical team members (regardless of their role, setting, or the tool they are using) are supported with information that facilitates optimal coordination among their decisions and actions. For example, discrepancies in recommendations about drug dosing and the like in resources used by patients, nurses, pharmacists, and physicians can create confusion and inefficiency. This means that although details presented can be optimized for the particular recipient type, potentially problematic inconsistencies should not be present.

For environments in which the same user is exposed to different systems, keep in mind also the importance of consistent information format and presentation. Users tend to rely on visual cues to prompt action. If critically important data, such as dosing information, are presented to the same user with different formatting or dosing units across dif-ferent systems, take extra care to "highlight" these differences for the user. Better yet, try and avoid inconsistencies altogether.

Because most institutions have many different CIS in play (often with different CDS interventions deployed in each) achieving this harmony can be challenging. It might be ideal to have a central repository of localized, vetted, consistent, maintained CDS knowledge assets (such as alerts, order sets, reference material) feeding all systems in an automated fashion. Although this scenario is not currently practical, it is consistent with a roadmap for national CDS efforts.[4]

Keep in mind that even when the same content is used in different systems (for example, alerting rules about patient allergies in CPOE, pharmacy systems and electronic medication administration records), different software, data feeds, and the like can cause inconsistent behavior. These problems can be avoided through mechanisms for providing "semantic interoperability," that is, approaches for ensuring consistent meaning of key knowledge and data elements across systems. Using terminology standards within the separate systems will help with this coordination but may not be sufficient to ensure complete semantic interoperability. Barriers to importing data or inherent discrepancies in database structure can exist that may make achieving this ideal impossible. If that is the case, manual processes for configuring independent systems in a manner that ensures proper rule behavior across each will be necessary.

Proactive KM approaches for monitoring and maintaining your CDS assets and their deployment can help identify and minimize important discrepancies in intervention behavior across ISs. The CIS inventory discussed in Chapter 4, page 86, and the CDS asset inventory described earlier are important components of such KM efforts.

Using Commercial Knowledge Bases

Many vendor-based CISs can be integrated with specific commercial knowledge bases for medication CDS. For example, these knowledge resources may include alerting capabilities for drug-allergy, drug-drug, drug-pregnancy interactions, and the like. Sometimes the CIS will offer a choice of third-party sources rather than only one integrated offering. When a choice is available, you should consider in making your selection how well each CDS resource and vendor's characteristics match your needs. Chapter 3 discusses Build versus Buy considerations (page 74); this section outlines some of the KM implications for the "Buy" decision. There are also review articles that address these issues.[5]

You should ask your CIS vendor which integrated medication-management knowledge bases are "supported." For specific commercial CDS offerings of interest, you should ask whether the CIS vendor has clients currently using the resource and seek details about the benefits and challenges that have been encountered in its use. Differences in ease of deployment and maintenance should be thoroughly explored. Again, consistent guidance across systems is also an important consideration in filling out your CDS portfolio.

The advantage to using a commercially-available knowledge base is that the cost of updating the underlying knowledge is shared by all clients of that vendor/source, typically rendering this option much more cost-effective for implementers. This advantage comes at several costs, which must be understood and managed actively for success. These include the potential for nuisance alerts with alerting applications, the need to understand the specific knowledge structure utilized, ongoing need to monitor and tailor the commercial content, and potential liability concerns (for example, related to manipulating the vendor-supplied content) addressed in Appendix B, Some Medico-legal Considerations.

Nuisance alerts are the result of overly-sensitive interaction checking, for example, due to conservative inclusion criteria. These false-positive alerts unnecessarily interrupt clinician workflow and can degrade end-user confidence in the CDS system. They can also contribute to information overload so that important interventions are lost in the noise (see Chapter 7, discussion of alerting and overrides, page

207). If the CIS and knowledge base structure are sufficiently transparent and configurable, it should be possible to significantly reduce the number of false-positive alerts. If not, tailoring alerts so that they are acceptable and valuable to end users can be very difficult.

Local tailoring of the commercial knowledge base should be governed by formal KM processes. Routine updates to the knowledge base by the third-party vendor should leave the local modifications intact. Ideally, new content should be segregated and highlighted so it can be reviewed to determine the extent to which local modification is necessary and easily applied as an update with or without modification, as appropriate.

Local modification may be associated with a greater legal responsibility for the knowledge content. KM processes should include addressing these issues with the organization's legal counsel (again see Appendix B) and ensuring that content modifications are governed by the organization's goals and are based on local circumstances, needs, and pertinent evidence. Ongoing evaluation to ensure that the locally adapted, vendor-supplied content is functioning as intended is another example of the need for a KM process that is rational, proactive, and defensible.

People and Infrastructure for Managing Knowledge Assets

The previous sections consider the aspects of knowledge assets that need to be managed; we now consider how to manage them.

Personnel

What individuals/committees are responsible for each CDS asset? Governance committees will define enterprise-wide strategies, clinical standards, and performance measures. They should likewise define a focal point of responsibility for the overall portfolio of CDS interventions used to address these elements. In larger organizations, roles such as the clinical director of ISs, CMIO and/or a CDS committee might assume responsibility for the CDS content portfolio.

In any case, an individual in a coordinating role, supported by a pertinent CDS governance committee (see Chapter 2, page 25), should work closely with various other stakeholders and positions to manage the individual elements and overall value of the organization's CDS content assets. These stakeholders include subject matter experts in the clinical domains covered by the CDS interventions, the IT groups responsible for developing and deploying the interventions, and the committees and positions responsible for the intervention effects (for example, pharmacy and therapeutics committee, quality/safety officer, and benefits realization team), among others. This coordinating and value realization role regarding the CDS assets is guided by the organization's broad and/or medication-specific CDS charter.

KM Tools

Many CDS interventions, such as alerts and order sets, may be delivered to end users through CIS, so understanding how these knowledge assets get integrated into these systems is very important. Likewise, the details of how these assets are maintained are important. For example, does content updating happen within the CIS or is the content exported, edited, and then re-imported? You should determine the export and input formats (such as Rich Text, HTML, or XML) that are available for pertinent CDS interventions in your CIS, and the extent to which the transfer is automated versus entirely manual. How are vocabularies and coding schemes handled and updated? Medical vocabularies and standard interfacing languages should be used when possible to facilitate interoperability.

You should also assess the tools (if any) that are currently used in your organization for managing the CDS asset inventory or related assets in other departments (for example, databases, spreadsheets, or lists in word processing documents). These simple tools may be a useful starting point if you have no other infrastructure in place for managing the asset inventory. To the extent that you are using completely independent applications or documents to track different CDS asset subsets, you will need to coordinate and integrate these catalogs to facilitate overall portfolio management as previously discussed. You may find that your needs will outgrow these relatively simple tools as your CDS program expands, or if you wish to include more collaboration management functionality.

Various general purpose tools are available to help manage key documents and related processes in your CDS program.[6] In addition, newer collaboration and content management tools are coming to market from various CDS vendors. At this early stage, these tend to focus on specific content types (for example, software tools for managing and maintaining order sets that come with the order set content), but more robust applications will likely follow. As noted earlier, most CIS vendors provide some tools for managing CDS content within their system, though these tools can vary in sophistication and usability. Often, the tools needed to search through the CDS content and assist with maintenance tasks are rudimentary or missing entirely. Unfortunately, there is little, if any, widely used "plug and play" interoperability of CDS content across CISs, making deploying CDS more resource intensive and difficult than it should be and limiting sharing of content between institutions. National attention is beginning to focus on addressing this challenge.[7,8]

Managing Processes and Decisions

So far in this chapter we have considered KM issues related to the CDS assets themselves and related to the people and tools used to manage these assets. We now consider KM functions related to processes and decisions that surround these assets. These include policies, standard operating processes, and governance needed to ensure CDS intervention portfolio quality, currency, appropriateness, and value.

Core Governance Processes

The governance structures and mechanisms your organization has established to handle its efforts to apply CDS in medication management provide the framework for how program decisions and processes are managed. Responsibility for coordinating these CDS activities should be assigned to some committee (see Chapter 2, page 25) with appropriate leadership—such as by a CMIO—and it should have formal sponsorship and active support from senior administration and clinical leadership.

It is imperative to communicate the committee's plans and decisions so that pertinent stakeholders are informed and can provide feedback and take appropriate action. You should explicitly establish ground rules for consensus building and coordinated action. A common problem such groups face is coming to agreement on a particular issue and then having members "go off and do their own thing," whether at the level of a hospital, unit or individual. Members must be committed to the consensus process and outcome, understanding that their way may not always prevail but that effectiveness depends on coordinated action.

Together with the CDS/medication management charter, these governance processes are the foundation for KM efforts, as they are for the CDS program itself. KM issues include the processes whereby this foundation is developed and maintained, and the manner in which it is documented and communicated. Likewise, the processes for addressing, documenting, and communicating subsequent key steps in the CDS process (such as selecting and prioritizing targets, mapping pertinent workflows, developing and deploying interventions, and monitoring and enhancing their effects) are also key ingredients in the KM effort. Figure 8-1 outlines some pertinent questions for the KM effort to address; these themes have also come into play throughout this book and its worksheets.

Updating Process

Sudden and dramatic changes in practice, such as the withdrawal of a widely used drug from the market or the announcement of practice-altering clinical trial results, highlight the importance of systematically approaching how an organization manages its overall CDS knowledge portfolio. These changes necessitate corresponding updates to pertinent components

across the entire CDS intervention suite, which your knowledge management mechanisms should enable in a timely and efficient manner. Otherwise, the credibility of specific CDS interventions, and the overall CDS program, can be called into question by end users. This can occur, for example, when a CDS intervention presents the user with a medication as the drug of choice in a particular situation after that drug has been withdrawn from the market.

Earlier in this chapter, we described various issues and approaches related to ensuring CDS intervention currency and appropriateness. From a process perspective, the question is how the updating function will be managed. For example:

- How will the review/updating frequency be determined?
- How will reviewers be credentialed, engaged, compensated, and supported in providing timely feedback?
- Who will determine whether/how to send reminders (automatic vs. manual) to responsible parties that their scheduled review date (and content "expiration") are approaching, execute this plan, and follow-up if reviews and updates are not provided in the timeframe necessary to ensure portfolio currency?
- If you will use third-party sources to help with keeping medication CDS content up to date, what is the process for evaluating the resources to ensure the content and editorial policies (approach to evidence assessment, updating, etc.) fit with your local needs and standards? Once initially deployed, what is the process for vetting regular updates?

Along similar lines, What role is there in your medication-management CDS efforts for alerting services to help proactively identify needed changes to CDS interventions? These include resources such as *The FDA Drug Safety Newsletter*[9] and ISMP's *Medication Safety Alert*,[10] which provide push notices that can be regularly reviewed for potential new or modified CDS interventions. The pharmacy and therapeutics committee may already review such newsletters. If so, mechanisms should be established to ensure that pertinent decisions made by this group are communicated directly to those managing the CDS content.

How you design your updating process to address these and related issues will depend on the priority your organization places on these critical tasks, and therefore the resources (such as people, time and money) devoted to them. Ideally, this should be considered early in CDS program development, or at least before subsequent major rounds of content creation or deployment. If your organization cannot maintain a particular CDS asset in at least a minimally acceptable way (as defined by your KM process), then you should seriously consider not deploying it in the first place.

Decision to Retire Interventions

The timing for retiring interventions is driven in part by results from the general content management and maintenance process (such as updating cycles) previously discussed. For example, as part of the regular updating cycle some content will be retired, such as recommendations within guidelines that are no longer in use or drug order items within order sets when drugs have been withdrawn. In a similar manner, new interventions may render old ones obsolete before a regular review cycle. Having a systematic approach to content maintenance allows these interactions to be tracked and managed as they occur. This becomes increasingly important as the CDS portfolio becomes large. With increasing interplay between a growing number of CDS interventions, the maintenance effort begins to grow exponentially rather than linearly, making a thoughtful approach even more critical.

The monitoring processes outlined in Chapter 7 may also suggest that consideration be given to withdrawing an intervention from the deployed portfolio. This can be useful in helping to keep the number of interventions that need to be managed more manageable. For example, if a strong suite of CDS interventions (such as standing orders) has completely eliminated the firing of a "safety net alert" for giving pneumococcal vaccine when

indicated, then you can consider retiring that alert. Alternatively, if an alert continues firing with an unacceptably high false-positive rate despite efforts to fix this, it might be appropriate to retire the alert and focus on other approaches to achieving the desired objective.

It is important to have a formal mechanism for addressing these issues and tracking the retired content and related decisions (such as who made them, when, and why). An appropriate governance committee should develop these mechanisms and review the decisions. Retired content should be archived so it can be retrieved as needed (for example, if required as backup for legal or quality improvement activities related to determining the information that was available at a particular point in time).

Versioning

Versioning functionality is required to track changes as content is updated, deleted, or modified over time and to maintain an audit trail for these actions. This functionality should include logging decision making across versions, including who was involved in the decision and why a particular course of action was chosen.

Versioning for deployed interventions is useful for a variety of purposes related to understanding how your asset portfolio is evolving over time. For example, to appreciate how end-user clinical decisions are influenced by CDS interventions (as discussed in Chapter 7, page 203) it is essential to make sure that you know the exact intervention content that was available during the examination period. If an intervention, such as an alert or order set, changes over time, these changes (as pertinent) must be factored into analyzing the effects. In other words, a rigorous versioning approach can help reconstruct what interventions were "live" at specific points in time for when this is needed for evaluation or other purposes.

Preserving superseded knowledge through versioning mechanisms helps to link knowledge to interventions even years after the intervention may have been used. Such version tracking may help clarify what happened during the course of a CDS intervention if this context is ever called into question (for example, in the case of a malpractice allegation regarding a decision that involved a CDS intervention).

In addition to content versioning, storing other specific intervention details (for example, recipient, patient, action taken by the recipient, and reason for intervention override, if the particular CIS allows these functions) in a log will help establish the intervention context. This information may become increasingly valuable for research purposes—for example, to help generate new clinical knowledge and enhanced best practices for CDS.[11]

Intervention Life Cycle Management

Managing a particular CDS intervention's life cycle is related to, but broader than, intervention versioning after launch. Previous chapters have outlined the various phases in this life cycle, and in each, KM issues related to intervention content and processes come into play. For example, processes such as conducting the opportunity assessment; establishing targets and baselines; and developing, launching, and evaluating interventions all generate data and decisions. How these are tracked and managed defines key elements of your KM environment, whether the approach is haphazard or proactive and finely tuned.

If you have used worksheets such as those outlined in previous chapters during the intervention life cycle, they will provide important documentation for major components of your knowledge management approach. As we mentioned in the introduction, you should consider consolidating key documents that reflect the status of work in process on all interventions in your program throughout their life cycle. This can be done in a physical "binder" for paper versions of worksheets you may have used and/or on a Web "portal," which can be easier to update and share. If appropriately managed and presented, this information can be very useful to enable the CDS team, governance entities, and other stakeholders to quickly gain a sense of the CDS program status, benefits, and challenges.

Accountability for Decision Capture

Determining who is responsible for driving and keeping track of the many critical decisions that drive the CDS initiative, where and how this information will be stored, who will have access to it and for what purposes, etc., is a foundational issue on which the entire CDS implementation rests. As noted earlier, these decisions flow from the CDS charter and initial governance decisions.

One approach is to have a core CDS governance entity appoint a "decision steward" who is accountable for driving discussion and identifying which decision points are critical to capture. This position should be well connected to relevant governance processes—such as those for IT, clinical care policies (related to medication management and other pertinent issues), and the CDS program. For smaller organizations, this may be a single individual with support from others more loosely affiliated with leadership structures. As organizational size and CDS sophistication increase, these decision management functions can be handled by a formal committee or workgroup that is positioned to triage the tasks and coordinate decisions according to institutional policies and procedures.

Once the decision steward is appointed, a team and mechanism can be developed for handling functions such as capturing and retaining critical data. When setting this up, consider how you can optimally address the following questions:

- If you return to the data two years later, how will you find the information trail that led to a particular decision about the CDS program or specific interventions?
- What process led to the decision? Consensus? Voting?
- If there is a sentinel event or other adverse patient outcome, can you demonstrate the pertinent CDS intervention used at the time and the decision process related to its development and deployment? As important as being able to ensure that the process was reasonable and justifiable, is there transparency of the sort that can be used to drive further improvements (as is routinely used

in other safety-critical sectors such as the airline industry)?

- Can you track who was involved in reaching decisions regarding particular content elements and their pertinent expertise? This information can be useful in continually enhancing how you engage pertinent stakeholders in critical decisions.
- What was the justification for taking a particular approach at that particular time? Again, this information can be used in driving continuous improvement in KM processes.

It will be much easier to reconstruct decision-making processes and outcomes as needed when a systematic approach for documenting these critical elements has been implemented thoughtfully and prospectively. Reconstructing the decision trail from a myriad of e-mail inboxes and meeting minutes is often time-consuming and challenging. As individuals transition to other roles or out of the organization, it may not even be possible to reconstruct the process in retrospect.

Collaborative Tools for Making and Documenting Decisions

Tools that help workgroups make and document decisions (for example, concerning developing, deploying, and evaluating CDS interventions) can be very helpful in facilitating collaboration among decision makers. One example is in helping organize discussion threads from an expert clinical review panel (such as one determining which DDIs will trigger interruptive alerting in a CPOE system). Collaboration tools should support and capture results from an explicit decision-making process. Traditional approaches such as e-mail, meeting minutes, and the like can be very cumbersome and limited, particularly in more robust CDS programs. General purpose collaborative tools—such as "Web 2.0"[12] technologies and related business tools,[13] some focused specifically on healthcare—are becoming much more powerful, user-friendly, and widely used.

These electronic collaboration tools can be used by clinical experts and other implementation team members to facilitate discussions and capture decisions (with associated rationale) that transpire in the tool's online forum. The systems can typically be configured to send automated notices to participants when there is new activity on the forum. Discussion threads can last days or months and can involve dozens of postings prior to a final decision.

Desirable functions to support KM needs for the CDS program include the capability to bring the discussion to a vote and document who was involved with the decision. Individuals involved should be allowed some flexibility in the conclusion they reach at a particular point (accept, decline, or not sure about a specific decision), especially in cases where the evidence basis for a particular decision may not be firmly established in the literature. Determining a recommended drug dose in a geriatric patient or patient with liver disease are examples. Considerable collaboration between the experts in your institution may be required to reach consensus on the appropriate approach to consistently dose medications in such cases—and effective tools can greatly facilitate this process. Organizations with rich experience managing the decision process note that there tend to be fewer disagreements with medication decisions than disagreements with workflow decisions, a matter in which it can be much harder to reach consensus.

Keep in mind that there is far more to the KM process than just having powerful collaboration tools. How the tools are used is more critical to success. For example, when decision stewards are used, the governance process can provide this role with the basis for formalizing decisions into CDS content and processes. The approach to managing online interactions will become more formal and refined as the decision steward becomes more adept at facilitation and the clinician experts become faster and more efficient at making decisions. Over time, this can become a highly effective collaboration mechanism for producing specific results needed for the CDS program.

It is important to recognize that clinical content and the technology for collaboration can be purchased, whereas the governance for such collaboration cannot. To be successful, this must be home-grown. Since optimizing the CDS governance role will be a learning experience within the organization, expect this to develop gradually over time as the pertinent roles (such as decision stewards) learn how to facilitate the process and leverage their position most effectively.

Ensuring That Interventions Are Useful

The CDS interventions you deploy are intended to support specific improvements to care processes and outcomes, so gathering feedback and creating a continuous improvement cycle are essential KM processes. Continuously monitoring intervention use and effects will provide insight into how users work with them and adopt them into their practice, and whether and how they deliver the desired value and benefits.

Chapter 7 outlines several key considerations for successful CDS program evaluation, including what should be measured, how it should be measured, who should do the measuring, and what should be done with the results. From a KM perspective, the central issue is how these processes are organized, documented, and improved. If the worksheets in Chapter 7 are used, they will provide some of this documentation. The tools for documenting intervention use and usefulness, the formal governance and management approaches for reviewing and addressing use and usefulness issues, and the like, define this important KM element.

As discussed in several previous chapters, the need for and usefulness of a specific CDS intervention can vary with many factors including the time, place, and the end-user type or individual. However, customizing CDS delivery based on these parameters can sometimes be problematic from a technical or a governance perspective. For example, the CIS might not permit such specificity or it may be resource intensive to configure, or the organization might not want to allow clinicians or departments to individualize certain order sets components or alert behaviors.

The KM issues here include the policies that determine whether and how tradeoffs are made to optimize intervention use, usefulness, and value. Best practice includes establishing review groups that include all pertinent stakeholders to develop institutional policy and care standards. Then, the decision support should be built in such a manner that it is as transparent to the end users as possible. If acceptable care is being provided, there should be no interruption to the clinical workflow unless the end user requests additional support. When the monitoring process detects a high degree of "bypass" behavior, the review group can evaluate the appropriate response. Depending on the situation, this may involve disabling the intervention, modifying the intervention, or education and dialog with end users. In any case, these changes are made according to formal organizational KM procedures.

Putting It All Together: Suggestions for Successful Knowledge Management

There are few, if any, organizations that have a long history of successful KM around their CDS efforts. Therefore, it is important to recognize that this is a relatively new clinical informatics domain that should evolve rapidly in the coming years. In summary, some suggestions for helpful practices include:

- Develop and empower a dedicated team to create (or obtain) and maintain CDS interventions. Ensure there is a published and transparent governance structure for this team.
- Engage clinical content experts to support the CDS team's work. It is not reasonable to expect the CDS team to have comprehensive clinical knowledge about all CDS interventions that will be deployed.
- Aim for a single reference version of knowledge with propagation to various interventions from that source. As a rule of thumb, acquire knowledge once, and use it consistently many times. Specific knowledge elements should be changed once (for example, in updating) and then that version should cascade through the CIS.

- Use KM tools suited to your needs, according to formal policies and procedures, to help manage CDS assets and processes.

- Utilize a collaboration environment that allows asynchronous discussion, capturing consensus, version tracking, and maintenance activities for KM. The maintenance activities should be automated to facilitate content currency, for example, through notifications about content expiration dates. It would be desirable to have automated notification when underlying CDS content needs to change based on regulations, drug withdrawals, new strong clinical evidence, and the like.

- Develop a formal process for migrating content from the KM environment into your CIS applications. Ask the CIS supplier for import specifications, and ensure that your KM tools export in these formats. Automate this process when possible.

- Develop a formal process for exporting deployed interventions from the CIS applications into the KM environment for updating (if the CIS does not provide adequate tools for this task).

- Because standards for KM are essential, try to use standard medical vocabularies for tagging your CDS assets and available interoperability standards for moving them across systems. These include (among many others):
  - Disease and procedure (SNOMED CT®, ICD-9/ICD-10[14])
  - Drug (NDC, RxNorm; commercial CDS vendors typically use these codes in their drug files)
  - Interoperability, such as those developed by the HL7 Clinical Decision Support Technical Committee[15] and addressed by the Health IT Standards Panel (HITSP)[16]

- Deploy tools that facilitate feedback on CDS interventions. Ideally, these can be accessed within the intervention, so that end users do not need to use a separate application to provide feedback.

- Consider approaches to generate new insights about clinical care and CDS effects from the clinical database, and use these to improve the delivery of care and CDS.

- Explore methods to share clinical content and strategies with other institutions to accelerate individual and collective progress toward priority objectives.

Further insights into best practices for KM can be gleaned from pioneering organizations that have outlined their knowledge management approaches.[17]

WORKSHEETS

Worksheet 8-1

CDS Knowledge Asset Inventory

In this chapter, we have recommended managing your deployed CDS interventions (and the subset focused on medication management) as a portfolio. In other worksheets throughout this guide, we've provided examples of key data about one or more interventions that you might record and track.

There is no "right way" to monitor a CDS portfolio; this worksheet is intended to provide another sampling of variables you might consider using to create an overview of your deployed CDS assets. Consider also other key dimensions outlined in this and previous chapters, and needs you have uncovered in your own organization. Data to complete this worksheet are available from various earlier worksheets.

Asset Name	Source/ Entity Responsible for Review (Version)	Delivery System	Go-live Date (Action)	Date of Last Review	Date of Next Review/ Review Frequency	Target Population, Role, Location	Target Medication Management Objective	Intervention Effects (Process/ Outcomes)	Actions/ Comments
Drug allergy alert trigger rules	CPOE alerts committee (v1)	CPOE	4/25/08	(none since launch)	5/25/08; annual	Prescriber entering orders for pediatric population in the wards	Eliminate preventable allergic reactions to drugs	Early feedback that triggering frequency is acceptable to end users; over-ride rate 30%; outcome data pending	Continue close monitoring
Drug-drug inter-action data-base	[commercial vendor]	CPOE, Pharmacy system	2/20/08	(none since launch)	2/20/08	Prescriber, pharmacist	Eliminate serious DDIs	Early feedback that triggering frequency is somewhat excessive; over-ride rate 70%; outcome data pending	Task force to monitor and consider options for further refinement

Worksheet 8-2

Decision Log

Clearly there are myriad decisions associated with all the components of a CDS program, and it is unrealistic to expect that trying to capture all of them in a single log would be possible or desirable. Nonetheless, there will be certain circumstances in managing CDS assets in which you will want to keep a record of the process and outcomes for key decisions. These are discussed in the chapter; examples include establishing the content and deployment characteristics for a high-stakes, interruptive alert.

Depending on the situation, you might track decisions using different tools and formats. Worksheet 8-2 is offered as a sample to help trigger your thinking about the occasions in which you may want to track key decisions and how you might do so. In this case, we've organized the decision log by the medication management objective.

Medication Management Objective	Decision Name	Decision Description	Decision Date	Decision Owner	Critical Decision Factors	Impact	Follow-up/ Comments
Reduce preventable allergic reactions	Interruptive allergy alert override	Make coded alert override reason a mandatory field when prescriber overrides an allergy alert	4/25/08	CPOE alerts committee	Coded reasons necessary to rapidly process data; plan reviewed with end user champions and stakeholders, who agreed to trial of this approach to enhance safety	May still get push-back from some physicians but approach consistent with alerting plan. Will provide communications/ support before/ during go-live	Revisit user response and log data in 3 months and re-evaluate whether mandatory override reason still necessary

CONCLUDING COMMENTS

We have emphasized two key KM functions pertinent to the subject matter of this guide; that is, (1) managing the decisions and processes that define CDS targets and ensure they are met, and (2) managing the CDS assets themselves. A thoughtful, proactive approach to these tasks from the CDS program outset (or at least subsequent improvement rounds) is foundational for successful efforts to improve medication use and outcomes with CDS. Keep in mind that KM tools and approaches for CDS are early in their evolution, so we are all learning as we go along (hopefully together).

You might find yourself describing to others (inside and outside your organization) *why* you are applying CDS to improving medication management. You might further outline *what* you are doing in this regard. When you get around to describing *how* you are doing and managing these CDS activities, you will be presenting your KM approach to the issues outlined in this chapter. Having considered these issues, together with similar ideas resonant throughout this entire guide, you will hopefully be able to provide a clear and compelling story for your program's why, what, and how. More importantly, you should have set your organization up to manage its CDS assets and processes in a manner that supports long-term success.

REFERENCES

1. Wikipedia. *Knowledge Management.* http://en.wikipedia.org/wiki/Knowledge_management, accessed 10/7/08.

2. See Glaser J, Hongsermeier T. Managing the investment in clinical decision support in Greenes RA, editor, *Clinical Decision Support: The Road Ahead.* London: Elsevier; 2007; p 405.

3. See, for example, Hongsermeier T, Kashyap V, Sordo M. Knowledge management infrastructure: Evolution at Partners Healthcare System (page 447). See also Rocha RA, Bradshaw RL, Hulse NC, et al. The clinical knowledge management infrastructure of Intermountain Healthcare (page 469). In Greenes RA, editor. *Clinical Decision Support: The Road Ahead.* London: Elsevier; 2007.

4. See, for example, American Medical Informatics Association. *A Roadmap for National Action on Clinical Decision Support, strategic objectives A and B.* http://www.amia.org/inside/initiatives/cds/, accessed 9/18/08.

5. Kuperman GJ, Reichley RM, Bailey TC. Using commercial knowledge bases for clinical decision support: opportunities, hurdles, and recommendations. *J Am Med Inform Assoc.* 2006; 13(4):369-371.

6. See, for example, Wikipedia. *Document Management System.* http://en.wikipedia.org/wiki/Document_management_system, accessed 9/18/08.

7. See, for example, U.S. Department of Health and Human Services. *AHIC April 2008 Meeting: Clinical Decision Support Recommendation Letter.* http://www.hhs.gov/healthit/documents/m20080422/6.2_cds_recs.html, accessed 9/18/08.

8. See, for example, attention by the American Health Information Community (AHIC) to order sets interoperability. http://www.hhs.gov/healthit/usecases/ordsets.html, accessed 9/18/08.

9. U.S. Food and Drug Administration. *FDA Drug Safety Newsletter.* http://www.fda.gov/cder/dsn/, accessed 9/18/08.

10. The Institute for Safe Medication Practices. *ISMP Medication Safety Alert!* http://www.ismp.org/Newsletters/acutecare/default.asp, accessed 9/18/08.

11. See, for example, American Medical Informatics Association. *A Roadmap for National Action on Clinical Decision Support, strategic objectives E and F.* http://www.amia.org/inside/initiatives/cds/, accessed 9/18/08.

12. Wikipedia. *Web 2.0.* http://en.wikipedia.org/wiki/Web_2, accessed 9/18/08.

13. Wikipedia. *Knowledge Management Enablers.* http://en.wikipedia.org/wiki/Knowledge_management#Knowledge_Management_enablers, accessed 9/18/08.

14 As of this writing, U.S. Department of Health and Human Services has proposed October 2011 as the date for transition to ICD-10 CM/PCS coding system. See CMS Web site: http://www.cms.hhs.gov/ICD10/04_Statute_Regulations_Program_Instructions.asp#TopOfPage. Updated 25 Aug 2008, accessed 12/15/08.

15 Health Level Seven. http://www.hl7.org/, accessed 9/18/08.

16 Health Information Technology Standards Panel (HITSP). *Welcome to www.HITSP.org.* http://www.hitsp.org/, accessed 9/18/08.

17 Greenes RA, editor. *Clinical Decision Support: The Road Ahead.* Section VI: Knowledge Management Approaches. London: Elsevier; 2007.

Epilogue

As pointed out in the preface, we suggest that you consider this guide to be a snapshot of a dynamic effort involving many people, rather than a static book in the traditional sense. The process that led to the guidance offered in the preceding pages did not resemble that typically used for a such a compilation; there was not one person sharing what he or she knows (as in a single-author text), a group of people dividing responsibility for a domain into discrete chunks (as in a multi-author text), or even a large panel deliberating on a topic with a small editorial team documenting this wisdom and synthesizing it into a publication.

Our process was different. Nearly 100 people with diverse perspectives and expertise contributed individual ideas much more directly into the mix, facilitated by various collaboration technologies such as wikis, Web 2.0 environments, and other shared document management tools. It took a writer, a developmental editing team, 13 associate editors, and the editor-in-chief to pull the resulting cacophony together into this guide.

The process was very messy, and the results have flaws. Nonetheless, we are very proud of this material and hope (perhaps expect, supported by comments from many reviewers) that this collection of thoughts and guidance on improving medication use and outcomes will prove valuable.

Rather than merely hoping that this effort creates real change, however, we are planning to follow our own advice on driving continuous PI. If one considers this guide as a CDS intervention (yes, we know this is a bit of a stretch), then recommendations provided in the previous chapters can be brought to bear in improving its use and usefulness. To some degree, we followed the recommendations in Chapter 2 on identifying and prioritizing opportunities prior to beginning this initiative. This convinced us that CDS for medication management is an important, top-priority topic, and led to our building the collaborations and processes that resulted in this guide. We (perhaps like you) have work to do getting up to speed with implementing recommendations in other chapters.

For example, we realize the need to learn more about the workflows that influence when and how the support offered by this guide is used. We need to know more about the infrastructure you have in place to implement these suggestions and what implications that has for successfully applying our recommendations. And indeed, we need to find out more about the specific challenges you are facing in trying to improve outcomes with CDS, and the potential information we could deliver, in what format, to which stakeholder, through which channel, and at which point in workflow to be most helpful in your efforts.

This guide is, therefore, is at least as much a question as it is an answer (perhaps like some of your own CDS interventions). We are not claiming to have provided all the answers, and our key question is, "To what extent is this material helpful?" In other words, we have ahead of us the critical evaluation work discussed in Chapter 7 applied to this guidebook. That is, we need to understand how this material has influenced the process and outcomes of your efforts to improve medication use with CDS, and the resulting implications for how we can do better in the next round. Harkening back to the earlier comment about how messy some of our processes were, we also have much to do in the way of our KM approach (applying concepts from Chapter 8) as well.

As we prepare to turn this manuscript over for production, we have also begun some exciting work toward addressing these issues. Nascent efforts include a newly formed HIMSS Clinical Decision Support Task Force, supported by the Scottsdale Institute and involving six participating care delivery organizations and other pertinent experts. This group is building on the framework and recommendations reflected in this guide to synthesize, implement, and evaluate CDS approaches to improving VTE prophylaxis. Our hope is to expand the initiative over time to include many more participating organizations and to outline optimal CDS approaches for other very specific and pressing PI challenges.

To deliver on the promise to continually refine and expand the material in this guide, we are building a wiki that readers can to use to give feedback about their efforts to apply the book's recommendations, to suggest content enhancements, and to engage in conversation with peers about questions, tips and strategies for applying CDS to improving medication use and outcomes.

So, just as this guide is part of an ongoing process, this epilogue is a beginning rather than an ending. We hope to collaborate with you on the journey of continually improving the value that CDS brings to healthcare. Please keep an eye on the HIMSS Web page at www.himss.org/cdsguide for further information about how we can work together going forward.

Appendix A

Using CDS to Enhance Safe and Effective Medication Use in the Small Practice Environment

Most healthcare delivery outside of self-care occurs in small physician practices. Medication errors, ADEs, and opportunities to improve medication use and outcomes are at least as great in these settings as they are in inpatient environments. For example, one study found that 21% of outpatient prescriptions contained at least one error,[1] and the IOM estimates that approximately 530,000 preventable drug related injuries occur each year among Medicare recipients alone in outpatient clinics.[2]

Office practices are increasingly adopting EMRs, in part to help increase patient care quality and safety. These benefits, however, do not come simply by implementing these systems; careful attention to their CDS components is required. For example, EMR use does not appear to be associated with improved performance on ambulatory quality indicators[3] (which include proper medication use) or reduced medication errors[4] without inclusion of CDS features focused on these objectives. The broad CDS definition, the "CDS Five Rights" approach to improving outcomes with CDS, and the opportunities for CDS in the medication-management cycle presented in Chapter 1 will provide a strong foundation for CDS efforts in small practice settings.

Although many scenarios and examples used in this book focus on hospital-based issues and systems, the underlying themes and guidance can be applied in many cases to outpatient care as well. This appendix expands discussions in earlier chapters to highlight some important CDS deployment considerations for those in small practices and other ambulatory settings.

Another resource that might be helpful in your efforts to apply the concepts in this guide to small practices is Doctors Office Quality-IT (DOQ-IT) University. This Centers for Medicare & Medicaid Services (CMS)-sponsored program provides an online educational program that includes modules to support care management and CDS in office practice.[5]

DISCUSSION
Governance, Charters, and Baseline Data

Small practices have far fewer numbers and types of stakeholders, so governance issues tend to be much simpler. The physicians are typically the stakeholders who take all the financial risk and are the primary executive decision makers. Generally, staffs are quite small and teamwork is inherent in a small practice, so there are rich channels for input and feedback in a well-run office. Nonetheless, consensus and engagement around targeted objectives is still critical to success. It is, therefore, important to identify which medication use targets are most appropriate for CDS-related efforts and ensure that all pertinent stakeholders are on board. Otherwise, just as in large organizations, detractors can seriously derail the program's success.

As with inpatient settings, there are increasing forces supporting CDS use to help improve outcomes in ambulatory practice. For example, many measures in CMS's Physician Quality Reporting Initiative (PQRI) involve effective outpatient medication use.[6] The growing numbers of pay-for-performance initiatives typically include many similar measures.[7]

The process for identifying, prioritizing, and defining baseline performance in areas targeted for CDS-enabled improvements is, therefore, just as important in outpatient and small practice settings as in hospitals and health systems. Documenting these processes explicitly can be a useful exercise. As with inpatient CISs, outpatient billing systems and electronic EMRs can likewise provide data for measuring baselines and progress for targeted processes and outcomes. A skim through Chapter 2 should yield useful tips for addressing these key issues.

Mapping Workflows

Workflow mapping, an important process change task, is generally easier to do in a small practice compared with a hospital because of the smaller size and scope and fewer participants. The change management team is the same as the implementation team, which is the same as the staff. As a result, the staff merely has to get together and discuss how to address the CDS intervention setup considerations addressed in Chapter 3. Workflow issues are critical to successful CDS deployment in ambulatory settings as well, so it's still important to give this careful consideration and to explicitly document old and new routines. This helps ensure that all affected staff are fully on board with the new routines and tools and adapt successfully. Keep in mind "upstream" and "downstream" activities that need to happen before and after physician-focused CDS for the intervention to have its intended effect. For example, if you will be using CDS to increase the rate of influenza vaccination, make sure you will have adequate supplies on hand, storage space for the vaccines, nursing time to administer the shots, and the like. Also consider other stakeholders (such as nursing, front desk staff, and patients) as potential CDS recipients in addressing specific targets (for example, through

policy-driven standing orders for vaccinations in appropriate patients).

Cataloging and Optimizing Available Information Systems and CDS Resources

Although the number and complexity of ISs and knowledge assets are far less in small practice settings, this infrastructure provides a foundation for deploying CDS interventions in these settings as well. Cataloging available resources can, therefore, be quite helpful. Consider "usual suspect" systems, such as an EMR or registry (if available), billing and scheduling systems, and others. On the CDS asset side, consider reference applications on the Internet or local computers, and CDS-related functionality in deployed clinical systems. Don't forget potential "low tech" options that might be in use, such as paper-based flowsheets, documentation templates, alerts (such as stickers on paper charts), reference information on wall charts and pocket cards, and the like.

Small practices can access CDS interventions and CIS in several ways. These include standalone systems within the practice itself, direct interaction with a larger health system's tools, and communication between the larger system's tools and the practice's local systems.

Within a medical practice, EMR, e-prescribing, and patient and clinician Web portals can enhance medication-related workflows with helpful tools and opportunities for decision support. For each of these systems, we outline several such features and CDS intervention possibilities that you might consider and cultivate in your practice.

EMR

- Comprehensive problem/medication lists, which support appropriate decision making and automated checking
- Drug interaction and allergy checking
- Drug and condition handouts for patients to help them understand their conditions and treatments, and become better informed and active participants in their care

- A drug lookup function to bring Internet-based resources to the point of care for prescribing and monitoring information
- Tools to authenticate who is accessing record functionality and content to support patient privacy and confidentiality and information interoperability. For example, the clinic's patient portal "authenticates" patients by validating their identity, then connects them to their own chart and allows them to review their own information and submit data for provider review (amounting to "automated filing" for the practice). Similarly, external laboratories interfaced with the EMR can authenticate results as belonging to a patient, which can then be automatically filed. These tools can help ensure that accurate data are rapidly available to support proactive CDS interventions, as well as relevant data display.

E-prescribing

- Automated systems for conveying prescriptions to pharmacy that may be integrated with EMRs to provide a "complete loop" of digital information flow, potentially eliminating input errors at the pharmacy site.
- Authentication with the pharmacy is automatic.
- Refill requests are streamlined.
- Opportunity for formulary support and checking (and safety checking if not integrated with an EMR).

Patient Portals

- These can be components of (or interfaced with) practice-based EMRs and are providing increasingly sophisticated tools to help patients more proactively manage their health. They allow patients to review medication lists and generally become more aware of the information physicians have entered into their charts. Also importantly, such portals can allow physicians to see drugs the patient is taking, including those of which the physician was previously unaware. Patient's ability to review their own outpatient EMR medication

list is a key factor for successful communication in the patient/physician/pharmacist triangle.
- Patients can request refills via the portal, selecting the medication from their EMR medication list and thus potentially reducing communication errors.
- Patient education about drugs, interactions and related safety and quality issues can be posted on the clinic portal, a trusted and readily accessible information source for the patient.

Besides patient portals that your practice may provide, keep in mind other types of PHRs that patients may be using. These are increasingly provided by software vendors, health insurance companies, and others. Patients will be using PHRs in greater numbers to manage information about their conditions and treatments, and if there's high use among your panel, you can consider ways to leverage these electronic, organized data for your CDS efforts. Also consider similar opportunities to leverage other home health aides, such as "smart pillboxes" that provide patients with text and voice alerts when medications are to be taken, and reminders when doses are missed. In a lower tech vein, the AHRQ provides an online brochure[8] on *How to Create a Pill Card* that can be used to help patients take their medications appropriately.

Although the floodgates may not be wide open, some hospitals are becoming more comfortable providing EMRs and related applications to physician practices, since anti-kickback and related regulations have been relaxed and clarified.[9,10,11] You might consider exploring this path with your hospital as part of your efforts to enhance CIS infrastructure for medication management CDS in your practice.

The following are some questions to consider addressing with health systems with which your practice participates:
- Does the healthcare system have a provider portal?
- Do provider portals give access to inpatient medications and labs for referral physicians without a hospital practice?

- Can discharge summaries, a key to medication management, be sent through a secure interface?
- Are there any health system-wide initiatives (help with change management, statistics, IT support, etc.) that can be made accessible to small practices?
- Are physicians with hospital practices able to access CPOE from their offices? Can it be integrated with their EMR?

Chapter 4, page 86, discusses conducting an inventory of available CIS and optimizing how these systems are used to support key steps around the medication management loop. Except, perhaps, for the sections on pharmacy verification and nurse administration, much of this material may trigger useful considerations for your practice-based medication CDS efforts.

CDS for Specific Objectives

Many safety and quality targets outlined in Chapter 5 are pertinent in the outpatient setting, though the infrastructure and resources available in small practices may not provide tools as robust for addressing them. Nonetheless, it may be worth reviewing the recommended approach for targets of interest (for example, preventing drug-allergy interactions or improving use of drugs addressed in quality measures) and adapting them as best as possible to available tools. A small sampling of implementation considerations for addressing specific targets from Chapter 5 that are pertinent to outpatient settings is listed next.

- Consider CDS approaches (such as alerts and relevant data display) for ensuring that patient allergy information is recorded and available for checking (automated, if possible) when drugs are prescribed (see page 122).
- Consider approaches to help ensure that a complete and accurate medication list is available (for example, see previous portal discussion). An accurate list not only helps appropriate clinical decision making but also decreases false-positive alerting from automatic medication safety checks.

- Consider alerts and other CDS approaches to decrease contraindicated medication prescribing for elderly patients[12] (see page 143), and support safer use of medications that frequently cause preventable admissions in this population[13] (see discussion and Table 5-7, page 145).
- Consider CDS approaches to more closely monitor drugs that frequently cause preventable ADEs and hospital admission (see discussion and Table 2-4, page 36).

Deployment

Implementing CDS for medication management in a small physician practice is easier in some respects than implementation in a large hospital or health system, especially in terms of change management surrounding deployment. A well-run small practice is already a streamlined, intimate group with shared knowledge about individual workflows. As a result, implementation tends to be simpler and more focused than in a larger system (assuming the requisite justification, planning, development, and change management have been appropriately addressed). Although the scale is much smaller, the key steps outlined in Chapter 6 are also important. These include intervention testing, communication, and training as needed, and seeking and responding to feedback.

Throughout this guide, we emphasize the role for diverse stakeholders in supporting CDS-related activities. An example pertinent to office practice is the successful role that nurses can play in facilitating CDS-mediated quality improvement in practices with EMRs. You should think creatively about this model and other approaches to fully engaging all stakeholders in optimizing your efforts.[14]

Measurement/Assessment

As can be the case in hospitals, small practices may feel that they do not have the time, money, or inclination to do in-depth measurements or assessments. As we stress in this book, if a problem or opportunity is significant enough to warrant the effort to apply CDS, then it is important to track intervention effects at some level on both care process and outcomes. This measurement may already be mandatory within the initiative prompting the CDS effort (for example, a public reporting or pay-for-performance initiative). EMR or registries may provide "canned" reports or have custom report generating capabilities that can be leveraged for these purposes.

Since all staff (and patients) in a practice are workflow participants, feedback on intervention effects (at least on process) is more immediate. The staff's intimate knowledge of their own workflows and the immediacy of many care processes can obviate the need for some formal intervention effects studies that might be required in hospitals. In any case, it might be fruitful to peruse the metrics discussion in Chapter 7, page 199, to ensure that the practice evaluates its CDS efforts in a manner that optimizes their value for medication use and outcomes, and practice efficiency.

Knowledge Management

Although CDS KM processes are much simpler in small practices than in hospitals, a systematic approach to documenting the key features and decisions related to the CDS program can be helpful. On the CDS asset side of KM, care in tracking the deployed CDS intervention portfolio, and in addressing CDS content currency and value, is equally important in both settings. Alerts, reference information, order sets, documentation tools, flowsheets and other interventions that are inconsistent with the best evidence and most current information can blunt value from these tools, or worse, potentially cause harm. Similarly, thoughtfully approaching and documenting the "why," "how," and "what" components of your CDS efforts focused on medication management can help ensure that they are successful. You may find useful pearls for this work in Chapter 8.

REFERENCES

1   Shaughnessy AF, Nickel RO. Prescription-writing patterns and errors in a family medicine residency program. *J Fam Pract.* 1989; 29(3):290-295.

2   Institute of Medicine. *Preventing Medication Errors: Quality Chasm Series.* Washington, DC: National Academies Press; 2006; http://www.iom.edu/?id=35961, accessed 9/18/08.

3   Linder JA, Ma J, Bates DW, et al. Electronic health record use and the quality of ambulatory care in the United States. *Arch Intern Med.* 2007; 167(13):1400-1405.

4   Gandhi TK, Weingart SN, Seger AC, et al. Outpatient prescribing errors and the impact of computerized prescribing. *J Gen Intern Med.* 2005; 20(9):837-841.

5   Meridian KSI Knowledge Center. *Welcome to the QualityNet eLearning Center.* http://elearning.qualitynet.org, accessed 10/8/08; alternatively, you can visit DOQ-IT University on the Masspro site at http://www.masspro.org/DOQITU/, accessed 12/15/08.

6   Centers for Medicare & Medicaid Services. *Physician Quality Reporting Initiative—Overview.* http://www.cms.hhs.gov/pqri/, accessed 9/18/08.

7   See, for example, the Bridges to Excellence programs: http://www.bridgestoexcellence.org/, accessed 9/18/08.

8   The How to Create a Pill Card brochure is available online from Agency for Healthcare Research and Quality (AHRQ) at: http://www.ahrq.gov/qual/pillcard/pillcard.htm. Updated Feb 2008, accessed 12/15/08.

9   iHealthbeat. *Hospitals Begin to take Advantage of Internal Revenue Service Rule.* http://www.ihealthbeat.org/articles/2008/5/16/Hospitals-Begin-To-Take-Advantage-of-Internal-Revenue-Service-Rule.aspx?topicID=54, accessed 9/18/08.

10 Center for Studying Health System Change. Grossman JM, Cohen G. *Despite Regulatory Changes, Hospitals Cautious in Helping Physicians Purchase Electronic Medical Records.* Issue Brief No. 123. Sept, 2008. http://www.hschange.org/CONTENT/1015/, accessed 10/8/08.

11 Health Data Management. *HDM Breaking News—CCHIT Quantifies EHR Incentives.* http://www.healthdatamanagement.com/news/electronic_medical_records_EMRs_EHRs26998-1.html. Sept 25, 2008.

12 Smith DH, Perrin N, Feldstein A, et al. The impact of prescribing safety alerts for elderly persons in an electronic medical record: an interrupted time series evaluation. *Arch Intern Med.* 2006; 166(10):1098-1104.

13 Budnitz DS, Shehab N, Kegler SR, et al. Medication use leading to emergency department visits for adverse drug events in older adults. *Ann Intern Med.* 2007; 147(11):755-765.

14 Nemeth LS, Wessell AM, Jenkins RG, et al. Strategies to accelerate translation of research into primary care within practices using electronic medical records. *J Nurs Care Qual.* 2007; 22(4):343-349.

Appendix B

Some Medico-legal Considerations

Legal issues are often cited as an important consideration in CDS implementation and even as an outright barrier by some. Liability and other legal matters surrounding CDS are complex and in flux as CDS and CISs mature. Consultation with legal counsel, peers, the literature and other sources can be very important in avoiding missteps. In the following paragraphs, we outline a few issues that are raised elsewhere this guide and point to further resources on the topic.

Commonly expressed legal concerns include the fear that a CDS intervention may increase liability exposure for clinicians and healthcare organizations. For example, could an allegation of malpractice be supported by evidence that a clinician ignored a pertinent alert? A review[1] on the topic noted that courts have treated CDS systems in the same way as a textbook that a clinician consults. The implication is that the supplied information supplements the clinician's judgment, and the clinician (not the CDS) is therefore responsible for care decisions and their results.

This same review suggests that organizations establish a policy on CDS tools that clarifies this intent to support rather then supplant clinical judgment and that they add language in contracts with CDS vendors to ensure that the knowledge bases are regularly updated. Similar considerations presumably apply to organizational responsibility for modifications made to commercial knowledge sources they have acquired (mentioned in Chapter 8, page 245).

A review on using commercial knowledge bases for CDS has recommended that, "To minimize risk, healthcare organizations create explicit policies and procedures regarding knowledge editing. Such policies should require that rule specifications be documented explicitly and that an identified individual or clinical committee be responsible for the content of the rule. The organization must assure that the edited knowledge is behaving as intended."[2]

Other related issues include how organizations deliver alerts to clinicians and manage the circumstances surrounding alert firing. These processes may include tracking how clinicians respond to the alert and whether and how they can indicate reasons for overrides. Evaluation metrics and KM approaches (discussed in Chapter 7, page 203, and Chapter 8, page 248, respectively) can help preserve the context of a specific CDS intervention instance, including the CDS content state at the time an intervention about a specific patient was delivered. If questions are raised about a clinician's decision involving a CDS intervention, say in a malpractice allegation, these techniques may help establish the exact intervention context to help others understand why a particular decision was made.

Chapter 6, page 179, touches on the issue of whether alert triggers, messages delivered, user response and the like become part of the record and/ or are retained in an archive or log, and this decision's implications for legal discovery. As we point out in the chapter, faulty CDS is itself a potential source of harm and liability, and careful testing (such as using approaches outlined in Chapter 6, page 181) is a key to managing this risk. In Chapter 7, page 207, we discuss issues related to handling alert overrides and documenting override reasons.

Organizations have addressed in various ways the fear that this type of detailed information about alert firing will be subject to legal discovery and used *against* clinicians or the organization. Some inactivate CDS intervention logging, thus removing this documentation source that might be discoverable in a legal action. This approach potentially limits an organization's ability to learn from and improve CDS intervention use (as discussed in Chapter 7). Others keep such logs but explicitly declare through policies that they are to be considered outside the official medical record (that is, to be used only for internal quality improvement initiatives) and thus, theoretically, not discoverable. It is questionable, though, whether such information could be prevented from legal discovery.

Although legal discussions about CDS most commonly address liability questions related to *using* CDS tools, they also frequently raise the issue of potential liability for *not using* (or *not making available*) such tools.[3,4] Malpractice is defined as a care standard violation, and some have suggested that the use of CDS in a given area may generally increase the clinical care standard because evidence (outlined earlier in this guide) indicates that such systems can improve care quality and reduce medical errors. Thus, from this perspective, *not* having a CDS program in place may increase malpractice liability because its absence might be cited in a legal action as evidence that an organization did not use available technology to prevent patient harm. The sources just cited note that there is precedent for such negligence or malpractice applying even in cases in which the technology is not yet widely adopted, as could be argued for some CDS intervention types such as alerts in CPOE.

In Chapter 7, page 199, we cite issues related to using CDS in quality improvement versus research initiatives and recommend consulting legal counsel and your organization's institutional review board about such matters as applicable.

In summary, this book outlines a careful approach to developing, testing, deploying, and monitoring CDS interventions to improve medication use. Although not intended in any way to represent legal advice, this systematic approach hopefully will be a useful component of your organization's efforts to address any legal issues and risks associated with CDS in this domain. As we noted earlier, legal issues around CDS are complex and in flux, so you should consult legal counsel as appropriate.

Peers in other organizations can also be a useful source of input—through your personal network, as well as through informatics-related professional society listservs or communities (such as those provided by HIMSS, Association of Medical Directors of Information Systems, AMIA, and SI). In addition to the references just cited, other literature sources may also provide useful background for legal considerations in CDS. A starting point for such exploration may include the following:

- American Health Information Management Association (AHIMA). *The New Electronic Discovery Civil Rule.* Available online at: http://library.ahima.org/xpedio/groups/ public/documents/ahima/bok1_031860. hcsp?dDocName=bok1_031860.
- Berner ES. Ethical and legal issues in the use of clinical decision support systems. *J Healthc Inf Manag.* 2002; 16(4):34-37.
- Fox J, Thomson R. Clinical decision support systems: a discussion of quality, safety and legal liability issues. *Proc AMIA Symp.* 2002:265-269.
- Klein SR. Welcome to the digital age: New federal e-discovery rules require digital records management. *J Healthc Inf Manag.* 2007; 21:6-7. http://www.jhimdigital.org/jhim/2007fall/?pg=8.
- Miller RA. Legal issues related to medical decision support systems. *Int J Clin Monit Comput.* 1989; 6(2):75-80.

- Miller RA, Gardner RM. Recommendations for responsible monitoring and regulation of clinical software systems. *J Am Med Inform Assoc.* 1997; 4(6):442-457.

Further reassurance regarding CDS intervention use is expected to come from the establishment of quality standards for software systems and knowledge bases, and health IT certification efforts based on such standards.[5]

REFERENCES

1   Klein SR, Jones JW. Clinical decision support programs can be risky business. *J Healthc Inf Manag.* 2007; 21(2):15-17.

2   Kuperman GJ, Reichley RM, Bailey TC. Using commercial knowledge bases for clinical decision support: opportunities, hurdles, and recommendations. *J Am Med Inform Assoc.* 2006; 13(4):369-371.

3   Annas GJ. The patient's right to safety—improving the quality of care through litigation against hospitals. *N Engl J Med.* 2006 May 11; 354(19):2063-2066.

4   Miller RA, Miller SM. Legal and Regulatory Issues Related to the User of Clinical Software in Health Care Delivery. Greenes RA, editor. *Clinical Decision Support: The Road Ahead.* London: Elsevier. 2007; pp 423-444; and Appendix B: Medico-legal considerations with CDS.

5   For example, the Certification Commission for Health Information Technology, http://www.cchit.org/, accessed 10/8/08.

Index